CINEMA SL

THE ADULTS ONLY GUIDE TO HISTORY'S
SICKEST AND SEXIEST MOVIES

EDITED BY
ROBIN BOUGIE

VOLUME

A
FAB
PRESS
PUBLICATION

CINEMA SEWER VOL. 3

FIRST EDITION PUBLISHED BY FAB PRESS, AUGUST 2011

FAB PRESS LTD
2 FARLEIGH
RAMSDEN ROAD
GODALMING
SURREY
GU7 1QE
ENGLAND, UK

WWW.FABPRESS.COM

A CIP CATALOGUE RECORD FOR THIS BOOK IS AVAILABLE FROM THE BRITISH LIBRARY.

ISBN 9781903254646

COVER ART BY THE ALWAYS AMAZING VINCE RAURUS. VISIT HIM AT:
WWW.VENIVIDIVINCE.COM

THIS BOOK IS DEDICATED TO:

CINEMA SEWER SUPER-FAN ELYSHA KLING, WHOM A FEW READERS MAY REMEMBER AS THE STAR OF THE "ONE NIGHT IN PARIS" COMIC FROM C.S #22. ELYSHA ALSO CAME UP WITH THE NEAT LITTLE MATH=SEX EQUATION IN MY "I LOVE NERDS" COMIC FROM VOL. 2. SHE DIED IN HER SLEEP ON MAY 8th, 2010. LYSH WAS A MATH/PORN/MOVIE/COMIC NERD, AND DESPITE OUR AGE DIFFERENCE, WE HAD A LOT IN COMMON -- ASIDE FOR THE LOVE OF MATH, THAT IS. I REMEMBER ONE TIME WE WERE CROSSING A BUSY INTERSECTION AND SHE REACHED OVER INSTINCTUALLY AND HELD MY HAND. DON'T GET ME WRONG -- IT WASN'T SEXUAL, IT WAS MORE LIKE SHE WAS MY KID SISTER. I LIKE THE MEMORY OF THAT TINY LITTLE MOMENT, THOUGH. IT SPEAKS SUBTLY ABOUT A REALLY COOL YOUNG WOMAN WHO WAS A GOOD FRIEND.

YOU WERE WISE BEYOND YOUR 21 YEARS, EK, AND I REALLY MISS YOU.

VISIT:
WWW.CINEMASEWER.COM
AND MY DAILY ART BLOG:
BOUGIEMAN. LIVEJOURNAL.COM

HOLY SHIT! PORNOGRAPHY

BY ROBIN BOUGIE ·2011·

QUEEN VICTORIA IN FULL EFFECT!

ONE OF THE THINGS THAT OFTEN ACTS LIKE A STUMBLING BLOCK FOR A PUBLICATION THAT DEVOTES MOST OF ITS PAGES TO FILMS THAT CAN ONLY REALLY BE CLASSIFIED AS PORNOGRAPHY, IS THE THE SOCIAL GHETTOISATION THAT THE LABEL BRINGS TO WHAT I WRITE AND DRAW ABOUT.

ON THE ONE HAND, I VIEW IT AS A BENEFIT. TICKLING THE HAIRY UNDERSIDES OF TABOOS AND CELEBRATING THE SLEAZY IS FAR MORE FUN THAN TOEING THE LINE. BUT ON THE OTHER HAND, BEING VIEWED AS LEGITIMATE IN ANY WAY SOMETIMES FEELS LIKE AN IMPOSSIBILITY. I CAN ONLY TAKE GROWN ADULTS GIGGLING (OR FREAKING OUT ABOUT) THE MOST BASIC INTERPRETATIONS OF SEXUALITY FOR SO LONG BEFORE I RUN OUT OF PATIENCE.

PART OF THAT IMMATURITY STEMS FROM IGNORANCE. BOTH LEGALLY AND SOCIALLY, OUR CULTURE DOESN'T SEEM TO KNOW WHAT PORN IS, WE JUST KNOW IT WHEN WE SEE IT. YOU WOULD THINK WE'D HAVE IT SUSSED OUT BY NOW, AS HUMANITY HAS USED EVERY SINGLE TECHNOLOGICAL STEP FORWARD TO RECORD THE ACT OF SEX.

MOST OF THE CONFUSION AND STUNTED DEVELOPMENT CAN BE EXPLAINED BY OUR MISCONCEPTION THAT PORNOGRAPHY HAS ALWAYS EXISTED -- WHEN THIS IS NOT TRUE AT ALL. PORNOGRAPHY IS AN INVENTION OF THE VICTORIAN ERA, A TIME OF STRICT MORAL VALUES THAT WERE IN STARK CONTRAST TO THOSE OF THE PREVIOUS GEORGIAN ERA (1714 TO 1830).

HUMAN HISTORY AND SEXUAL IMAGERY CERTAINLY TRACE FAR FURTHER BACK THAN THE MID 1800s, BECAUSE FOR AS LONG AS OUR SPECIES HAS BEEN ABLE TO DRAW OR WRITE, WE'VE CRAFTED SEXUAL AND SEX-THEMED IMAGES AND STORIES. IN OUR LIFE TIMES WE HAVE SEEN PORN DEFINED, CATAGORIZED, AND CONTEXUALIZED EVERY WHICH WAY, BUT WHAT IS SO OFTEN IGNORED IS THAT AT ITS ESSENCE, PORNOGRAPHY IS SIMPLY THE INHERITANCE OF VICTORIAN VALUES AND SENSIBILITIES. IN THE GRAND SCHEME OF HISTORY THESE ARE VERY YOUNG -- VIRTUALLY BRAND NEW -- CULTURAL PRETENTIONS.

SO THAT IS WHERE AND WHEN THE CONCEPT OF PORN ORIGINATES, BUT HOW DID QUEEN VICTORIA'S LOYAL SUBJECTS COME UP WITH IT?

ONE DAY IN ITALY, A LOWLY PEASANT STUMBLED UPON THE ANCIENT ROMAN CITY OF POMPEII. BURIED BY THE ERUPTION OF MOUNT VESUVIUS NEARLY 17 CENTURIES PRIOR, THE RAVIOLI-MUNCHERS QUICKLY SET TO WORK -- REVEALING THE LONG FORGOTTEN CITY FROM THE VOLCANIC ASH. AS EXCAVATORS DUG, THEY REVEALED A REMARKABLY PRESERVED DOCUMENT OF ANCIENT ROMAN LIFE, RIGHT DOWN TO THE FRESCOES ON THEIR WALLS, AND THE SCULPTURES AND ART THAT THEY DECORATED THEIR HOMES WITH.

BA-DOING

HOT!

BUT AS THE EXHUMING OF THIS LONG-DEAD URBAN CORPSE WENT DOWN, SOMETHING AMAZING AND TOTALLY UNEXPECTED TOOK PLACE. THE WORKERS CLEARING AWAY

THE DIRT FOUND THEMSELVES ABSOLUTELY DISGUSTED, AND THE PEEPS RUNNING THE COUNTRY WEREN'T TOO THRILLED EITHER. WHAT THEY EXPECTED WERE ARTEFACTS FROM A NOBLE PEOPLE WHO WERE THE MOST ADVANCED OF THEIR TIME, BUT WHAT THEY ACTUALLY LAID EYES ON WAS, IN THEIR OPINION, AN ANCIENT SOCIETY THAT WAS CONTAMINATED WITH VILE DEBAUCHERY.

FOR THE VERY FIRST TIME, EUROPE WAS MADE TO NOT ONLY RE-EVALUATE THEIR PAST AND TRACE THEIR ROOTS AND CULTURE IN UNCOMFORTABLE WAYS, BUT THEY WERE ALSO FORCED TO PONDER WHO THEY WERE THEMSELVES. BY ALL ACCOUNTS, THIS WAS NOT AN ENJOYABLE EXPERIENCE, AND THE GENESIS OF THIS SOCIAL UPHEAVAL WAS VIEWED AS A VERY DANGEROUS NEW THREAT.

A STATUE OF PAN HUMPING A GOAT: THE FIRST PIECE OF PORNOGRAPHY IN HUMAN HISTORY

I KNOW I WOULDN'T HAVE LIKED TO HAVE BEEN THE POOR MESSENGER WHO HAD TO DELIVER THE FACT TO A PRUDISH MODERN EUROPE THAT THEIR PARTY ANIMAL ANCESTORS HAD ABSOLUTELY NO QUALMS WITH DECORATING EVERY PART OF THEIR SURROUNDINGS WITH HARDCORE IMAGERY. THIS WASN'T A BOOB HERE AND THERE, THIS WAS PEOPLE FUCKING, SUCKING, TAKING IT IN THE ASS, TEA-BAGGING, JERKING EACH OTHER OFF, DOGGY-STYLING, FUCKING PROSTITUTES, FUCKING PIGS, FUCKING GOATS, FUCKING CHILDREN, FUCKING SLAVES, ETC AND SO ON. KEEPING IN MIND THAT EVEN UTTERING THE WORD "LEG" WAS CONSIDERED OFF-COLOR IN POLITE VICTORIAN SOCIETY (THE ACCEPTABLE TERM WAS "LIMB") AND YOU BEGIN TO SEE THE CONTRAST.

THIS CLASH OF CULTURES LED TO A NUMBER OF DISCOVERIES BEING QUICKLY REBURIED. A WALL FRESCO WHICH DEPICTED PRIAPUS, THE GOD OF SEX AND FERTILITY WITH HIS GIANT AMAZING WANG WAS COVERED WITH PLASTER, AND WAS ONLY DISCOVERED AGAIN IN 1998 AFTER A RAINSTORM REVEALED IT.

THOSE SALTY OL' ROMANS DIDN'T JUST SOCK THIS ART AND DECORATION AWAY IN THEIR BEDROOMS. IT WAS IN EVERY PART OF THE HOUSE, AS WELL AS IN PUBLIC SPACES AND SLAVES QUARTERS. THE ROMANS CLEARLY VIEWED PAINTINGS OF GIANT COCKS SLIDING INTO WELL-LUBRICATED ORIFICES AS BEAUTIFUL, AND NOT DIRTY OR SHAMEFUL WHATSOEVER. VICTORIAN INTELLECTUALS COULDN'T COMPREHEND THIS CONCEPT, AND ASSUMED THAT THE SEXUAL IMAGES MUST HAVE BEEN ENJOYED IN SECRET. IN REALITY, THE ROMANS DIDN'T EVEN HAVE A WORD FOR "PRIVACY". THEY WERE A SOCIAL PEOPLE, AND DID EVERYTHING OPENLY. THE CONCEPT OF HIDING AWAY AND ENJOYING GUILTY SHAMEFUL PLEASURES WAS TOTALLY INCOMPREHENSIBLE TO THEM.

ALL OF THIS NOT TO SAY THAT THE ROMANS WERE UNLIKE EVERY SOCIETY SINCE THE DAWN OF TIME, AND DIDN'T HAVE STRICT RULES AND SOCIAL REGULATIONS PERTAINING TO KNOCKIN' BOOTIES. OF COURSE THEY DID -- BUT THEY WERE BASED AROUND THE ACT ITSELF, NOT SOMETHING HARMLESS LIKE A PAINTING OF SOMEONE GETTING THEIR FREAK ON.

FOR INSTANCE: IT WAS FELT THAT ONE SHOULD NOT PUT ANOTHERS GENITALS INTO YOUR MOUTH UNLESS YOU WERE A WHORE OR SLAVE. THE MOUTH HAD SIGNIFICANT VALUE TO THE ROMANS, AND THEIR SOCIETY HAD A FIXATION ON THE PURITY OF IT. THIS WAS YOUR METHOD OF SPEECH AND HOW YOU DISPLAYED NOT ONLY YOUR EMOTION, BUT YOUR INTELLECT. IT WAS YOUR MOST IMPORTANT TOOL TO PROVE YOUR WORTH AS A VALUED CITIZEN. TO USE YOUR ORATORY HOLE THE WAY YOU'D USE YOUR FUCK HOLES WAS CONSIDERED DOWNRIGHT WEIRD.

PRAYING AT THE ALTAR OF PRIAPUS, SUPER-DONGED MEGA-GOD OF SEXY TIMES

THE FIRST OBJECT OF ART TAKEN FROM POMPEII, STUDIED, AND LABELLED AS PORN -- INDEED THE FIRST EXAMPLE OF PORNOGRAPHY IN HUMAN HISTORY -- WAS AN AMAZING MARBLE STATUE OF THE GOD PAN SCREWING THE SNOT OUT OF A FEMALE GOAT, BOTH OF WHOM LOOKED AS IF THEY WERE LOVING EVERY MINUTE OF IT.

A PLAN WOULD HAVE TO BE DEVISED. IT COULDN'T BE DESTROYED THANKS TO ITS HISTORICAL VALUE, REBURYING WASN'T AN OPTION NOW THAT THE EXCAVATION WAS THE TALK OF EUROPE, AND IT CERTAINLY COULDN'T BE DISPLAYED. THE ONLY OTHER FEASIBLE OPTION WAS TO HIDE IT AWAY UNDER LOCK AND KEY. METAL DOORS WERE BUILT OVER THE GORGEOUS MURALS FOUND ALL OVER POMPEII, AND IN 1849, A BRICKED-OVER DOORWAY TO A ROOM IN A GALLERY BECAME KNOWN AS "THE SECRET MUSEUM".

THE CREATION OF THIS PLACE IN THE CITY OF NAPLES WAS INTEGRAL IN THE INVENTION OF THE CONCEPT OF PORN. WHEN WE LABEL IMAGES OR ART AS "DIFFERENT", AND TUCK THEM AWAY UNDER THE PRETENCE OF PROTECTING PEOPLE, WE ARE CENSORING -- AND CENSORSHIP AND PORNOGRAPHY ARE INSEPARABLE. INDEED, THIS WAS THE FIRST EXAMPLE IN ACTION OF OUR SOCIETIES LONG-STANDING BELIEF THAT IMAGES OF SEX WILL CAUSE AN INDIVIDUAL DAMAGE, AND WILL ALSO PROVOKE DISTURBANCE AND A LACK OF MORALS IN SOCIETY AT LARGE.

NOW THAT THIS KINDA THING WAS GOING DOWN, IT NEEDED TO BE QUALIFIED AND QUANTIFIED. UP UNTIL THEN, THERE WASN'T EVEN A WORD TO DESCRIBE IMAGES ON THE BASIS OF THEIR SEXUAL CONTENT, SO WHEN THE WORD "PORNOGRAPHY" FIRST APPEARED IN A ENGLISH MEDICAL DICTIONARY IN 1857, IT WAS SOME WATERSHED SHIT.

DAY-UM, THESE ROMANS WUZ CRAY-ZEE!

ART HISTORY 'N' SHIT

TO CELEBRATE THIS BRAND NEW WAY IN WHICH GOVERNMENT WOULD STRIVE TO POLICE THE PEOPLE, THE VICTORIANS LAUNCHED THE VERY FIRST OFFICIAL CAMPAIGN AGAINST PORNOGRAPHY.

"THE OBSCENE PUBLICATIONS ACT" WAS PASSED BY PARLIAMENT IN 1857. I DOUBT THEY KNEW IT AT THE TIME, BUT THIS INTERVENTION BY THE STATE IN THE CONSUMPTION OF SEXUAL IMAGERY WOULD WIND UP AS ONE OF THE MOST HISTORICALLY SIGNIFICANT UNDERTAKINGS OF PRUDISH STIFF UPPER-LIPPERY **EVER**, AND IT WOULD AFFECT HUMANS IN EVERY CIVILISED COUNTRY FOR HUNDREDS (AND PERHAPS EVEN THOUSANDS) OF YEARS.

IT WAS A LEGAL PRECEDENT THAT CREATED A BRAND NEW STRUCTURE AROUND THE ACT OF LOOKING AT SEXUAL IMAGERY OR NUDITY. THESE WERE OUTLANDISH AND FANCIFUL THEORIES THAT ARE STILL VERY POPULAR TO THIS DAY -- SUCH AS THE IDEA THAT THE VIEWING OF OBSCENE IMAGES WILL MAKE YOU AN ADDICT. OR THAT PORN WILL MAKE YOU DEGRADE YOURSELF WITH THE DAMAGING ACT OF MASTURBATION, AND MASTURBATING WILL THEN MAKE YOU LOOK AT MORE PORN, AND SO ON AND SO ON INTO AN ENDLESS VORTEX OF SIN THAT ENDS ONLY WHEN THE

MY RECREATION OF A PAINTING ON A WALL OF A PUBLIC BATH (KNOWN AS THERMS) IN POMPEII. IT WAS PAINTED IN 79 BC.

PERSON IS PUT IN A MADHOUSE OR A CASKET.

WITH THE INVENTION OF THIS ORIFICE-POUNDING, ENGORGED, AND LUBRICATED NOTION, VICTORIAN MORALITY AND ITS OBSESSION WITH SEXUAL RESTRAINT BECAME THE NORM IN EUROPE; THANKS TO THE PROMINENCE OF THE BRITISH EMPIRE DUE TO THEIR RIGOUROUS COLONISATION EFFORTS IN THE AMERICAS AND ELSEWHERE, THESE NEW RULES AND VALUES SPREAD ACROSS THE PLANET LIKE WILDFIRE.

JUST LIKE BEING BORN INTO A CULT, MANY OF US NOW GROW UP, LIVE OUR LIVES, AND DIE -- NEVER QUESTIONING WHY PORNOGRAPHY SHOULD BE KEPT SEPARATE, CONTROLLED, AND VIEWED AS TABOO. THE MAJORITY OF US SIMPLY ACCEPT THAT AS THE WAY THAT IT IS, AND THAT IS HOW IT MUST HAVE ALWAYS BEEN.

SO WHAT BECAME OF THE SECRET MUSEUM? WELL, IT WAS PREDICTABLY CLOSED TO THE PUBLIC FOR OVER A HUNDRED YEARS, ONLY BRIEFLY BEING MADE ACCESSIBLE AGAIN AT THE END OF THE 1960s (DUE TO THE SEXUAL REVOLUTION), BEFORE BEING CLOSED UP FOR ANOTHER 30 YEARS. THE MUSEUM WAS FINALLY OPENED PERMANENTLY ONLY IN THE YEAR 2000, AND NOWADAYS YOU CAN GO TO THE NAPLES NATIONAL ARCHAEOLOGICAL MUSEUM AND CHECK OUT OL' PAN FUCKING HIS GOAT ON ANY DAY OF THE YEAR EXCEPT CHRISTMAS DAY.

COULD IT BE THAT WE MIGHT LIVE LONG ENOUGH TO WITNESS THE GHOSTS OF QUEEN VICTORIA AND HER STUFFY LEGISLATORS FINALLY BEING FORCED TO LOOSEN THEIR 150 YEAR GRIP ON MODERN FREE-THINKING SOCIETY?

STAY TUNED PORN FANS

AND:

WITH THAT WEDGE OF HISTORICAL CONTEXT PACKED INTO PLACE, PLEASE ALLOW ME TO WELCOME ALL OF YOU TO CINEMA SEWER BOOK THREE! MY HOPE IS THAT THIS ONE WILL KICK THE ASSES OF THE PREVIOUS VOLUMES, OR AT THE VERY LEAST HOLD ITS OWN IN TERMS OF ENTERTAINMENT VALUE.

PRETTY MUCH THIS WHOLE THING WAS WRITTEN AND DRAWN BY ME, BUT I'D BE REMISS IF I DIDN'T MENTION ALL OF THE OTHER EXCELLENT CONTRIBUTORS, SUCH AS:

(IN NO PARTICULAR ORDER) CHRIS ENG, BRANDON GRAHAM, MORITAT, REBECCA DART, SHAWN JOHNS, KAZIMIR STREZEPEK, MIKE SULLIVAN, PHIL BARRETT, DOCTOR BIOBRAIN, D.J. BRYANT, TED DAVE, BEN NEWMAN, DAVID PALEO, TIM GRANT, JOSH SIMMONS, JOSEPH BERGIN THE THIRD, SEAN ESTY, COLIN UPTON, MIKE MYHRE, TIMOTEO, DON GUARISCO, AND YET ANOTHER BOOTY-SMASHIN' COVER BY MR. VINCE RAURUS: WWW.VENIVIDIVINCE.COM

THIS BOOK COLLECTS THE BEST OF ISSUES #17 TO #20 (ORIGINALLY PUBLISHED 2005 TO 2007) AS WELL AS MOUNDS OF BRAND NEW CRUD THAT I'VE PUT TOGETHER OVER THE LAST YEAR JUST FOR THIS BOOK!

ANYWAY -- HOPE YOU ENJOY IT!

ROBIN BOUGIE
WWW.CINEMASEWER.COM
☆ ☆ ☆ ☆ ☆ ☆ ☆ ☆ ☆ ☆

LITTLE MISS DANGEROUS

TEXT: ROBIN BOUGIE
ART: PHILIP BARRETT

ONE OF THE DEFINING MOMENTS IN THE SHAPING OF MY EXPLOITATIONAL TASTES IN ENTERTAINMENT CAME WHEN I WAS 12 YEARS OLD. AT THAT TIME, MOST OF MY TV AND FILM WATCHING INTEREST DIDN'T GET MUCH CRAZIER THAN STUFF STARRING THE MUPPETS, BUT I ALSO INDULGED IN MIAMI VICE ON FRIDAY NIGHTS AT 9:00.

MIAMI VICE WAS THE FIRST TV DRAMA THAT WATCHED LIKE A MOVIE/MUSIC VIDEO, AND I ADORED IT. THE LIGHTS WOULD GO OUT AND THE VOLUME WOULD GET CRANKED UP, AND I'D IMMERSE MYSELF INTO THE 1980'S COKED OUT UNDERWORLD OF MIAMI FOR AN HOUR.

IT WASN'T UNTIL A FEW MONTHS BACK (WHEN THE DVD BOX SET CAME OUT) THAT I REVISITED A LOT OF THESE EPISODES FROM THE SERIES, AND I REMEMBERED THAT IT WAS THE ONE STARRING '80S FLASH-IN-THE-PAN SINGER FIONA THAT HAD THE BIGGEST EFFECT ON ME THEN, AND I WAS SURPRISED TO FIND I WAS A LITTLE SHAKEN UP STILL.

FIONA WAS A CROSS BETWEEN TEEN POP IDOL TIFFANY, AND LONG HAIRED METAL QUEEN LEE AARON (ALTHOUGH NOT EVEN CLOSE TO BEING AS WELL KNOWN AS EITHER) AND DESPITE HAVING NO ACTING EXPERIENCE, SHE VERY CONVINCINGLY PLAYED A TEEN PROSTITUTE IN A 2ND SEASON EPISODE ENTITLED; 'LITTLE MISS DANGEROUS'.

SHE'S A CRAZED WHORE WHO'S MURDERING HER TRICKS, AND SHE FALLS IN LOVE WITH VICE COP RICARDO TUBBS (PHILIP MICHAEL THOMAS) WHO DESPITE HER JEALOUS PIMP, TRIES TO HELP HER OFF THE STREETS. HE DOESN'T REALISE THAT SHE'S A BLOODTHIRSTY MENTAL CASE AS SOON AS HER CLOTHES COME OFF.

OK, SO HERE WE HAVE A CHARACTER THAT'S IMPLIED TO BE UNDERAGE. A HOOKER, AND WHO DOES LIVE SEX SHOWS ON A FUCKING BURNING STAGE.

...SHE PULLS OUT A GUN AND BLOWS HER HEAD OFF!

IT TURNED OUT TO BE A FAIRLY EASY BIT OF DETECTIVE WORK. SHE'S NOW A HOUSEWIFE IN NEW JERSEY AND WAS HAPPY TO TELL ME ALL ABOUT MAKING THE EPISODE.

BUT THE CRAZY PART WAS YET TO COME. THE FINALE IS THIS INTENSE NAIL-BITING SCENE WITH PIL'S 'ORDER OF DEATH' PLAYING, WHERE FIONA GETS NAKED, CHAINS TUBBS TO A BED, AND WHILE HE SCREAMS AND FREAKS OUT...

THAT SHIT WAS SOOOO HEAVY - ESPECIALLY FOR 1986 CONSERVATIVE REAGAN-ERA TV-LAND. UPON RE-LIVING THE SLIGHT MENTAL TRAUMA I HAD THE FIRST TIME AROUND, I DECIDED I WAS GONNA TRACK FIONA DOWN AND TELL HER WHAT AN EFFECT SHE HAD ON ME.

"THE DIRECTOR LEON ICHASO, PICKED ME UP AT MIAMI INTERNATIONAL. HE WAS A WILD MAN. I LOVED HIM. HE CALLED ME MILKY."

"WE ENDED UP DRIVING THROUGH THE AIRPORT ON SOME TARMAC OR RUNWAY TO THE SET OF THE EPISODE THAT WAS CURRENTLY BEING FILMED. IT WAS VERY DISORIENTATING AND A BIT FRIGHTENING."

"I'VE ALWAYS REMEMBERED HIM COS HE HAD A WEIRD NAME AND HE WAS VERY INTENSE AND BEAUTIFUL. I THINK THEY BOTH ALREADY KNEW HE HAD TO GO HOME BECAUSE HE HAD AN INFECTION IN HIS ARM, BUT THEY WANTED ME TO MEET HIM ANYWAY."

"LARRY JOSHUA CAME FROM NEW YORK TO PLAY CAT. I DIDN'T MEET HIM UNTIL WE WERE DOING A SEX SCENE TOGETHER ON CAMERA!"

"THEN WE HAD CUBAN SANDWICHES AND TINY STRONG COFFEES SOME-WHERE IN MIAMI. LATER, MAYBE THE SAME NIGHT, LEON TOOK ME TO MEET THE GUY WHO WAS GOING TO PLAY CAT (HER PIMP-ED), VIGGO MORTENSEN."

"LEON COACHED ME THE NEXT DAY IN HIS HOTEL SUITE WHICH WAS BRILLIANT BECAUSE WHEN WE WERE ACTUALLY FILMING THERE WAS NO TIME FOR ANY KIND OF ACTING HELP. IT WAS SETTING UP SHOTS AND ACTION, ACTION, ACTION!"

WHEN I TOLD FIONA HOW SHE HAD STARTED ME ON A 20 YEAR OBSESSION WITH THE SEX TRADE WHEN SHE FUCKED MY YOUNG ASS UP WITH HER OVER SEXED HOOKER/PSYCHO PORTRAYAL, AND HOW IT WAS POSSIBLE THAT CINEMA SEWER WOULDN'T EVEN EXIST IF NOT FOR THAT EPISODE - SHE SIMPLY SAID:

"I THOUGHT EVERY TV SHOW WAS ABOUT A PROSTITUTE."

END!

9

ENTER THE NINJAS:

THE RISE AND FALL OF GOLAN + GLOBUS

BY: ROBIN BOUGIE · 2010 ·

THE STORY OF CANNON IS THE STORY OF A DECADE. THE 1980s. ISRAELI COUSINS MENAHEM GOLAN AND YORAM GLOBUS MOVED TO AMERICA AND BOUGHT THE CANNON GROUP IN 1979 FROM DENNIS FRIEDLAND AND CHRISTOPHER DEWEY FOR A MERE $350,000. CANNON WAS A TINY LITTLE PRODUCTION HOUSE AT THE TIME, BUT WITHIN ONLY FIVE YEARS MENAHEM AND YORAM HAD TRANSFORMED IT INTO CALIFORNIA'S BIGGEST INDEPENDENT FILM COMPANY, WITH REVENUES REACHING $150 MILLION. AMAZINGLY, THREE SHORT YEARS AFTER THAT, THEY HAD PISSED IT ALL AWAY.

THEY USED TO SAY THAT IF YOU WERE HUNGRY, DESPERATE, AND TALENTED, THERE WAS A PLACE FOR YOU AT CANNON. MENAHEM AND YORAM ACHIEVED WHAT THEY DID WITH THEIR UPSTART PRODUCTION HOUSE BY HIRING THE HIGHEST QUALITY DIRECTORS AND WRITERS THEY COULD DRUM UP, AND THEN GETTING THEM TO MAKE LOW BUDGET, QUICKLY MADE, CROWD-PLEASING THEATRICAL PRODUCT. IT WAS A FORMULA THAT ROGER CORMAN HAD INVENTED, BUT THAT GOLAN AND HIS COUSIN PERFECTED.

ON TOP OF PRODUCING CONTENT FOR A QUARTER OF WHAT HOLLYWOOD FILM COMPANIES WERE, GOLAN AND GLOBUS ALSO REDUCED COSTS AND MAXED OUT PROFITS BY TALKING NAME-BRAND STARS INTO FORFEITING THEIR LARGE PAYCHEQUES IN RETURN FOR A SLICE OF THE PIE. THIS PROFIT-SHARING GAME PLAN WORKED GREAT, BECAUSE IT NOT ONLY MADE THEM POPULAR WITH STARS, BUT IT WAS ALSO BACKED UP BY THE FACT THAT CANNON SAFEGUARDED AGAINST LOSS BY SELLING CABLE, HOME VIDEO, AND OVERSEAS EXHIBITION RIGHTS PRIOR TO PRODUCTION.

AT CANNON, CREATIVITY WAS KING. GOLAN AND GLOBUS AFFORDED AN UNHEARD OF AMOUNT OF ARTISTIC FREEDOM TO FILMMAKERS WHO COULD WORK WITHIN THEIR BUDGETARY CONSTRAINTS, TO THE POINT WHERE THEY OFTEN DIDN'T EVEN BOTHER READING THE SCRIPTS OF THE MOVIES THEY PRODUCED. INSTEAD, THEY WOULD RELY ON THE QUALITIES OF THE PEOPLE THEY HIRED, AND THE MONEYMAKING ABILITY OF THE IDEAS PRESENTED BY THOSE PEOPLE. THEIR NICKNAME WAS "THE GO-GO BOYS", AND THEIR UNORTHODOX MANNER OF MAKING MOVIES GARNERED THEM A TINSELTOWN REP FOR WILDLY FLYING BY THE SEAT OF THEIR PANTS.

TOBE HOOPER, DESPITE THE FLOPPING OF HIS FIRST CANNON GROUP OUTING (THE SCI-FI VAMPIRE GOREFEST KNOWN AS LIFEFORCE) CLAIMED THAT "CANNON WAS REALLY A GOOD COMPANY TO WORK FOR, SINCE BOTH YORAM AND MENAHEM LOVED THE MOVIES AND THE FILMMAKERS, AND REALLY TREATED THEM WELL. IT SEEMED MORE, WHEN I WAS THERE, LIKE MAYBE WHAT THE OLD SYSTEM WAS LIKE. I MISS THAT KIND OF SHOWMANSHIP AND RISK TAKING."

GOLAN AND GLOBUS, CIRCA 1986

IN 1985/1986 CANNON PRODUCED 72 FILMS, MORE THAN ANY OTHER FILM COMPANY

IN AMERICA, AND AS THEIR THEATRICAL ROSTER GREW, SO DID THEIR BUDGETS AND THEIR FINANCIAL BURDENS. UNFORTUNATELY, WHEN CANNON ACQUIRED PRODUCTION COMPANY THORN EMI AND THE 6TH LARGEST THEATRE CHAIN IN THE COUNTRY (COMMONWEALTH), THEY HAD BIT OFF MORE THAN THEY COULD CHEW. THESE RISKY MOVES CRIPPLED THE GOLAN AND GLOBUS EMPIRE, WHICH WAS GROWING LEGENDARY ON THE BACK OF EVENTS SUCH AS GOLAN AND JEAN LUC GODARD SIGNING A MILLION DOLLAR CONTRACT ON A FUCKING COCKTAIL NAPKIN OVER LUNCH IN CANNES. ON TOP OF THAT WAS 'OVER THE TOP' -- A HIGHLY ENGAGING FLOP STARRING SYLVESTER STALLONE AS A RUGGED ARM-WRESTLING TRUCK DRIVER TRYING TO WIN THE LOVE OF HIS PREP-SCHOOL SON. UNWISELY, CANNON PONIED UP A RECORD $13 MILLION DOLLAR SALARY FOR STALLONE, AND ENDED UP TAKING IT RIGHT IN THE ANUS WHEN BOX OFFICE RECEIPTS WERE FAR LOWER THAN PREDICTED. A 17 MILLION DOLLAR BUDGET FOR THE LIVE-ACTION MASTERS OF THE UNIVERSE MOVIE DIDN'T HELP MUCH EITHER.

NEAR BANKRUPTCY IN 1988, THE GO-GO BOYS HAD GONE AND RUN OUT OF OPTIONS. HANDING CONTROL OF THE COMPANY OVER TO ITALIAN FINANCIER GIANCARLO PARRETTI WAS A LAST-DITCH EFFORT, AND TURNED OUT TO BE YET ANOTHER REALLY BAD PLAY. THE BRASH MOGUL WOULD GO ON TO BUY MGM FOR 1.3 BILLION, FIRE EVERYONE, RUN THE COMPANY INTO THE GROUND, AND END UP IN JAIL FOR MISUSE OF CORPORATE FUNDS. GOLAN GOT OUT WHILE HE COULD AND DISSOLVED THE GOLAN-GLOBUS PARTNERSHIP, WHILE GLOBUS AND PARRETTI CHANGED THE COMPANY NAME TO PATHE COMMUNICATIONS. A YEAR LATER LOAN PAYMENTS WERE DEFAULTED ON, LAWSUITS CAME ROCKETING IN FROM ALL DIRECTIONS, AND EVERYTHING THAT WAS LEFT OF CANNON GOT SWALLOWED UP WHOLE BY AN MGM STUDIO THAT WAS NOW OWNED BY A FRENCH BANK.

BY 1993 PARRETTI WAS A MEMORY, AND GLOBUS TEAMED UP WITH CHRISTOPHER PEARCE TO TRY TO GET THE CANNON-BALL ROLLING ONCE MORE, BUT IT WAS NOT TO BE. AFTER A YEAR OF FALSE STARTS AND DIRECT-TO-VIDEO BUSTS (SUCH AS HELLBOUND, CHAIN OF COMMAND, AND STREET KNIGHT), THEY LET THE NOW-BELOVED CANNON NAME, LOGO, AND LEGEND REST IN PEACE.

"IF YOU MAKE AN AMERICAN FILM WITH A BEGINNING, A MIDDLE AND AN END, WITH A BUDGET OF LESS THAN FIVE MILLION DOLLARS, YOU MUST BE AN IDIOT TO LOSE MONEY."
- MENAHEM GOLAN

NOW IT'S TIME FOR: **CINEMA SEWER'S 50 MUST-SEE GOLAN-GLOBUS CANNON PRODUCTIONS!**
OK! (DRUM ROLL) HERE WE GO IN ORDER OF THE RELEASE DATE OF EACH FILM!

THIS IS GONNA BE FUUUN!

THE APPLE
(1980. DIR: MENAHEM GOLAN)
THIS IS THE ONE THAT STARTED IT ALL! A COUPLE OF NAIVE TEENS FROM MOOSE JAW, SASKATCHEWAN COMPETE IN THE SUPER FUTURISTIC 1994 WORLDVISION SONG CONTEST. MEGACONGLOMERATE BIM AND ITS DEVILISH LEADER MR. BOOGALOW SOON COME CALLING, AND OFFER FAME IN RETURN FOR SOULS. PACKED WITH GLITTERY, OUTRAGEOUS COSTUMES, CATCHY SONGS, EYE-POPPING SETS, AND WONKY FUTURE-SLANG, THIS LUSH DISCO ATROCITY WILL FLIP YOUR GOURD! IT CERTAINLY WASN'T VERY WELL-LIKED WHEN IT FIRST CAME OUT, THOUGH. REPORTEDLY DURING ITS PREMIERE AT THE PARAMOUNT THEATRE IN HOLLYWOOD, AUDIENCES THREW THEIR FREE SOUVENIR SOUNDTRACKS AT THE SCREEN, CAUSING SERIOUS DAMAGE. SHORTLY THEREAFTER AT A SCREENING THAT GOLAN AND GLOBUS ATTENDED IN MONTREAL, THE AUDIENCE ERUPTED INTO A LOUD CHORUS OF BOOS. AS THE LIGHTS CAME UP, GOLAN WAS NOWHERE TO BE FOUND, BUT WAS DISCOVERED LATER ON THE ROOF OF HIS DOWNTOWN HOTEL, PONDERING SUICIDE. GLOBUS

THE POWER OF ROCK...IN 1994.

THE APPLE

SCHIZOID

TALKED HIS COUSIN DOWN, AND THE REST IS HISTORY. FELLOW APPLE FANATICS: LOOK FOR AN EPISODE OF THE UK 'KITCHEN NIGHTMARES,' WHERE GORDON RAMSAY HELPS APPLE STAR ALLAN LOVE GET A FISH AND CHIP RESTAURANT OFF THE GROUND. IT'S THE BEST EPISODE OF THE SERIES.

SCHIZOID (1980 DIR: DAVID PAULSEN)
OH MAN, I ADORE KLAUS KINSKI. IT'S TOUGH NOT TO, BECAUSE HE WAS SO DAMN NUTTY. THE CAMERA LOVES CRAZY PEOPLE, ESPECIALLY WHEN THEY ARE INCREDIBLY CHARISMATIC BUG-EYED THESPIANS AND PLAY WEIRD PERVERTS. HERE, KLAUS RUNS A THERAPY GROUP THAT HE USES AS HIS PERSONAL DATING SUPPLY, AND ALSO SEEMS TO HAVE AN UNHEALTHY INTEREST IN HIS OWN TEENAGE DAUGHTER (DONNA WILKES, THE CHICK FROM ANGEL!). WHEN THE FEMALE MEMBERS OF THE GROUP START GETTING HACKED APART BY A KILLER ARMED WITH SCISSORS, POOR OL' KLAUS HAS SOME SPLAININ' TO DO...

NEW YEAR'S EVIL (1980 DIR: EMMETT ALSTON)
MY PICK FOR THE BEST TITLE OF ANY OF THE CANNON GROUP EFFORTS. BEGINS ON NEW YEAR'S EVE WHERE PUNK KROQ DISC JOCKEY DIANE SULLIVAN (AKA BLAZE) IS HOSTING A PARTY-PACKED COUNTDOWN INTO THE NEW YEAR. SHIT GOES AWRY, HOWEVER, WHEN A RIDICULOUS FOZZIE BEAR SOUNDING-MOTHERFUCKER ANNOUNCES THAT HE'S GONNA MURDER A SLUT EACH TIME THE CLOCK STRIKES 12 IN ONE OF THE WORLD'S VARIOUS TIME ZONES, CULMINATING IN DIANE'S HORRIFIC DEMISE. NOT A VERY SCARY SLASHER MOVIE, BUT A FUN ONE. WHAT OTHER MOVIE PURPORTS THAT "SPIN OUT AND BOIL YOUR HAIR" IS COMMON SLANG FOR PUNKERS, OR WOULD SHOW THE KILLER SUCCESSFULLY PICKING UP A NUBILE YOUNG KNIFE-HOLDER BY INVITING HER TO A PARTY AT ERIK ESTRADA'S HOUSE? HONESTLY.

DON'T DARE MAKE NEW YEAR'S RESOLUTIONS... UNLESS YOU PLAN TO LIVE!

NEW YEAR'S EVIL

A Cannon Films Release

WARRIORS OF A LOST MARTIAL ART!
ENTER THE NINJA
FRANCO NERO • SUSAN GEORGE • SHO KOSUGI
RESTRICTED   WARNING: FREQUENT GORY VIOLENCE—

ENTER THE NINJA (1981 DIR: MENAHEM GOLAN)
HERE IT IS, THE MOVIE THAT LAUNCHED NOT ONLY THE 1980S NINJA CRAZE, BUT THE LEGENDARY CANNON ACTION MOVIE FILMOGRAPHY AS WELL. MAYBE NOT AS ASTONISHINGLY BOOTY-KICKING AS SOME OF THE CINEMATIC NINJA IDIOCY IT INSPIRED, BUT THIS IS STILL AN UNUSUALLY FUN AND FRANTIC GRADE-D ACTIONFEST THAT ONLY COST A MILLION AND A HALF SMACKERS. SOUTH AFRICAN ALT-RAP-RAVE GROUP DIE ANTWOORD RECENTLY HAD A HIT SONG CALLED "ENTER THE NINJA" THAT WAS NAMED IN HONOR OF THIS JAMMIN' FRANCO NERO CLASSIC.

THE LAST AMERICAN VIRGIN (1982 DIR: BOAZ DAVIDSON)
THREE TEENAGE BOYS SHARE A COMMON SINGULAR GOAL IN THIS FILM: TO JAM THEIR BONERS INTO SOME HAIR PIE, AND BOY DO THEY GET INTO SOME CRAZY MISADVENTURES IN THEIR QUEST TO DO SO. PERHAPS THE BEST 1980S TEEN MOVIE, AND SOME (ESPN'S BILL SIMMONS, FOR INSTANCE) HAVE EVEN CITED IT AS ONE OF THE MOST UNDERRATED AMERICAN FILMS EVER MADE. SERIOUSLY.

10 TO MIDNIGHT (1983 DIR: J. LEE THOMPSON)
I'M CONVINCED THAT ANYONE WHO HAS BEEN AWESOME IN THE LAST 30 YEARS HAS APPRECIATED CHARLES BRONSON'S MOUSTACHIOED CHARMS. IN HIS FIRST OF MANY MOVIES HE'D MAKE FOR GOLAN/GLOBUS, CHARLIE BUSTS THE NUTS OF A SERIAL KILLER WHO LIKES TO GET NAKED AND DRIVE KNIVES INTO THE TENDER TORSOS OF PRETTY YOUNG COEDS. EBERT CALLED IT "SCUMMY", AND NOTED THAT THE PEOPLE WHO MADE IT "SHOULD BE ASHAMED OF THEMSELVES" -- SO YOU KNOW DAMN WELL THAT YOU NEED TO SEE IT! ALSO OF NOTE IS THAT THIS FILM IS BASED ON TWO REAL-LIFE CASES: RICHARD SPECK'S BRUTAL SLAUGHTER OF 8 STUDENT NURSES, AND THAT OF TED BUNDY, TO WHOM ACTOR GENE DAVIS BEARS A STRIKING RESEMBLANCE.

400 years of training in the art of sudden death... unleashed on 20th century America.

REVENGE OF THE NINJA

REVENGE OF THE NINJA (1983 DIR: SAM FIRSTENBERG)
IF YOU WOULD PAY HARD-EARNED MONEY TO SEE NIMBLE NINJAS DUKE IT OUT WITH A VARIETY OF EXOTIC WEAPONS, THIS POOP IS GONNA HAVE YOU BRAYING LIKE A DONKEY AS YOU PUNCH YOUR GENITALS WITH GLEE. IT STARS GOOD OL' SHO KOSUGI, WAS SHOT IN UTAH (WHERE ELSE?) AND FEATURES A MARTIAL-ARTS GRANDMA, GRATUITOUS CHILD VIOLENCE, DISEMBOWELLINGS, THROWING STARS EMBEDDED IN EYE SOCKETS, UNEXPECTED NUDITY, AND A GHETTO STREET GANG THAT IS EERILY REMINISCENT OF THE VILLAGE PEOPLE. I'D ALSO BE REMISS IF I DIDN'T MENTION BLONDE BABE CATHY (ASHLEY FERRARE) WHO APPEARS IN A SHORT RED ROBE FOR A WORKOUT WITH THE NINJA IN QUESTION. "WELL, IF YOU WANT TO WORK OUT, YOU FORGOT YOUR PANTS" HE EXCLAIMS. AS THEY START SPARRING, HER TINY LIL' ROBE RIDES UP TO GRATUITOUSLY REVEAL THAT CATHY ISN'T JUST A BLONDE... SHE'S A NATURAL BLONDE! BOOOO-YAAA!

THE SEVEN MAGNIFICENT GLADIATORS (1983. DIR: CLAUDIO FRAGASSO)
YOU CAN GUESS THAT YOU'RE IN FOR A SWEET TREAT WHEN THE SCREENWRITING CREDIT POPS UP AND CLAUDIO FRAGASSO'S NAME APPEARS. THIS ITALIAN SCHLOCK-KING SPORTS SOME OF THE BEST '80S GENRE SCRIPTS AROUND: HELL OF THE LIVING DEAD, STRIKE COMMANDO, TROLL II, AND THE OTHER HELL TO NAME JUST A FEW. HERE HE HAS A NEARLY NAKED LOU FERRIGNO RUN AROUND WITH A SWORD, WHICH SHOULD KEEP YOU GAY FELLOWS HAPPY. DON'T FRET, MY LESBIAN SISTERS, THERE ARE SOME LOVELY GREASED-UP CLEAVAGE-HEAVERS THAT WRESTLE ONE ANOTHER FOR YOUR ENTERTAINMENT AS WELL.

YOUNG WARRIORS (1983. DIR: LAWRENCE D. FOLDES)
HEY, COOL! A STRANGE SEQUEL TO THE AWESOME 1979 DRIVE-IN HIT, MALIBU HIGH! WHAT STARTS AS A GOOFBALL FRAT COMEDY THEN TRANSFORMS INTO A DISTURBING RAPE/VIGILANTE THRILLER AND THEN MORPHS YET AGAIN INTO A BIZARRE '80S ACTION MOVIE WHERE PRETTY BOY JOCKS DRIVE AROUND WITH A POODLE (??) AND BLOW AWAY SCUMBAGS. ONLY IN CANADA COULD THIS IDIOTICALLY ENTERTAINING PORKY'S/DEATH WISH MISHMASH BE SHAT INTO EXISTENCE. MORE PEOPLE NEED TO HIP THEMSELVES TO THIS FUN LITTLE TIME-WASTER AS IT IS FAR TOO UNKNOWN FOR MY LIKING.

HERCULES (1983. DIR: LUIGI COZZI)
THIS MOVIE STARS LOU FERRIGNO AND SYBIL DANNING'S TITS. HIGHLIGHTS: HERCULES THROWS A BEAR INTO OUTER SPACE. YOU WANT MORE? FRANKLY, THAT SHOULD BE ALL YOU NEED TO GET EXCITED ABOUT THIS, BUT HE ALSO HAS GROWN MAN HANDS WHEN HE IS AN INFANT, WALKS ACROSS A RAINBOW BRIDGE, FIGHTS WITH GIANT STOP-MOTION ROBOTS, WINS A WOMAN AS A PRIZE FOR CLEANING UP CRAP FASTER THAN ANY LIVING MAN EVER HAS, AND MEETS THE KING OF AFRICA WHO RIDES AROUND WITH HIS HONKY BITCHES INSIDE A MOBILE ELEPHANT SKELETON. DID I MENTION THAT THIS IS NOT A COMEDY? MY WIFE REBECCA AND I WATCHED THIS WHOLE FUCKING THING WITH OUR PIE HOLES AGAPE, A MUST SEE. ABSOLUTELY.

MISSING IN ACTION (1984. DIR: JOSEPH ZITO)
I REMEMBER STANDING IN THE VIDEO STORE AND STARING BUG-EYED AT THE VHS BOX FOR THIS WHEN I WAS A KID -- AND JUST ACHING TO SEE IT. WE DIDN'T EVEN OWN A VCR AT THE TIME, BUT CAN YOU BLAME ME? RESPLENDENT WITH A GIANT MACHINE GUN IN PLACE OF HIS PECKER, CHUCK NORRIS CONFIDENTLY STRUTS IN THE FOREGROUND AS A GREEN HUEY LANDS IN FRONT OF A BURNING JUNGLE INFERNO. FILMED BACK TO BACK WITH PART TWO, THIS WAS ACTUALLY THE TRUE SEQUEL, BUT WAS RELEASED FIRST WHEN GOLAN AND GLOBUS DECIDED IT WAS THE SUPERIOR FILM. DIANNE HOLECHEK WOULD DISAGREE, HOWEVER. SHE WAS CHUCK'S

WIFE FOR 30 YEARS, AND NORRIS SAYS SHE CITED THIS AS HER LEAST FAVOURITE OF HIS MOVIES.

LOVE STREAMS (1984 DIR: JOHN CASSAVETES)
DEFINITELY UNLIKE ANY OTHER FILM IN THE CANNON LINE, BUT FANS OF CASSAVETES KNOW WHAT WE'RE TALKING ABOUT HERE: LOW-KEY ARTHOUSE THAT DOESN'T STINK IT UP LIKE AN OUTHOUSE. CASSAVETES AND REAL-LIFE SPOUSE GENA ROWLANDS TEAM UP AS A TROUBLED BROTHER AND SISTER BUT THE PLOT ISN'T THE DRAW HERE, IT'S THE EMOTIVE, EXPLOSIVE, NATURALISTIC PERFORMANCES. "IT WAS TWO HOURS LONG WHEN HE SCREENED IT FOR ME THE FIRST TIME", GOLAN SAID IN AN INTERVIEW WITH CHRISTOPH HUBER. "I SUGGESTED HE SHOULD TAKE OUT HALF AN HOUR SINCE IT SEEMED QUITE WONDERFUL, BUT ALSO A BIT BORING AT THAT LENGTH. HE AGREED, BUT WHEN HE SHOWED ME THE NEW CUT, IT WAS HALF AN HOUR LONGER !". CANNON RELEASED THE FILM UNCUT.

MAKING THE GRADE (1984 DIR: DORIAN WALKER)
AN UNFAIRLY FORGOTTEN EIGHTIES FISH-OUT-OF-WATER COMEDY THAT POKES FUN AT WEALTHY PREPPIES? YES PLEASE! HIGHLIGHTS INCLUDE: BRUSHING YOUR TEETH WITH COCA-COLA, A DUCK CORPSE THROWN THROUGH A WINDOW, A MOB THUG THAT LOOKS LIKE RASPUTIN, A SYNTH-HEAVY SCORE BY BASIL "CONAN" POLEDOURIS, RAD '80S DANCE MOVES, MANY HETEROSEXUAL YOUNG MEN SHAMELESSLY WEARING PINK AND YELLOW SWEATERS, AND A TIGHT CAST OF JUDD NELSON, ANDREW DICE CLAY, AND GORDON JUMP.

EXTERMINATOR 2 (1984 DIR: MARK BUNTZMAN)
YOU KNOW WHAT IS MISSING FROM YOUR LIFE RIGHT NOW? A TASTELESS MOVIE ABOUT A FLAMETHROWER-WIELDING VIGILANTE WHO ROASTS THE FACES OFF OF NEW YORK LOWLIFES ! ADMITTEDLY NOT AS SEEDY AS THE ORIGINAL, PART TWO STILL HAS ENOUGH CHEESY CHARMS TO EASILY WIN OVER THE CINEMA SEWER ARMY. NAMELY: AN F'N SWEET ELECTRONIC SCORE, MARIO VAN PEEBLES AS A PUNK GANG LEADER NAMED X, A DRUG DEALER ON ROLLER SKATES, ZIPPY BREAKDANCING, AN ARMOURED BATTLE-READY GARBAGE TRUCK, AND ALL KINDS OF WICKED PYROTECHNICS.

NINJA III: THE DOMINATION (1984 DIR: SAM FIRSTENBERG)
WHILE THE FIRST TWO NINJA MOVIES PLAYED IT STRAIGHT UP (NOW TELL ME), HERE GOOD OL' GOLAN/GLOBUS TRIED TO NOT ONLY CHOP-SOCKY THEIR WAY TO BOFFO BOX OFFICE, BUT ALSO CASH IN ON THE SUCCESS OF FLASHDANCE. YES, FLASHDANCE. DON'T ASK, JUST WATCH ! HIGHLIGHTS: A MAGIC FLOATING NINJA SWORD BACKED BY DISCO LASER LIGHTS AND DRY ICE, A LOVE SCENE WHERE V8 IS POURED ON BOOBIES AND SLURPED OFF (GROSS), AND ENOUGH LEG-WARMER AND LEOTARD-CLAD DANCING AND NINJA BATTLING TO CHOKE IRENE CARA!

THE LEGEND LIVES! HERCULES

BREAKIN'
(1984. DIR: JOE SILBERG)
"FOR THE BREAK OF YOUR LIFE ! PUSH IT TO POP IT ! ROCK IT TO LOCK IT ! BREAK IT TO MAKE IT !" THAT IS WHAT BREAKIN'S PRINT ADVERTISING TAGLINE SCREAMED LIKE A DRILL SERGEANT WITH TOURETTES, BUT BREAKIN' HAD NO MILITARY CHOPS TO BACK THAT UP -- INSTEAD THEATERGOERS WERE TREATED TO AN OVERLY ENERGETIC BREAKDANCE VERSION OF WEST SIDE STORY. LOOK FOR AN ODDBALL CROWD CAMEO EARLY ON BY A YOUNG FROLICING JEAN-CLAUDE VAN DAMME WHO COULD ONLY LAND ACTING WORK AS AN EXTRA AT THAT POINT IN HIS CAREER, AND WAS CLEARLY JUST TRYING TO PAY SOME RENT AS HE SPAZZ-DANCED FOR THE CAMERA MAN'S ATTENTION.

BREAKIN' 2: ELECTRIC BOOGALOO (1984. DIR: SAM FIRSTENBERG)
HOW COULD THE CREATORS OF BREAKIN'2 HAVE

KNOWN WHEN THEY DUBBED THEIR SEQUEL "ELECTRIC BOOGALOO" THAT THE SUBTITLE WOULD PASS INTO COMMON ENGLISH LANGUAGE USAGE ANYTIME AN IMAGINARY SEQUEL WAS FACETIOUSLY SCOFFED ABOUT? IF YOU LIKE YOUR CINEMA INDISTINGUISHABLE FROM A LIONEL RICHIE MUSIC VIDEO, LOOK NO FURTHER THAN THIS GOOD NATURED MUSICAL HOLOCAUST, WHICH, FOR MY MONEY, SURPASSES THE ORIGINAL QUITE HANDILY.

KING SOLOMON'S MINES (1985. DIR: J. LEE THOMPSON)

YET ANOTHER SOLID AND QUICKLY-PACED OFFERING FROM ONE OF CANNON'S MOST PROLIFIC DIRECTORS (THE ALWAYS RESOLUTELY DEPENDABLE J. LEE THOMPSON) AND THIS ONE STARS A YOUNG SHARON STONE WHO IN HER PRIME WAS WORTH HER FAIR SHARE OF PENILE SALUTES. SET IN THE WILDS OF TURN OF THE CENTURY AFRICA, THIS WAS BIRTHED AMONGST THE FETID LITTER OF RAIDERS OF THE LOST ARK CLONES, AND IS PROBABLY THE MOST SHAMELESS RIP-OFF OF THE WILDLY POPULAR SPIELBERG/LUCAS FRANCHISE. THE FILM ALSO FEATURES AN ENTERTAINING JERRY GOLDSMITH SCORE, WHICH, IN ORDER TO CUT COSTS, THE SEQUEL WOULD USE AS WELL.

RUNAWAY TRAIN (1985. DIR: ANDREY KONCHALOVSKY)

THE SETTING: A RUNAWAY TRAIN IN THE DEAD OF WINTER ROCKETS TOWARDS OBLIVION. THE PLAYERS: TWO ESCAPED CONVICTS AND A CUTE YOUNG FEMALE RAILWAY WORKER. THE VERDICT: FROM START TO FINISH, THIS MOVIE (WHICH HAPPENS TO BE GOLAN AND GLOBUS' PERSONAL FAVOURITE FROM THEIR OWN FILMOGRAPHY) WILL ENTHRAL AND KEEP YOU GUESSING FROM MINUTE ONE TO MINUTE 112. IT'S WRITTEN BY BOTH LEGENDARY JAPANESE DIRECTOR AKIRA KUROSAWA AND BANK ROBBER (TURNED WRITER AND ACTOR) EDDIE BUNKER, AND NOMINATED FOR A BUNCHA OSCARS. LOOK FOR A YOUNG DANNY TREJO IN HIS FIRST ROLE.

MISSING IN ACTION 2: THE BEGINNING (1985 DIR: LANCE HOOL)

IT'S BEARDED JINGOISTIC, XENOPHOBIC, ULTRA PATRIOTIC CLAPTRAP AS ONE ONLY FINDS IN A VIOLENT CHUCK NORRIS WAR FILM FROM THE '80S, AND YOU'LL LOVE EVERY SECOND OF IT. FRANKLY, IT'S ABOUT AS EASY TO TAKE SERIOUSLY AS THE SATURDAY MORNING RAMBO CARTOON FROM THE SAME ERA, AND THAT HELPS IT WORK AS EXPLOITATION. SOON-TECK OH IS SUPER AS AN OVER-THE-TOP TORTURE-HAPPY VILLAIN 'FRANCOIS' AND HIS SLUTTY CAMBODIAN JUNGLE WHORES ARE A REALLY NICE TOUCH, AS IS THE SCENE WHERE NORRIS ATTACKS A WILD RAT WITH JUST HIS TEETH. ALSO: ANY MOVIE THAT HAS THIS MANY CHARACTERS GET FUCKING BURNT TO DEATH WITH A FLAME THROWER IS OK IN MY BOOKS.

HERCULES 2 (1985 DIR: LUIGI COZZI)

BECAUSE ONE WAS JUST NOT ENOUGH! WHERE ELSE DOES THE HERO OF A MOVIE GROW SO HUGE THAT HE CAN STEP BETWEEN THE EARTH AND THE MOON WHEN THEY START GETTING UPPITY WITH ONE ANOTHER? WHAT OTHER FILM GIVES YOU SOUND AND VISUAL FX THAT ARE ATARI 2600 QUALITY? NONE HAVE THE BALLS TO, THEY WOULDN'T DARE. WELL THIS MOVIE DOES, AND IT ALL CULMINATES IN A CHEESEFEST LASER LIGHT SHOW IN THE SKY AS COLOURFUL OUTLINES OF THE CHARACTERS ARE ANIMATED ONTO AN OUTER SPACE BACKDROP. THEY DO BATTLE AS LASER GORILLAS, DINOSAURS, SNAKES, AND WHAT THE HELL IS GOING ON IN THIS FUCKING MOVIE? ASTONISHMENT, THAT'S WHAT. BE A BETTER PERSON BY PARTAKING IN IT.

DEATH WISH 3 (1985 DIR: MICHAEL WINNER)

I CAN'T DECIDE IF THIS IS THE BEST OF THE DEATH WISH MOVIES, THE BEST CANNON MOVIE EVER MADE, THE BEST BRONSON MOVIE OR ALL THREE! THIS TIME OUT, PAUL KERSEY'S ARMY BUDDY IS GAKKED BY GHETTO GOONS, AND HE AND AN APARTMENT BUILDING OF LOW-RENT FAMILIES AND SENIORS DECIDE TO TURN THEIR BLOCK INTO A WAR ZONE. YES, THE STREETS OF

THE SOUTH BRONX ARE SPLASHED WITH CRIMSON AS NEARLY 80 PEOPLE ARE BEATEN, STABBED, SHOT, RAPED, AND BLOWN TO SMITHEREENS WITH A BAZOOKA. THE DIALOGUE IS SILLY, THE ACTION IS DELIRIOUS, AND THE CONCEPT IS ABSOLUTE MADNESS. A MUST-VIEW.

LIFEFORCE (1985 DIR: TOBE HOOPER)
SEXY SPACE VAMPIRES AS A THEME, AND AN ARMY OF FX CREATORS, MODEL BUILDERS, AND PROSTHETIC MAKEUP ARTISTS THAT, ALL TOLD, CONSISTED OF 156 INDIVIDUALS. THAT IS ALL I SHOULD HAVE TO SAY TO YOU, BUT I WILL ALSO ADD THAT I LOVED THE POOP OUT OF THIS ONE.

THUNDER ALLEY (1985 DIR: J.S. CARDONE)
DO YOU LIKE TO ROCK? DO YOU PERHAPS LIKE TO WITNESS OTHER PEOPLE WHEN THEY ROCK? WELCOME TO YOUR MOVIE WHICH FOLLOWS A BAND CALLED 'MAGIC' AND THEIR STRATOSPHERIC RISE TO STARDOM. THE NAKED GROUPIES ARE NICE, BUT WATCH OUT FOR THE DRUG OVERDOSING, BOYS! '70S HEARTTHROB LEIF GARRETT STARS.

INVASION U.S.A. (1985 DIR: JOSEPH ZITO)
CHUCK NORRIS IS HERE TO SUCK YOUR MAN-TITS AND TONGUE YOUR LADY-BALLS, AND YOU BETTER NOT HAVE ANYTHING TO SAY ABOUT IT, OR HE'LL CHOMP THEM OFF AND SPIT THEM AT THE SUN! CHUCK IS MATT HUNTER, A ONE-MAN ARMY WHO IS LITERALLY EVERYWHERE AT ONCE WHEN ALL OF THE TERRORISTS ON EARTH DECIDE TO TEAM UP AND INVADE THE USA AS A UNIFIED FORCE. READ THAT AGAIN AND CONSIDER HOW CRAZY IT IS, AND YOU'LL BE CLOSER TO UNDERSTANDING WHY THIS IS THE SINGLE GREATEST NINETY MINUTES OF THE CHUCK NORRIS FILMOGRAPHY.

INVADERS FROM MARS (1986 DIR: TOBE HOOPER)
TOBE HAD A DECENT BUDGET AND A HOST OF TALENTED CREW MEMBERS AND STILL MANAGED TO SHIT THE BED SOMEHOW WITH THIS ONE. I MEAN, STAN WINSTON DID AMAZING CREATURE FX WORK HERE, BUT HIS HARD WORK IS MOSTLY RUINED BECAUSE HOOPER INSISTS ON SHOWING US EVERYTHING. BRIGHTLY LIT FULL FIGURE CAMERA SHOTS OF SLOW, WADDLING BIG-MOUTH ALIENS DOES NOTHING AT ALL TO INSPIRE TERROR OR EVEN TENSION. IT'S INTERESTING TO CLOSELY COMPARE THIS WITH ANOTHER 1980S REMAKE OF A '50S HORROR CLASSIC, JOHN CARPENTER'S THE THING. WHILE HOOPER TRIED TO RECREATE AND FAILED, CARPENTER BROUGHT GORY FRESHNESS TO THE TABLE AND THE RESULTS ARE LEGENDARY.

OVER THE TOP (1986. DIR: MENAHEM GOLAN)
SYLVESTER STALLONE IS LINCOLN HAWK, A BROKE-ASS ARM WRESTLING TRUCK DRIVER WHO JUST WANTS A LITTLE LOVE FROM HIS YOUNG SON, PLAYED BY "WORST NEW STAR" RAZZIE AWARD RECIPIENT, DAVID MENDENHALL. TOGETHER THEY GO ON A ROAD TRIP AND HAVE THRILLING POWER-BALLAD TESTOSTERONE ADVENTURES ON THEIR WAY TO THE BIG ARM WRESTLING CHAMPIONSHIPS IN VEGAS. FAR MORE FUN THAN MOST PEOPLE GIVE IT CREDIT FOR -- IN FACT I DEFY YOU NOT TO ENJOY IT. GO AHEAD, SEE IF YOU'RE UP TO THE CHALLENGE.

52 PICK-UP (1986. DIR: JOHN FRANKENHEIMER)
EVEN THE MAINSTREAM CRITICS AT THE TIME LOVED THIS ONE, AND THEY USUALLY GAVE BAD REVIEWS TO CANNON RELEASES VIRTUALLY SIGHT UNSEEN! DON'T LET THAT SCARE YOU OFF, THOUGH, BECAUSE YOU'LL BE MISSING A STUNNER. BASED ON THE WORK OF AUTHOR ELMORE LEONARD, ROY SCHEIDER STARS AS A SUCCESSFUL BUSINESSMAN IN 1986'S 52 PICK UP. BUT HIS SEEMINGLY HAPPY MARRIAGE IS THREATENED WHEN HIS AFFAIR WITH A NUDE MODEL IS DISCOVERED BY A TRIO OF

CHARLES BRONSON in a MICHAEL WINNER film "DEATH WISH 3"

BRONSON AND FRIEND BLOW AWAY PENCIL NECK SLIMEBALLS!

VIOLENT EXTORTIONISTS. THIS TAUT, SCUZZY THRILLER GOES BALLS-DEEP THANKS IN LARGE PART TO THE GENUINELY SCARY PERFORMANCE OF CLARENCE WILLIAMS THE THIRD. EASILY IN MY TOP FIVE CANNON PRODUCTIONS OF ALL TIME.

AMERICA 3000 (1986 DIR: DAVID ENGELBACH)
THE POSTER TAGLINE SCREAMS ABOUT "AN OUTRAGEOUS POST-NUKE ADVENTURE", AND YOU BETTER BELIEVE THIS HAIRY MEN VS GORGEOUS AMAZONIAN WOMEN ALL-OUT BATTLE OF BLISTERING RAGE IS TOTALLY "HOT PLASTIC". HIGHLIGHT: A MATTED MANSQUATCH NAMED 'ARRRG' WHO DANCES AROUND WITH A THOUSAND YEAR OLD GHETTO BLASTER. A PERFECT MOVIE FOR A FRIDAY NIGHT PIZZA PARTY WITH YOUR BESTEST PALS.

AVENGING FORCE (1986 DIR: SAM FIRSTENBERG)
THIS IS MICHAEL DUDIKOFF'S FINEST HOUR, WHICH FRANKLY ISN'T SAYING MUCH BECAUSE, WELL, HE'S MICHAEL DUDIKOFF. THAT'S NOT TO SAY THAT AVENGING FORCE DOESN'T ROCK SOME BALLS THOUGH, CASE IN POINT: DUDIKOFF AND A KID FALL ABOUT THREE STORIES OUT OF A BUILDING. IT WAS SUCH A CRAZY SLICE OF NECK-SNAPPINGLY RAD FOOTAGE, I ASSUMED THE BAD GUYS WERE JUST PUTTING THE BRAT OUT OF HIS MISERY WHEN THEY BLEW HIS ASS OFF AFTER HE LANDED. OR HOW ABOUT WHEN DUDIKOFF'S GRANDPA GETS BLOWN UP BY A BOMB? SERIOUSLY, THIS IS THE KIND OF MOVIE WHERE, AFTER THE VILLAINS (WHO WEAR NINJA OUTFITS AND S+M GEAR) KIDNAP A LOVELY YOUNG LADY, THEY DON'T HOLD OUT FOR A SWEET RANSOM, THEY SIMPLY AUCTION HER ASS OFF AT SOME CAJUN HOE-DOWN IN THE SWAMP.

DANGEROUSLY CLOSE (1986 DIR: ALBERT PYUN)
I'VE BEEN SEARCHING FOR THIS ONE FOR A COUPLE YEARS NOW, AND HAVE CONSISTENTLY COME UP SHORT. LIKE SO MANY CANNON PRODUCTIONS, THIS HAS NEVER COME OUT ON DVD, AND FINDING THE OLD OUT-OF-PRINT VHS IS QUITE A CHALLENGE. BUT HEY, THE THRILL OF THE HUNT IS PART OF THE JOY OF BEING A MOVIE NERD, RIGHT? ACCORDING TO ONLINE REVIEWS, DIRECTOR ALBERT PYUN SERVES UP WHAT BASICALLY AMOUNTS TO MAKING THE GRADE (POOR KID GOES TO A RICH SCHOOL) BUT WITHOUT THE COMEDY AND WITH MORE GANG VIOLENCE. FROM WHAT I UNDERSTAND, FANS OF HEATHERS AND PUMP UP THE VOLUME SHOULD ENJOY IT, AND PRETTY MUCH EVERYONE ELSE WON'T.

NO ONE THOUGHT IT COULD EVER HAPPEN HERE... AMERICA WASN'T READY... BUT HE WAS
CHUCK NORRIS
INVASION U.S.A.

THE CANNON GROUP, INC. PRESENTS CHUCK NORRIS IN A GOLAN-GLOBUS PRODUCTION JOSEPH ZITO FILM INVASION U.S.A. ALSO STARRING RICHARD LYNCH · MELISSA PROPHET · DIRECTOR OF PHOTOGRAPHY JOAO FERNANDES MUSIC BY JAY CHATTAWAY · STORY BY AARON NORRIS, JAMES BRUNER · SCREENPLAY BY JAMES BRUNER & CHUCK NORRIS PRODUCED BY MENAHEM GOLAN AND YORAM GLOBUS · DIRECTED BY JOSEPH ZITO
CANNON RELEASING CORPORATION
READ THE PAPERBACK FROM PINNACLE BOOKS
R RESTRICTED
MCMLXXXV CANNON FILMS, INC.

MURPHY'S LAW (1986 DIR: J. LEE THOMPSON)
PEPPERONI BREATH! DINOSAUR DORK! SNOT RAG! CHARLES BRONSON IS JACK MURPHY ("THE ONLY LAW I KNOW IS JACK MURPHY'S LAW, AND THAT LAW IS THAT YOU DON'T FUCK WITH JACK MURPHY!!") AN ALCOHOLIC COP WHO IS FRAMED AND HANDCUFFED TO A YAPPY TEENAGE REDHEAD DELINQUENT (PLAYED BY KATHLEEN WILHOITE) WHO IS FOND OF PG RATED INSULTS. "WHO TALKS LIKE THAT?" KATHLEEN EXCLAIMED IN AN ONLINE INTERVIEW IN 2010. "THEY DIDN'T WANT ME TO SWEAR TOO MUCH. LAST TIME I CHECKED, SWEARING IS KIND OF CENTRAL TO BEING A 'POTTY MOUTH.' I HAD A BLAST THOUGH, EXCEPT AFTERWARDS WHEN I WAS DOING A PLAY IN NEW YORK AND EVERY TIME I WENT DOWN TO TIMES SQUARE, SOMEONE WOULD FOLLOW ME AND SAY, 'HEY, HEY, SCROTUM CHEEKS, JIZZ BREATH ...'"

COBRA (1986 DIR: GEORGE P. COSMATOS)
EPIC. JUST EPIC. OK, MAYBE 'EPIC' IS ACTUALLY THE WRONG WORD SINCE THIS ONE WAS ON MANY

"WORST FILM OF THE YEAR" LISTS WHEN IT CAME OUT, BUT I THINK HISTORY IS PROVING NICELY THAT 99% OF THE CRITICS IN THE '80S HAD NO FORESIGHT, OR PULSE FOR THAT MATTER. SYLVESTER STALLONE STARS AS THE TITULAR BOUNTY HUNTER, AND HE WAS WOOED INTO THE ROLE BY CANNON WITH 10 MILLION SMACKEROONIES AT A TIME WHEN SUCH PAY DAYS WERE MOSTLY UNHEARD OF. STALLONE PILES UP A BODY COUNT OF 52 WHILE PLAYING OPPOSITE HIS REAL LIFE WIFE (AT THE TIME), BRIGITTE NIELSEN, A WOMAN THAT GLOBUS CLAIMS STALLONE WAS AFRAID OF. TWAS BEAUTY WHO TAMED THE BEAST.

ALLAN QUARTERMAIN AND THE LOST CITY OF GOLD (1986 DIR: GARY NELSON)
THE SEQUEL TO THE PREVIOUSLY MENTIONED KING SOLOMON'S MINES, WHICH IT WAS FILMED CONCURRENTLY WITH. AS EXPECTED, THIS IS MORE OF THE SAME, BUT THIS TIME WITH ADDED JAMES EARL JONES, HENRY SILVA, AND CASSANDRA PETERSON (BETTER KNOWN AS "ELVIRA"). LACKS THE WHOOPIEDOO THRILL-RIDE ASPECT OF THE FIRST INSTALMENT, AND SLOWS DOWN ESPECIALLY WHEN THEY ARRIVE AT THE CITY OF GOLD. WORTH A WATCH, BUT I'D RANK IT NEAR THE BOTTOM OF THIS TOP 50 LIST.

THE TEXAS CHAINSAW MASSACRE 2 (1986 DIR: TOBE HOOPER)
IT WAS AN ODD AND BALLSY CHOICE TO GO WITH A COMEDIC SEQUEL TO ONE OF THE MOST HARROWING AND LEGENDARY HORROR FILMS IN AMERICAN HISTORY, BUT THAT IS EXACTLY WHAT TOBE HOOPER DID, AND IT ACTUALLY WORKS. THE CAST IS GREAT (DENNIS HOPPER, CAROLINE WILLIAMS, BILL MOSELEY) EVEN THOUGH ONLY ONE OF THEM (JIM SIEDOW) APPEARED IN THE FIRST INSTALMENT. SOME OF THE GORY HIGHLIGHTS ARE: LEATHERFACE IN A TRUCK, CHOPPING ANOTHER DRIVER'S HEAD IN HALF WHILE BOTH VEHICLES ARE IN MOTION, A WOMAN WEARING A SEVERED FACE, CHAINSAW-AS-PENIS AND CAPITALISM-THROUGH-CANNIBALISM REFERENCES, AND BLOODTHIRSTY REDNECKS APLENTY. I HAVE A FEELING THIS IS ONE OF ROB ZOMBIE'S FAVES, BECAUSE IT SURE SEEMS TO BE WHAT HE'S AIMING FOR IN MANY OF HIS MOVIES.

THE NAKED CAGE (1986 DIR: PAUL NICHOLAS)
OK, SUGAR-TITS, HEAR ME NOW: NAKED CAGE IS A TOTAL MUST-SEE! CONSIDERED BY MANY GENRE FANS TO BE THE LAST GREAT WOMEN-IN-PRISON MOVIE (A GENRE THAT SAW ITS REAL HEYDAY IN THE '70S), SHARI SHATTUCK AND ANGEL TOMPKINS STAR IN THIS ASS-CRACKIN LITTLE SPITFIRE OF A DRIVE-IN FILM ABOUT A SPUNKY YOUNG LADY WHO IS FALSELY ACCUSED OF A BANK ROBBERY, AND THEN FORCED TO ENDURE THE 1980S' GLAM-FUELED INDIGNITIES OF A CORRUPT WOMEN'S PRISON.

THE COVER OF THE HUNGARIAN 'COBRA' COMIC BOOK

THE DELTA FORCE (1986 DIR: MENAHEM GOLAN)
WELCOME TO THE JEWIEST ACTION MOVIE OF THE '80S! CHUCK NORRIS TROTS OUT HIS AWESOME ONE-MAN-ARMY-ON-A-DIRTBIKE-WITH-MISSILES SHTICK FOR THE FINALE, BUT FOR THE MOST PART THIS IS ACTUALLY A SEMI-REALISTIC HOSTAGE CRISIS THRILLER LOADED WITH ALL THE POLITICAL INTRIGUE AND GLOBE-HOPPING THE GENRE DEMANDS. ALSO, AS MENTIONED: LOTS AND LOTS AND LOTS OF JEWISHNESS. OY, IT'S THE PERFECT ACTION MOVIE FOR ROSH HASHANAH! THE MOVIE WAS ACTUALLY BASED ON THE REAL LIFE 1985 TWA HIGHJACKING, AND AS ONE MIGHT EXPECT MANY MOMENTS IN THE FILM ARE DRAWN FROM THE ACTUAL INCIDENT, SUCH AS WHEN A U.S. SERVICEMAN IS BEATEN TO DEATH

BY THE TERRORISTS, AND THEN
DUMPED OUT OF THE PLANE ON TO
THE RUNWAY. OF COURSE, WHEN OL'
LEE MARVIN AND CHUCK NORRIS
CATCH UP WITH THE THE BADDIES,
THE WHOLE THING TRANSFORMS INTO
A PATRIOTIC REVENGE FANTASY.
JACKIE BROWN'S ROBERT FORSTER
IS FLIPPIN' AWESOME AS THE LEGITIMATELY
FRIGHTENING TERRORIST RINGLEADER.

The Siege...The Ordeal...The Rescue...
CHUCK NORRIS LEE MARVIN
THE DELTA FORCE

BARFLY (1987. DIR: BARBET SCHROEDER)
HMM... WHEN I LOOK AT THE TITLE, I
ALWAYS READ IT AS "BARF-LY"-- WHICH
IS ODDLY FITTING GIVEN THE SUBJECT
MATTER HERE. ALONG WITH ANGEL
HEART AND THE WRESTLER, THIS
STANDS AS THE FINEST PERFORMANCE
OF MICKEY ROURKE'S CAREER, AND
ONE OF THE BEST OF FAYE
DUNAWAY'S AS WELL. MICKEY
AND FAYE PLAY THE LIKEABLE
TITULAR SOCIETAL REJECTS WHO
REALLY SEEM TO THRIVE IN THEIR
ABJECT MISERY, POVERTY, AND
ALCOHOLISM. THE SCRIPT IS BY
CHARLES BUKOWSKI (THE ONLY
ONE HE EVER WROTE FOR
HOLLYWOOD), A MAN WHO CERTAINLY
KNEW THESE CHARACTERS AND WALKED
MANY A MILE IN THEIR SHOES. SPEAKING OF
BUKOWSKI -- HAVE A LOOK FOR HIM IN 1977'S
SUPERVAN. HE APPEARS, UNCREDITED I MAY ADD,
AS A JUDGE FOR A WET T-SHIRT CONTEST.

THE BARBARIAN BROTHERS (1987 DIR: RUGGERO DEODATO)
KNOWING WHAT I KNOW ABOUT JUST HOW BAD A BARBARIAN MOVIE CAN ACTUALLY BE, IT FEELS
SATISFYING TO REPORT ON HOW STUPIDLY ENTERTAINING THIS CONAN RIP-OFF IS. IT WAS
AFTER ALL, DIRECTED BY THE TERRIFIC RUGGERO "CANNIBAL HOLOCAUST" DEODATO, AND
WRITTEN BY JAMES SILKE. SILKE IS, AMONG OTHER THINGS, THE AUTHOR OF THE FRANK
FRAZETTA DEATH DEALER PAPERBACK NOVELS -- WHICH ARE ACTUALLY PRETTY DECENT SWORD
N' SORCERY BOOKS. HIS MOVIE STARS TWIN HIMBO BODYBUILDERS NAMED PETER AND DAVID
PAUL, AND THESE OILY, WAXED OAFS COME ACROSS EVERY BIT AS MORONIC AS SWORD-SWINGIN'
BARBARIANS WOULD IN REAL LIFE. A FUN, EXCITABLE GOOFJUICER THAT CAN ALSO DOUBLE AS
GAY PORN IF YOU'RE HOUSE SITTING AT YOUR STRAIGHT FRIENDS PLACE, AND HE DOESN'T
HAVE THE INTERNET.

TOUGH GUYS DON'T DANCE (1987 DIR: NORMAN MAILER)
YOU KNOW THAT YOUTUBE CLIP THAT WENT VIRAL A YEAR OR SO AGO? THE HILARIOUS ONE
CALLED "WORST LINE READING EVER" THAT HAS RYAN O'NEAL ON THE BEACH YELLING "OH GOD!!
OH MAN!!" OVER AND OVER AGAIN? WELL, THAT MELODRAMATIC WAD OF THESPIAN PHLEGM
ORIGINATES FROM THIS BIZARRE LITTLE GEM. ISABELLA "BLUE VELVET" ROSSELLINI AND WINGS
"VICE SQUAD" HAUSER LAWRENCE "RESERVOIR DOGS" TIERNEY, AND PENN "BULLSHIT!"
JILLETTE ARE ALSO ON DISPLAY FOR YOUR AMUSEMENT. HANDS DOWN ONE OF THE STRANGEST
FILMS MADE IN AMERICA IN THE EIGHTIES.

SHY PEOPLE (1987 DIR: ANDREY KONCHALOVSKIY)
TAKE THE DIRECTOR OF RUNAWAY TRAIN, THE SCREENWRITER OF THE TENANT, THE
CINEMATOGRAPHER OF THE MISSION THE SETTING OF DELIVERANCE, A KILLER SOUNDTRACK BY
TANGERINE DREAM -- AND THEN CAST MARTHA PLIMPTON AS A WILD DRUG ADDICTED TEEN WHO
FALLS IN LOVE WITH A REDNECK WHO IS KEPT IN A CAGE. THERE, YOU JUST CREATED SHY
PEOPLE. IT'S ALSO WORTH NOTING THAT BARBARA HERSHEY WON BEST ACTRESS AT CANNES 1987
FOR HER ROLE HERE. WHY IS THIS MOVIE SO HARD TO FIND?

MASTERS OF THE UNIVERSE (1987 DIR: GARY GODDARD)
HERE'S A MOVIE THAT HAS BEEN UNFAIRLY DISMISSED AND MADE FUN OF OVER THE YEARS,
WHICH IS KINDA HUMOROUS, CONSIDERING IT IS MILES BETTER THAN THE BELOVED SATURDAY
MORNING TV CARTOON IT WAS MADE TO CASH IN ON. DIRECTOR GODDARD WANTED MATTHEW
MODINE FOR HE-MAN, BUT GOLAN AND GLOBUS WANTED DOLPH LUNDGREN, WHO KINDA STINKS THIS
UP EVERY TIME HE OPENS HIS MOUTH. DUDE CANNOT ACT. NO MATTER, THOUGH -- THERE IS
PLENTY MORE TO KEEP YOUR ATTENTION. STICK AROUND AFTER THE CREDITS, BECAUSE
SKELETOR'S HEAD POPS OUT AND SAYS "I'LL BE BACK!", SETTING THE STAGE FOR A SEQUEL
THAT (ALONG WITH CANNON'S PLANS FOR A SPIDER-MAN ADAPTATION) WAS SHIT-CANNED WHEN
GOLAN AND GLOBUS COULDN'T SCRAPE ENOUGH DOUGH TOGETHER TO PAY MATTEL AND MARVEL
FOR THE RIGHTS.

STREET SMART (1987 DIR: JERRY SCHATZBERG)
EVER WONDER HOW MORGAN FREEMAN FIRST GOT NOTICED? WELL, IT WAS IN THIS MOVIE, AND
IF YOU CAN IMAGINE IT, HE PLAYS A SCARY-ASS TIMES SQUARE PIMP WHO BITCHSLAPS
CHRISTOPHER REEVE AROUND. TONS OF GREASY NEW YORK STREET LOCATIONS, TRASH-TALKIN'
WHORES, AND A BATTLE OF WITS BETWEEN A SAVVY JOURNALIST AND ONE OF THE MOST CUNNING
PUSSY HUSTLERS IN FILM HISTORY. SURELY ONE OF THE BEST AND MOST GENUINELY THRILLING

MOVIES ON THIS LIST, AND A FILM THAT I WATCH AT LEAST ONCE EVERY COUPLE YEARS.
SOUNDTRACK BY THE TALENTED MILES DAVIS. CANADIANS: LOOK FOR SOME MONTREAL IN THIS!

GOR (1987 DIR: FRITZ KIERSCH)

GOR IS BASED ON A BUNCH OF SHITTY SCI-FI NOVELS WHICH HAVE BEEN CO-OPTED INTO A
FETISHY SEXUAL SUBCULTURE. "GORIANS" IS WHAT THEY CALL THEMSELVES. LOOK 'EM UP. IN THE
MOVIE A NERDY SCIENTIST IS TRANSPORTED TO ANOTHER PLANET WHICH IS ON THE OTHER SIDE
OF THE SUN AND REMAINS CONTINUALLY HIDDEN FROM US HERE ON EARTH. WHILE THERE, HE GOES
BUCKWILD AND GETS HIS BATTLE ON WITH BARBARIAN WARLORDS WHO KEEP ALL WOMEN AS
SUBMISSIVE PETS. THIS IS BY NO MEANS IN THE TOP OF THE CLASS ON THIS LIST, BUT IT SURE
IS AN ASS-LOVERS DREAM. I'VE WATCHED PILES OF THESE FANTASY-SCI-FI DINGLEBERRIES, AND
EVEN IN THE ONES WHERE THERE IS SOME SCANTILY-CLAD BARBARIAN WOMAN WARRIOR IN A
CHAINMAIL BRA, THERE IS ALWAYS SOME KIND OF LOIN CLOTH THING THAT COVERS UP HER
HINDER. NOT SO HERE -- EVERY CHICK IN THIS ENTIRE CRUSTY MOVIE IS IN SOME KIND OF
THONG. ASS <u>APLENTY</u>! FOLLOWED UP BY A SEQUEL MADE TWO YEARS LATER THAT WAS ROASTED
ON MST3K.

DEATH WISH 4: THE CRACKDOWN

(1987 DIR: J. LEE THOMPSON)
THE FIRST OF THE DEATH
WISH MOVIES NOT TO BE
DIRECTED BY MICHAEL
WINNER AND A MUCH LOWER
BUDGET WOULD SEEM LIKE A
RECIPE FOR DISASTER, BUT
THIS SEQUEL HOLDS ITS OWN
VERY NICELY. J. LEE
THOMPSON PROVED ONCE
AGAIN THAT HE WAS ONE OF
THE MOST DEPENDABLE
DIRECTORS THAT EVER
WORKED FOR CANNON, AND
ALSO THE MOST PROLIFIC,
WITH 8 CANNON PRODUCTIONS
IN HIS FILMOGRAPHY. YEAH,
HE WAS EARNING HIS KEEP
BY CHURNING OUT B MOVIES,
BUT THE GUY WAS NO SLOUCH.
J. LEE DIRECTED THE
ORIGINAL 1962 CAPE FEAR
WHICH IS A SUPERIOR FILM
TO SCORSESE'S 1990S
REMAKE. ANYWAY, IN DEATH
WISH 4 BRONSON'S STEP
DAUGHTER GOES TO A VIDEO
ARCADE AFTER DARK AND
YOU ALL KNOW WHAT THAT
MEANS! AFTER HER FUNERAL,
BRONSON IS HIRED BY A
VERY MYSTERIOUS SHADY
INDIVIDUAL TO GO ON ONE OF
HIS ALWAYS INVIGORATING
VIGILANTE VENDETTAS
AGAINST THE CRIMINAL
UNDERWORLD. ALSO: PERHAPS
IT WAS THE RAVAGES OF OLD
AGE, BUT BRONSON LOOKS
LIKE KINDA AN OLD LADY IN
THIS MOVIE.

UNDERCOVER

(1987. DIR: JOHN STOCKWELL)
YES, THE DIRECTOR IS THE
SAME JOHN STOCKWELL
THAT STARRED IN CHRISTINE
(1983) AND MY SCIENCE
PROJECT (1985). ACTUALLY,

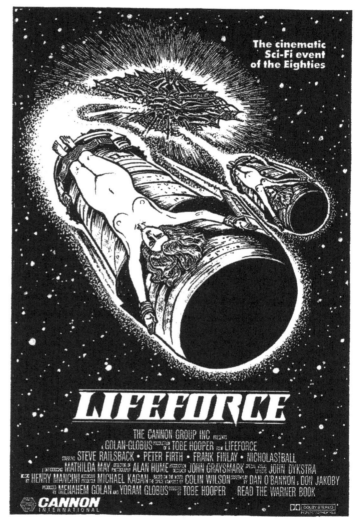

The cinematic
Sci-Fi event
of the Eighties

LIFEFORCE

THE CANNON GROUP INC PRESENTS
A GOLAN-GLOBUS PRODUCTION OF A TOBE HOOPER FILM LIFEFORCE
STARRING STEVE RAILSBACK · PETER FIRTH · FRANK FINLAY · NICHOLAS BALL
INTRODUCING MATHILDA MAY DIRECTOR OF PHOTOGRAPHY ALAN HUME PRODUCTION DESIGNER JOHN GRAYSMARK SPECIAL VISUAL EFFECTS JOHN DYKSTRA
MUSIC BY HENRY MANCINI ASSOCIATE PRODUCER MICHAEL KAGAN BASED ON THE NOVEL THE SPACE VAMPIRES BY COLIN WILSON SCREENPLAY BY DAN O'BANNON AND DON JAKOBY
PRODUCED BY MENAHEM GOLAN AND YORAM GLOBUS DIRECTED BY TOBE HOOPER READ THE WARNER BOOK
CANNON INTERNATIONAL

I'VE BEEN SEARCHING FOR THIS FOR AGES, BUT STILL CAN'T GET MY MITTS ON IT. IT HASN'T
LANDED A DVD RELEASE, SO I GUESS I'LL HAVE TO LUCK INTO A USED VHS COPY OR A
BOOTLEG DVDR SOMEWHERE. I DON'T DOUBT FOR A SECOND THAT IT BELONGS ON THIS LIST
THOUGH, BECAUSE IT LOOKS TO BE TERRIFIC. I WILL CONTINUE MY VISION QUEST, AND REVIEW IT
LATER ON. IT'S BASICALLY 21 JUMP STREET (UNDERCOVER COPS POSING AS HIGH SCHOOL KIDS)
IN BALTIMORE, AND JENNIFER JASON LEIGH CO-STARS IN IT. I HEART HER PRETTY HARD.

BLOODSPORT (1988 DIR: NEWT ARNOLD)

I SAW THIS WHEN MY WIFE AND I WERE 17, AND WE WERE BOTH LIKE: "HOLY LABIAS, THAT
MOVIE WAS QUITE AWESOME. WHO IS THIS VAN DAMME DUDE?". GOLAN WAS THE ONE THAT
DISCOVERED HIM, AND THIS WAS THE FILM THAT STARTED THE BALL ROLLING ON CLAUDE'S
CAREER: "I WENT TO A FRENCH RESTAURANT IN LOS ANGELES WITH MY WIFE. WE ORDERED
TURTLE SOUP AND THIS GOOD-LOOKING FRENCH GUY APPROACHES US WITH A BOWL IN EACH
HAND. 'MONSIEUR GOLAN?' HE ASKED. WHEN I SAID, 'OUI' HE KICKED ABOVE MY HEAD WITH HIS

LEG WITHOUT THE SOUP BOWLS MOVING AN INCH! WHEN I ASKED HIM TO REPEAT THAT, HE DID. SO I SAID, COME TO MY OFFICE TOMORROW MORNING!

HERO AND THE TERROR (1988 DIR: WILLIAM TANNEN)

A NECK-SNAPPIN' SERIAL KILLER (WITH A KILL COUNT OF 64 WOMEN) REFERRED TO IN THE PRESS AS "TERROR" ESCAPES THE INSTITUTION HE'S BEING IMPRISONED IN BY DRIVING A VEHICLE OFF A 400 FOOT CLIFF. THEY ALL THINK HE'S DEAD, BUT CHUCK NORRIS KNOWS BETTER BECAUSE HE'S THE HERO. THANKS TO POOR EDITING THIS IS SLOWER AND LESS ENGAGING THAN MANY OF CHUCK'S CANNON PROJECTS, BUT THANKFULLY IT UTILISES AN EFFECTIVE HORROR ELEMENT INTO ITS COP-THEMED SUSPENSE THRILLER STORYLINE. IT'S A FORMULA THAT WOULD NET SILENCE OF THE LAMBS FIVE ACADEMY AWARDS ONLY 3 YEARS LATER.

KINJITE: FORBIDDEN SUBJECTS (1989 DIR: J. LEE THOMPSON)

THIS IS THE BEST OF THE CROP OF FILMS MADE IN THE LAST COUPLE YEARS OF THE GOLAN GLOBUS PARTNERSHIP, AND IT IS A THEATRICAL EXPERIENCE THAT ROGER EBERT CALLED "SLIMY", "DISTASTEFUL", AND "THOROUGHLY UNPLEASANT". CHARLES BRONSON IS BACK AS A WORLD-WEARY COP WHO GRITS HIS TEETH THROUGH DAY AFTER SOUL-CRUSHING DAY -- AND THIS TIME HE DOESN'T JUST HATE THE SAVAGE PUNKS THAT ARE MESSING UP HIS TOWN, HE HATES ASIANS TOO! THIS IS THE KIND OF SEEDY EXPLOITATION MOVIE THAT INSENSITIVELY USES CHILD PROSTITUTION AS A STORY DEVICE JUST TO GET A CHEAP INDIGNANT RISE OUT OF THE AUDIENCE. IN OTHER WORDS: AN AWESOME ONE! HIGHLIGHTS: BRONSON BEATS A MAN WITH A LARGE PINK DILDO, AND MAKES ANOTHER EAT A ROLEX WATCH.

CYBORG (1989 DIR: ALBERT PYUN)

IT'S ANOTHER JEAN CLAUDE VAN DAMME VEHICLE, AND WHILE CYBORG ISN'T AS EPIC AS BLOODSPORT, IT IS STILL BETTER THAN MOST OF HIS NON-CANNON EFFORTS THAT AUDIENCES WOULD HAVE FLUNG AT THEM THROUGHOUT THE 1990S LIKE SO MUCH GORILLA POO. DIRECTOR ALBERT PYUN HAD LOFTY PLANS FOR THIS PLAGUE-RAVAGED APOCALYPTIC ACTION FILM (HE WANTED TO MAKE IT BOTH DIALOGUE FREE AND BLACK AND WHITE) BUT CANNON PUT THEIR FOOT DOWN AND DEMANDED THAT IT APPEAR MORE COMMERCIALLY VIABLE. THEY WERE DESPERATE AT THIS POINT, AND COULDN'T ABIDE ANOTHER BOMB. THE FILM IS ALSO LEGENDARY FOR BEING THE SET ON WHICH JCVD ACCIDENTALLY TOOK JACKSON 'ROCK' PINCKNEY'S EYE OUT DURING A SCENE WHERE THE TWO ACTORS FOUGHT WITH SWORDS. PINCKNEY TOOK VAN DAMME TO COURT, AND EVENTUALLY WON AN UNDISCLOSED AMOUNT OF MONEY IN A SETTLEMENT WITH THE BELGIAN ACTION STAR. THE MOVIE WAS A HIT (BUDGET: $500,000. GROSS: OVER $10 MILLION DOLLARS), BUT IT WAS TOO LITTLE TOO LATE FOR GOLAN AND GLOBUS, WHO HAD ALREADY LOST THEIR COMPANY BY THE TIME THE MONEY CAME IN.

THERE WE GO... THAT'S **FIFTY**!!

ON THE THIRD WEEKEND IN NOVEMBER OF 2010, MANHATTAN'S LINCOLN CENTER PRESENTED A CANNON FILMS RETROSPECTIVE, AND SCREENED A DOZEN OF G'N'Gs FINEST EFFORTS, INCLUDING THE APPLE, BARFLY, 52 PICK-UP, RUNAWAY TRAIN, SHY PEOPLE, STREET SMART, TEXAS CHAINSAW MASSACRE PART 2, AND TOUGH GUYS DON'T DANCE.

GOLAN AND GLOBUS HADN'T BEEN SEEN TOGETHER IN 20 YEARS, BUT THEY PATCHED UP THEIR VARIOUS DIFFERENCES AND APPEARED AT THE RETROSPECTIVE, DOING TWO HOUR LONG Q+A'S, AND EVEN APPEARING AT AN APPLE-RELATED DISCO PARTY WHERE FANS OF THE MOVIE WERE FURNISHED WITH BOOZE AND BIM MARKS.

ALSO APPEARING BEFORE THE BARFLY SCREENING WAS FRENCH FILMMAKER BARBET SCHROEDER WHO TOLD THE STORY OF THE DAY HE LEARNED OF CANNON'S TERMINAL FINANCIAL WOES, AND WAS THEN TOLD THAT HIS FILM COULD HAVE TO BE PUSHED BACK ON THE SCHEDULE. SCHROEDER THEN GRABBED A BLACK AND DECKER SAW, BUST INTO CANNON'S OFFICES, AND TOLD GOLAN AND GLOBUS THAT HE WOULD HACK OFF ONE OF HIS FINGERS IF THEY DARED TO PUT THE RELEASE OF HIS SEVEN-YEAR LABOUR OF LOVE INTO JEOPARDY. THE MOVIE WAS FINISHED ON SCHEDULE, AND TURNED A HANDSOME PROFIT ON VHS.

— BOUGIE

BOGUS CELEBRITY NUDES REVEALED!

BY D.J. BRYANT
&
ROBIN BOUGIE

DETECTIVES IN THEIR '40S NOIR CINEMA INCARNATION DON'T USUALLY ANNOUNCE THEIR PRESENCE BY YELLING OUT TO ANYONE WHO WILL LISTEN ABOUT THEIR ABILITY TO SOLVE CRIMES...

BUT A 65 YEAR OLD WISCONSIN MAN NAMED ED LAKE WHO IS BETTER KNOWN TO PHOTOSHOP DEVOTEES AS "THE FAKE DETECTIVE", DOES JUST THAT ON HIS BEAT -- THE INTERNET.

HIS CLAIM TO UNDERGROUND FAME IS THAT ED USES ALL HIS FREE TIME DEBUNKING FAKE AND PHOTOSHOPPED NUDES OF CELEBRITIES THAT HE FINDS IN NEWS GROUPS AND IN OTHER SHADOWY ONLINE ALLEYWAYS.

ALL RETIREES NEED SOME KINDA HOBBY, AND FOR ED IT'S "PROTECTING THE INNOCENT, DEFENDING THE TRUTH, AND RECOVERING THE SULLIED REPUTATIONS OF BEAUTIFUL DAMSELS IN DISTRESS", OR SO HE SAYS IN HIS SITE'S MISSION STATEMENT.

ED DOESN'T LIKE TO SEE HIS FAVORITE FEMALE ACTRESSES, OR ANY CELEB LADIES TAKEN ADVANTAGE OF DIGITALLY BY UNDERHANDED HACKERS. THESE WOMEN ARE BEING DISROBED AND DIGITALLY RAPED ACCORDING TO ED, AND THE MOST PREDOMINANT VICTIM IS NONE OTHER THAN GILLIAN (X-FILES) ANDERSON.

THERE ARE AT LEAST 500 NUDE FAKES OF GILLIAN ANDERSON OUT THERE, AND SHE'D NEVER POSE IN THE NUDE!

SAYS ED, WHO FIRST STARTED HIS CRUSADE OF INTERNET CHIVALRY BECAUSE OF THE STOIC ACTRESS.

"ONE DAY I CAME ACROSSED SOME PICTURES OF GILLIAN THAT DIDN'T LOOK REAL. I COULDN'T BELIEVE SHE WOULD POSE WAY. I LOOKED THEM OVER AND FOUND OUT THAT THREE OF THEM HAD THE SAME HEAD SHOT. I DECIDED TO LET EVERY-BODY ELSE IN THE WORLD KNOW ABOUT IT!"

HA!

ANDERSON, UNLIKE SOME MAINSTREAM FEMALE MOVIE STARS, COULDN'T GIVE A SHIT ABOUT THE FAKE NUDES ONE WAY OR ANOTHER.

HEY GILL, I FOUND ANOTHER ONE!

THAT'S NICE JULES.

SOME PEOPLE DON'T APPRECIATE THE FAKE DICK'S EFFORTS...

HE'S REALLY RUINING THE MAGIC OF THIS WHOLE THING! IT'S LIKE SOMEONE RUINING A JOKE, OR TELLING YOU THE ENDING OF A MOVIE. SOMETIMES YOU DONT WANT TO KNOW HOW THE RABBIT GOT IN THE HAT!

Trixy
Amateur Faker of Photos

I'M SORRY, THIS WHOLE THING GETS ME REALLY EMOTIONAL.

Most of the time, fakes are easy to spot, either because they were unconvincingly tampered with, or because the concept is simply unrealistic. Bouncy teen heart-throb Britney Spears has had her perky anus cornholed thousands of times in this fake-photo world.

And I just saw Celine Dion while surfing for porn last night -- the diva was resplendent with an 8-inch cock and pendulous shaved balls!

But these oddball photo-chops aren't the pictures that the Fake Detective is the most concerned about. It's the hoaxes that try hard to make viewers think they are looking at an actual actress in a compromising position.

It's a new form of post modern art, and the Fake Detective is its ultimate critic, assigning grades to every photographic myth that he dubunks.

For years Ed Lake toiled in near total obscurity, tirelessly honing his craft with the help of visitors to his site, but since being featured in Wired magazine a couple years ago, he's found himself happily enjoying a few fleeting seconds of fame.

One can only imagine that being brought out of his mouldy basement and into the limelight (however briefly) is only going to strengthen his resolve to 'do the right thing', and bring fakers to justice.

THE END.

Visit: www.fake-detective.com

"PUBLIC ENEMIES IN SKIRTS!"

The early years of the Chicks-in-Chains movie

IF ONE WANTED TO SEARCH OUT A SHITLOAD OF FILMIC IMAGERY OF SEXUALLY ACTIVE, SERIOUSLY DANGEROUS, AND SOCIALLY DEVIANT FEMALES, THEN THE WOMEN IN PRISON GENRE WOULD BE THE PLACE TO LOOK. I'M SURE A PSYCHOLOGIST COULD BREAK THESE MOVIES DOWN TO THEIR ESOTERIC FUNDAMENTALS (BONDAGE, POWER, MISOGYNY, LATENT HOMOSEXUALITY, RAPE FANTASIES, ETC) BUT THE RIDDLE OF THEIR ALLURE IS SIMPLE: A HORDE OF NO-NONSENSE, SHIT-KICKING BITCHES WHO ARE OFTEN DISROBED WHILE IN SQUALID CONDITIONS.

THE FEMALE PRISON MOVIE WAS FIRST CONCEIVED AS FAR BACK AS THE LATE 1920s IN THE FORM OF SOMEWHAT DOUR MORALITY TALES THAT SEEM VERY TIMID AND TAME BY TODAY'S STANDARDS. DEMURE FILMS LIKE **THE GODLESS GIRL** (1929), **LADIES OF THE BIG HOUSE** (1931), **LADIES THEY TALK ABOUT** (1933), AND **CONDEMNED WOMEN** (1938). LIKE FILMDOM'S EARLY GANGSTER FILMS, THE FIRST WAVE OF CLASSIC W.I.P. CINEMA WAS SIMPLY THERE TO BEAT AUDIENCES OVER THE HEAD WITH THE GOODY-GOODY MESSAGE! "CRIME DOES NOT PAY!".

THE LATTER PART OF THIS DECADE SAW A FILM, **WOMEN IN PRISON** (1938), DIRECTED BY LAMBERT HILLYER, ABOUT A FEMALE PRISON WARDEN (MARTHA WILSON) WHOSE DAUGHTER ANN WAS AN INMATE IN THE VERY SAME PRISON HAVING BEEN FRAMED FOR MANSLAUGHTER. THAT SAME YEAR, WILLIAM McGANN DIRECTED **GIRLS ON PROBATION**, WHICH WAS A PRETTY SHITTY FEMALE PRISON DRAMA, BUT WAS NOTABLE SINCE IT STARRED A YOUNG SUSAN HAYWARD AND RONALD REAGAN.

THE LATE 1930s BOASTED PRISON FILMS SUCH AS **MARKED GIRLS** (1938) WHICH WAS A DECENT ATTEMPT AT BRINGING FRANCIS CARCO'S NOVEL "PRISONS DE FEMMES" TO FILM. IN IT, AN ORPHAN GIRL IS DROPPED ON HER ASS IN JAIL WHERE SHE SOMEHOW MANAGES TO MARRY A WEALTHY BUSINESSMAN VIA HER "UNDERWORLD CONNECTIONS". ONLY IN THE MOVIES LADIES, ONLY IN THE MOVIES.

THE 1940s SAW ANOTHER BURST OF W.I.P FILMS, SUCH AS **CONVICTED WOMAN** (1940) DIRECTED BY NICK GRINDE, WHICH PRESENTED AN ODD CONCEPT: PRISONER SELF GOVERNMENT. THAT SAME YEAR, ROBERT FLOREY CAME OUT WITH **WOMEN WITHOUT NAMES**, IN WHICH A POOR COUPLE ARE FALSELY ACCUSED OF MURDERING A COP. THE FELLA IS SENTENCED TO DEATH ROW, AND THE DAME TO LIFE IN PRISON.

IT WASN'T UNTIL 1950 WHEN DIRECTOR JOHN CROMWELL BROUGHT THEATERS A FILM CALLED **CAGED**, VIA PARAMOUNT PICTURES, THAT A W.I.P FILM BLASTED THE BUTTOCKS OFF THE

Startling!
BEYOND BELIEF!
Shocking!
YOU MAY FAINT . .

ILLUSTRATIONS PROVIDED BY: KAZIMIR STRZEPEK

FORLORN MELODRAMA AND WASN'T AFRAID TO INDULGE A LITTLE IN EROTICALLY CHARGED SCENARIOS, A DARK VIEW OF SOCIAL HOPELESSNESS, AND THE TRADEMARK EXPLOITATION THEMES THAT FANS OF THE GENRE HAVE COME TO KNOW AND ADORE. HELL, THIS OUTSTANDING SHIT EVEN GOT NOMINATED FOR SOME OSCARS.

LET'S TAKE A BREAK FROM OUR HISTORY LESSON FOR A MINUTE AND EXAMINE THE TRADEMARKS THAT WOULD COME TO CHARACTERISE EVERYTHING ABOUT THIS PSYCHOTRONIC CINEMA SUB GENRE, TRADEMARKS THAT WERE EXPERTLY COMPILED BY WRITER JIM MORTON IN "INCREDIBLY STRANGE FILMS" (RESEARCH BOOKS, 1986): "BY THE END OF THE '60S THE ARCHETYPAL ROLES OF THE W.I.P. FILMS HAD BEEN ESTABLISHED, I.E. THE QUEEN BEE: DOMINANT FEMALE PRISONER THAT LORDS IT OVER THE OTHERS. THE NEW FISH: USUALLY THE LEAD ACTRESS, IN JAIL FOR THE FIRST TIME. THE SADISTIC WARDEN: MORE OFTEN THAN NOT THE ONE WHO PROVES TO BE THE ROOT OF ALL EVIL AND UNREST IN THE PRISON. THE HOOKER WITH THE HEART OF GOLD: A STREET SMART DAME WHO KNOWS THE ROPES AND BEFRIENDS THE NEW FISH FOR BETTER OR WORSE. THE DYKE GUARD: SOMETIMES NAMED "RUBY"; NO FILM WOULD BE COMPLETE WITHOUT ONE."

IN **CAGED**, THE NEW FISH IS PLAYED BY ELEANOR PARKER, AND SHE ARRIVES INNOCENT AND LEAVES THE CRUDE PRISON AT THE END OF THE FILM AS A SICK, HARDENED CRIMINAL. HOLLYWOOD HAD NEVER SEEN ANYTHING OF THE SORT, NOR HAD THEY SEEN THE POSITION OF POWER (THE HEAD MATRON PLAYED BY HOPE EMERSON) AS A

SADO-LESBIAN MAE WEST PARODY WHO RULES OVER THE IMPRISONED LADIES WITH A SEXUAL GRIP OF IRON -- SHAVING ONE GIRL'S HEAD TO PROVE HER DOMINATION OVER HER. SO POWERFUL AND MEMORABLE WERE THE IMAGES AND SEQUENCES IN THIS FILM, THE GENRE WOULD AGAIN VISIT THEM TIME AND TIME AGAIN IN FILMS LIKE **SO YOUNG, SO BAD** (1950), **HOUSE OF WOMEN** (1962) AND LATER IN **REFORM SCHOOL GIRLS** (1986).

The most daring movies of their kind!

THE LESBIAN SUBTEXT WAS EVEN MORE IN-YOUR-FACE IN 1955'S NOIR-STYLE **WOMEN'S PRISON** STARRING IDA LUPINO AS THE FUCKED UP WARDEN "AMELIA VAN ZANT", WHO IS SO MONSTROUSLY VILE, YOU CAN'T HELP BUT CHEER HER ON JUST TO SEE WHAT SHE'LL COOK UP NEXT (IDA BEATS AUDREY TOTTER'S CHARACTER TO **DEATH**, YO!). THE SAME COULD BE SAID FOR AN ALLIED ARTISTS COPYCAT FILM **BETRAYED WOMEN** (1955) WHICH SHOWCASED A BRUTAL PRISON GUARD NAMED 'DARCY' - PLAYED BY SARA HADEN.

THE NEXT CRUCIAL HISTORICAL FOOT--NOTE IN THE GENRE'S EARLY YEARS WAS THE SUDDEN INFLUX OF B-FEATURES TO CASH IN ON THE YOUTH MARKET WHICH WERE LINED UP OUTSIDE DRIVE-IN'S IN HORDES. THIS SAW THE MELDING OF THE JUVENILE DELINQUENT FILM AND THE WOMEN IN PRISON CINEMATIC EXPERIENCE -- AND THE STAR THAT SPEARHEADED THIS MOVE WAS THE B'S ANSWER TO MARILYN MONROE, THE INCOMPARABLE MAMIE VAN DOREN. DESCRIBED BY WARNER BROS. AS "THE GIRL BUILT LIKE A PLATINUM

POWERHOUSE". IT WAS MAMIE'S TWO W.I.P. FILMS OF 1957 **UNTAMED YOUTH** AND **GIRLS TOWN** (MADE THRU MGM) THAT SOLIDIFIED VAN DOREN'S STATUS AS THE QUEEN OF THE B'S.

1957 ALSO SAW CUTE GLORIA CASTILLO STAR IN A W.I.P. J.D. FILM CALLED **REFORM SCHOOL GIRL**, WHICH WAS REMADE IN 1994 FOR TV STARRING MATT "FRIENDS" LEBLANC. THE OPENING 20 MIN. OF THE ORIGINAL VERSION ARE SO GLORIOUSLY SLIMEY AND OUT-OF-CONTROL, THE REST OF THE FILM CAN ONLY SUFFER IN COMPARISON. GLORIA'S BOYFRIEND STEALS A CAR, RUNS OVER SOME POOR BASTARD, AND FRAMES HIS INNOCENT YOUNG GIRLFRIEND FOR THE CRIME! GLORIA, HARDENED BY THE SYSTEM, TURNS INTO A RAW, ANTISOCIAL, HOSTILE LITTLE BITCH, AND THE WORLD WEEPS. NEXT!

THE REST OF THE DECADE AND THE BETTER PART OF THE '60S SAW MUCH LESS IN THE WAY OF W.I.P. FILMS WITH A FEW EXCEPTIONS HERE AND THERE SUCH AS BARRY MAHON'S **VIOLENT WOMEN** (1960), A.I.P.s **WHY MUST I DIE?** (1960) AND THE 1962 US. FILM **HOUSE OF WOMEN**, WHICH MARKED A FURTHER SHIFT TOWARDS THE GREAT SCENE-CHEWING CAMPY "BABES BEHIND BARS" VISION OF THE WOMEN'S PRISON GENRE. IN THE UK, FILMS SUCH AS **SO EVIL SO YOUNG** (1961) WITH JILL IRELAND, AND THE NAUGHTY **SCHOOL FOR UNCLAIMED GIRLS** (1969) -- WHICH HAD SOME SURPRISING BRIEF FULL FRONTAL NUDITY -- ALSO CONTINUED THIS TREND.

Plus BUT DESPITE THE FACT THAT FEW FILMS WERE BEING MADE, THE

NO ESCAPE.. FROM THE VIOLENCE OF THEIR OWN DEPRIVED SEX

VIOLENT WOMEN

starring
JENNIFER STATLER
JO ANN KELLY
Pamela Perry · Elinor Blair

W.I.P. RAFT WOULDN'T SINK WHILE CAST ADRIFT IN THE '60S LIKE IT SHOULD HAVE. IN MY OPINION IT'S BECAUSE THEY WERE HEROICALLY RESCUED FROM THE CINEMA AND TAKEN ASHORE BY THE "MEN'S ADVENTURE" PULP MAGAZINES SO POPULAR AT THE TIME. READERS GASPED AT THE SIGHT OF NAZIS AND PRISON WARDENS TORMENTING HORRIFIED CHAINED FEMALES, AS THIS WAS IMAGERY PREVIOUSLY UNSEEN IN ANY FORM OF MEDIA. THE MOTIF BECAME A PERENNIAL FAVOURITE SUBJECT FOR THE SALTY SEMI-PORNOGRAPHIC COVERS OF POINTEDLY WILD "TRUE ADVENTURE" MAGAZINES SUCH AS **ARGOSY, MAN'S STORY, DARING,** AND **MEN TODAY**.

WHEN VIEWED IN THIS CONTEXT, IT'S EASY TO RECOGNIZE THE W.I.P. FILM GENRE AS A MORE EXPLICIT VARIANT OF THE SAME DAMSELS-IN-DISTRESS SEXUAL FANTASY, BUT IRONICALLY, IT WAS LIBERAL SEXUALITY OF THE TIME THAT WASHED IT ALL AWAY.

IN 1968, THE BOTTOM FELL OUT OF THE MEN'S ADVENTURE MAG BUSINESS WHEN A SERIES OF COURT CASES MADE MORE GRAPHIC, PHOTO-BASED PORNOGRAPHY EASIER TO DISTRIBUTE. OVERNIGHT THE BRILLIANT PAINTED COVERS AND TEXT STORIES COVERING A MYRIAD OF CONTEMPTIBLE STORYLINES WERE TRANSFORMED INTO THE GIRLIE MAGAZINES WE KNOW TODAY, REPLETE WITH BARED NIPPLES AND ROUND NAKED ASSES. PUBIC HAIR, AND SPREAD ASS AND BEAVER SHOTS WOULD FOLLOW BEFORE TOO LONG.

TO THE UNTRAINED EYE, IT WOULD SEEM THAT THE MEN'S ADVENTURE MAGAZINE CROAKED RIGHT THEN, BUT IS IT ANY COINCIDENCE THAT 1969 WAS THE BIRTH OF THE MODERN WOMEN IN PRISON FILM? THE CONTENT OF THE MEN'S ADVENTURE MAGAZINES HAD SIMPLY CHANGED VENUES, AND THE FILM THAT STARTED THE THIRD (AND SO FAR, FINAL) WAVE OF W.I.P. CINEMA?

JESS FRANCO'S **99 WOMEN**.

PERHAPS THE MOST INTERESTING THING ABOUT THIS SEMINAL GENRE EFFORT IS THAT (DESPITE THE TITLE) ONLY 3 FEMALE

PRISONERS ARE ACTUALLY ONSCREEN. THE CAST IS FUCKING **TOPS**, AND I THINK THE FILM RANKS WITH FRANCO'S BEST WORKS. AS THE SADISTIC WARDEN "THELMA DIAZ", MERCEDES McCAMBRIDGE STRUTS AROUND AN ISLAND PRISON OFF THE PANAMANIAN COAST UNINTENTIONALLY LOOKING LIKE NAPOLEON IN A THRIFT STORE WIG, AND DEALING OUT NASTY PUNISHMENTS (SURPRISINGLY KEPT OFFSCREEN). SHE YELLS CRAZY DIALOG WITH UNRESTRAINED FURY -- SUCH AS "PRISON IS A PLACE FOR THE PUNISHMENT OF CRIMINALS! IT'S NOT MEANT TO BE A HAPPY PLACE!!"

HER THREE PRISONERS (MARIA ROHM, ELISA MONTES, LUCIANA PALUZZI) ARE SENTENCED TO THE ISLAND HELL ONLY TO ENCOUNTER TORTURE, RAPE, AND FORCED LESBIANISM. WHILE THE TRIO ARE MISTREATED AND DEHUMANISED -- THIS ONE COMPARED TO MOST ANY OTHER WIP FEATURE TO COME LATER SEEMS PRETTY CLASSY IN ITS DEPICTION OF SAID EVENTS. WHEN SYMPATHETIC WARDEN CAROLL (MARIA SCHELL) REPLACES DIAZ, THE GIRLS PRESUME THAT THEIR SAD CIRCUMSTANCES WILL CHANGE. THEY DON'T, SO THE LADIES DECIDE TO MAKE GOOD THEIR GETAWAY.

THERE ARE MANY DIFFERENT VERSIONS OF **99 WOMEN** WITH VARIOUS RUNNING TIMES (THE CENSORED U.K. CUT REPORTEDLY RUNS ONLY 70 MIN.) BUT BLUE UNDERGROUND'S EXCELLENT DVD RELEASE REPRESENTS THE MOST COMMON VERSION, WHICH IS CONSIDERED THE "UNRATED DIRECTOR'S CUT". B.U. HAS ALSO RELEASED A X-RATED FRENCH VERSION (WITH A LITTLE HARD SEX SHOT BY BRUNO MATTEI) WHICH IS INTERESTING, BUT ISN'T BETTER THAN THE SOFTER VERSION AND IS MISSING SOME OF THE EXTRA FEATURES FOUND ON THE DIRECTORS CUT.

IN ALL HONESTY, THE "SLEAZE" IN THIS MOVIE IS REALLY TAME BY TODAY'S STANDARDS, ALTHOUGH IT DOESN'T SUFFER FOR IT, AND FRANCO WOULD EVENTUALLY HATCH FAR FIERCER SEXUALLY EXPLICIT WIP CREATIONS, SUCH AS **BARBED WIRE DOLLS**, **ILSA THE WICKED WARDEN**, AND THE INCREDIBLE **SADOMANIA**. WHAT SETS IT APART THOUGH, IS THAT THIS WAS THE VERY FIRST OF THE WIP GENRE TO CATER TO THE SLEAZE HOUNDS, AND IT INSPIRED THE MAD BUMRUSH OF SIMILAR FEMME JAILBIRD CELLULOID THAT CAME OUT OF THE U.S., EUROPE, SOUTH AMERICA, AND ASIA OVER THE NEXT 20 YEARS BEFORE UNCEREMONIOUSLY DYING OFF.

-BOUGIE '06

SCRUBBERS (1982) A NASTY BRITISH REFORM SCHOOL (AKA "A BORSTAL") FOR GIRLS PROVIDES THE SETTING FOR THIS HEAVY HANDED DRAMA ALL ABOUT TWO INMATES -- ONE HOPING TO FIND SANITY AND LESBIAN LOVE IN THE PRISON, THE OTHER DESPERATE TO BE REUNITED WITH HER INFANT.

WHILE LIVING COOPED UP IN THE FILTHY BORSTAL LIKE DOGS, THEY COPE WITH ALL KINDS OF SHIT (AT ONE POINT DOING SO BY MAKING A LARGE BANNER OUT OF MASKING TAPE AND GARBAGE BAGS THAT SAYS "HELL HOLE BITCHES".) AND BY TALKING N' SINGING IN REALLY FUCKING ANNOYING BRITISH SLANG. YEAH, I CAN'T RECOMMEND THIS. -BOUGIE

CINEMA SEWER

BOOK REVIEWS

IN THE CONVENTIONAL '50S IT WAS TOUGH FOR LESBIANS TO FIND ANY MENTION OF THEMSELVES, LET ALONE ANYTHING REMOTELY POSITIVE. ALL THAT CHANGED WITH THE ARRIVAL OF THE LESBIAN PULP NOVEL. WITH THEIR GORGEOUS, SEXY COVER ART AND LURID STORIES SOMETIMES SET IN WOMEN'S PRISONS, LESBO PULP BECAME A REFUGE IN A CULTURE OF UPTIGHT HOMOPHOBIA FOR MANY LESBIANS. IMAGINE THE NEW FOUND SENSE OF ACCEPTANCE AS RUG-MUNCHERS COULD FOR THE FIRST TIME BE INTRODUCED TO OTHERS OF THE SOFTER SEX THAT ENJOYED BUMPIN' UGLIES WITH FELLOW CHICKS.

PULP NOVELS WERE DESIGNED TO BE READ AND QUICKLY TOSSED OUT, BUT MANY DYKES PASSED THESE BOOKS FROM PERSON TO PERSON, CHERISHING AND HOLDING THEM IN HIGH REGARD. MANY LATTER-DAY SAPPHIC CITIZENS HAVE A HEALTHY INTEREST IN PULPS FROM THIS ERA, DRIVING THE PRICES UP DURING AUCTIONS ON EBAY, AND **TOTALLY SCOOPING MY ASS** ON MANY OF THESE RARE WIP PULP TITLES WHICH HAVE NOW BECOME VALUED PUBLICATIONS.

ONE SUCH COLLECTORS ITEM IS REED MARR'S 1957 PULP **WOMEN WITHOUT MEN** (GOLD MEDAL BOOKS), BUT IN THIS CASE I WAS THE ONE DOING THE FUCKIN' SCOOPING. WOOT! BETTER LUCK NEXT MY LESBIAN HOMEBOYS! I AM THE EBAY KING. WHEEEE-HA-HA-HA! YOU GOTTA GET UP PRETTY EARLY IN THE A.M. IFFIN' YOU WANNA BALL WITH ME! ☺

"THE UGLY AND THE BEAUTIFUL, THE DEPRAVED AND THE INNOCENT, THE DANGEROUS AND THE FRIGHTENED," READS THE BACK COVER BLURB. "THEY SHUFFLED THROUGH THE DAYS IN BAGGY, GREY COTTON -- THE WOMEN WHO SOCIETY HAD IMPRISONED IN KENNETANK PENITENTIARY."

"KENNETANK, WHERE EVIL FLOURISHED AND FEAR RULED, AND EVEN THE WARDEN WAS HELPLESS TO STOP IT. FOR BEHIND IT'S WALLS THE HABITUAL THIEF CALLED "THE QUEEN" REIGNED -- HER WEAPONS TERROR AND COERCION, TWISTED LOVES AND PASSIONATE HATES.

"SOON SHE WOULD HAVE A NEW COURTIER -- OR ENEMY. MARY HALLOWAY WAS COMING TO KENNE--TANK, AND THE PRISON BUZZED EXCITEDLY AT THE NEWS. FOR MARY WAS A CELEBRITY -- THE BEAUTIFUL STAR ATTRACTION OF THE RECENT VICE TRIALS. KENNETANK WAS WAITING FOR HER, AND SO WAS THE QUEEN -- THE GREY GROSS SPIDER WEAVING A WEB THAT COULD IMPRISON MARY

WOMEN CAGED LIKE ANIMALS ...

MORE DEGRADINGLY THAN ANY CELL IN THE WORLD".

OK OK, SO MAYBE THE RAUNCHY QUEEN WHOSE "CRUELTY AND LUST TRAPS HER FELLOW HAPLESS INMATES" WASN'T EXACTLY THE MOST POSITIVE PERSONA FOR A LESBIAN TO BE PORTRAYED UNDER, BUT THIS TOUGH-AS-NAILS SISTER IS A REALLY FUCKING ENTERTAINING CHARACTER NONETHELESS.

SHE HOLDS THE ENTIRE PRISON IN HER GRASP UNTIL SUPERSTAR MARY SNATCHES THE CROWN AND CONTROL OF THE PRISON -- WITH GENTLER HANDS (AND LIPS - ROWR!). BUT SUGAR SWEET CAN'T POSSIBLY LAST IN A SAVAGE PLACE "WHERE WOMEN ARE CAGED LIKE ANIMALS AND BECOME AS BEASTS", AND BEFORE THE END, MARY TRANSFORMS INTO THE POWER-CORRUPTED TYRANT SHE TOPPLED. IT'S READING ABOUT WHAT CAUSES HER TO TURN FROM NAIVE TO JADED THAT PROVIDES THE THRILLS HERE, AND I LOVE A TALE THAT ISN'T AFRAID TO SPIT IN MY EYE TO REMIND ME THAT SOMETIMES THE WORLD IS INDEED AN AWFUL PLACE.

ALSO WITH A DEPRESSING SLANT IS NEDRA TYRE'S **REFORMATORY GIRLS** (AKA "HALL OF DEATH"), WHICH HAS THE SETTING OF A STATE INSTITUTION FOR DELINQUENT DAMSELS. "THE READER HAS NEVER, AND WILL NEVER ENTER THE DOOR OF SUCH A DREADFUL EDIFICE AS PORTRAYED IN THE BOOK" WROTE REVIEWER LILLIAN GREGSON NOT LONG AFTER THE BOOK WAS RELEASED IN 1960. SHE GOES ON TO PRAISE TYRE'S SKILL IN "EVOKING THAT SMELL OF MASS FEMALE, THE MASS FEAR IN THIS HOUSE OF DETENTION, WHICH WILL LINGER LONG AFTER THE LAST PAGE IS TURNED".

FROM THE BACK COVER OF NEDRA TYRE'S: "REFORMATORY GIRLS"

UNFORTUNATELY, I DON'T THINK I SMELLED ANY LINGERING FEMALE SMELLS LIKE LILLIAN DID. THIS ONE IS DIFFERENT THAN ANY OF THE OTHER WIP PULPS I'VE READ, IN THAT IT TELLS THE STORY FROM THE P.O.V. OF ONE OF THE GUARDS RATHER THAN ONE OF THE INMATES.

THIS IS THE 1ST PERSON ACCOUNT OF "MISS MICHEALS", DETAILING HER HORRIFIC TRAVAILS BEHIND THE WALLS OF THE REFORMATORY -- AN ANXIETY-PACKED EXPERIENCE DUE TO HER FELLOW MATRONS: THE "TALL, COMMANDING AND CRISP" MRS SPINKS (WHO IS FOND OF SCREAMING "WE ARE HERE TO **PUNISH THEM!**") THE ENORMOUS MRS GRINDLEY, THE "IMMACULATE" MISS LYNCH, AND MISS PIERCE -- "WHO SEEMED PERPETUALLY TO SWEAT, EVEN IN THE DEAD OF WINTER."

"WE EARNED OUR LIVING FROM THE SUFFERING OF DEFENCELESS GIRLS, AND WE WERE PART OF A PLOT TO PUNISH WHEN WE SHOULD HAVE BEEN TRYING TO HELP." MISS MICHEALS LAMENTS IN HER OVERLY SANCTIMONIOUS WAY. THE GIRLS IN THE REFORMATORY, AGED 14 TO 17, ALL FROM "BROKEN HOMES", AND FOR THE MOST PART INCARCERATED FOR THE SERIOUS CRIME OF "BEING PROMISCUOUS", (IT SURE WAS A DIFFERENT TIME) ARE PORTRAYED AS INNOCENT VICTIMS -- AND VERY REPENTANT. I'M TALKING INNOCENT TO THE POINT OF SAINTHOOD. MEANING: NO SENSATIONAL TENDER-TEEN-LESBO-RUTTING.

IN FACT THE WHOLE THING READS WAY MORE LIKE **DEAD POET'S SOCIETY**, THAN **CAGED HEAT**, WHICH IS ALL FINE AND GOOD, BUT IT SURE LEFT MY EXPLOITATION TOOTH PRETTY MUCH UNQUENCHED. THAT'S NOT TO SAY IT'S NOT ONE OF THE BETTER WRITTEN BOOKS REVIEWED HERE, BUT THE FACT THAT IT IS SET IN A REFORMATORY FOR GIRLS IS TOTALLY SECONDARY TO THE PLOT. I MEAN, BLAH, LET'S JUST SAY I WAS IN THE MOOD FOR SOMETHING ELSE.

I FOUND THAT "SOMETHING ELSE" IN THE FORM OF ONE OTHER PULP PRISON BOOK, WITH THE TITLE OF **PRISON GIRL**. I REVIEWED IT WITH THE EXCELLENT ILLUSTRATIVE HELP OF MY PAL PHIL BARRETT, AND IT'S ON THE FOLLOWING PAGE. ENJOY!

TRUCK STOP WOMEN (1974)

A BUSHEL OF "DOUBLE CLUTCHIN' GEAR JAMMIN' MAMAS" RUN THEIR OWN LITTLE SMUGGLING AND PROSTITUTION RING OUT OF A TRUCKSTOP, AND EVEN FIND THE TIME TO KICK THE SNOT OUTTA ANY MAN WHO DARE INTERFERE. THE MOB DECIDES THEY WANT A TASTE OF THE ACTION, AND IT'S A MOVE THAT PROVIDES FOR AN ALL-OUT WAR BETWEEN THE RURAL GALS AND THE CITIFIED GOONS.

HIGHLIGHTS: SOME DOORKNOB GETTING TRAMPLED IN A TRAILER FULL OF CATTLE, AN 18-WHEELER GOING OFF A VERY TALL CLIFF, REDNECK GIRLS WITH GUNS, A NUDITY PACKED MUSICAL MONTAGE ABOUT THE JOYS OF TRUCKIN', AND AN ODD BUT NOT-SO-SUBTLE FEMINIST SUBTEXT, AND THE SASSY AND FREQUENTLY UNCLAD 1970 PLAYBOY PLAYMATE OF THE YEAR - CLAUDIA JENNINGS (**UNHOLY ROLLERS, GATOR BAIT**) IN A STARRING ROLE.

POLITICAL TRIVIA: PRESIDENTIAL HOPEFUL PHIL GRAMM GOT INTO SOME TROUBLE IN THE '96 CAMPAIGN WHEN IT WAS REVEALED THAT HE DID QUITE A BIT TO HELP FINANCE TRUCK STOP WOMEN IN HIS APPARENTLY LESS CONSERVATIVE DAYS.

MOVIE POSTER ARTIST JOSEPH SMITH, WHO WAS ALSO RESPONSIBLE FOR THE AWESOME POSTER ART FOR **PHANTASM**, **LADY FRANKENSTIEN**, AND **EARTHQUAKE** PULLED OUT ALL THE (TRUCK) STOPS WITH HIS ASS KICKING DESIGN FOR THE **TRUCK STOP WOMEN** POSTER. GOD... IF ONLY ARTISANS LIKE SMITH WERE STILL IN CHARGE OF PUTTING TOGETHER THE AESTHETICS OF MODERN DAY AD CAMPAIGNS - RATHER THAN THE CURRENT CROP OF UNCREATIVE RETARDED HALF WITS WHO EXCLUSIVELY USE LAME PHOTOSHOP TECHNIQUES AS A SUBSTITUTE FOR ARTISTIC TALENT.

NO RIG WAS TOO BIG FOR THEM TO HANDLE!

Double-clutchin'... gear-jammin' mamas who like a lot of hi-jackin' by day... a lot of heavy truckin' by night!

TRUCK STOP WOMEN

CLAUDIA JENNINGS · LIEUX DRESSLER · DENNIS FIMPLE JENNIFER BURTON · GENE DREW · PAUL CARR

WENZELL BROWN
PYRAMID BOOKS

PRISON GIRL

1958

THE BACK COVER BLURB READS: "LINDA WAS NOT YET EIGHTEEN, YET THIS WAS HER LIFE: THE METALLIC CLANG OF A CELL DOOR. EVEN WHEN SHE SLEPT THE GRAY LIFE OF PRISON CREPT AROUND HER, AND SHE HEARD THE HARSH VOICE OF A LADY-LOVER:"

LINDA HAD BEEN CONVICTED OF NO CRIME YET THIS WAS HER LIFE - THIS WAS:

PRISON

SO PLAY IT EASY KID, AND BE NICE TO ME!

WHAT YOU NEED'S AN OLD WOMAN TO TAKE CARE OF YA...

OH SWEET MOTHER OF DIRTY PAPER-BACKS, THIS TAWDRY PAGE-TURNER BROUGHT THE NOISE IN MORE WAYS THAN EXPECTED. THIS IS THE CLASSIC GOOD-GIRL-GONE-BAD STORY, BUT THIS TIME IT'S THANKS TO HER JUNKIE BOYFRIEND WHO BUSTS OUT THE HIPSTER LINGO:

BUT THERES SO MUCH MORE... WE'VE GOT THE ANGELIC PAROLE OFFICER, THE VIOLENT QUEEN BEE WHO RUNS THE PRISON WITH AN IRON FIST, AND THE GOOD GIRL'S SASSY-ASS NEMESIS...

COOL IT BABYCAKES!

ADD TO THAT THE PREREQUISITE LUNCHROOM BRAWL, A JAILBREAK, PLENTY O' LESBIAN UNDERTONES AND YOU'RE IN TRASHY PAPERBACK HEAVEN. THIS BOOK REALLY IS THE BEST OF BOTH WORLDS - ALL THE TEENAGE GUM-CHEWING THRILLS OF A JUICY JD PULP AND ALL THE NIGHTMARISH TITILLATION OF THE BEST W.I.P. MOVIES.

REVIEW: ROBIN BOUGIE   ART: PHIL B '06

RAPE SQUAD
AKA "ACT OF VENGENCE" 1974

THIS GETS THE CINEMA SEWER **FIST PUMP** OF APPROVAL!

RAPE SQUAD (1974) OPENS WITH A WOMAN GETTING ATTACKED AND RAPED BY A HOCKEY MASK WEARIN' SEXUAL PREDATOR IN A BUTT-UGLY ORANGE JUMPSUIT WHO PREDATES MICHAEL MYERS AND JASON VORHEES BY A FEW YEARS. THIS FREAKY FOUL-MOUTHED FUCK-MONKEY FORCES HIS PREY TO SING "JINGLE BELLS" WHILE HE DOES THE DIRTY DEED. CREEEEPY!

IF THIS DIDN'T CONTAIN TRACES OF NUTS AND NUDITY, I'D SWEAR BY THE WAY THAT IT'S SHOT THAT IT WAS AN NBC FRIDAY NIGHT TV MOVIE! NO SURPRISE THEN THAT DIRECTOR BOB KELLJAN WENT ON THE NEXT YEAR TO DIRECT TV'S **STARSKY AND HUTCH**, AND THEN LATER HELMED TV'S **WONDER WOMAN**, AS WELL AS EPISODES OF **CHARLIE'S ANGELS**.

THE POOR VICTIM GETS ZERO SYMPATHY FROM THE JADED CHAUVINIST PIGGIES DOWN AT POLICE H.Q., NOR DO ANY OF THE 'JINGLE BELL' RAPISTS' MANY OTHER VICTIMS – AND IT'S AT THIS POLICE STATION POW-WOW THAT THESE PISSED OFF WOMEN BOND TOGETHER TO FORM A MOST UNLIKELY SUPER HERO TEAM -- **THE RAPE SQUAD!!**

THEY TAKE KARATE LESSONS, FORM A CLUBHOUSE, SMASH A DUMMY IN THE NARDS WITH NIGHTSTICKS, DISPENSE ADVICE TO OTHER RAPE VICTIMS, POUR INDELIBLE BLUE DYE ON A SWINGERS COCK + BALLS, SHOUT AT MEN WHO WHISTLE AT THEM, KICK A PIMP UNCONSCIOUS, AND EVENTUALLY TRACK DOWN 'JINGLE BELLS' AND HAVE A CRAZY MIDNIGHT SHOWDOWN AT AN ABANDONED ZOO WITH THE MASKED MAN WHO RAPED ALL OF THEM IN THEIR INFURIATED ASSES! WOW!

THIS TOTALLY UNUSUAL FILM IS SCRIPTED BY DAVID KIDD (AS ("BETTY CONKLIN"), AND WHILE IT'S NOT AN OLD-STYLE SEXIST MOVIE (DESPITE THE FACT THE LADIES GET THE IDEA TO FORM THEIR ANTI-RAPIST GUERRILLA UNIT WHILE THEIR BOUYANT NAKED BREASTS LUSCIOUSLY FLOAT AND BOB IN A HOT TUB), IT'S FAR FROM A FEMINIST MOVIE EITHER. THIS IS PURE, SLEAZY EXPLOITIVE FUN! AND I... **LOVE IT!**

SEE? SEE? MORE FIST PUMPING!

PUMP PUMP

RAPE SQUAD IS BANNED IN A HALF DOZEN COUNTRIES, WHICH IS FRANKLY RATHER SILLY. I MEAN, DESPITE MY LURID DESCRIPTIONS OF THE EVENTS THAT TRANSPIRE, THE FILM IS NOT EXCESSIVLY GRAPHIC OR ANYTHING.

← BAD MAN!

RAPE SQUAD MEMBER JO ANN HARRIS, WHO BREATHED LIFE INTO ADORABLE RETARD RALPH WIGGUM DURING THE FIRST 3 SEASONS OF THE SIMPSONS - BEFORE NANCY CARTWRIGHT TOOK OVER THE ROLE.

LOVELY CONNIE STICKLAND PLAYS TERESA, A CUTE COCKTAIL WAITRESS WHO GETS 'SURPRISE SEXED'.

JENNIFER LEE AS NANCY. SENSE HER FURY, PLEASE.

THE VENUS AND THE FOX
VANCOUVER'S TWIN PALACES OF SIN

BOUGIE · 2006 ·

THE TWO THEATRES, AS THEY APPEARED IN CINEMA SEWER ISSUE #2.

THE VENUS THEATRE IS WHAT ONE MIGHT CALL "A DISGUSTING SHITHOLE". LOCATED IN VANCOUVER, BRITISH COLUMBIA AT 720 MAIN STREET, IN WHAT MOST REFER TO AS THE ROUGHEST, MOST DEPRESSING NEIGHBOURHOOD IN ALL OF CANADA, THE VENUS IS THE KIND OF ENTERTAINMENT VENUE WHERE IT HELPS TO BE A TOTAL BAD-ASS TO EVEN CONSIDER WALKING IN THE DOOR -- HECK, THERE'S A SCARY BIKER BAR RIGHT NEXT DOOR.

SO WHY WOULD SOMEONE FOREGO A NICE, RELAXED JERK-OFF SESSION PROVIDED BY YOUR HOME ENTERTAINMENT SYSTEM FOR THIS INHOSPITABLE LEVEL OF HELL?

THE LEVEL OF DANGER, THAT'S WHY. THE STREETWALKING HOOKERS. THE DRUGS. THE SLEAZE, THE GRIME, THE SMELL OF SWEAT AND SEX. OH, AND THE PIZZA... THEY SOLD STALE, CARDBOARD-LOOKIN' PIZZA FOR 99 CENTS A SLICE IN THE LOBBY UNTIL JUST A YEAR OR SO AGO. I NEVER WORKED UP THE STEEL NERVE TO PUT IT IN MY MOUTH.

THIS CLASSIC TWO TIERED BUILDING (AT ONE TIME A MAJESTIC VAUDEVILLE THEATRE CALLED THE IMPERIAL, WHICH OPENED IN 1912) IS NOW THE KINDA SMUT DEN PEOPLE WRITE HORROR STORIES ABOUT. THE UPPER BALCONY IS WHERE MOST OF THE PUBLIC DEBAUCHERY HAPPENS, AND YOU TAKE YOUR LIFE IN YOUR HANDS GOING UP THOSE STAIRS. A VALID FEAR OF TOUCHING ANY SURFACE IN THE PLACE WITH YOUR BARE HANDS IS QUICKLY INTERCHANGED WITH CONCERN FOR TRIPPING AND FALLING DUE TO THE ONLY LIGHT BEING PROVIDED BY A CRAPPY OLD FASHIONED 3-LIGHT VIDEO PROJECTION SYSTEM FLICKERING HARDCORE PINK IMAGES.

THE SCENE IS A TAD NIGHTMARISH. CHAIRS HELD TOGETHER WITH SILVER DUCT TAPE, WADS OF USED TOILET PAPER ON THE FLOOR, CONSTANT

AT ONE POINT (AS EVIDENCED BY THIS AD) THE VENUS FEATURED LIVE STRIPPERS AS WELL AS XXX MOVIES AT THE SAME TIME.

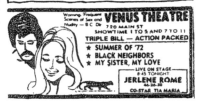

EERIE MOANING CRACKLING OUT OF THE SOUNDSYSTEM SPEAKERS, THE HAZY STENCH OF PISS IN THE AIR, AND AT ANY GIVEN TIME A GUY BEING SUCKED ON BY A STREET HOOKER OR ANOTHER GUY. HUMANOID SHAPES IN THE SAFETY OF THE DARKNESS TAKE IN ALL THE ACTION -- LEERING AND WAITING.

COUPLES CAN RENT A VIP ROOM AND WATCH MOVIES IN PRIVATE, BUT MOST FREAKS JUST CRASH OUT ON THE FILTHY COUCH POSITIONED AT THE BOTTOM OF THE BALCONY SEATING. HERE THEY SMOKE SOME ROCK, GET THEIR COCKS SUCKED, OR WATCH SOMEONE ELSE GETTING A BJ. IT'S BUYER BEWARE AS THE WHORES ARE MOSTLY DISEASED, PRACTICALLY FERAL, AND HAVE BEEN KNOWN TO RIP OFF THEIR CUSTOMERS. THE LATE '90s XXX VIDEO PLAYING ON THE SCREEN SEEMS QUITE SECONDARY AND JUST THERE FOR ATMOSPHERE.

RUMOR HAS IT THE OWNERS ARE GETTING READY TO SELL THE PROPERTY, WHICH WILL NO DOUBT LEAD TO IT BEING BULLDOZED. HALF A MILLION DOLLAR CONDOS HAVE SPRUNG UP ALL AROUND THE BLOCK THE

VENUS INHABITS, AND WITH THE REAL ESTATE MARKET AS HOT AS IT IS IN VANCOUVER RIGHT NOW, THE SMART MONEY IS ON ITS DEMISE COMING MUCH SOONER THAN LATER. I'LL BE VERY SURPRISED IF THE VENUS SURVIVES INTO 2008, IN FACT. GAME OVER.

FURTHER UP THE HILL ON MAIN STREET AROUND THE 2300 BLOCK IS MY NEIGHBOURHOOD XXX THEATRE -- THE FOX. I LIVE ABOUT 7 BLOCKS AWAY BUT FOR YEARS NEVER VENTURED ANYWHERE NEAR IT SINCE IT WAS OBVIOUS THAT ONLY GAY DUDES WENT THERE TO CRUISE AROUND FOR OTHER GAY DUDES. LIKE THE VENUS, IT SEEMED LIKE ASKING FOR TROUBLE TO EVEN BUY A TICKET, BUT AS I GOT MORE ENTRENCHED IN PUBLISHING CINEMA SEWER, GETTING TO KNOW THE PLACE ON AN INTIMATE LEVEL BECAME A PRIORITY. I WOULD GO ON TO SEE SOME OF MY FAVOURITE PORN MOVIES TO THIS DAY IN THE FOX -- MOVIES SHOWN 365 DAYS A YEAR AND STARRING NAKED LUMINARIES SUCH AS SEKA, JOHN HOLMES, SERENA, AND JAMIE GILLIS. IT WAS TREMENDOUS.

MY FIRST EXPERIENCE AT THE FOX WASN'T SO HOT THOUGH. I WALKED IN OFF THE STREET AND ASKED FOR AN INTERVIEW WITH THE FIRST PERSON THAT I SAW -- THE MAN BEHIND THE COUNTER AT THE TICKET BOOTH -- WHICH GOT ME KICKED OUT ALMOST BEFORE I COULD FINISH MY OPENING LINE. I MEAN, IF THE CHINESE DUDE (WHO I LATER FOUND OUT WAS A FELLOW NAMED MR. LI) WORKING THERE HAD A BROOM IN HIS HAND, I'M POSITIVE HE WOULDA BEAT ME OVER THE HEAD WITH IT AS HE CHASED ME OUT THE DOOR.

QUITE BY CHANCE I LATER BEFRIENDED A GUY THAT WOULD GO ON TO BECOME A CINEMA SEWER CONTRIBUTOR AND STAGE HIS OWN SUCCESSFUL "RETURN TO PORNO CHIC" EVENTS AT THE FOX -- DMIDTRUI OTIS. HE CAME INTO THE MUSIC STORE I WAS WORKING IN AND ASKED FOR PORN SOUNDTRACKS, AND WE LATER FOUND THAT WE HAD A MUTUAL INTEREST IN THE HISTORY OF THIS GENRE, AS WELL AS THE FOX. THIS WAS A HISTORY THAT OVER THE YEARS WE WOULD EXCITEDLY SHARE WITH ONE ANOTHER AS WE DEDUCED

THE FOX, CIRCA 2006

MORE AND MORE OF ITS TIMELINE. PARTNERS IN GRIME.

OUR FIRST EXCITING DISCOVERY (WELL OK, IT WAS DMIDTRUI'S DISCOVERY, BUT "OUR" SOUNDS BETTER) WAS THAT THIS UNASSUMING LITTLE SHIT-SCAB OF A THEATRE HAD OUTLIVED THOUSANDS OF OTHER 35mm PORN HOUSES ACROSS THE CONTINENT. BY THE MID-TO-LATE '80s, THE ADVENT OF THE VCR HAD MASSACRED THE ADULT MOVIE THEATRE LANDSCAPE, WITH THE FEW SURVIVORS CONVERTING TO VIDEO PROJECTION WHEN THE 35mm PORN PRINT DISTRIBUTION SERVICE CRUMBLED INTO NOTHING. THAT MEANT NO FILM PRINTS, AND NO PRINTS MEANT NO THEATRES.

PREVIOUSLY THE "SAVOY CINEMA" IN THE EARLY '80s, WHERE OWNER/OPERATOR SEAN DALY PROGRAMMED 3D MOVIES LIKE **THE STEWARDESSES**, AND **HOUSE OF WAX**, THE VENUE BECAME THE FOX AFTER A FEW YEARS WHEN AN EAST INDIAN FAMILY BOUGHT THE BUSINESS AND TURNED IT INTO A SMUT PALACE. INSTEAD OF RELYING ON A DISTRIBUTOR LIKE MOST XXX HOUSES, THEY BOUGHT OVER 150 ADULT FILM PRINTS TO ROTATE IN WEEKLY GROUPS OF TWO THROUGHOUT THE YEAR. A FEW SEASONS AFTER THAT MRS. LI AND HER HUSBAND BOUGHT THE WHOLE OPERATION, AND LI'S COUSIN ENDED UP BUYING THE AFOREMENTIONED VENUS THEATRE DOWN THE HILL AS WELL.

WITH THE LABORIOUS AND THANKLESS DUTY OF FILM PROJECTION COMPARED WITH THE

OH, THE STORIES THE FOX'S PROJECTIONIST BATHROOM COULD TELL IF ONLY IT COULD TALK...

UTTER EASE OF STICKING A VHS TAPE OR A DVD IN A PLAYER, NONE OF THE OTHER REMAINING FUCK-SHACKS ON THE CONTINENT STILL HAD THE GORGEOUS FLICKER OF PROJECTED FILM ON A CELLULOID SILVER SCREEN. THE FOX WAS NOW IT. A DINOSAUR. WE WERE QUITE ASTOUNDED.

DMIDTRUI PUT IN WEEKS OF DETECTIVE WORK TO MAKE ABSOLUTELY SURE THERE WEREN'T ANY OTHER SCREENS STILL REGULARLY PLAYING 35mm PORN ON THE CONTINENT, AND DESPITE A FEW FAKERS (THERE WAS ONE IN TORONTO THAT COMES TO MIND) HE WAS ABLE TO ANNOUNCE THE FACT THAT THIS INDEED WAS THE LAST ONE DURING A BEER AND SWEAT-SOAKED SOLD OUT SCREENING OF **DEEP THROAT** AND **BEHIND THE GREEN DOOR**.

IT WAS SATURDAY, JUNE 16th 2001 -- AND IT WAS AN ENORMOUSLY AWESOME EVENING FOR ME BECAUSE IT WAS THE NIGHT VANCOUVER WAS REINTRODUCED TO THAT STINKY DEN OF SIN SO DEAR TO MY HEART. FOR DECADES BARELY ANYONE ASIDE FROM CHRONIC MASTURBATORS (THE ELDERLY SKID-ROW VARIETY) HAD VENTURED THROUGH ITS DOORS, AND NOW THERE WAS A LINE UP OF NEARLY EVERYONE I KNEW GOING DOWN THE FUCKING BLOCK, WITH ABOUT 70 PEOPLE TURNED AWAY AT THE DOOR. THE REGULAR RAINCOATERS WERE TOTALLY CONFUSED.

"JESUS CHRIST!" ONE OL' BOOZE HOUND EXCLAIMED AS HE WALKED INTO THE LOBBY. "I'VE BEEN GOIN' HERE FOR ABOUT 20 YEARS N' I'VE NEVER SEEN ANYTHING LIKE **THIS**!"

I SOLD $140 WORTH OF CINEMA SEWERS TO THE MASSES, AND POSITIONED AS I WAS NEXT TO THE MEN'S BATHROOM, I HAD THE TRUE PLEASURE OF SNORTING LUNGFULS OF FESTERING STENCH ALL EVENING. VANESSA DEL RIO ONCE TOLD ME SHE LOVED GOING INTO MEN'S ROOMS IN PORN THEATRES CUZ THE PHEROMONE-HEAVY SMELL OF MEN'S PISS MAKES HER HORNY. SHE WOULD <u>LOVE</u> THE FOX. WALKING THROUGH THE DOOR TO THAT DANK, GRAFFITI-SCRAWLED SHIT-PIT IS LIKE BEING BOXED IN THE FACE WITH A GLOVE MADE OF CUM AND URINE.

THE SCREENING AREA ITSELF, PACKED WITH SWEATING, SCANTILY CLAD PATRONS ALSO BEGAN TO GIVE OFF A RANK ODOUR, BUT I COULDN'T STOP SMILING. THIS TYPE OF SEEDY ATMOSPHERE IS THE WAY THESE MOVIES WERE **MEANT** TO BE SEEN! THESE PEOPLE WOULDN'T FORGET THIS NIGHT. THEY WERE TOURISTS IN A DEN OF DEPRAVITY, A PLACE MOST OF THEM WOULDN'T SET FOOT IN NORMALLY, BUT ONE THAT WAS MADE "SAFE" FOR ONE NIGHT BY THE EFFECT OF "A HAPPENING".

STEPPING INTO THE FOX CINEMA WAS LIKE NO OTHER FILM EXPERIENCE I'VE EVER HAD, BUT I CAN ONLY ASSUME THAT IT WAS LIKE LEGENDARY TIME SQUARE GRINDHOUSES SUCH AS THE AVON, THE GLOBE, AND THE LYRIC. THIS WAS A CUM-ENCRUSTED TIME CAPSULE THAT GLIDED ONE BACK TO A 1970s CINEMA-GOING EXPERIENCE THAT DIDN'T EXIST ANYMORE FOR A GENERATION OF FILM FANS OBSESSED WITH IMMACULATE DVD TRANSFERS AND THX SURROUND SOUND. IT WAS NASTY. IT WAS DIRTY. IT MADE US FEEL ALIVE.

OUR EXPERIENCE WATCHING FILMS SEATED AMONGST THE USUAL PATRONS ON ANY GIVEN NIGHT (AS WELL AS OUR TRIPS UPSTAIRS TO THE PRODUCTION BOOTH ONCE DMIDTRUI HAD BEFRIENDED THE LI'S) TOLD US THAT THE QUALITY OF THE PRINTS ON HAND RANGED FROM ABYSMAL TO PRETTY DECENT. TAKING INTO ACCOUNT THAT MOST OF THEM HAD BEEN PLAYED OVER AND OVER FOR 15-20 YEARS, THEY'D HELD UP VERY WELL.

SURVIVING A NIGHT AT THE FOX WAS EASIER ONCE YOU KNEW THE UNWRITTEN RULES. THE MIDDLE OF THE ROOM IS A "NO MANS LAND". SIT THERE AND YOU'RE USUALLY SAFE FROM BEING APPROACHED BY GENTLEMEN ACHING TO SUCK YOUR BALLS. THE CRUISING ITSELF GOES LIKE SO: YOU GO FOR A SAUNTER AND FIND A SUITABLE PARTNER IN THE FIRST, OR LAST FEW ROWS IN THE BACK. THEN YOU SIT DOWN A COUPLE SEATS AWAY FROM THEM SO THIS "PATRON OF THE ARTS" CAN SIZE YOU UP. IF HE MOVES CLOSER, THAT MEANS "ROCK ON!" AND THE PAIR WILL OFTEN MOVE TO SOME SEATS IN THE FIRST ROW OR TWO WHERE BLOWJOBS N' HANDJOBS TAKE PLACE. ONCE THE DIRTY DEED IS DONE, GENTS USUALLY LEAP FROM THEIR SEATS AND BOLT FOR THE REAR EXIT. FRIENDLY CHITCHAT OF ANY KIND IS FROWNED UPON, IT SEEMS.

"I LOVED THAT BACK EXIT. <u>EVERYONE</u> EXITED THROUGH THERE" MY GAY PAL SPUZZ TOLD ME WHEN I ASKED HIM ABOUT CRUISING THE FOX. "TO BE SEEN EXITING WAS LIKE A MAJOR THING".

SPUZZ TOLD ME LOTS OF FUNNY STORIES ABOUT BEING GROPED IN THE DARK, THE TIME A GUY BROUGHT A GIRL IN AND HOW EVERYONE TOOK TURNS BANGING HER, AND ABOUT THE OLD FART WHO GOT IN TROUBLE FOR LEAVING HIS DICK HANGING OUT THE FRONT OF HIS PANTS.

NOoooo, MY VENUS NOooooooo

☆UPDATE:
SURE ENOUGH, THEY TORE THE VENUS DOWN AND BUILT CONDOS BEFORE 2008 WAS EVEN OVER. OH, THEN A SHITTY HIPSTER CLOTHING BOUTIQUE MOVED IN NEXT TO THE FOX AND BEGAN BOO-HOOING TO THE CITY AND THE LOCAL PRESS ABOUT THE PROSTITUTES. ITS DAYS ARE NUMBERED, SURELY.

I WITNESSED SOME PRETTY AMAZING SITUATIONS AND MET SOME INTERESTING PEOPLE AT THE FOX MYSELF. WATCHING DMIDTRUI ALMOST GET IN A FIST FIGHT IN THE LOBBY WITH TWO FEMALE THEATER-GOERS WRACKED WITH RIGHTEOUS INDIGNATION AND FURIOUSLY DEMANDING THEIR MONEY BACK AFTER WITNESSING SEX MIXED WITH VIOLENCE IN 1977's **DISCO DOLLS**, WAS ONE SUCH EXPERIENCE.

ANOTHER WEIRD ONE WAS DURING A SCREENING OF 1985's **A COMING OF ANGELS** (A GREAT PORN VERSION OF **CHARLIE'S ANGELS**). A CREEPY REPROBATE WHO REEKED OF WHIZ SNUCK IN THE BACK DOOR, WALKED RIGHT UP TO ME AND ANNOUNCED THAT HE DETESTED PORN. THE MERE IDEA THAT A PORN THEATRE EXISTED IN HIS HOOD GAVE HIS RAGE FUEL ENOUGH TO ".. COME DOWN HERE AND FUCKIN' FIREBOMB THIS PLACE." EVEN STRANGER, WHEN CONFRONTED FOR SNEAKING IN, HE CONTENTEDLY COUGHED UP $8 AND CALMLY TOOK A SEAT (???).

"I-I.. I'M GONNA COME DOWN HERE AND FUCKIN' **FIREBOMB** THIS PLACE!"

IN AUGUST 2002 RON JEREMY SHOWED UP FOR A NIGHT OF PORN TRAILERS -- AND THAT WAS QUITE A SCENE. WITNESSING USUALLY CHASTE GIRLS I KNEW PULL THEIR TITS OUT FOR A HAIRY, OLD, SHORT GUY -- WHO IF HE WASN'T FAMOUS, COULD EASILY BE CONFUSED FOR A TRUCKER -- WAS RATHER BIZARRE. BUT HERE THEY WERE, FLIPPING THEIR SWEATER PUPPIES OUT FOR RONNIE, OR DASHING UPSTAIRS TO THE PROJECTIONIST'S BOOTH TO DOUBLE-TEAM HIS DONG IN THE TINY PRIVATE BATHROOM. AFTER THAT WE WENT TO THE TEMPLETON CAFE DOWNTOWN ON GRANVILLE WHERE RON GOT **YET** ANOTHER BLOWJOB FROM ANOTHER SCENESTER. WOW, THAT'S SOMETHING TO BRAG ABOUT, YOU GOT TO SUCK THE COCK OF A FAT, SWEATY, UNFUNNY CHEAPSKATE.

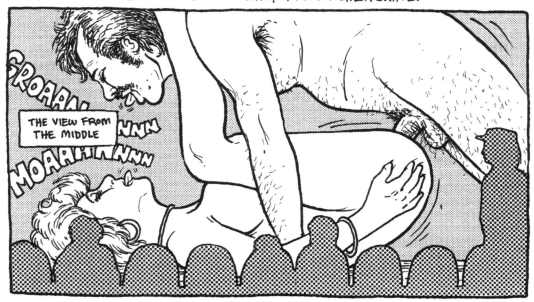

GROARRRNNN
MOARHANNNN
THE VIEW FROM THE MIDDLE

SOON AFTER, KIER-LA JANISSE (CURATOR OF THE CINEMUERTE FILM FEST AND THEN EMPLOYEE OF THE EXCELLENT BLACK DOG VIDEO ON CAMBIE STREET) AND SEVERAL OTHER PARTNERS ARRANGED TO TAKE OVER THE FOX ON THE WEEKENDS AND MAKE THE FOX INTO A CULT MOVIE GRINDHOUSE UNDER THE NAME "CRIMINAL CINEMA". THIS WAS A FANTASTIC IDEA WHICH EXCITED ME TO NO END. UNFORTUNATELY, IT WAS AN IDEA THAT THE LI'S CAPITALISED UPON BY CHARGING AN OVERINFLATED RENTAL FEE, PRICING KIER-LA AND CO. RIGHT OUTTA BUSINESS.

WHY NO ONE COME SEE **EL TOPO**?

THEY MADE A VALIANT EFFORT TO MAKE THE PLACE A LITTLE MORE HOSPITABLE BY RIPPING OUT THE NOTORIOUS ELEVATED SEATING AREA AT THE BACK -- WHICH WAS BY THEN A TRASHED MASS OF BROKEN MOVIE SEATS. THEY ALSO SLAPPED NEW PAINT ON THE WALLS, PUT A NEW CARPET IN THE LOBBY, AND ARRANGED FOR AN AMAZING MURAL OF OF SCOTT BAIO TO BE PAINTED IN THE GIRLS ROOM, ALL AT NO FEE TO THEIR CHEAP-ASS LANDLORD.

BUT IT WASN'T THE LI'S THAT KILLED CRIMINAL CINEMA. IT WAS DUE TO A TOTAL LACK OF SUPPORT FROM LOCAL MOVIEGOERS. NONE OF THE PEOPLE WHO'D BEEN PLEADING FOR A RETRO GRINDHOUSE THAT WOULD PLAY CLASSIC CULT AND EXPLOITATION PRINTS SHOWED UP. MY WIFE AND I SAW INCREDIBLE RARE SCREENINGS OF **EL TOPO**, **BRING ME THE HEAD OF ALFREDO GARCIA**, **GIMMIE SHELTER**, AND **STREETS OF FIRE** WITH AN AVERAGE OF TEN PEOPLE IN A ROOM THAT CAN EASILY FIT 300.

"CROWD"

ADVERTISING WAS GOOD, ADMISSION WAS ONLY $5, AND THERE WAS POPCORN AND CHEAP BEER ON TAP. THE ONLY THING MISSING WERE PEOPLE WHO WOULD BRAVE THE FOX, PEOPLE WHO WEREN'T SCARED TO WALK THROUGH THE DOOR, PEOPLE WHO WEREN'T DISGUSTED BY WHAT THEY THOUGHT IT STOOD FOR.

FILM ENTHUSIAST AND CINEMA SEWER READER KIERAN SUMMED UP THE SITUATION:

"I WENT TO THE SHOWING OF **BRING ME THE HEAD OF ALFREDO GARCIA**. I GOT THERE EARLY WITH KIER-LA, DARREN, AND SOME OTHERS FROM THE BLACK DOG CREW. AFTER DOWNING A FEW BEERS AND CHATTING, WE RAN OUTSIDE FOR A QUICK SMOKE BEFORE THE SHOW BEGAN. THE OTHERS FINISHED FIRST, AND I WAS THE LAST TO GO IN, EXTINGUISHING THE SMOKE. DARREN CALLS TO ME "COME ON, IT'S STARTING", AND JUST AT THAT MOMENT, A WELL-DRESSED WOMAN IS WALKING PAST THE DOORS AND MUTTERS:

"YEAH, YOU DON'T WANNA BE LATE FOR THE CIRCLE-JERK, PERV."

I WAS JUST FUCKIN' <u>SPEECHLESS</u>. I LAUGHED AND FELT EMBARRASSED/ ASHAMED AT THE SAME TIME."

FEAR OF INCIDENTS IDENTICAL TO THE ONE KIERAN EXPERIENCED WERE A MAJOR FACTOR IN KEEPING PEOPLE AWAY, BUT I DON'T CARE TO ALLOW SUPPOSED FILM FANATICS TO USE IT AS AN EXCUSE. TO THIS DAY I HAVE NOT FORGIVEN THE MOVIE GEEKS IN THIS CITY FOR DROPPING THE BALL ON THAT ONE.

BUT THE REAL HEARTBREAK WAS YET TO COME.

FRIDAY, JULY 17th 2003 WAS THE LAST DAY THE FOX SCREENED 35mm PRINTS BEFORE SWITCHING OVER TO A DVD PROJECTION SYSTEM. THE MOVIE THEATRE STILL EXISTS TODAY, SCREENING MODERN XXX DVDS, BUT THAT DAY WAS WHEN AN ERA CAME TO AN END AND THE CURTAIN DREW ON A LONG, SORDID LINEAGE OF PORNOGRAPHIC HISTORY.

THE FOX: ADULT MOVIE HOUSE FOR NEARLY TWENTY YEARS, AND THE LAST (AND PERHAPS LONGEST RUNNING) 35mm PORN THEATRE EVER.
—BOUGIE

The Cool and the Crazy (1958)

A NO GOOD POT HEAD DELINQUENT NAMED BEN (SCOTT MARLOWE) ARRIVES IN A SMALL TOWN HIGH SCHOOL, TAKES OVER THE LOCAL GANG, AND GETS THE KIDS HOOKED ON "THE KILLER WEED" WITH MALEFIC RESULTS. HILARIOUSLY, NASTY BEN PRESSURES THE IMPRESSIONABLE HICK TEENS TO JOIN HIM IN A CRAZY RAMPAGE THROUGH TOWN, AGITATING AND MORTIFYING THE VANILLA POPULACE.

THIS '50s J.D. ANTI-DRUG MOVIE WAS ORIGINALLY FOISTED ON THE PUBLIC VIA A DRIVE-IN DOUBLE BILL WITH A FUN LITTLE BIKER MOVIE CALLED **DRAGSTRIP RIOT**, AND STARS A MOTLEY CREW OF NOBODIES - SOME OF WHOM LOOK OLD ENOUGH TO HAVE TEENAGERS OF THEIR OWN. THE COOL AND THE CRAZY MAY NOT BE ENTERTAINING FOR

Seven savage punks on a weekend binge of violence!

COOL THE AND CRAZY

SCOTT MARLOWE   GIGI PERREAU   DICK BAKALYAN   DICK JONES

THE REASONS THE FILMMAKERS ORIGINALLY HOPED FOR, BUT IT SUCCEEDS IN SPITE OF ITSELF AS A HISTORICAL BIT OF "DEVILS WEED" PROPAGANDA, AND THUS: A TRUE CULT CLASSIC.

SHOOTING THE FILM IN KANSAS CITY ENDED UP BEING PROBLEMATIC FOR THE PRODUCTION, AS STARS RICHARD BAKALYAN AND DICKIE JONES WERE ROUGHED UP A LITTLE AND ARRESTED BY KANSAS CITY POLICE FOR VAGRANCY AS THEY STOOD ON THE STREET SMOKING BETWEEN TAKES. THE HAYSEED COPS SPOTTED THIER MEDIUM LENGTH HAIR AND LEATHER JACKETS, AND LATER TOLD THE LOCAL PRESS THAT THEY WANTED TO "GET THEM OFF THE STREETS" BEFORE THEY "INFESTED THE LOCAL YOUTH."

DIRECTED BY WILLIAM WITNEY, WHO STARTED HIS CAREER IN 1935 AS "HOLLYWOOD'S YOUNGEST DIRECTOR" (HE WAS 21) ALSO HELMED J.D. FILMS SUCH AS **JUVENILE JUNGLE**, AND **YOUNG AND WILD** (BOTH 1958). WITNEY'S LAST FILM BEFORE HE RETIRED WAS THE INSANE AND AMAZINGLY POLITICALLY INCORRECT RACEPLOITATION COMEDY **DARKTOWN STRUTTERS** FROM 1975. TO SEE IT IS TO NEVER FORGET IT.

—BOUGIE '06

CELEBRITIES ★ ARE WHORES!

Ahhh, celebrities and their camera time. They fight & claw and virtually kill to get right into the public's face as much as possible. They'll fuck, suck and even film themselves doing it — as long as they can safely take the role of innocent victim later on.

But it's no good to get all freaky if no-one sees it! You've gotta leak that tape to the public 'accidentally', to sustain that craving for more fame and money. Is there no depravity they won't stoop to in order to further their careers?

Of course they all plead ignorance when the media comes calling. They screech and cry foul as they count the millions that roll in due to their sexy "bad-girl/bad-boy" image making headlines across the nation.

All celebrities are whores, and the stakes are rising every year. In order to stay king-shit of crap mountain, you gotta be willing to give more of yourself to the public.

Take for instance the Paris Hilton sex tapes. It's no accident that this media blitz fell into place right just as practically unknown Paris was only days away from launching a new reality tv show. This was no coy and naive little millionaire princess who was "hurt" that the nation was suddenly obsessed with her.

THE STORY - IN ORDER TO STAY ON THE FRONT PAGE WHERE HILTON AND HER PUBLICISTS NEEDED IT TO BE - HAD TO GET PROGRESSIVELY MORE LURID. AS THE STORY HEATED UP, IT WENT FROM ONE VIDEO, TO HILTON APPEARING IN AT LEAST 10 AMATEUR XXX HUMP TAPES, AND THEN THE HORNY HEIRESS ALSO FILMING A TRYST WITH PLAYBOY PLAYMATE NICOLE LENZ WHICH SHE PURPORTEDLY SHOWED PROUDLY TO FRIENDS AND CONTEMPORARIES.

BEFORE YOU KNEW IT HILTON AND HER SEX PARTNER RICK SALOMON WERE RAKING IN MILLIONS VIA SELLING THE FOOTAGE TO THE PUBLIC THROUGH A PORN WEBSITE, AND THE DVD VERSION HAD ROCKETED UP THE CHARTS TO BE THE BIGGEST XXX DVD OF THE YEAR.

AVA CADELL:

IT'S NO COINCIDENCE THAT ALL THE CELEBRITIES WHO TAPE THEMSELVES JUST HAPPEN TO HAVE PERFECT BODIES. THEY WANT PEOPLE TO SEE THEM. THEY WANT PEOPLE TO SAY: 'WOW! SHE'S HOT!'

L.A.-BASED SEX THERAPIST

DAMN RIGHT. WHY ELSE WOULD LIL' PARIS VAINLY JOCKEY FOR NUDE CAMERA TIME WITH SALOMON WHEN HE COAXES HER TO FACE FORWARD SO "THEY CAN SEE HOW PRETTY YOU ARE." IT'S ALL ABOUT BEING 'SEEN'. IT'S ALL ABOUT BEING 'SOMEBODY'. IT'S ALL ABOUT BEING 'HOT'.

IT'S NOT AS IF THESE CELEBS DON'T KNOW THAT THERE IS A HUGE MARKET FOR THIS KIND OF MATERIAL. PAMELA ANDERSON AND TOMMY LEE OF MOTLEY CRUE MADE THEMSELVES FROM *JUST* STARS INTO MEGA-CELEBRITY HOUSEHOLD NAMES WITH THE "STOLEN" PORN TAPE THAT SURFACED IN 1997. THE TAPE ITSELF SPAWNED A COTTAGE INDUSTRY AND BECAME ONE OF THE HIGHEST GROSSING MODERN-DAY XXX RELEASES.

DIDN'T YOU LOVE THE WAY PAM AND TOMMY "FOUGHT" TO HAVE THE TAPE SUPPRESSED? AS IF SETTING UP MEGA MARKETING CAMPAIGNS AND PROFITING LIKE KINGS OFF THE ROCKETING SALES FIGURES THAT THEIR DULL COPULATION FOOTAGE PRODUCED IS EQUAL TO PROTECTING YOUR LOST HONOR.

IN FACT, OTHER THAN THE REVELATION THAT CELEBS HAVE HARD/SOGGY GENITALIA LIKE THE REST OF US, DULL AND BORING SEX FOOTAGE IS THE ONE AND ONLY THING THAT ALL THESE TAPES HAVE IN COMMON.

ROCKER VINCE NEIL, COLIN FARRELL, TOM SIZEMORE, "SCREECH" FROM "SAVED BY THE BELL", ROB LOWE, FIGURE SKATER TONYA HARDING, THE RATHER SOPHOMORIC ANAL INTRUSION OF A GROUPIE BY A COUPLE OF MEMBERS OF THE 80'S GIRL BAND THE GO-GO'S...

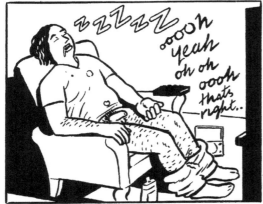

ZZZZZZ ...oooh yeah oh oh oooh thats right..

A LOT OF TIMES, PEOPLE ARE SO INTO THEMSELVES, THEY WANT TO HAVE A VISUAL RECORDING. THEY WANT TO BASK IN THE GLOW.

PSYCHOLOGIST STANLEY TEITELBAUM ON THE SUBJECT OF EGOTISTS FILMING SEX.

AND BY RELEASING THESE TAPES TO THE GENERAL PUBLIC, WHO CLAMOR AND BEG FOR JUST A MORSEL - JUST A GLIMPSE OF THE 'REAL' - THESE EGO-MANIACAL CULTURE-VULTURES FEED THAT HUNGER AND EMPTINESS INSIDE OF THEMSELVES.

SO DON'T BE SURPRISED IF YOU SEE OPRAH WINFREY PRYING OPEN HER FAT ASS TO TAKE A LARGE PISTACHIO PUDDING ENEMA, OR THE INSANE GRIN OF MARTHA STEWART PEERING OUT FROM UNDERNEATH GALLONS OF FETID SPUNK IN A VIDEOTAPED BUKKAKE SESSION.

YOU GO GIRL!

WE ALL BASK IN THEIR GLOW - THAT CATHODE RAY OF CELEBRITY SKIN.

HEY! FOR MORE PHIL BARRETT COMICS...... WWW.BLACKSHAPES.COM

VICE SQUAD

BOUGIE '06

AFTER I SAW THE ATMOSPHERIC **DEATHLINE** (AKA "RAW MEAT"), I WAS ROCKED OUTTA MY SOCKS AND WANTED TO INTERVIEW ITS DIRECTOR, GARY SHERMAN. AFTER I SAW THE GOTHIC **DEAD AND BURIED**, I WAS ASTOUNDED BY HOW UNDERRATED IT WAS, AND WANTED VERY BADLY TO INTERVIEW GARY SHERMAN. BUT IT WASN'T UNTIL I

SAW **VICE SQUAD** (AN OVER-THE -TOP 1982 EXPLOITATION COP MOVIE THAT MADE ME WET MY PANTS WITH ENTHUSIASTIC EXCITEMENT) THAT INTERVIEWING SHERMAN BECAME A SERIOUS PRIORITY.

WALSH, IN THE EXPLOSIVE, VIOLENT FINALÉ OF VICE SQUAD

LAST YEAR AT FANTASIA FEST 2006 IN MONTREAL, I WAS STANDING IN THE LOBBY AFTER A FILM SCREENING WITH GENRE FILM JOURNALIST ANDY MAURO, AND HE COMMENTED OFFHANDEDLY THAT GARY SHERMAN WAS ON THE PREMISES. AT FIRST I THOUGHT HE MUST BE TALKING ABOUT SOMEONE ELSE, SINCE I HAD NO IDEA SHERMAN HAD A NEW MOVIE OUT, WHICH IS ALMOST ALWAYS WHY ANY GIVEN DIRECTOR WOULD BE AT THE FILM FESTIVAL.

"SURE, IT'S CALLED **39**. IT'S SCREENING TOMORROW NIGHT. I SAW IT A COUPLE DAYS AGO AT THE AFTERNOON PREVIEW, IT'S THIS SERIAL KILLER THING. HEY LOOK, HE'S STANDING RIGHT OVER THERE...OVER BY THE THEATRE DOORS.. NO <u>THOSE</u> DOORS."

SURE ENOUGH SHERMAN WAS STANDING THERE, SEEMINGLY WITH NO ONE TO TALK TO. NO ONE ELSE SEEMED TO KNOW WHO HE WAS. I HADN'T FIGURED ON DOING ANY INTERVIEWS AND HAD NOT BROUGHT ANY KIND OF RECORDING DEVICE.

"YOU CAN USE MY RECORDER", ANDY SAID, SOOTHING MY FRANTIC AGITATION. 5 MIN LATER WE'D ARRANGED TO MEET GARY AT HIS HOTEL ROOM THE FOLLOWING AFTERNOON FOR A LIL' CHINWAG.

WINGS HAUSER AS RAMROD

THE NEXT AFTERNOON ARRIVED, AND I APPEARED ALONE AT THE HOTEL WHERE SHERMAN, A FRIENDLY BALDING GUY WITH GLASSES USHERED ME INTO HIS DARKENED ROOM. WE CHATTED FOR A BIT OFF THE RECORD, AND THEN HE SAT ME DOWN AT A DESK, FLIPPED OPEN A LAPTOP, PUT SOME EARPHONES ON ME, TURNED OUT THE LIGHTS, AND SAID "I'LL BE BACK IN AN HOUR AND A HALF."

THE SCREEN POPPED INTO MOTION, AND IT WAS **39**, A PSEUDO-DOCO STYLE NAIL-BITER ABOUT AN INSANE PSYCHOPATH THAT CHAINS VICTIMS UP IN A GARAGE AND VIDEOTAPES HIMSELF AS HE TORTURES, RAPES, AND KILLS THEM IN HORRIFIC WAYS. THINK OF **HENRY: PORTRAIT OF A SERIAL KILLER**, EXCEPT WITH WAY MORE KILLING. MY BACK WAS TO THE DOOR... I COULDN'T HEAR ANYTHING OTHER THAN THE SCREAMING AND SOBBING IN THE EARPHONES, AND I SUDDENLY GOT <u>VERY</u> CREEPED OUT.

WHAT IF IT WASN'T REALLY GARY SHERMAN? WHOSE HOTEL ROOM WAS I IN? MAYBE THIS WAS SOME FREAK WHO'D PERFORMED IDENTITY THEFT AND TRICKED FEST ORGANISER MITCH DAVIS! I DUNNO WHAT FUCKING GARY SHERMAN LOOKS LIKE, DO YOU?! WHAT IF THIS MANIAC WAS NOW SHOWING ME FOOTAGE OF WHAT HE

42

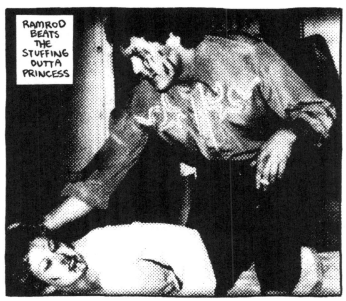

RAMROD BEATS THE STUFFING OUTTA PRINCESS

WAS GONNA DO TO ME?! WITH THE ONLY LIGHT IN THE ROOM COMING FROM THE SCREEN RIGHT IN FRONT OF MY FACE, THE FILM WAS HAVING ITS WAY WITH ME.

DON'T GET ME WRONG, **39** ISN'T **THAT** GREAT OF A MOVIE, AND CERTAINLY NOT THE BEST MOVIE I SAW AT 2006's FANTASIA FESTIVAL, BUT THE ACT OF WATCHING IT WAS CERTAINLY THE MOST INVOLVING AND MENTALLY DISTURBING ASPECT OF MY TRIP TO QUEBEC -- THANKS TO MY OWN STUPID OVERACTIVE IMAGINATION.

GARY APPEARED BEHIND ME, EXACTLY WHEN HE SAID HE WOULD, NOT WITH AN AXE OR A STRAIGHT RAZOR -- BUT WITH ANDY. I GATHERED MYSELF TOGETHER, AND WE RELAXED ON THE ROOM'S TWO IMMACULATE BEDS LIKE WE WERE AT A 12 YEAR OLD'S SLEEPOVER, AND BEGAN A RECORDED CONVERSATION. ANDY ASKED HIM ABOUT **39** FOR SOME HORROR WEBSITE HE WAS WRITING FOR, AND I ASKED HIM ABOUT **VICE SQUAD**.

AHHH... **VICE SQUAD**. (SMILES) WHERE DO I BEGIN? HOW DO I PROPERLY CONVEY TO YOU JUST HOW FUCKING INCREDIBLE THIS MOVIE IS? V.S. ROCKETS INTO ACTION WITH WHAT MAY BE ONE OF THE FINEST OPENING CREDIT SEQUENCES IN 1980s CINEMA: A VERITÉ NEON MONTAGE OF SHITTY HOLLYWOOD STREET LIFE JAM-SMOOSHED WITH SKEEZY WHORES, DANGEROUS PIMPS, DUBIOUS JOHNS, STRUTTING COPS, CREEPY CHICKENHAWKS, LEATHERMEN, HOBOES, TRANNIES N' BIKERS -- ALL SET TO AN INCREDIBLE SONG ("NEON SLIME") SCREAMED BY THE FILM'S STAR AND VILLAIN, WINGS HAUSER.

THE MOVIE FOLLOWS "PRINCESS" (SEASON HUBLEY), A CARING MOM WHO LEAVES HER YOUNG TODDLING WITH A NANNY SO SHE CAN PROWL THE STREETS TURNIN' TRICKS AS A NO-NONSENSE WHORE. HER FIRST JOHN OF THE NIGHT TURNS OUT TO BE AN UNDERCOVER COP. BUT PRINCESS MAKES HIM BEFORE SHE EVEN GETS IN THE CAR:

"DO I LOOK LIKE A COP?" HE ASKS DEFIANTLY.
PRINCESS FLASHES A SEXY GRIN. "DOES A TEDDY BEAR HAVE COTTON BALLS?"

AS KICK-ASS AS PRINCESS IS, SHE'S NO "RAMROD". I GIGGLED WHEN I HEARD WINGS HAUSER WAS THE STAR OF VICE SQUAD, ASSUMING THAT HIS NAME MEANT CRAP WAS ON ITS WAY, BEING AS EVERYTHING ELSE I'VE SEEN HIM IN WAS TERRIBLE. **DEAD WRONG.** THIS WAS WINGS'S FIRST STARRING ROLE, AND HIS PERFORMANCE AS RAMROD-- THE PSYCHOTIC COWBOY WHO GETS OFF MUTILATING WOMEN ... IS SO GRITTY AND INSANE, IT BURNS ITS SIGNATURE ON YOUR PSYCHE WHETHER YOU WANT IT BURNED OR NOT.

LOWBROW IS THE THEME, AND PRINCESS GOES ON FUCK-DATES WITH A TOE-SUCKER, A PISS DRINKER, A NECROPHILIAC, A PARAPLEGIC, AND ALL THE WHILE

RAMROD STALKS HER (FOR REASONS YOU'LL HAVE TO WATCH THE MOVIE TO FIND OUT), CUTTING THE NUTS OFF FRED "RERUN" BERRY, N' HACKING APART A COUPLE HOOKERS IN THE PROCESS. IT'S UP TO HARD-NOSED DETECTIVE WALSH (GARY SWANSON) TO GET TO PRINCESS FIRST, AND HE'S EQUIPPED WITH PLENTY OF AMAZING LINES AS WELL:

"BLINK YOUR EYES MOTHERFUCKER, AND YOU DIE IN THE DARK."

THE MOVIE PLAYS OUT VIRTUALLY IN REAL TIME -- AS ONE LONG, HEART-STOPPING EXPLOITATIONAL GOONSHOW CHASE SCENE (ONE THAT 1984's **TERMINATOR** OWES A NOD TO) ON THE FOUL, SECRETION-SOAKED PAVEMENT OF HOLLYWOOD BLVD.

VICE SQUAD WAS INITIALLY CONCEIVED AS A SERIES OF VIGNETTES CULLED FROM THE REAL-LIFE EXPERIENCES OF AN L.A. BEAT COP NAMED KENNETH PETERS. IT WAS TO

WALSH THREATENS TO PUT PRINCESS' YOUNG DAUGHTER INTO FOSTER CARE.

BE A HARD, DIRECT LOOK AT A REAL UNDERGROUND WORLD OF CRIME. GARY SHERMAN INSTEAD HONED IT DOWN TO ONE LINEAR NARRATIVE, EFFECTIVELY CHARGING UP THE INTENSITY AND MAKING THE CHARACTERS AND SITUATIONS INTO EXAGGERATED VIRAL VERSIONS OF REALITY. THE EFFECT IS MESMERISING.

(THANKS TO ANDY MAURO FOR TRANSCRIBING THIS INTERVIEW WITH GARY SHERMAN)

RB: I ACTUALLY DIDN'T SEE VICE SQUAD UNTIL FAIRLY RECENTLY. I SAW IT AT A MIDNIGHT SCREENING AT CINEMUERTE IN VANCOUVER.

GS: They screened a print? Wow.

RB: IT WAS PRETTY AMAZING TO SEE IT WITH AN AUDIENCE.

GS: I haven't seen it with an audience since it was released.

RB: THE EFFECT OF THAT EARLY SCENE WITH HAUSER BUSTING INTO THE HOOKER'S ROOM,.... NINA BLACKWOOD, WASN'T SHE AN MTV --?

GS: Yeah, she was the first VJ.

RB: SO HE BUSTS IN AND DOES THAT WHOLE PHYSICAL AND VERBAL DEBASEMENT THING AND TORTURES HER WITH A COAT HANGER. THE EFFECT ON THE AUDIENCE WAS -- PEOPLE WERE JUST FROZEN IN THEIR SEATS. IF THAT'S HOW IT'S AFFECTING TODAY'S AUDIENCE, HOW DID IT AFFECT AUDIENCES BACK IN '82?

GS: People didn't know how to react to it. In the same way they didn't know how to react to Deathline. It was so far beyond anything else that existed in terms of how real it was. Unintentionally I started a whole new genre of films. Walter Hill says he wouldn't have made 48 Hrs. if he hadn't seen Vice Squad.

RB: WOW.

GS: It was such an ego trick for me when I did Vice Squad. I got calls from John Milius and Martin Scorsese saying 'Wow, where in the fuck did this come from?' People in Hollywood were fighting about it. One of the major executives at Paramount at the time told me, 'Boy did you cause a problem last night.' I said, 'Whaddya mean I caused a problem last night?'. Dawn Steel and Martin Scorsese got into a screaming match about Vice Squad. We were at a Paramount dinner and everyone was talking about what films were going to get nominated for an Oscar, and Marty said the picture that deserves to be best picture is Vice Squad, and Dawn says 'Are you out of your fucking mind?! That was the most evil movie I've ever seen, that was the most anti-woman movie I've ever seen.' She just went on and on, and Marty says 'Well, you didn't understand it.' I wasn't there, so I can't quote them, but people reacted pretty violently to it. I actually lost a picture because of it. I was signed to do a picture at Paramount that John Milius was going to produce and finally Dawn Steel saw it and the picture got cut. She said 'Not only do I not want to work with him, I wouldn't even sit in a room and take a meeting with the person that made Vice Squad'.

RB: WOW. SEE, TO ME THAT'S THE SIGN OF AN IMPORTANT MOVIE IF IT CAN DIVIDE PEOPLE LIKE THAT.

GS: Anyway, she and I eventually made up and we were going to make a picture together, but that never happened. She got sick and passed away. The reviews on Vice Squad were one extreme or the other, it was either no stars or five stars. Vincent Canby loved it, he did a four or five page article in the Sunday New York times. Richard Corliss in Time or Newsweek gave it five stars and the title of the review was 'State of the R.' He said this is the best film of its genre that's ever been made.

RB: WELL, I THINK IT'S ONE OF MY FAVOURITE FILMS OF THE '80S. I THINK I'D PUT IT IN MY TOP 5.

GS: Thank you.

RB: JUST TO KISS YOUR ASS. (LAUGHS)

...The Real Story.
VICE
SQUAD ®
AVCO EMBASSY PICTURES

GS: It's one of my favourite films of mine. I took a terrible script in which I loved the story and hated the script, very much like 39. We changed it and tweaked it and fixed then got out on the floor and filmed something different than the script anyway.

RB: THE CHARACTER OF RAMROD, NOT TO GUSH TOO MUCH MORE, IS SUCH A GREAT VILLAIN. I THINK HE MIGHT BE ONE OF THE BEST VILLAINS IN ANY MOVIE I'VE EVER SEEN. YOU JUST HATE HIM SO MUCH. YOU WANNA SEE HIM GET HIS COMEUPPANCE.

GS: Well, thank you very much. Walter Hill said to me, 'I should really hate you, because nobody's going to be able to create a better villain than Ramrod'. He was going to use Wings in a film and said he couldn't after seeing him as Ramrod.

RB: SPEAKING OF WHICH, WHAT HAPPENED TO WINGS? I'VE NEVER SEEN HIM DO ANYTHING OF THAT QUALITY SINCE. NOT TO BE MEAN TO THE GUY, BUT HE'S KIND OF A JOKE NOW ISN'T HE?

GS: It's hard for me to talk about this. I like Wings as a person, but I think he threw his career away after Vice Squad. I knew Wings socially. He was married at that time to Nancy Locke. You Dead and Buried fans know who Nancy Locke is, she was the Mom with the little boy in the haunted house. I had known her from television, and Nancy and I were pretty good friends, and I thought she was a pretty good actress, so I gave her a part in D&B. At the time Wings was playing Greg Foster in the Young and the Restless and he would come up to Mendocino where we were shooting.

RB: YA! <unintelligible and frankly odd excitement>

GS: Wings himself is a puppy, a teddybear, but there was a dark side to Wings that I got to know...I used to drink back then, I don't drink anymore, I haven't drank for 12 years. But, back then I used to drink and do other stuff. So we'd go out and get plastered together. I was more cognoscente even when we were drunk than he was and he would spill the beans to me, and I got to see a lot of what went on inside him. So I had seen him in these weird situations where he was really smashed, and it could get really ugly. I thought, 'I wonder if he can conjure that up without drinking?', and he said he would kill to do the part. He had to convince me he could do it, and he did.

It was a studio picture, and the studio had final approval of everything. They had a bunch of names they threw at me that they wanted to play Ramrod. They wanted to go with a name person, and I said 'I want to go with Wings Hauser', and one of the executives said 'Greg Foster from the Young and the Restless?!'. I just brought him in to do a reading. I set up a situation with the entire executive staff of a studio sitting at a long table in a conference room, and he's got to come in and convince them. Wings came into the room in character, and scared the FUCK out of those executives. He was ready to rip the wallpaper off the walls. At one point he grabbed Bob Rehme, he was the president of the Academy at one time, a big guy and a great man, and Bob just yells 'Ok you got the part, get your hands off of me!' Wings says 'Oh, you don't think I'm bad, you don't think I'm bad?' and he takes off his belt and wraps it around his hand and starts smashing shit on the table.

I did some really terrible things to Wings to get that performance out of him. I knew some stuff that was going on in his head, and I used that. I did the same thing with Season.

RB: SHE WAS GREAT TOO!

GS: Susan was unbelievable. I think it's probably the best thing she's ever done too.

IN ABOUT 5 SECONDS, RAMROD IS GONNA STUFF HIS FINGERS IN HER MOUTH...

RB: YEAH, I'VE NEVER SEEN HER IN ANYTHING SINCE.

GS: Well, she had a problem afterwards that kept her from working for a long time. She was going through a custody battle for her kid, and in order to get custody she had to stop working to prove she was a stay at home Mom. It took like 2.5 years. I don't know the details... it's too bad because she was very talented, and she missed that niche and never really got back into it. Too bad, because she was great in Vice Squad, she was great in Hardcore. Both pictures were hits, and she should have been a superstar.

RB: SO MUCH OF THE FILM IS SHOT AT NIGHT, AND HAS THAT DIRTY NEON LOOK TO IT.

GS: Well, I wanted a dirty gritty look to it. I had the best cinematographer, John Alcott, shooting it. He shot 2001, Barry Lyndon, Clockwork Orange, etc, he was Kubrick's DP. We had shot commercials together in London and we were really good friends and had worked together a lot, and I was convinced that nobody could give me the look I needed except John Alcott. He was brilliant at lighting actors in low-light situations. He would stand next to the camera and focus a mini-maglight in the actors eyes so no matter how dark it got there was always some light in the actors eyes. You watch Vice Squad there's not a shot where there's not a glint in the actors eyes. That's one of the things that makes Ramrod so evil, that there's always something going on in his eyes.

END

SUPERSTARLET A.D. (2000, Dir. By J.M. McCarthy)

A MODERN SEXPLOITATION FILM SET IN THE POST-APOCALYPTIC RUINS OF "FEMPHIS" WHERE MEN HAVE DE-EVOLVED INTO FAT ANGRY NEANDERTHALS, WHEREAS THE LADIES ARE GORGEOUS, STACKED, AND WEAR THE ONLY CLOTHING TO HAVE WITHSTOOD THE SAVAGE RAVAGES OF TIME IN THIS NEW VIOLENT WORLD: FRILLY VINTAGE UNDERGARMENTS AND STOCKINGS!

CURSED WITH A HATRED FOR HAIR COLORS OTHER THAN THEIR OWN, WOMEN HAVE BANDED TOGETHER INTO BEAUTY GANGS. ARMED WITH HUGE MACHINE GUNS, THE BLONDE PHAYRAYS, THE BRUNETTE SATANAS, AND THE PISSED-OFF REDHEAD TEMPESTS ARE CONSTANTLY AT EACH OTHERS THROATS. ONE GANG HOWEVER, IS DIFFERENT: THE SUPERSTARLETS. DIRECT DESCENDANTS OF 1950s BURLESQUE LEGENDS, THESE GALS WEAR THEIR GRANDMOTHERS' FILM REELS ON THEIR BACKS AND SEARCH ANCIENT GRINDHOUSE MOVIE THEATERS.

GORGEOUSLY SHOT IN HIGH CONTRAST BLACK AND WHITE, WHICH KINDA MAKES THE HAIR COLORS MEANT TO DELINEATE THE GANGS HARD TO DISTINGUISH. THEIR CHARACTERS ARE ALSO INTERCHANGEABLE. EVERYONE SPEAKS THE SAME MONOTONE, POST-MODERN ESOTERIC DIALOGUE, AND HAVE THE SAME EXPRESSION AS THEY RECITE IT. IF YOU DON'T MIND THAT, YOU'LL LOVE THE QUIRKY TN'A CRAZINESS IN THE WASTELAND OF **SUPERSTARLET A.D.**

TROMA'S PACKAGING IS DOWNRIGHT TERRIBLE, I SHOULD ADD. IF I HADN'T GOTTEN A SCREENER COPY IN THE MAIL, I WOULD HAVE NEVER THOUGHT TO BUY A COPY, AND THAT IS A SHAME. J.M. McCARTHY IS ONE OF THE MOST TALENTED AMERICAN ARTISTS TO CREATE PORN COMICS IN THE 1990s -- WHY DIDN'T TROMA GET THE DIRECTOR TO DRAW A COVER? WOULDA BEEN BETTER THAN THE SHITTY 2 COLOR PHOTO MONTAGE THEY COBBLED TOGETHER.

MR. T IS COLD HARD STEEL!
HE'LL GIVE YOU PEACE OF MIND...
PIECE BY PIECE!

TROUBLE MAN

TWENTIETH CENTURY-FOX   COLOR BY DE LUXE®   R

WEEEE! IVAN DIXON'S 1972 BLAXPLOITATION CLASSIC IS ONE OF MY FAVES, NOT ONLY FOR MARVIN GAYE'S ASTONISHING SCORE, BUT FOR ITS BAD ASS STORY, CHARACTERS AND DIALOGUE.

ONE CAT...
WHO PLAYS LIKE
AN ARMY!

TROUBLE MAN

HIS FRIENDS CALL HIM MR. T...
HIS ENEMIES CALL FOR MERCY!

20TH CENTURY-FOX Presents TROUBLE MAN
Starring ROBERT HOOKS
Co-Starring PAUL WINFIELD · RALPH WAITE
WILLIAM SMITHERS · PAULA KELLY · JULIUS HARRIS
Produced by JOEL D. FREEMAN · Executive Producer
JOHN D. F. BLACK · Directed by IVAN DIXON · Written by
JOHN D. F. BLACK · Music by MARVIN GAYE
COLOR BY DE LUXE® ·   R
Original MARVIN GAYE SCORE
Available On MOTOWN RECORDS

"THIS IS PETE COCKRELL. I WANT TO TALK TO CHALKY."

"T" PLAYED BY THE COOL AND CRAZY ROBERT HOOKS!

"THIS IS 'T'. CHALKY'S DEAD. .... NOW I'M COMIN' TO GET YOUR HONKY ASS!"

TRAILER: "HE CARRIES TWO GUNS... ONE TO STOP TROUBLE... AND ONE TO START IT!!"

"SHOULD I BE WORRIED FOR YOU..?"

"YEAH, WORRY. THAT'S REAL GOOD FOR YOU AND IT HELPS A LOT. SHIIIT, BABY, THERE'S NEVER NOTHIN' TO WORRY 'BOUT... BE COOL."

THAT'S WHAT I'M TALKIN' 'BOUT!!!

47

HUZZAH CHRIS ENG'S ALONE IN THE DARK

"THERE IS NO THEORY OF EVOLUTION. JUST A LIST OF CREATURES CHUCK NORRIS HAS ALLOWED TO LIVE."
"GUNS DON'T KILL PEOPLE. CHUCK NORRIS KILLS PEOPLE."
"CHUCK NORRIS DOES NOT SLEEP. HE WAITS." — CHUCKNORRISFACTS.COM

BY THIS POINT YOU'VE READ THE CHUCK NORRIS FACTS. EVERYBODY'S READ THEM. YOUR GRANDMOTHER READ THEM MONTHS AGO, THEN SNORTED DERISIVELY WHEN SHE SAW THE JOHNNY-COME-LATELY EMO KIDS WEARING THE T-SHIRTS. CHUCK NORRIS AND HIS AMAZING ABILITIES HAVE BEEN SO LAUDED LATELY IT'S ALMOST TIME FOR A BACKLASH... BUT NOT BEFORE WE GET A FEW LAST FACTS OUT OF THE WAY -- AS EXPLORED IN THE TIMELESS TRUCKER CLASSIC **BREAKER! BREAKER!**

FACT: CHUCK NORRIS LOVES DESTROYING THE LIVES OF SOUTHERN COLONELS, OR MEN WHO DRESS UP LIKE SOUTHERN COLONELS. LIKE JUDGE TRIMMINGS -- THE EVIL, SHAKESPEARE-SPOUTING, PUPPET-TALKING, DRUNKEN JUDGE/DICTATOR OF THE SMALL BACKWOODS TOWN OF 'TEXAS CITY' WHO KIDNAPPED CHUCK'S LIL' BROTHER (AND HIS BIG-RIG SHIPMENT OF TV DINNERS) WHILE TRYING TO SHAKE HIM DOWN FOR $250. IF TRIMMINGS DIDN'T HAVE THE COLONEL WARDROBE ALREADY, CHUCK WOULD HAVE DRESSED HIM UP IN SOME BEFORE LAYING HIS RIGHTEOUS VENGEANCE DOWN.

A Bean Store Dolly with easy curves and a Million Miler with an easy smile ...they had an 18-wheeler with ears ...and a grudge!

STARRING
CHUCK NORRIS
7 Time Karate
World Champion!

BREAKER! BREAKER!
The CB battle cry of The Great Trucker's War

AN AMERICAN INTERNATIONAL RELEASE

BREAKER! BREAKER! starring CHUCK NORRIS with GEORGE MURDOCK
TERRY O'CONNOR · EXECUTIVE PRODUCERS - SAMUEL SCHULMAN AND BERNARD TABAKIN
MUSIC COMPOSED BY DON HULETTE · SCREENPLAY BY TERRY CHAMBERS
PRODUCED AND DIRECTED BY DON HULETTE
COLOR PRINTS BY MOVIELAB · A PARAGON FILMS PRODUCTION

PG PARENTAL GUIDANCE SUGGESTED
SOME MATERIAL MAY NOT BE SUITABLE FOR PRE-TEENAGERS

FACT: CHUCK NORRIS ARM WRESTLES PIRATES, BUT ONLY AFTER DINNER. SURE, THEY TRIED TO MAKE EVERYONE BELIEVE THEY WERE TRUCKERS BUT HOW DO YOU EXPLAIN THE SWASHBUCKLING HAT ONE OF THEM WAS WEARING? NO, THE FACT IS THEY WERE PIRATES WHO WANTED TO SHOW THE WORLD THEY WERE THE BEST AT ARM WRESTLING. EXCEPT THEY SHOWED UP WHILE CHUCK WAS EATING HIS DINNER, SO HE ASKED THEM TO COME BACK LATER. CHUCK ONLY ALLOWS HIS MEALS TO BE INTERRUPTED BY ANACHRONISMS AT LEAST A THOUSAND YEARS OUT OF PLACE, AND ONLY BY GROUPS OF A LEGION OR MORE.

FACT: EVEN A HORDE OF REDNECKS ISN'T ENOUGH TO FAZE MR. CHARLES NORRIS. I MEAN, CHRIST, THEY SENT HALF THE TOWN AFTER HIM AND HE STILL MANAGED TO TAKE MORE THAN HALF OF THEM OUT. THEN HE HID UP ON A ROOF AND JUMPED DOWN JUST SO HE COULD TAUNT THE JUDGE! MAN, CHUCK'S BALLS ARE SO BIG THEY AFFECT TIDAL PATTERNS. AND THEN, AFTER HE'S DONE BASHING IN THE SKULLS OF THE CALIFORNIAN PITCHFORK BRIGADE, HE HEADS -- WHERE? OVER TO THE BAR TO POUND BACK A FEW COLD ONES? NO. OVER TO THE JUDGE'S HOUSE TO LAY EVEN MORE SMACK DOWN? NO. OVER TO THE HOUSE OF THE CUTE WAITRESS HE MET EARLIER? YES, BUT NOT FOR THE REASON THAT YOU THINK.

FACT: CHUCK NORRIS IS INTERESTED IN MORE THAN YOUR BODY. AND PROOF POSITIVE OF THAT IS NESTLED IN CHUCK HEADING OVER TO THE WAITRESS'S HOUSE TO ENGAGE IN A ROMANTIC MONTAGE WITH HER. THERE WAS NO SEX -- NOT RIGHT

AWAY, ANYWAY -- JUST THE NEED FOR THEM TO WALK THROUGH THE TALL GRASS AND TALK AND LAUGH AND RELAX ON A TREE SWING AND THINK ABOUT HOW WONDERFUL AND SIMPLE LIFE TRULY IS, AND NOT THE FACT THAT CHUCK HAD JUST BRUTALLY BEATEN UP HALF OF THE PEOPLE IN TOWN WHO WERE ABOUT FIVE MINUTES AWAY AND LUSTING FOR HIS BLOOD. CHUCK NORRIS DOESN'T CARE ABOUT THAT -- HE CARES ABOUT YOU. HOW ARE *YOU* FEELING? ARE YOU CHILLY? WOULD YOU LIKE TO BORROW HIS JACKET?

FACT: CHUCK NORRIS'S MEDITATION POWERS ARE RECHARGED BY THE WEARING OF SEQUINED JUMPSUIT. I'M NOT SURE HOW THE SATIN /SEQUINS CHANNEL THE CHI THAT FLOWS THROUGH CHUCK'S CHAKRAS LIKE THE MIGHTY NIAGRA, BUT THEY MUST, BECAUSE HE WOULDN'T WEAR A SEQUINED JUMPSUIT WITHOUT GOOD REASON. THEY PROBABLY HELP HIM TO FOCUS HIS TIME CONTROL ABILITIES. YOU DIDN'T KNOW HE HAD THOSE, DID YOU?

FACT: CHUCK NORRIS CAN CONTROL TIME, MAKING YOUR ASS-KICKING THAT MUCH MORE PROLONGED AND BRUTAL. I MEAN, COME ON -- HOW DRAMATIC IS IT GOING TO BE IF HE JUST WALKS UP AND DROPS YOU IN 2.4 SECONDS? CHUCK IS A MAN WHO SAVOURS HIS VICTORIES AND THERE'S NO BETTER WAY TO SAVOUR THEM THAN BY BREAKING ALL THE KNOWN TEMPORAL LAWS SO HE CAN WATCH THE LOOK OF PAINED ASTONISHMENT ON YOUR FACE AS HIS FOOT ROUNDHOUSES TOWARD YOU IN SLOW MOTION AND DULLY THUDS UPSIDE YOUR IGNORANT HILLBILLY HEAD. NOT ONLY THAT, BUT HE'LL DO IT ARTFULLY, COAXING A HORSE TO RUN SLOWLY BY IN THE BACKGROUND, SYMBOLICALLY GALLOPING THIS WAY AND THAT AS YOUR HEAD WISHES IT COULD END IT'S PRIVATE HELL AND JUST QUIETLY FALL OFF.

FACT: CHUCK NORRIS'S FRIENDS ARE MORE STEADFAST AND PSYCHOTIC THAN YOURS. IF SOMEONE YOU KNEW CALLED OUT ON A CB TO TELL THE TRUCKER COMMUNITY YOU'D BEEN CAPTURED AND WERE ABOUT TO BE EXECUTED BY A BUNCH OF REDNECKS, HOW MANY OF THEM DO YOU THINK WOULD COME TO YOUR AID? ONE OR TWO, MAYBE. IF IT WERE CONVENIENT AND YOU WERE EXTREMELY LUCKY. BUT CHUCK GOT PRETTY MUCH EVERY TRUCK IN CALIFORNIA BARRELING THROUGH TEXAS CITY, BLARING THE AIR HORNS. AND THEN WHEN THEY COULDN'T FIND HIM THEY JUST DECIDED TO GIVE THE HICKS A TASTE OF TRUCKER JUSTICE... BY RAZING THE TOWN TO THE GROUND. THEY DIDN'T GET OUT OF THEIR TRUCKS -- GOD NO -- THEY JUST DROVE THROUGH EVERYTHING IN SIGHT -- PEOPLE, BUILDINGS, THE LOT. WHILE THE EVIL JUDGE WAS ENJOYING SOME POST-COITAL AFTERGLOW WITH HIS GOOD LADY WIFE, THEY PLOWED RIGHT THROUGH HIS HOUSE. BY THE END OF IT ALL, CHUCK FOUND HIS BROTHER AND GOT A BUNCH OF TRUCKERS TO SET A SMALL CALIFORNIA TOWN ON FIRE.

AND THAT'S HOW HE FOUNDED BURNING MAN IN 1977.

EXCEPT IT WAS BURNING <u>MEN</u>. AND WOMEN. AND HOUSES. AND IT WASN'T MUCH OF A PARTY.

BUT THAT'S A FACT.

-CHRIS ENG · 2006 -

TRIVIA!!

STEPHEN KING TRIED TO TALK STANLEY KUBRICK OUT OF CASTING JACK NICHOLSON IN THE LEAD FOR THE 1980 ADAPTATION OF HIS BOOK, SUGGESTING EITHER MICHAEL MORIARTY OR JON VOIGHT INSTEAD.

THE TIMBERLINE LODGE ON MT. HOOD IN OREGON REQUESTED THAT KUBRICK NOT USE ROOM 217 (AS SPECIFIED IN THE BOOK), FEARING THAT NO ONE WOULD EVER STAY IN THE ROOM AGAIN. IT WAS CHANGED TO ROOM 237, WHICH DOESN'T EXIST IN THE HOTEL.

THE LINE "HERE'S JOHNNY!!!" WAS AD-LIBBED BY JACK NICHOLSON, AS WAS THE THROWING AROUND OF THE TENNIS BALL INSIDE THE OVERLOOK HOTEL.

ACCORDING TO STEPHEN KING (WHO DOESN'T CARE MUCH FOR KUBRICK'S VERSION OF HIS STORY) THE TITLE IS INSPIRED BY THE JOHN LENNON SONG "INSTANT KARMA" WHICH FEATURES THE CHORUS: "WE ALL SHINE ON".

YOUNG ACTOR DANNY LLOYD (WHO CROAKS "REDRUM" 43 TIMES) DIDN'T KNOW HE WAS WORKING ON THE SET OF A HORROR FILM.

KELLY NICHOLS IS A BIG COMIC NERD

BORN MARIANNE WALTER IN 1956, KELLY NICHOLS BEGAN HER SMUT CAREER AS A NUDE MODEL IN THE 1970S, AND PARLAYED HER SELECTION AS A PENTHOUSE PET OF THE MONTH INTO AN IMPRESSIVE CAREER IN THE ADULT FILM BIZ -- WITH MANY STARRING ROLES TO HER CREDIT. SHE DID DOUBLE PENETRATIONS AND TOOK IT IN THE ASS AT A TIME WHEN THAT WASN'T VERY COMMON, AND ALSO MADE A FEW CAMEOS IN NON-PORN EXPLOITATION MOVIES, SUCH AS **THE TOOLBOX MURDERS** (1978). IT TOOK FUCKING THE ASSISTANT DIRECTOR TO GET THE GIG TO DOUBLE FOR JESSICA LANGE IN **KING KONG** (1976).

NICHOLS STARRED IN OVER 50 ADULT FILMS, WAS AWARDED THE BEST ACTRESS AWARD BY THE ADULT FILM ASSOCIATION OF AMERICA FOR HER ROLE IN 1983'S **IN LOVE** AND IN 1996 WAS INDUCTED INTO THE EROTIC LEGENDS HALL OF FAME. ADD TO THAT IS YEARS WORTH OF CREDITS AS A MAKE-UP ARTIST AND A RECENT HARDCORE COMEBACK INTO THE MILF GENRE (CHECK OUT **SEASONED PLAYERS 8** AND **MASTURBATION NATION 4: THE MILF EDITION**) AND YOU'VE GOT A PRETTY NIFTY PORNO LADY. HOWEVER, WHAT REALLY ENDEARED KELLY TO MY HEART WAS NOT THE AMOUNT OF COCK SHE COULD CRAM INTO HER VARIOUS OPENINGS, BUT THE INTERVIEW SHE DID IN A FANZINE FROM 1984 WHERE SHE WAS OUTED AS A COMIC BOOK AND SCI-FI NERD.

MY HOMEYS AND HOMETTES, KEEP IN MIND THAT AT THE TIME FEMALES THAT WOULD ADMIT THEY WERE INTO COMIC BOOKS WERE A RARITY, AND UNLIKE TODAY, IF YOU SAW A VAGINA-OWNER AT A COMIC CONVENTION -- 99 TIMES OUT OF 100 SHE WAS PAID TO BE THERE AS A BOOTH BABE. NICHOLS ON THE OTHER HAND WAS A BIG FAN OF KIRBY AND BUSCEMA -- WHICH AUTOMATICALLY MAKES HER ONE OF THE ALL-TIME COOLEST CLASSIC PORN STARS AS FAR AS THIS COMIC GEEK IS CONCERNED.

HERE IS A PORTION OF THE INTERVIEW:

☆☆☆☆☆☆

Kelly Nichols: "My father had two large boxes of pulps from the late 40s and 50s -- "Amazing", "Fantastic", "Analog" -- in mint condition, that he had saved as a boy. When I was about 8, my five brothers and I used to take them into our rooms and read them for hours on end. The boys grabbed them because it was their first glimpse of those large, milky-white female protuberances. I got into them because I thought the art was fantastic. I love the erotic covers and the drawings. One of the reasons I loved Vampirella so much was because of the art -- just fantastic. That started my interest in becoming an artist of some sort."

WHICH OF THE OLD PULPS DID YOU LIKE?

K.N: "The only one who stayed in my mind was Virgil Finlay, because I liked his particular scratchboard style and the stippling that he did. I was into the actual stories as well. That's where I discovered Heinlein and Lester Del Ray. After I got hooked on science fiction, it got to the point where I would go to the library and my stomach would actually hurt because I couldn't check out all the books I wanted to check out. It was a positive thing to center on. It increased my vocabulary until I had the highest vocabulary throughout grade school and high school. In high school I was very alienated from my peer group, the only girl -- and kind of a tomboy. This love of mine just helped it along."

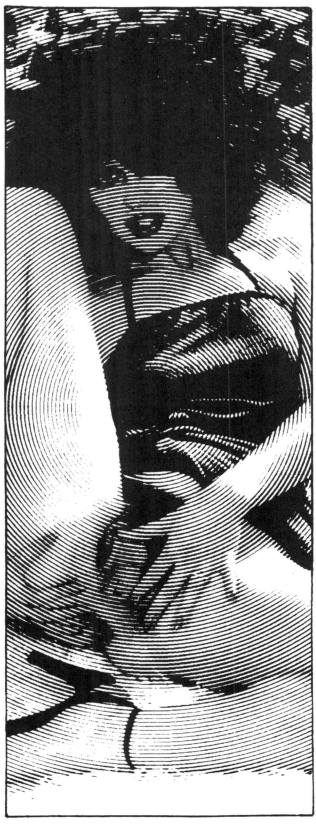

WERE YOU INTO THE MARVEL SUPERHEROS OF THE PERIOD?

K.N: "We put a fortune in pulp magazines in our club house behind the garage. We didn't sufficiently cover them, and they got rained on. Stupid us, we didn't learn our lesson. Within two years we'd built up a collection of DC and Marvel comics and had done the same thing. We had a big collection too. I saved my milk money and was buying comics like there was no tomorrow. I started off with DC because at the time Marvel was going through a kind of 'Dingo' period. I mean, they didn't quite know what to do with Captain America, and they were introducing heroes who were killed off right away because they weren't selling. But then, all of a sudden the Silver Surfer came out and I went nuts over it. I saw that, and went out of my way to buy more Marvel than DC. Those old Jack Kirby/Stan Lee issues had more to offer. I met Stan Lee once, by the way. He was at this party and he kept on saying 'I want to talk about your interest in comics and in being an artist".

DID YOU DRAW YOUR OWN COMICS AS A KID?

K.N: "Oh, yes. I was a real doodler. It was one of the things that helped me get through grade school. I was also a real Trekkie. My first Hollywood crush was on Leonard Nimoy, which then got transferred to Captain Kirk. My girlfriend and I would write whole stories about "Star Trek". I wrote one that was 900 pages. We would illustrate them, too. There was a whole lot of sublimated sex in there."

HAVE YOU GONE TO MANY COMIC CONVENTIONS?

K.N: "I hate them."

WHY?

K.N: "They're rip-offs. They generally charge too much, both for entry and what they're selling. They're generally only worthwhile if there's some special function that you want to go to, like a dress up night or a guest speaker you want to see. "

YOU SAID YOU WANTED TO DRAW COMIC STRIPS WHEN YOU WERE A KID. I'VE SEEN THE LITTLE MISTER ZEN CHARACTER YOU'VE CREATED. HAVE YOU DONE ANYTHING WITH HIM YET?

K.N: "I don't know what I will do with him yet. I'd like to draw comic books rather than a comic strip. I'd like to draw the women in sexy outfits. I'd love to draw the men in Teen Titans, and think of new outfits for the guest stars. I was really good at human anatomy because I used to draw the bunched-up muscles I would see in The Silver Surfer and other comics. In anatomy class, when we went into the muscles, I didn't even know the names of the muscles but I already knew how to draw them."

IF YOU COULD BE ANY SUPER-HEROINE, WHICH ONE WOULD YOU BE?

K.N: "The Black Widow. She's hot!"

WHAT HAVE YOU SEEN IN COMICS LATELY THAT YOU LIKED?

K.N: "Twisted Tales. I have an affinity for horror tales. I love H.P. Lovecraft."

YOU KNOW, YOU DON'T FIT WHAT I WOULD ASSUME IS THE STEREOTYPE OF A PORNO ACTRESS. ONE WOULD EXPECT THEM ALL TO BE DUMB BIMBOS, AND YOU'RE CERTAINLY NOT.

K.N: "There are a lot of girls in this business that are very bright -- Samantha Fox, Veronica Hart. There are, I would say, a small percentage of the women who are very serious about their acting, and are very intelligent."

HOW DOES IT FEEL TO BE A PORNO CELEBRITY?

K.N. "Strange."

MY FRIENDS, CLEARLY THE THING TO DO HERE IS DRAW COMICS THAT HAVE MISS NICHOLS IN THEM SOMEHOW. I'LL START, AND Y'ALL CAN FOLLOW MY LEAD. Y'KNOW, IT COULD BE A MEME. AN UNDERGROUND IN-JOKE, KINDA LIKE "ANDRE THE GIANT HAS A POSSE" OR PEDOBEAR, EXCEPT WITH MORE KELLY NICHOLS! SO YEAH, IF YOU DRAW COMICS, STICK KELLY IN THERE EVERY SO OFTEN AND EVENTUALLY IT IS GONNA GET BACK TO HER AND BLOW HER MIND. SHE IS, AFTER ALL, A BIG NERD.
— BOUGIE

THE FINAL SIN (1977)

"ULTRA-RARE SMUT-FEST WITH A WHEELCHAIR BOUND PERVERT PLAYING SICK GAMES WITH HIS WIFE, KIDS, AND GUESTS. INCLUDES SOME GOOD OLD FASHIONED FUNTIME RAPE, BONDAGE, AND A DASH OF INCEST."

THAT PLOT SYNOPSIS ON THE CINEMA-DE-BIZARRE WEBSITE WAS ENOUGH TO CATCH MY ATTENTION AND ENTICE ME TO ORDER THIS XXX SHOT-ON-FILM OBSCURITY FROM MASTER PORNOGRAPHER, CECIL HOWARD -- AND AM I EVER GLAD I DID! THIS WAS OUTRAGEOUS, ENTERTAINING, GORGEOUSLY MADE, AND PERVY FROM BEGINNING TO END.

RICHARD STRONG, WHO I'D NEVER HEARD OF BEFORE, WAS AN ABSOLUTE REVELATION AS "DADDY", A FOUL-MOUTHED SICK FUCK ON WHEELS WHO TOOTLES AROUND HIS MANSION BARKING DEMENTED DEMANDS AT HIS WIFE, TEENAGE DAUGHTER, AND STEP-SON AS THEY GEAR UP FOR AN INSANE ASYLUM EVENING OF "SEXUAL FUN AND GAMES". THIS WAS HIS ONLY STARRING ROLE, AND IT IS CERTAINLY A SHAME, BECAUSE RICHARD STRONG HAS ALL THE TWISTED LUNATIC CHARISMA OF A JAMIE GILLIS, A ZEBEDY COLT, OR A GEORGE PAYNE. THE SEQUENCE WHERE A MALE GUEST NAMED BUSTER IS HUMILIATED AND ABUSED BY LINDA WONG (WEARING A STRAP-ON) AS "DADDY" BELLOWS "FUUUCK HIIIMM!!! FUUCKK HIIIMM!!!" OVER AND OVER HAD MY EYES BUGGING OUT.

SCREW MAGAZINE CALLED IT "A MINDBLOWING MAELSTROM OF VIOLENT INCESTUOUS EROTIKA" AND I COULDN'T AGREE MORE.

WEIRD, HOT AND DEEP . . . WILL BE TALKED ABOUT FOR YEARS TO COME
—R.L. Smith/FLICK MAGAZINE

SEXUALLY BEYOND ANYTHING YOU'VE EVER SEEN
R. Allen Leider, ELITE.

Super Quality
Ⓧ Adult Film

THE FINAL sin

Starring Linda Wong

RATED X

BIANCA TRUMP

WHITE SUPREMACIST

BUXOM BRUNETTE SENSUALIST BIANCA TRUMP WAS ONE OF THE 1990S' MOST VISIBLE PORN STARS, FREQUENTLY TURNING IN MEMORABLE PERFORMANCES WITH JERRY SPRINGER ON TV AND HOWARD STERN ON RADIO WHERE SHE BOASTED ABOUT HER LEGIONS OF ADORING FANS, HER $1,200 PER HOUR PROSTITUTION WAGE, AND HOW HAPPY SHE WAS LIVING IN HER "MANSION WITH A WINE CELLAR."

KNOWN IN THE INDUSTRY AS A BOX COVER GIRL, BIANCA'S NAME AND PICTURE ON THE FRONT OF AN X-RATED VIDEO GUARANTEED SALES. TO CAPITALIZE ON HER ASSETS, BIANCA SURGICALLY BALLOONED HER BREASTS TO SICKENING PROPORTIONS AND UPPED HER RATE FOR BOFFING WEALTHY FANS ACCORDINGLY.

SO WHY DID SHE GIVE IT ALL UP TO JOIN THE KU KLUX KLAN?

BLACK ON WHITE SUPREMACIST

DART + GRAHAM '06

JUST A FEW YEARS AGO, BIANCA BILLED HERSELF AS "THE LATIN PRINCESS OF PORN". THAT SEEMS SO LONG AGO NOW. THESE DAYS SHE'S MORE LIKELY TO BE SEEN SHOOTING AT MEXICAN BORDER JUMPERS THAN PLAYING ONE IN A XXX MOVIE.

SHE WAS BORN ON NOV. 7th 1972 IN BROOKLYN, NEW YORK -- THE YOUNGEST OF SEVEN CHILDREN AND THE ONLY GIRL. IT WAS A "WONDERFUL CHILDHOOD" BIANCA CLAIMS. "AND I NEVER HID ANYTHING FROM MY FAMILY. WE GET ALONG PERFECTLY."

SWARTHY-SKINNED BIANCA MARRIED YOUNG AND LOST HER VIRGINITY DURING HER HONEYMOON. AT 18 SHE BEGAN DANCING AT THE DEJA VU PEELER BAR IN SPOKANE, WASHINGTON, ALONGSIDE HER ROOMMATE "MONA LISA." EVENTUALLY HER BRIEF MARRIAGE ENDED IN DIVORCE.

THIS CASH-FOR-GASH LIFESTYLE LED BIANCA TO MEET WITH THE CELEBRATED JIM SOUTH AT WORLD MODELING WHO GOT HER GLISTENING CROTCH SHOTS IN POPULAR STROKE MAGS SUCH AS HUSTLER AND PENTHOUSE.

SOON ENOUGH, 19 YEAR OLD BIANCA WAS BLOWING SKIN FLUTES FOR A PAYCHECK BEYOND HER WILDEST DREAMS IN HER FIRST ADULT VIDEO **TWO OF A KIND**. SHE WOULD GO ON TO APPEAR IN OVER 250 SEX VIDEOS AND 30 MEN'S MAGAZINES OVER THE NEXT 8 YEARS. BIANCA TRUMP, IN FACT, BECAME A STAR -- AND, SUBSEQUENTLY, ONE OF THE HIGHEST PAID VIDEO VIXENS-TURNED-PRIVATE ESCORTS EVER.

THEN, AROUND 2002, BIANCA TRUMP DISAPPEARED.

A YEAR LATER THE RAVEN-MANED RAVISHER REEMERGED IN THE PUBLIC EYE AS AS WENDY IWANOW (HER BIRTH NAME), A FIRE-BREATHING, NEO-NAZI TATTOO ARTIST AND FUCK-TOY FOR AMERICA'S WHITE RACIST UNDERGROUND. THE UTTER INSANITY WAS REVEALED WHEN IWANOW WAS ARRESTED IN THE SPOKANE, WASHINGTON AIRPORT ON AN OUTSTANDING WARRANT FOR FORGERY ON NOVEMBER 7th 2003 WHILE TRAVELING WITH ARYAN NATIONS' FUEHRER, RICHARD BUTLER.

BUTLER HAD NO IDEA THAT HIS BUXOM LIL' EVA BRAUN HAD ONCE USED HER SILICONE-ENHANCED FIGURE TO COAX CUM IN FUCK FLICKS   SUCH AS
LITTLE WHITE GIRL, BIG BLACK MAN. I KNOW GIRLS WHO DROP OUTTA PORN LIKE TO REINVENT THEMSELVES BUT POOR WENDY CERTAINLY HAD SOME 'SPLAININ' TO DO ABOUT THE PREVIOUS DECADE'S WORTH OF BLACK JIZZ AND LESBIAN TWAT GOO SHE'D INGESTED IN FRONT OF CAMERAS.

THIS WAS AN AWE-INSPIRING ABOUT FACE OF CAREERS. BUBBLY, SOFT-BODIED BIANCA TRANSFORMED INTO HARDENED, INK SPLATTERED WHITE SUPREMACIST WITH A BETTY PAGE HAIRCUT. AS JOURNALIST CALI RUCHALA NOTED, "IN JUST UNDER A YEAR, SHE WENT FROM A HIGH-PRICED ESCORT AND SOUTH FLORIDA TABLOID SUPERSTAR TO A BITCH FOR THE ARYAN NATIONS."

BIANCA WASN'T ITALIAN OR HISPANIC, AS THE PORN RAGS AND ONLINE INTERVIEWS OFTEN DECLARED, RATHER A MIX OF SEVERAL EUROPEAN O FLAVORS (MOSTLY HUNGARIAN). ALTHOUGH IT'S TRUE THAT SHE'S ALWAYS DISPLAYED A STEREOTYPICAL LATIN TEMPER WHILE CLASHING IN ONLINE USENET MESSAGE GROUPS WITH FANS, CRITICS, AND AN INFAMOUS UGLY FLAME WAR WITH RETIRED PORN STAR BRANDY ALEXANDRE.

THE FIRST SIGN THAT SOMETHING WAS VERY ROTTEN WAS IN JUNE 1995 WHEN FT. LAUDERDALE, FLORIDA POLICE ARRESTED A TWENTY-TWO -YEAR-OLD TRUMP AND TWO OTHER EX-CONS IN THE PISTOL-WHIPPING ROBBERY OF TWO MEN.

DETECTIVES TOLD THE LOCAL PAPERS THAT TRUMP HATCHED THE PLAN IN MAY OF THAT YEAR WHEN ONE OF THE VICTIMS EMPLOYED HER THROUGH AN ESCORT SERVICE AND "PAID HER $200 FROM A SECRET STASH OF CASH TUCKED IN A PILE OF NEWSPAPERS IN HIS CLOSET."

ACCORDING TO POLICE, SHE MADE A NOTE OF THE LOCATION AND ASSUMED THAT THE JOHN KEPT A FAT WAD OF GREENBACKS. SHE RELAYED THE SCAM TO HER SUITCASE PIMP, WHO RECRUITED TWO OTHER YOUNG MEN, ASSURING THEM OF AN EASY RIP-OFF.

IN LOVE with THE CLAN

© BRANDON GRAHAM 2006

BUT WHEN THE TWO MOOKS BUSTED INTO THE APARTMENT, THEY FOUND ONLY $60, AND FLEW INTO A RAGE, BEATING AND THREATENING TO KILL A COUPLE GUYS INNOCENTLY TRYIN' TO WATCH SITCOMS ON TV. POLICE CAUGHT THE THIEVES SHORTLY AFTERWARD WITH THEIR PATHETIC HAUL IN TOW. BIANCA WAS REVEALED TO HAVE DESIGNED SEVERAL SUCH ROBBERIES OF HER CUSTOMERS.

AROUND THE SAME TIME THAT BIANCA/WENDY MADE A VIDEO WHEREIN SHE INSERTED HER FINGER INTO A DEFORMED MAN'S PENIS, SHE BOASTED TO JOURNALIST LUKE FORD THAT SHE LIVED IN A PALATIAL MANSION IN "ONE OF THE MOST AFFLUENT NEIGHBORHOODS IN THE COUNTRY", BUT THOSE CLAIMS WERE A TAD EXAGGERATED. HER ADMITTEDLY LARGE HOME AT 3916 WESTVIEW IN PALM BEACH, FLORIDA WAS GUARDED BY TWO HUGE DOBERMANS AND LOCATED IN A DUMPY HOOD MOSTLY POPULATED BY MIDDLE-CLASS MINORITIES, A FACT THAT WAS LATER REVEALED TO HAVE BEEN A <u>HUGE</u> ISSUE FOR IWANOW.

WHEN SHE WASN'T FUCKING FOR $$, BIANCA SEEMED TO SPEND HER FREE TIME CLASHING WITH BLACK NEIGHBORS OVER BOUNDARY LINES AND SKIN COLOR. THE DOWNRIGHT UNCIVIL WAR RESULTED IN MORE THAN 140 CALLS TO 911, AND SPILLED OVER INTO VANDALISM AND BRUTAL VIOLENCE.

"I'M SUBMISSIVE WHEN IT COMES TO SEX, BUT I'M VERY DOMINANT WHEN IT COMES TO SPEAKING MY MIND."

... BIANCA ONCE TOLD AN INTERVIEWER, TRUE DAT; SHE WAS KNOWN AROUND HER 'HOOD FOR SCREAMING:

"STAY AWAY FROM MY HOUSE, YOU LITTLE **NIGGERS**!"

...AT KIDS WALKING BY HER HOUSE ON THEIR WAY HOME FROM SCHOOL.

THE TWO-YEAR BATTLE, WHICH BEGAN WITH SILLY JIBBA-JABBA OVER TREES AND PROPERTY LINES, BECAME (ACCORDING TO THE LOCAL PAPER) "THE WORST DISPUTE WEST PALM BEACH'S POLICE FORCE HAS EVER HAD TO REFEREE."

THE NADIR OCCURRED WHEN DOMINANT-MINDED MISS IWANOW DECIDED TO FLING A GALLON OF WHITE PAINT ALL OVER HER ENEMIES' FRONT PORCH. FIFTEEN OUTRAGED CITIZENS THEN BANDED TOGETHER AND PULLED BIANCA'S CRAZY WHITE ASS OUTTA HER CAR AND BEAT THE CRAP OUTTA HER.

AFTER THIS MOB ASSAULT (WHICH NETTED HER

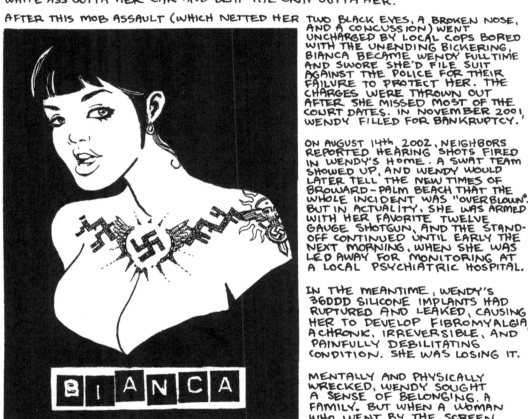

ILLUSTRATION BY: MORITAT '06

TWO BLACK EYES, A BROKEN NOSE, AND A CONCUSSION) WENT UNCHARGED BY LOCAL COPS BORED WITH THE UNENDING BICKERING, BIANCA BECAME WENDY FULLTIME AND SWORE SHE'D FILE SUIT AGAINST THE POLICE FOR THEIR FAILURE TO PROTECT HER. THE CHARGES WERE THROWN OUT AFTER SHE MISSED MOST OF THE COURT DATES. IN NOVEMBER 2001, WENDY FILLED FOR BANKRUPTCY.'

ON AUGUST 14th, 2002, NEIGHBORS REPORTED HEARING SHOTS FIRED IN WENDY'S HOME. A SWAT TEAM SHOWED UP, AND WENDY WOULD LATER TELL THE NEW TIMES OF BROWARD-PALM BEACH THAT THE WHOLE INCIDENT WAS "OVERBLOWN". BUT IN ACTUALITY, SHE WAS ARMED WITH HER FAVORITE TWELVE GAUGE SHOTGUN, AND THE STAND-OFF CONTINUED UNTIL EARLY THE NEXT MORNING, WHEN SHE WAS LED AWAY FOR MONITORING AT A LOCAL PSYCHIATRIC HOSPITAL.

IN THE MEANTIME, WENDY'S 36DDD SILICONE IMPLANTS HAD RUPTURED AND LEAKED, CAUSING HER TO DEVELOP FIBROMYALGIA, A CHRONIC, IRREVERSIBLE, AND PAINFULLY DEBILITATING CONDITION. SHE WAS LOSING IT.

MENTALLY AND PHYSICALLY WRECKED, WENDY SOUGHT A SENSE OF BELONGING. A FAMILY. BUT WHEN A WOMAN WHO WENT BY THE SCREEN NAME "WENDYFL" POSTED HER DOLLED-UP SLUTTY PICTURE TO A PROMINENT ONLINE WHITE SUPREMACIST GROUP, SHE WAS IMMEDIATELY MET WITH HOSTILITY FROM UGLY, SOCIALLY REJECTED SKINHEADS WHO ASSUMED SHE WAS FAR TOO FOXY TO BE ONE OF THEM.

WENDY WAS EVENTUALLY BANNED FROM THE SITE, BUT ONLY A FEW MONTHS LATER SHE WAS ABLE TO RETURN WITH HER GRUNGY NEW BIKER-BITCH LOOK AND A NEW NAME TO GO WITH IT: "TATTOOGIRL1488". REINVENTED AS A SPUNKY TATTOO ARTIST HAWKING HER WARES, WHATEVER RESERVATIONS THE BITTER SKINHEADS PREVIOUSLY HAD WITH HER SEEMED TO DISAPPEAR. WENDY HAD FOUND A NEW HOME.

IN A FLASH, WENDY RENOUNCED THE SEX TRADE, DUMPED HER BOYFRIEND, TOOK OFF FOR CHICAGO, REMOVED HER IMPLANTS, AND TOOK UP TATTOOING FULL TIME. THINGS SEEMED TO BE LOOKING UP FOR THE FORMER CUM QUEEN WHO HAD ONCE BEEN NOMINATED AS THE "MOST OUTRAGEOUS GUEST" IN THE HISTORY OF THE JENNY JONES SHOW.

WHITE-POWER WENDY MAY HAVE BEEN PROUD OF THE AMOUNT OF HATRED SHE RESERVED FOR THE BETTER PART OF THE EARTH'S POPULATION, BUT BY ALL ACCOUNTS SHE WAS AT THIS POINT A VERY LONELY WOMAN--ACHING TO BE NEEDED BY SOMEONE.

WENDY POSTED A PERSONAL AD WITH THE BYLINE "SINGLE AND JADED" IN JUNE 2003 ON THE MESSAGE BOARDS OF STORMFRONT.ORG. "I AM HEADING TO INDIANA ON MONDAY WITH THE HOOSIER SKINS TO TATTOO AT SS."

AFTER LESS THAN TWO MONTHS GIVING FREE MOUSTACHE RIDES TO HIGH PROFILE MALE RACISTS IN CHICAGO, OUR SLUTTY FUN-LOVIN' GAL WAS ON THE MOVE AGAIN, SEEN POSTING ONLINE TO HER NAZI PEN PALS THAT SHE WAS NOW IN INDIANA AND THAT SHE "JUST WANTED EVERYONE TO KNOW THAT IT IS SUPERCOOL HERE, A SOLID GROUP OF GUYS, AND A GREAT LITTLE WHITE TOWN. I HOPE TO SEE MORE AWARE PEOPLE RELOCATING HERE IN THE FUTURE."

BUT THE WOMAN WHO HAD ONCE SELF DIAGNOSED HERSELF AS "A LITTLE CRAZY" WAS SWITCHING SEIG-HEILING BOYFRIENDS MORE OFTEN THAN SHE CHANGED HER SCUMMY UNDERWEAR. WENDY'S BELOVED "HOOSIER STATE SKINS" GREW BORED OF HER GROUPIE PRESENCE AND TOLD HER TO "ACHTUNG BABY".

THE BELEAGUERED YOUNG DRIFTER TAGGED ALONG THROUGH THE FRINGE OF THE WHITE POWER MOVEMENT IN THE LAST HALF OF 2003, WANDERING FROM CHICAGO TO INDIANA TO ARIZONA, TO THE ARYAN NATIONS COMPOUND IN HADLEY, IDAHO.

ALL THIS COUCH SURFING CAME AT A PRICE, AS WENDY REPORTEDLY USED A STOLEN GAS STATION CREDIT CARD AND SIGNED BOGUS CHEQUES WHILE TRAVELING -- WHICH LATER PROVIDED THE BASIS OF THE FORGERY CHARGES AGAINST HER.

IT'S BEEN SAID WHEN YOU'RE A CARD CARRYING MEMBER OF THE KKK, YOU NEVER HAVE TO SLEEP IN A MOTEL IN MANY PARTS OF MIDDLE AMERICA -- AND AFTER BEDDING DOWN WITH SOME FELLOW "BROTHERS" FOR A WEEK OR TWO SOMEWHERE IN ARIZONA, WENDY WENT FOR A DRUNKEN NIGHT ON THE TOWN WITH A TRUCKER NAMED JEREMY (WHO BY NO COINCIDENCE IS AN ARYAN NATIONS LEADER) AND SOME MONOSYLLABIC INBRED DOOFUS WHO LATER POSTED HIS RAMBLING ACCOUNT OF THAT NIGHT ON SLASHDOT.ORG.

"ME AND JEREMY KICKED SOME MEXICAN GIRL OUTTA [A BAR] BECAUSE SHE WAS BEING RUDE TO SOMEONE. AND SOME GIRL STARTED A VERBAL THING WITH JEREMY AND [WENDY AND JEREMY] BOTH ENDED UP CURSING HER OUT, I WAS TOO DRUNK TO SAY ANYTHING SO SHE CAME UP TO ME AND STARTED TALKING TO ME ABOUT GOD KNOWS WHAT. EVENTUALLY WE ALL LEFT, STARTED THROWING SHOPPING CARTS IN THE STREET AND PISSING ON CARS AND WHATNOT... WHO THE HELL KNOWS. I DON'T REMEMBER MUCH EXCEPT WHEN JEREMY N ME PICKED UP SHOPPING CARTS AND HEAVED THEM INTO THE ROAD [WENDY WAS] LAUGHING HYSTERICALLY. NEXT MORNING I WOKE UP FEELING TERRIBLE NOTHING TOO BIG HAPPENED THOUGH, EXCEPT WENDY DRANK AS SOON AS SHE WOKE UP, THATS ONE THING I HATE ABOUT THIS GIRL, SHE ALWAYS HAS A GODDAMN CIGARETTE OR A BEER HANGING OUTTA HER MOUTH. SHE IS SUCH A WASTOID."

"AFTER THAT, I WAS CONVINCED I DON'T WANT TO BE THERE

56

ANYMORE, SO I STARTED TALKING TO PEOPLE AND ABOUT 3 PEOPLE ACTUALLY KNOW HER AND KNOW WHAT SHE IS ABOUT. I DON'T THINK SHE BELIEVES IN SHIT. WENDY DRINKS AND DRIVES AND ALWAYS STARTED PROBLEMS WITH ME. SHE CHANGED COMPLETELY AND I TRIED TO EXPLAIN HOW I WAS FEELING BUT SHE DIDN'T WANT TO HEAR IT. NEXT DAY I TOLD WENDY I WAS GOING TO LEAVE EARLY, SHE JUST SAID OK. THEN SHE MADE ME FOOD BUT I REFUSED IT, OBVIOUSLY BY THEN I DIDN'T TRUST HER. I WAS JUST TOO AFRAID OF ZACH AND THE FACT THAT WENDY WAS SHOWING HER TRUE SELF. BEFORE THEN I'D EATEN MOLDY BREAD AND GOTTEN REALLY SICK AND SHE DIDN'T CARE, JUST SAID "OH COME ON, CHEESE IS MOLD BUT YOU DON'T GET KILLED BY THAT". NOT TO MENTION THERES 50,000 TYPES OF MOLD, WHAT A FUCKING IDIOT. WHITE PRIDE MY ASS, HER PROFILE ON RINGO SAYS SOME GARBAGE ABOUT TAKING CARE OF PEOPLE AND COOKING AND CLEANING... WHAT FUCKING EVER, ALL SHE DOES IS COMPLAIN ABOUT HER FUCKING DIVORCE AND ABSOLUTELY USES MEN FOR WHAT EVER PURPOSE THEY CAN BE USED FOR. GUESS I JUST WASN'T COOL ENOUGH FOR HER ANYMORE AND SHE DIDN'T MIND THROWING A TRUE WHITE OUT IN THE COLD. SHE IS A TRAITOR AND I LOOK DOWN ON PEOPLE LIKE HER."

REGARDLESS OF HER RIPPLING WAKE OF UNIMPRESSED WHITE DUDES, WENDY WAS MOVING UP THE LADDER -- ONE FUCK AT A TIME. SOMEWHERE ALONG THE ROAD A COUPLE MONTHS LATER, SHE SPREAD THIGHS AND SWALLOWED UP PASTOR RICHARD BUTLER -- THE ARYAN NATIONS WRINKLY DEMIGOD. SHE COULD CLIMB NO HIGHER.

ENTRUSTED WITH MAKING DRUG DEALS, RUNNING A FAKE ID OPERATION, NOT TO MENTION BEING EXPECTED TO HELP ORGANIZE HIGH-PROFILE EVENTS -- WENDY HAD ATTAINED HER THRONE AS THE QUEEN OF THE SKINHEADS. SHE WAS THE PASTOR'S HOT LITTLE HUMP-BUDDY, AND HE WAS HER POWERFUL GERIATRIC, SHRIVELED-COCK MEAL TICKET.

BUTLER WAS THE ULTIMATE PRIZE, BUT WHEN HER OUTSTANDING WARRANTS FINALLY CAUGHT UP WITH HER, THE OBLIVIOUS PASTOR WAS SCANDALIZED. HE WASN'T JUST TRAVELING WITH A WANTED FELON, BUT ONE WHO'D MADE A HIGH PROFILE CAREER AS A LATINA LOVER OF ALL RACES. THE SHIT MAGNET HAD INFILTRATED THEIR RANKS, AND THE BROTHERHOOD WAS BESIDE ITSELF WHEN THE NEWS BROKE. SHE'D NEVER TOLD ANY OF THEM ABOUT HER RACE-TRAITOR XXX YEARS AS BIANCA TRUMP.

THE DEBACLE PROMPTED RICK SPRING, THE ARKANSAS STATE LEADER OF THE BROTHER--HOOD TO SEND OUT AN OPEN LETTER TO ALL ARYAN NATIONS MEMBERS AND ALLIED WHITE NATIONALIST ORGANIZATIONS IN ORDER TO CIRCLE THE WAGONS AND STEM THE TIDE OF GOSSIP AND CONFUSION:

"CONCERNING THE ARREST OF WENDY IWANOW, WHO WAS TRAVELING WITH PASTOR BUTLER ON NOVEMBER 7th 2003: FOLLOWING THE SCRIPTURAL TEACHINGS OF THE BIBLE, PASTOR BUTLER TRIES TO HELP EVERYONE WHO IS WHITE AND SEARCHING TO CHANGE THEIR LIFE FOR THE BETTER. IN THE LAST 30-PLUS YEARS PASTOR BUTLER HAS SACRIFICED EVERYTHING FOR WHAT HE BELIEVES IN. IN OUR WORLD THERE ARE VERY FEW WHO CAN COMPARE. HE HAS BEEN GIVEN BAD ADVICE FROM TIME TO TIME AS WELL, BECAUSE HE IS SUCH A TRUSTING AND SINCERE MAN. AND NOW, ONCE AGAIN, HIS OVER-GENEROSITY TO A WOMAN WHO PURPORTED TO BE "WHITE POWER" BUT TURNED OUT TO BE A FORMER PORN STAR, IS THE SUBJECT OF MANY JOKES. MEASURES

HAVE BEEN PUT INTO PLACE SO THAT THIS WILL NOT HAPPEN AGAIN. STOP SPENDING TIME FIGHTING IN CHATROOMS AND POINTING FINGERS, ENTERTAINING THE JEW."

I'VE BEEN LAYING WITH A JEW-FUCKER! AAAKK MY HEART!!

WENDY, WHO'D SPENT FALL 2003 PROMOTING ARYANFEST AND PROMISING HALF-PRICE SWASTIKA TATS AT THE EVENT FOR ALL HER RACIST BROTHERS N' SISTERS, WAS NOW BANNED FROM THE KEGGER/BBQ/TAILGATE PARTY SHE'D CO-ORDINATED AFTER THE HATE-FILLED MASSES LEARNED SHE'D FORNICATED WITH DIRTY LESBOS, AFRICAN AMERICANS, AND EVEN (GASP) RON JEREMY -- A FAT HAIRY **JEW**!!

AS SUSY BUCHANAN OF THE PHOENIX SUN TIMES WROTE (AND LET ME THANK HER NOW FOR HER HELP WITH THIS ARTICLE) "RULES ARE RULES, EVEN FOR THE CLOSE PERSONAL FRIEND OF A NEAR DEITY. SUCKING BLACK DICK GETS A GIRL BANNED FROM NAZI PARTIES."

BIG SURPRISE -- THE EXPOSURE OF IWANOW'S BLACK-ON-WHITE MISGIVINGS CAUSED HER INTERNET LIFELINE OF INTOLERANCE TO ACT INTOLERANT. ONE OF HER NET PALS NAMED "FRITZ" SUMMED UP THE OUTRAGE BY POSTING "ONCE YOU GO BLACK, WE WON'T LET YOU COME BACK!"

AS ODD AS WENDY'S CASE IS, IT'S NOT THE FIRST TIME THE ARYAN NATIONS HAVE BEEN INVOLVED IN THIS KINDA SHIT. CATHERINE DANIELS AT AGE 16 WAS INVOLVED IN AN INFAMOUS S+M SEX SCANDAL IN ARKANSAS, AND TALKED ABOUT HER KINKY RACIST SEX ISSUES WITH THE MEDIA. ALTHOUGH DANIELS CONVERTED TO WHITE NATIONALISM, SHE LATER CLAIMED TO HAVE BEEN ABUSED AND RAPED BY HER SKINHEAD BUDDIES. SHE'S SINCE MOVED TO THE CARIBBEAN AND IS NOW "SEXUALLY INVOLVED" WITH A PROMINENT BLACK LAWYER.

AS OF LATE 2004 BIANCA/WENDY WAS STILL AWAITING TRIAL, WHICH WAS THE LAST I HEARD OF ANYTHING TO DO WITH HER STORY UNTIL APRIL OF 2006 WHEN SHE PLEA BARGAINED AND CUT A DEAL WITH PROCECUTORS UNDER CHARGES OF KIDNAPPING ASSAULT AND FORGERY. SHE MIGHT HAVE BEAT THE RAP, BUT IN JUNE 2006 SHE WAS PULLED OVER IN SPOKANE WA. WHILE ATTEMPTING TO PROVE SHE WASN'T CARRYING A GUN, WENDY DUMPED HER PURSE ON THE HOOD OF THE CAR AND 3 GOLF-BALL SIZED BUNDLES OF METH FELL OUT.

ON NOVEMBER 29th 2006, IWANOW WAS ORDERED TO PAY $602 RESTITUTION AND SPEND 43 MONTHS IN PRISON.

PASTOR BUTLER KICKED THE CAN DUE TO OLD AGE, OR MAYBE IT WAS OUT OF SHEER FRUSTRATION WITH WENDY. POLICE REPORTED THAT IWANOW MISSPELLED THE WORD "LICENSE" ON MANY OF THE FAKE ID'S SHE MADE.

"I HAVE NO IDEA WHAT I WANT TO BE WHEN I'M 40 YEARS OF AGE" WENDY ONCE TOLD A REPORTER. "I'M A LIVE-FOR-THE-DAY KIND OF GIRL. I'M A NORMAL PERSON LIKE ANYONE ELSE."

NORMAL IS IN THE EYE OF THE BEHOLDER, BUT FOR A SISTER LIKE WENDY, WHO HAS LIVED HER LIFE IN A SAVAGE AND UNCONVENTIONAL WAY, HER TRUTH WILL BE TOLD IN THE PERMANENT LETTERING EMBLAZONED ACROSS THE TOP OF HER TITS THAT READS:

"NEVER FORGIVE, NEVER FORGET".

BOUGIE '07

SEX BOX IS ONE OF THE MOST BRUTAL, CRAZY, KINKY, HARD-TO-WATCH MODERN PORN SERIES I'VE WITNESSED. WEAPONS, DISTURBING COSTUMES, CONSTANT PISSING, FISTING, ROUGH FUCKING, AND ABOVE ALL : **SCREAMING**!! IT'S ALL CONSENSUAL, BUT DESIGNED TO LOOK LIKE IT AIN'T. TO DATE THERE ARE ABOUT 30 VOLUMES OF THIS SAVAGE GERMAN XXX SERIES, WITH THE FIRST ONE APPEARING IN 2004. FOR CLOSERS ONLY, BECAUSE THIS IS LIKE SOMETHING THAT WOULD APPEAR ON A VIDEODROME BROADCAST. -RB

HOW I BECAME AN ACTION MOVIE STAR IN INDONESIA:
THE AWESOME STORY OF PETER O'BRIAN

PLOP DOWN ON THE RUG AND LET ME TELL YOU A LITTLE YARN ABOUT A GOOD NATURED GUY FROM A POOR FAMILY IN NEW ZEALAND NAMED PETER O'BRIAN. HE'S THE KIND OF HUMBLE, AVERAGE JOE THAT MAKES YOU FEEL LIKE THERE ARE MORE NICE PEOPLE THAN MEAN PEOPLE IN THE WORLD, AND IN 1984 HE DECIDED TO GO ON A GLOBE-HOPPING ADVENTURE WITH HIS BEST FRIEND, CRAIG GAVIN.

"I HAD A TICKET TO TRAVEL THE WORLD", PETER TOLD GGTMC.COM. "AND INDONESIA WAS MY SECOND PORT OF CALL. I WAS SCHEDULED TO STAY FIVE DAYS IN JAKARTA, BUT AFTER TWO DAYS HERE I COULDN'T STAND IT."

JUST HOURS BEFORE HE AND CRAIG WERE ABOUT TO BOARD A PLANE AND LEAVE, PETER SUDDENLY REALISED HE WAS BEING WATCHED BY SIX INDONESIAN GUYS, WHOM HE PRESUMED WERE VIOLENT THUGS. THE MEN FOLLOWED HIM TO THE HOTEL WHERE HE WAS STAYING, AND WAITED FOR HIM OUTSIDE. WHEN HE WENT OUT TO TRY AND GET SOME LUNCH, THEY CONFRONTED HIM.

THE MEN CLEARLY WANTED SOMETHING FROM HIM, AND SUGGESTED THAT HE SHOULD GET IN A CAR WITH THEM AND TAKE A LITTLE RIDE. PETER WAS VERY ON EDGE ABOUT THE WHOLE THING, A STATE OF MIND THAT DIDN'T CHANGE WHEN THE CAR PULLED UP AT A MANSION WITH SECURITY GUARDS POSTED OUTSIDE. SOON ENOUGH THOUGH, EVERYTHING WAS EXPLAINED.

"FUUUCK YOU!!"

THE AMAZING PETER O'BRIAN IS ARMED WITH A GUN AND A RUBBER BALL IN 1986's RAMBU

"(THEY WERE) FILM SCOUTS. AT THE TIME THEY WERE LOOKING FOR A RAMBO LOOK-A-LIKE AND THERE I WAS. THEY ACTUALLY THOUGHT I WAS SLY, POOR BASTARDS. ANYWAY, THE NEXT THING YOU KNOW, I'M DOWN AT RAAM PUNJABI'S FILM STUDIO DOING A FIGHT SCENE WITH THIS CHINESE FIGHTER."

RAPI FILMS MAY HAVE DECIDED THAT THEIR PROSPECTIVE LEADING MAN LOOKED LIKE A LOW-RENT STALLONE, BUT IN REALITY HE ACTUALLY RESEMBLED ADULT CONTEMPORARY MUZAK KING KENNY G. ALSO, PETER WASN'T A MARTIAL ARTIST OR A TRAINED ACTOR. HE WAS JUST A GUY ON VACATION. PRODUCER RAAM PUNJABI DIDN'T KNOW THIS THOUGH, AND PETER WISELY KEPT IT TO HIMSELF, AND EVEN FIBBED A LITTLE ABOUT HIS ACTING EXPERIENCE.

"THEY STOPPED THE FIGHT SCENE AFTER SEVERAL MINUTES, AND ASKED ME INTO RAAM'S OFFICE TO SIGN A CONTRACT AS A LEADING MAN."

THE MOST BIZARRE DAY OF HIS LIFE BEHIND HIM, PETER WENT BACK TO HIS HOTEL ROOM WHERE HE TOLD HIS BUDDY CRAIG THE WHOLE CRAZY STORY. CRAIG REACTED BITTERLY.

"HE SAID, 'OH, NOW YOU'RE GOING TO BE A BIG MOVIE STAR IN INDONESIA AND FORGET ALL ABOUT ME.'"

ACCORDING TO O'BRIAN CRAIG WAS INTO ALL KINDS OF CRIMINAL SHIT. ONE OF THE SKILLS OF HIS TRADE WAS TO BE AN EXPERT MANIPULATOR, AND PETER, KIND-HEARTED SOUL THAT HE IS, WAS NO MATCH FOR THE WELL-TIMED EMOTIONAL BLACKMAIL. OUR HERO WENT BACK TO THE FILM

STUDIO THE NEXT DAY AND TOLD HIS NEW EMPLOYERS THAT HIS FRIEND CRAIG HAD TO WORK ON THE MOVIE TOO, EVEN THOUGH HIS PAL WAS A LITTLE PAUNCHY, COULDN'T FAKE HIS WAY THROUGH A MARTIAL ARTS FIGHT NEARLY AS ADEPTLY AS PETER, AND WAS HARDLY THE MOVIE STAR TYPE. "IT'S BOTH OF US OR NEITHER OF US", PETER WARNED, AND WENT BACK TO HIS HOTEL ROOM.

"THE NEXT THING, I GET THE CALL SAYING, 'OK, WE'LL KEEP HIM HERE AS YOUR MANAGER AND WHO KNOWS, MAYBE WE MIGHT FIND A ROLE FOR HIM'."

THEY WOULD. SOMEHOW (I'M GUESSING DUE TO THAT MANIPULATIVE CHARM OF HIS) CRAIG WOULD END UP CO-STARRING AS A DRUG KINGPIN AND AN EVIL ARCH NEMESIS FOR PETER. CHEEKILY, THE INDONESIANS NAMED CRAIG'S CHARACTER 'MR WHITE'.

THUS BEGAN THE UNLIKELY FILM CAREER OF PETER O'BRIAN (KNOWN TO HIS TINY GROUP OF RABID FANS AS PO'B) WHICH WOULDN'T RESULT IN SUPERSTARDOM, BUT CERTAINLY WOULD PRODUCE A HANDFUL OF THE MOST AMAZING INDONESIAN ACTION FILMS EVER PRODUCED. THIS IS ALL THANKS IN NO SMALL PART TO O'BRIAN'S BOUNDLESS ON-SCREEN ENERGY, ODDBALL FACIAL CONTORTIONS, AND CONFUSED DOE-EYED FIGHT STARES THAT ARE LEGENDARY AMONGST THE FEW CULT FILM FANS THAT HAVE WITNESSED THEM.

PO'B STEPPED IN FRONT OF THE CAMERA AND DONNED THE RED HEADBAND AS **RAMBU** (AKA "THE INTRUDER"), AN AMAZING RAMBO RIP OFF. THE OPENING SCENE IS A HIGHLIGHT, AND DEPICTS A SPEEDING CAR RUNNING OVER AN OLD WOMAN ON A COUNTRY ROAD IN THE MIDDLE OF NOWHERE. AS THE DRIVER AND HIS SALTY PASSENGER GET OUT TO CALL HER A "BITCH" FOR GETTING IN THEIR WAY, RAMBU SUDDENLY APPEARS AND BEGINS "BEATING" THEIR CAR WITH A STEEL PIPE TO SHOW HIS DISPLEASURE CONCERNING THEIR POOR DRIVING ETIQUETTE.

THEY PAY OFF THE OLD LADY FOR THE DESTRUCTION OF THE ONLY THINGS SHE OWNED (WHICH APPARENTLY CAN FIT IN A SMALL BASKET UNDER HER ARM?) AND THEN RAMBU SAVAGELY FUCKS THEM OVER WITH A RUBBER BALL THAT HE THROWS AND CATCHES AGAIN WITH COMEDIC ACCURACY. THE MEN, ASSES SOUNDLY WHOOPED, LOUDLY INFORM HIM THAT THEY ARE INDEED BAD GUYS, AND THAT THEY WON'T FORGET THIS. THEIR CHAGRIN INFORMS THE REST OF THE HAM FISTED PLOT -- A STORY THAT WOULDN'T BE OUT OF PLACE AS THE THREE PAGE RESULT OF A 12 YEAR OLD'S URGE TO WRITE A MOVIE SCRIPT.

OTHER HIGHLIGHTS: RAPE AND ITS SUBSEQUENT AND EXPECTED REVENGE, A TEENAGE SLAVE GIRL THAT SPITS IN MR WHITE'S FACE (PROMPTING HIM TO COLDLY MONOTONE "IF YOU CAN'T EVEN LOVE YOURSELF, WHY SHOULD I LOVE YOU?" BEFORE SHOOTING HER IN THE BACK), A BALLS-OUT THREE-WHEELED TUK-TUK CART BATTLE, A STUNT DUDE WHO GETS KICKED RIGHT THE FUCK OUT A WINDOW, AND A ROCKET LAUNCHER THAT MAKES A LASER SOUND EFFECT WHEN FIRED. THIS MOVIE RULES HARD ENOUGH TO MAKE YOUR ANUS CLENCH INVOLUNTARILY -- ALTHOUGH I SUGGEST YOU VOLUNTEER AND MAKE IT EASY ON YOURSELF.

THE SECOND OF PETER'S CRUDE, GRITTY ACTION EPICS WAS **THE STABILIZER**, AND IT MAY WELL BE HIS BEST. HERE, O'BRIAN PLAYED A COP NAMED PETER GOLDSON, AND HIS HOMEY CRAIG GAVIN PLAYED A BLOODTHIRSTY EVIL-TYPE DUBBED GREG RAINMAKER. RAINMAKER PROVES HIS BOUNDLESS VILLAINY BY KIDNAPPING A DRUG-INVENTING PROFESSOR, AND STABBING WITH HIS POINTY SPIKE SHOES. I'LL TELL YOU WHAT I WOULD DO WITH SPIKE SHOES. I'D KICK ME SOME GRAPEFRUIT.

THE DIABOLICAL MR. WHITE (CRAIG GAVIN) MISTREATS SLAVE GIRLS IN THE INTRUDER FROM 1986.

THERE IS SO MUCH TO LIKE HERE: WE'VE GOT EXPLOSIONS GALORE, MOTORCYCLE STUNTS, AN INDONESIAN GUY WHO LOOKS LIKE MR.T, A GARDENER KILLED WITH HIS OWN WEEDWACKER, KUNG-FU CHICKS, TORPEDOES, AND MORE NON-STOP ACTION THAN YOU CAN SHAKE PETER'S FLOWING CURLY MULLET AT. HELL, AT ONE POINT PO'B (DOING A STUNT THAT HE RANKS AS HIS PERSONAL FAVOURITE MOMENT OF HIS CAREER) JUMPS 40 METERS FROM A HELICOPTER INTO A LAKE, KNOCKING HIMSELF UNCONSCIOUS. DUDE GOES BALLS OUT 100%.

PETER WOULD DO 8 MOVIES ALTOGETHER (CHECK OUT THE YOUTUBE TRAILER FOR THE 1988 MOVIE **LETHAL HUNTER** WITH CHRISTOPHER MITCHUM), AND EVEN GOT TO WORK WITH BONER-COAXING BUTTOCK-POUNDER CYNTHIA ROTHROCK IN A PRODUCTION SHE MADE IN JAKARTA IN 1991. THE FILM IS CALLED **ANGEL OF FURY**, AND IT'S A FULL-TILT CRACKER.

"SOME OF THE INDONESIAN ACTORS WERE A BIT TERRIFIED OF HER BECAUSE SHE WAS REALLY INTO FULL CONTACT, AND THEY DON'T LIKE BEING HIT. SO SHE SAID TO ME, 'LOOK I'LL TELL YOU WHAT. WE'VE GOT THIS SHOT AND THERE ARE THIRTEEN KICKS TO THE HEAD. IS IT OK IF I JUST KICK YOU IN THE HEAD THIRTEEN TIMES? BECAUSE I DON'T THINK YOU'LL REMEMBER THE COMBINATIONS. HOPEFULLY I WON'T KNOCK YOU OUT.' AND I JUST SAID, 'LET'S GO AHEAD. DO IT'. SHE WAS REALLY HAPPY."

TODAY PETER IS A 7TH GRADE TEACHER IN INDONESIA. IT WAS A THRILL FOR ME AS HIS FAN TO FIND HIM ON FACEBOOK, AND WITNESS HIS STUDENTS GOING ON THE SOCIAL NETWORKING SITE AND DISCOVERING FOR THE FIRST TIME THAT THEIR BELOVED TEACHER (WHOM THEY CALL "PAK PETER") WAS A FORMER LEADING MAN IN ACTION CINEMA.

"I NEVER IMAGINED BEING A MOVIE STAR." PETER O'BRIAN RECENTLY SAID IN AN INTERVIEW. "WHEN I DID IT, I LOVED IT. I THOUGHT, 'MAN, I'D DO THIS FOR FREE!'".

WHAT'S WITH ALL THE NEGATIVE VIBES, MAN? BOUGIE -2011-

A COMMON ASSUMPTION IS THAT I HAVE LOTS OF PROBLEMS WITH CENSORSHIP FROM RIGHT WING RELIGIOUS ZEALOTS WHO DON'T APPROVE OF THE CONTENT IN MY COMICS AND CINEMA SEWER -- BUT IT ISN'T SO. FOR EVERY SINGLE PISSY CONSERVATIVE, I HAVE EXPERIENCED A RUN IN WITH 20 FROM THE FAR LEFT. OH, HOW THEY LOVE TO CONFRONT ME, WITH THEIR DISGUST FOR "HATE SPEECH", AND PORN THAT DEPICTS "BAD VIBES", "UNNATURAL SEX", "PATRIARCHAL OPPRESSION", OR WHATEVER CATCH PHRASE THEY'RE USING TO DESCRIBE OFF-PUTTING KINK THAT DOESN'T PERSONALLY FLOAT THEIR GROOVY GRANOLA BOAT OF HIPPY-LUV. THESE ARE THE SAME PEOPLE WHO WILL INFORM YOU THAT YOU'RE A CLOSET PEDO IF YOU'RE ATTRACTED TO A WOMAN WITH A SHAVED PUSSY, AND THEIR PLENTIFUL NUMBERS HAVE A LOT TO DO WITH WHERE I AM SITUATED: THE PACIFIC NORTHWEST.

CASE IN POINT: A WOMAN IN PORTLAND AT THE STUMPTOWN COMICS CONVENTION GOT UP IN MY GRILL ABOUT HOW SHE WAS SO OPEN MINDED AND INTO PORN, AND YET THOUGHT THAT DRAWINGS OF SEX MIXED WITH VIOLENCE IN ANY CAPACITY HAD NO PLACE IN A HEALTHY SOCIETY. SHE WAS ANGRY WITH ME FOR BEING THERE, AND INFORMED ME OF MY "SICKNESS". I CERTAINLY DON'T THINK EVERYONE SHOULD HAVE TO SEE OR LIKE PORN THAT DOESN'T DO IT FOR THEM, BUT THAT STYLE OF INDIGNANT INTOLERANCE DOESN'T SIT RIGHT WITH ME. SHE WASN'T THE ONLY ONE TO LECTURE ME ABOUT HOW WOMEN DON'T WANT THEMES OF DOMINANCE IN THEIR PORN, AND YET IT IS MY FEMALE READERSHIP WHO ARE THE MOST SHAMELESS AND VOCAL ABOUT THEIR TITILLATION WHEN VIEWING IT.

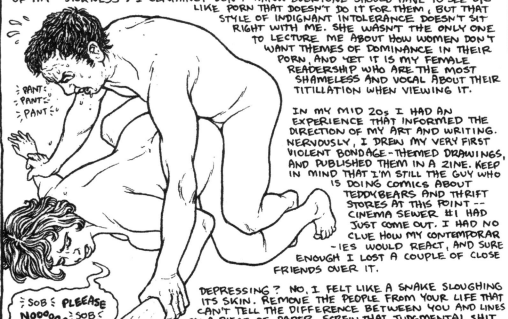

IN MY MID 20s I HAD AN EXPERIENCE THAT INFORMED THE DIRECTION OF MY ART AND WRITING. NERVOUSLY, I DREW MY VERY FIRST VIOLENT BONDAGE-THEMED DRAWINGS, AND PUBLISHED THEM IN A ZINE. KEEP IN MIND THAT I'M STILL THE GUY WHO IS DOING COMICS ABOUT TEDDY BEARS AND THRIFT STORES AT THIS POINT -- CINEMA SEWER #1 HAD JUST COME OUT. I HAD NO CLUE HOW MY CONTEMPORAR -IES WOULD REACT, AND SURE ENOUGH I LOST A COUPLE OF CLOSE FRIENDS OVER IT.

DEPRESSING? NO, I FELT LIKE A SNAKE SLOUGHING ITS SKIN. REMOVE THE PEOPLE FROM YOUR LIFE THAT CAN'T TELL THE DIFFERENCE BETWEEN YOU AND LINES ON A PIECE OF PAPER, SCREW THAT JUDGMENTAL SHIT.

PANT PANT PANT

SOB PLEEASE NOOOOOO SOB

END

AFTER OVER 3 JAZZY MINUTES OF EXTREMELY COOL '60S FOOTAGE OF THE HIGH AND LOW LIGHTS OF LOS ANGELES URBAN NIGHT TIME SCENERY (COURTESY GORGEOUS BLACK AND WHITE CINEMATOGRAPHY BY STAN LANDERS) IT'S TIME FOR THE SWINGIN' SLEAZINESS OF:

OVER 18... ...AND READY!

WRITTEN BY ROBIN BOUGIE

DRAWN BY DAVID PALEO

LYN (MARY McREA) IS A BORED SECRETARY WHO SPENDS HER AFTERNOONS BANGING THE KEYS FOR HER BOSS, THE SNARKY MR BARNEY MERRIT (LARRY MARTINELLI- WHO ALSO APPEARED IN LEE FROST'S INFAMOUS LOVE CAMP 7), A PRODUCER OF SOFTCORE ADULT FILMS.

BUT WHAT THIS YOUNG BLACK HAIRED LASS REALLY WANTS TO DO IS ACT, AND BEFORE LONG SHE'S PESTERING THE SEXPLOITATION MOGUL INTO GIVING HER THE STARRING ROLE IN HIS LATEST DICK STIFFENER.

I'M SURE I COULD SATISFY YOU, MR MERRIT

BUT IT'S NOT LYN'S RATHER FAT ASS, POT BELLY, AND CHUNKY RACK ALONE THAT HAVE GOT BARNEY INTERESTED. HIS WIFE, BILLIE MERRIT, (PLAYED BY MARGO STEVENS) - A SCARY LOOKING SUBURBAN DYKE WHO IS THE BRAINS AND MONEY BEHIND THE OPERATION- IS INSTANTLY JUICY FOR THE YOUNG SECRETARY, AND PULLS THE APPROPRIATE STRINGS.

I WANT HER. GET HER FOR ME, BARNEY

WHEN THEIR LATEST LEADING LADY MAKES AN APPEARANCE AT THE MALIBU HOME OF THE CONSTANTLY BICKERING SLEAZE-MERCHANTS, SHE FINDS OUT THAT SOME EXTRACURRILAR BOFFING IS EXPECTED.

YOU GOTTA TURN OFF THE FREEZE LYN, AND START PLAYING BAAAALL!

APPREHENSIVE, LYN ENDS UP COMPLYING WITH THE WET, SLOPPY MATING. AFTER ALL, THIS IS THE BIG TIME.

THERE'S SOME RUGGED STUFF IN THIS FILM, AND I FIGURE YOU OUGHTA GET IN SOME REHEARSAL!

MEANWHILE, BILLIE THE LESBIAN COUGAR HAS FULLY REELED LYN INTO HER INTRICATE WEB OF POOL PARTIES AND SAPPHIC BEACH ROMPS IN THE BUFF. BEFORE THE ROOKIE PORN PRINCESS KNOWS WHAT HIT HER, SHE'S LIVING IN BILLIE AND BARNEY'S MALIBU HOME AND THE OLD BATTLE AXE IS GROPING HER EXPOSED TITS AND RUNNING HER MOUTH OVER SOME PREVIOUSLY PRIVATE PROPERTY. BAM! INNOCENCE CRUSHED!

YOUTHFUL GERRY (GARY M. FOX) IS A UP N' COMING NUDIE PHOTOGRAPHER THAT'S FALLEN HEADS OVER MUFFINS FOR LYN, AND HE DOESN'T WANT TO SEE HIS DREAM GIRL CHEWED UP N' SPIT OUT BY THE SENIOR PORNOGRAPHERS BEFORE HE CAN GET A CHANCE AT DOING SO WITH HIS CAMERA.

THOUSANDS OF GIRLS LIKE YOU COME HERE WITH A DREAM, ONLY TO HAVE IT SHATTERED BY REALITY

REALITY REARS HIS UGLY HEAD ON THE FIRST DAY OF SHOOTING AS POOR HUMILIATED LYN IS MUGGED RAPED, BOUND NAKED AND THEN WHIPPED ON CAMERA. BUT IT'S ALL JUST ACTING, RIGHT LYN?

IT'S WORTH NOTING THAT THE ENTIRE CAST OF OVER 18...AND READY! IS COMICALLY WOODEN IN THEIR DELIVERY. IT'S STRANGE WATCHING LYN'S NON REACTIONS TO HER LIFE SLOWLY CRUMBLING INTO DEGENERACY, AND IT'S IRONIC THAT ACTRESS MARY MC CREA WAS PROBABLY LIVING THE LIFE OF THE CHARACTER SHE WAS UNCONVINCINGLY TRYING TO PLAY.

end

IN THE SUMMER OF EIGHTY ONE, THE LEGENDARY PRINCE BEGAN WORKING ON MATERIAL FOR A GIRL GROUP HE WAS PLANNING CALLED THE HOOKERS. HE CAME UP WITH THE CONCEPT FOR THE GROUP (THREE SINGERS WHO DRESS LIKE PROSTITUTES, AND SING ABOUT BEING NAUGHTY IN BED), AND BEGAN WORKING ON TRACKS IN HIS HOME STUDIO BEFORE THE GROUP WAS EVEN ASSEMBLED. WHILE ATTENDING THE AMERICAN MUSIC AWARDS SHOW IN JANUARY OF 1982, PRINCE MET DENISE MATTHEWS, A BEAUTIFUL MODEL, AND ACTRESS FROM NIAGARA FALLS, CANADA. THROUGH TEARS, DENISE HAD BEGGED HER AGENT AT WILLIAM MORRIS FOR BACKSTAGE ACCESS TO THE EVENT, AND HE COULDN'T SAY NO.

THE TWO WENT IMMEDIATELY TO THE MEN'S ROOM TOGETHER AND EXCHANGED CLOTHING AND WHO KNOWS WHAT ELSE. WITHIN DAYS PRINCE WAS REGULARLY BEDDING DENISE, AND HAD PLACED HER AS THE FRONT PIECE IN THE HOOKERS, WHICH WERE RENAMED VANITY 6 AFTER DENISE'S NAME WAS CHANGED TO VANITY. PRINCE ORIGINALLY HAD RENAMED HER VAGINA, BUT THE YOUNG WOMAN (NOT SURPRISINGLY) BALKED AT THE NAME, AND TOLD HIM TO COME UP WITH SOMETHING ELSE.

VANITY 6 TOURED WITH PRINCE, AND WENT ON TO HAVE A COUPLE OF HIT SINGLES - "NASTY GIRL" BEING THEIR SIGNATURE TRACK. IN AUGUST 1993 SHE WAS CAST TO PLAY THE MUSICAL AUTEUR'S LOVE INTEREST IN THE FILM "PURPLE RAIN", BUT BROKE TIES WITH HIS PURPLENESS (MATTERS CONCERNING THEIR RELATIONSHIP AND MONEY WERE THE TWO REASONS CITED BY REPORTERS AT THE TIME) TO PURSUE A SOLO CAREER. PRINCE CHOSE 22 YEAR OLD PATRICIA KOTERO FOR THE LEAD ROLE IN BOTH HIS MOVIE AND THE NEWLY NAMED APOLLONIA 6.

VANITY'S PARTY-ANIMAL BED-HOPPING ANTICS ARE LEGENDARY EVEN TODAY. ABOVE AND BEYOND PRINCE, SHE ALSO SHAGGED ADAM ANT, EL DEBARGE, AND BILLY IDOL IN THE 1980S, WHEN THEY WERE ALL AT THE HEIGHT OF THEIR FAME. SHE WAS ALSO ENGAGED TO MOTLEY CRUE BASSIST NIKKI SIXX IN 1987. SIXX'S BOOK, "THE HEROIN DIARIES: A YEAR IN THE LIFE OF A SHATTERED ROCK STAR" GIVES DETAILED ACCOUNTS OF HIS BIZARRE DRUG-FUELED ADVENTURES WITH THE PROUDLY SLUTTY SINGER.

"WE USED TO SIT IN MY HOUSE WATCHING TV AND SNORTING COKE AND POINTING OUT GIRLS THAT WE'D LIKE TO FUCK. THEN I'D PHONE THE MOTLEY OFFICE AND THEY'D GET US THE GIRLS NUMBERS SO WE COULD CALL THEM. IT WAS A SICK LIL' GAME WE PLAYED, NEVER REALLY REALISING WE WERE PLAYING WITH PEOPLE'S LIVES. WE SAW VANITY ON MTV, AND WHEN PETE SAID, "DUDE, THAT'S PRINCE'S OLD GIRL" I SAID, "EXCELLENT, HE'S GOT A TINY DICK." THE OFFICE RANG VANITY AND ARRANGED FOR US TO MEET. SHE OPENED THE DOOR NAKED, WITH HER EYES GOING AROUND IN HER HEAD. SOMEHOW I HAD A FEELING THAT WE JUST MIGHT HIT IT OFF."

SIXX IS A NOTORIOUS BAD BOY OF HEAVY METAL, BUT IT WAS ACTUALLY VANITY WHO TAUGHT HIM HOW TO FREEBASE, AND FOR THE NEXT YEAR THE TWO HURTLED TOGETHER INTO A COCAINE CHASM OF PARANOIA, DEBAUCHERY, AND NEAR DEATH EXPERIENCES. ONE NOTEWORTHY OCCASION OCCURRED WHILE THE TWO WERE LAYING NAKED IN BED, AND SIXX DECIDED THAT SINISTER EVIL VOICES WERE CLOSING IN ON THEM. TO SCARE THEM AWAY, HE BEGAN BLASTING HIS .357

VANITY:

THE DEADLIEST SIN!

MAGNUM THROUGH THE DOOR, BUT THE VOICES CONTINUED, UNAFRAID OF HIS THREATS OF VIOLENCE.. TURNS OUT THEY WERE SIMPLY COMING OUT OF A RADIO.

SIXX'S DIARY ENTRIES ALSO DETAILED THE END OF THE RELATIONSHIP BETWEEN THE TWO EGOMANIACAL MUSIC STARS, WHOSE TASTES IN MUSIC, FOOD, RELIGION, AND MOVIES WERE POLAR OPPOSITES FROM DAY ONE.

"COULD I PAY SOMEONE TO KILL MY GIRLFRIEND? VANITY CAME TO REHEARSAL. . . JESUS, I TRY MY BEST TO LOOK NORMAL AROUND THE BAND AND THEN SHE SHOWS UP LIKE THAT. A YEAR AGO, I WOULD HAVE BEEN ASHAMED AT HER CACKLING, THROWING THOSE FUCKING PRINCE DANCE MOVES AND HANGING OFF MY NECK WHILE I WAS TRYING TO PLAY. HER EYES WERE FUCKED. . . ..SHE MUST HAVE BEEN FREEBASING ALL NIGHT. I TOLD HER TO SHUT THE FUCK UP AND SHE GOT IN MY FACE AND ASKED WHAT I WAS GONNA DO. WHAT COULD I DO? I JUST TURNED AND WALKED OUT OF REHEARSAL. LEFT HER THERE WITH THE GUYS IN THE BAND."

MANY OF HER INTERVIEW APPEARANCES ON SHOWS LIKE SOUL TRAIN, MERV GRIFFIN, GARRY SHANDLING, THE TONIGHT SHOW, AND THE UK'S THE LATE LATE BREAKFAST SHOW HAD THE STINK OF DRUG USE ALL OVER THEM AS WELL. BETWEEN TRULY AWKWARD PASSES AT HOSTS, INAPPROPRIATE ANECDOTES ABOUT FANS BITING HER NIPPLES ON STAGE AND ERRATIC BODY LANGUAGE, VANITY WOULD BADLY LIP-SYNCH TO HER OWN OFF PITCH POP SONGS. IT'S WORTH NOTING THAT SHE MADE MOST OF THESE PROMOTIONAL APPEARANCES IN OUTFITS THAT WOULDN'T LOOK AT ALL OUT OF PLACE IN A BROTHEL.

NIKKI SIXX AND VANITY ENJOY THE TWO THINGS THEY HAD IN COMMON: THEIR ENTHUSIASM FOR SEX AND DRUGS.

"DO I, UM, HAVE SOMETHING ON MY LIPS?" QUERIED GARRY SHANDLING IN THE MIDDLE OF AN INTERVIEW AS VANITY POKED HIM ON THE MOUTH WITH HER OUTSTRETCHED FINGERS, CLEARLY INTERRUPTING HIM IN THE MIDDLE OF A SENTENCE.

"NO. I JUST WANTED. . . TO TOUCH THEM." WAS HER SPINNY REPLY.

SHE HAD A LOUSY SINGING VOICE, BUT VANITY WASN'T ACTUALLY ALL THAT BAD OF AN ACTRESS -- AND MANAGED TO GET CAST IN A STRING OF DECENT ACTION AND EXPLOITATION MOVIES, MOST OF WHICH UTILISED HER WILLINGNESS TO GET NAKED AND REALLY DIVE INTO PLAYING NASTY GIRLS AND DRUG ADDICTS. LIKE KEANU REEVES, VANITY WAS AT HER BEST WHEN THE SCRIPT CALLED FOR HER TO PLAY HERSELF. THE RANGE WAS LIMITED.

UNFORTUNATELY, AS THE '80S CAME TO A CLOSE VANITY'S FILM CAREER FLATLINED. HER REPUTATION FOR BEING A HIGH MAINTENACE JUNKIE WAS CATCHING UP WITH HER, TRYING THE PATIENCE OF FRUSTRATED DIRECTORS, AND SOURING HER BIDS FOR WORK. SHE WAS WORKING ON A 3RD SOLO ALBUM, BUT IT WAS NEVER FINISHED. SHE WAS ALSO REPORTEDLY UP FOR A PART IN 1988'S THE LAST TEMPTATION OF CHRIST, BUT DIDN'T MANAGE TO LAND IT.

AFTER 1989, SHE ONLY DID GUEST APPEARANCES ON TV SHOWS, MADE-FOR-TV DREK AND DIRECT-TO-VIDEO CRAP. NEEDLESS TO SAY, DEPRESSION BEGAN TO TAKE HOLD, AS DID HER CRACK ADDICTION. RUMOURS ARE THAT SHE EVEN HAD A SPECIAL BEEPER THAT WAS DESIGNATED ONLY FOR HER DEALER AS WELL AS A LIMO RESERVED FOR HIS LATE-NIGHT DELIVERIES TO HER HOME.

FINALLY IN 1994, SUICIDE WAS JUST ABOUT ALL SHE EVER THOUGHT ABOUT. VANITY EVENTUALLY COVERED UP ALL THE MIRRORS AND WINDOWS OF HER TOWNHOUSE, AND LOCKED HERSELF INSIDE WHILE ON A CRACK BINGE. SHE DIDN'T ANSWER THE DOOR OR THE PHONE FOR DAYS, AND RESIGNED HERSELF TO DEATH. LUCKILY, ONE OF HER FEW REMAINING FRIENDS CAME TO CHECK ON HER, AND CALLED 911.

VANITY HAD TEMPORARILY GONE BLIND AND DEAF, AND DOCTORS GAVE HER THREE DAYS TO LIVE. IN A BID TO SAVE HER LIFE, THEY REMOVED BOTH OF HER KIDNEYS, AND SHE SPENT MONTHS IN INTENSIVE CARE.

AFTER LEAVING THE HOSPITAL, SHE FELT FULLY RESURRECTED, AND BECAME A BORN AGAIN CHRISTIAN. FINISHING EVERY SENTENCE WITH "HALLELUJAH" INSTEAD OF "WANNA FUCK?" IS A BIG CHANGE, BUT VANITY HAS ALWAYS BEEN A WOMAN OF EXTREMES. SHE THEN APPEARED ON THE 700 CLUB, AND PLEASED THE HOST -- NOT BY MAKING HER USUAL AWKWARD SEXUAL INNUENDOES -- BUT BY SPILLING TALES ABOUT THE EVILS OF HOLLYWOOD. HALLELUJAH!

"ALL I HAD BECOME WAS THUS PAINTED ON MY FACE --VANITY." "I LOWERED MYSELF TO THAT OF A SQUATING DOG, DARE I SAY SUCKING UP HIS OWN VOMIT."

DENISE MATTHEWS, FROM HER "LUXURIOUS COFFEE TABLE BOOK", BLAME IT ON VANITY.

TANYA'S ISLAND

VANITY

RICHARD SARGENT

"THERE WAS A TIME THAT I WAS MAKING ACTION JACKSON, AND I WAS CRYING. I DIDN'T WANT TO TAKE OFF MY CLOTHES, AND THEY SAID: 'WELL YOU HAVE TO, OR YOU'RE NOT GOING TO DO THE FILM'. AND GUESS WHAT? I GAVE IN, BECAUSE I WAS NOT WALKING WITH GOD. AND MY GOODNESS, IT HURT SO BAD."

SHE'D NOW COME TO A PLACE IN HER LIFE WHERE SHE WASN'T CRAZY FOR DRUGS -- BUT CRAZY FOR GOD. TRADING IN ONE ADDICTION FOR ANOTHER. VANITY TURNED HER BACK ON EVERYTHING THAT WASN'T HARDCORE EVANGELICAL CHRISTIANITY, AND THEN REVERTED TO HER BIRTH NAME, DENISE MATTHEWS. WHEN YOU USE HARD DRUGS FOR SUCH A LONG TIME, IT MESSES UP THE CHEMISTRY OF YOUR BRAIN.

SHE THREW OUT EVERY SHRED OF EVIDENCE OF HER FORMER LIFE, AND TO THIS DAY REFUSES TO WATCH MOVIES OR OWN A TELEVISION. SHE DOESN'T LISTEN TO MUSIC ANYMORE, INSTEAD PLAYING SCRIPTURE READINGS IN HER CAR OR LISTENING TO SERMONS. SHE NOW SPENDS HER TIME AS A PREACHER, AND FROWNS UPON SEX BEFORE MARRIAGE.

PLAYING AN ABUSED HOOKER IN **52 PICK UP** (1986)

HOMOSEXUALITY, DRUGS, NUDITY, AND WHEN SHE GIVES AN ALL-TOO-RARE INTERVIEW, SHE DOMINATES IT THE WAY ALL RELIGIOUS EXTREMISTS DO -- TAKING THE STANCE THAT SHE HAS ALL TO TEACH AND NOTHING TO LEARN.

FOR AWHILE SHE CLAIMED SHE WAS NO LONGER ACCEPTING ROYALTY CHEQUES FROM THE MUSIC AND MOVIES SHE'D TURNED HER BACK ON, BUT WHEN ASKED ABOUT IT AGAIN IN 2010 BY BLOGTALKRADIO.COM, DENISE ADMITTED THAT SHE'D NEVER ACTUALLY TURNED THOSE CHEQUES AWAY. THE LUDICROUS CONTRADICTION OF HER CONTINUING TO LIVE OFF THE AVAILS OF VANITY, WHILE CONDEMNING EVERY ASPECT OF HER PREVIOUS LIFESTYLE SEEMED LOST ON HER.

REGARDLESS OF HER CONFLICTING JUNKIE-SLUT AND HOLY-ROLLER LIFESTYLES, VANITY WAS CERTAINLY ONE FINE-ASS FOX IN THE EIGHTIES, AND MADE SOME OUTSTANDINGLY ENTERTAINING MOVIES DURING HER HEDONISTIC HEYDAY. I'D LIKE TO TAKE A MOMENT HERE TO BABBLE ABOUT A FEW OF MY FAVOURITES:

TANYA'S ISLAND (1980)
SWEET FUCK THIS HAS TO BE (AND I DON'T SAY THIS LIGHTLY) ONE OF THE SINGLE CRAZIEST CANADIAN-MADE MOVIES OF ALL TIME. THIS MEMORABLE CELLULOID HEMORRHOID MAKES ME DAMN PROUD TO BE A CANUCK, AND I WISH I'D SEEN IT BEFORE I MADE MY "TOP 20 CANADIAN FILMS OF ALL TIME" LIST IN CINEMA SEWER BOOK 2. A TWENTY YEAR OLD VANITY (CREDITED HERE AS D.D. WINTERS) IS NAKED FOR ABOUT 50% OF THE RUNTIME, AND LIVES ON AN DESERTED ISLAND WITH A BEARDED PAINTER WHO DOESN'T MUCH CARE FOR THE FACT THAT HIS GAL PAL HAS FALLEN IN LOVE WITH A GORILLA. THAT'S RIGHT, IT'S A HARLEQUIN ROMANCE NOVEL STYLE FORBIDDEN DESIRE STORY ABOUT A KOOKY BITCH IN LUST WITH A SIMIAN, AND YES -- THERE IS GORILLA-ON-GIRL DOGGYSTYLE PENETRATION ON DISPLAY. A MUST-SEE, MY FRIENDS.

THE LAST DRAGON (1985)
YO! HE AIN'T BRUCE LEE, HE'S BRUCE LEROY! WELCOME TO WHAT MAY WELL BE THE LAST TRUE BLAXPLOITATION MOVIE EVER MADE (NOT INCLUDING SPOOFS AND HOMAGES). TAIMAK, JULIUS CARRY, AND VANITY (ALSO NOMINATED HERE FOR A RAZZIE AWARD FOR "WORST ORIGINAL SONG" FOR "7TH HEAVEN") CARRY THE PICTURE, AND WHAT A PICTURE IT IS! I CONSIDER THE LAST DRAGON TO BE A NEAR-PERFECT BLEND OF LASER-INFUSED

You READY TO FUCK SOME SHIT UP, VANITY?

YOU BET, DADDY. LET'S DO IT.

ACTION JACKSON

ASS-KICKS, SILLY BLACK STEREOTYPES, '80S FASHION, CAMPY SYNTH/DRUM MACHINE-BASED MUSIC, AND AMAZING ONE-LINER SHIT-TALK! US KIDS WHO GREW UP IN THE '80S WERE OBSESSED WITH THIS DIPPY POPCORN MOVIE, AND WATCHING IT AGAIN RECENTLY, I CAN FULLY UNDERSTAND WHY. EVEN OL' FUN HATING ROGER EBERT LOVED IT, POINTING OUT THAT THE MOVIE IS "A FUNNY, HIGH-ENERGY COMBINATION OF KARATE ROMANCE, ROCK MUSIC, AND SENSATIONAL SPECIAL EFFECTS".

NEVER TOO YOUNG TO DIE (1986)
OH MY GOD. OH MY GOD. OH MY GOD. I'M SORRY, I'M STILL TRYING TO PICK MY JAW UP OFF THE FLOOR AFTER WATCHING THIS MOVIE, WHICH WAS MY TRUE IMPETUS FOR DECIDING TO DEVOTE A NICE BIG ARTICLE TO VANITY IN THESE PAGES. IN FACT, I'M NOT GONNA SAY ANYTHING ABOUT NEVER TOO YOUNG TO DIE RIGHT NOW. WE'LL DEVOTE SOME SPACE SPECIFICALLY FOR IT OVER ON PAGE 85. GO CHECK THAT OUT, AND I'LL MEET YOU BACK HERE WHEN YOU'RE ALL DONE, POR QUE?

52 PICK-UP (1986)
CHECK OUT MY ARTICLE ON CANNON FILMS PRODUCTIONS EARLIER IN THIS BOOK FOR MORE ON THIS, ONE OF MY FAVE FILMS OF THE '80S. THE MOVIE FEATURES SOME OF VANITY'S MOST ACCOMPLISHED ACTING, ALBEIT IN A FAIRLY MINOR ROLE AS A PROSTITUTE WHO SELLS INFORMATION. THE LITTLE MONEY SHE GETS FOR SELLING OUT TO ROY SCHEIDER'S CHARACTER CERTAINLY ISN'T WORTH THE RAW PSYCHOLOGICAL TORTURE AND TRAUMA VANITY MUST ENDURE AT THE PAWS OF THE LEGITIMATELY SCARY CLARENCE WILLIAMS THE THIRD. I DUNNO WHAT BECAME OF THAT ACTOR, BUT HE'S GENUINELY FRIGHTENING.

I WATCH THIS MOVIE AT LEAST ONCE EVERY COUPLE OF YEARS, AND IT SEEMS TO GET BETTER EVERY TIME. LOOK FOR WALK-ON ROLES FOR CLASSIC PORN STARS JAMIE GILLIS AND AMBER LYNN, WHO WERE DATING AT THE TIME.

ACTION JACKSON (1988)
I KNEW THIS MOVIE EXISTED FOR TWO DECADES BEFORE I FINALLY GOT AROUND TO BUYING IT FOR $2 OUT OF A DVD BARGAIN BIN IN A LOCAL DOLLAR STORE. WHAT A NICE SURPRISE! ACTION JACKSON IS ONE OF THOSE LATE 1980s VEHICLES THAT PROVIDED A JUMPING OFF POINT FOR A STUNT-MAN WHO WAS WANTING TO DIRECT, IN THIS CASE--CRAIG BAXLEY. CRAIG CASTS CARL WEATHERS IN THE TITLE ROLE AND PULLS OUT ALL THE STOPS, PROVIDING BLAZING GUNS, SLASHING KNIVES, TORTURE, BARE TITTIES, SADISM, COOKED FLESH, EXPLOSIONS, SNAPPING BONES, ELECTROCUTION BY CHRISTMAS LIGHTS, TESTICLES IN A JAR, SHATTERING GLASS, AND OUT OF CONTROL VEHICLES SMASHING THROUGH THE STREETS (AND BUILDINGS) OF DETROIT. ON TOP OF ALL THAT, YOU HAVE A YOUNG SHARON STONE A COUPLE OF YEARS AWAY FROM SUPERSTARDOM, AND LOVELY VANITY AS A JUNKIE IN THE LAST MAJOR ROLE OF HER ACTING CAREER. SHE WAS

VERY UNFAIRLY NOMINATED FOR A "WORST ACTRESS" RAZZIE AWARD FOR THIS PERFORMANCE, DESPITE BEING A TOTAL SCENE-STEALER. ANYWAY, CHECK IT OUT. THIS PULSE-POUNDING REGAN-ERA ACTION FEST IS TO CARL WEATHERS WHAT REMO WILLIAMS WAS TO FRED WARD.

-BOUGIE. 2010

CINEMA SEWER
DUSK to DAWN

HAAAAYYY REMEMBER IN THE FIRST BOOK WHEN I SHARED A WHOLE BUNCH OF DUST-TO-DAWN MULTIPLE BILL AD-MATS FROM MY MOVIE AD COLLECTION AND BABBLED LIKE A GOOBER ABOUT DRIVE-INS FOR A COUPLE OF PAGES? LET'S ☆ DO THAT AGAIN! ☆

THE GRAVEL CRUNCHED BELOW THE TIRES OF OUR CAMARO AS WE LOOKED FOR THE KEY SPOT TO DROP ANCHOR AND TAKE IN A DOUBLE, TRIPLE, OR EVEN AN ALL-NIGHT SHOW

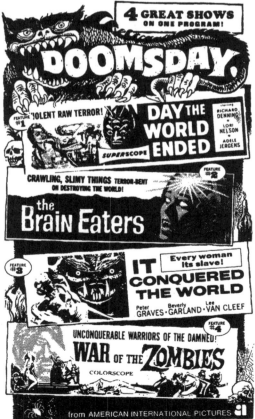

OF DERANGED FEATURE FILMS. IT WAS A TRUE TREAT IN THE DAYS BEFORE A CINEMATIC HOME FORMAT EXISTED -- UNLESS YOU COUNT GETTING TO SEE THE OCCASIONAL EDITED MOVIE ON TV.

THE DELICIOUS AROMA OF POPCORN, HOTDOGS, NACHOS, AND SOFT SERVE ICE CREAM TREATS WAFTING FROM THE SNACK BAR WAS NEARLY IMPOSSIBLE TO IGNORE. AN EARLY VERSION OF THE SLURPEE CALLED THE SLUSH PUPPY WAS A POPULAR CHOICE WITH YOU AND YOUR SISTER. A LOGO OF A DROOPY-EARED DOG IN A BLUE SWEATER WITH A GIANT 'S' EMBLAZONED ON THE FRONT STOOD WATCH OVER THE MACHINE THAT DISPENSED THE BRIGHTLY COLOURED FROZEN DRINK. THREE SIPS IN, AND YOUR TONGUE WAS DYED BRIGHT RED.

SNEAKING IN WAS A KEY PART OF THE ADVENTURE. THE TRUNK MOVE WAS POPULAR, ALTHOUGH YOU WONDERED EXACTLY WHY WHEN YOU WERE CRAMMED INTO THE TRUNK OF THAT 1961 CHEVROLET, WORRIED THAT YOUR PALS WOULD SOMEHOW FORGET ABOUT YOU. GOOD THING YOU WEREN'T CLAUSTROPHOBIC.

SHIT, YOUR FRIEND GARY OFTEN SNUCK IN BY DRIVING IN THROUGH THE EXIT, AND WHEN HIS FRIENDS ASKED HIM HOW HE PULLED IT OFF, HE JUST LAUGHED AND EXPLAINED HOW HE TOOK CARPET OUT OF A DUMPSTER FROM ACROSS THE STREET, LAID IT OVER THE TIRE SPIKES, AND DROVE RIGHT ON IN. WE WEREN'T GONNA MISS NIGHT OF THE BLOOD BEAST AND BLACK SUNDAY JUST BECAUSE WE WERE LOW ON CASH, WERE WE?

SHOOT TO KILL

4 SUPER SHELL-SHOCKERS!

SHOW!

R

1 PROGRAMMED TO KILL!
COLOR
KISS & KILL

2 SHELLEY WINTERS
Bloody Mama
The INCREDIBLE SAGA of "MA" BARKER!
COLOR by MOVIELAB

3 THEY HAD GUTS, GUNS and ONE GAL BETWEEN THEM!
KILLERS THREE COLOR by DELUXE
ROBERT WALKER · DIANE VARSI

4 KISSING and KILLING!
BARBARA HERSHEY as
BOXCAR BERTHA
COLOR BY DELUXE

SPACE-TACULAR SHOW!

CONQUERORS FROM A DYING WORLD INVADE EARTH!
THEY CAME FROM BEYOND SPACE
IN COLOR
AN EMBASSY PICTURES RELEASE

PLUS

The virgin sacrifice to the gods of a ghastly galaxy!
The TERRORNAUTS
IN COLOR
AN EMBASSY PICTURES RELEASE

FEATURE #1
BORIS KARLOFF
HIS FINAL EVIL ROLE
CHRISTOPHER LEE
The CRIMSON CULT
COLOR GP

FEATURE #2
SHOCK! AFTER SHOCK!
BLACK SUNDAY

FEATURE #3
EDGAR ALLAN POE'S GP
The CONQUEROR WORM COLOR
VINCENT PRICE

FEATURE #4
EDGAR ALLAN POE'S
Haunted PALACE
VINCENT PRICE
PATHÉCOLOR PANAVISION

from AMERICAN INTERNATIONAL PICTURES

FEATURE #1
EDGAR ALLAN POE'S
The MASQUE of the RED DEATH — COLOR

FEATURE #2
CAT GIRL

FEATURE #3
DAY THE WORLD ENDED
SUPERSCOPE

FEATURE #4
A NIGHTMARE OF TERROR AND SHOCK!
HORROR HOUSE
COLOR GP
FRANKIE AVALON JILL HAWORTH

from AMERICAN INTERNATIONAL PICTURES

72

SIGH -- REMEMBER HOW WE BROUGHT BLANKETS TO LAY ON, OR SET UP LAWN CHAIRS TO RELAX IN ON MUGGY JULY NIGHTS? THE LITTLE ONES WOULD COZY UP ON THEIR PARENTS' LAPS, DECKED OUT IN THEIR LITTLE FOOTY PYJAMAS.

OUR EYES BUGGED OUT AS WE GOSSIPED AT SCHOOL ABOUT HOW THE TRI-CITY DRIVE-IN IN LOMA LINDA (WITH ITS SCREEN THAT FACED THE I-10, SO AS TO ATTRACT PASSERS-BY) CAUSED A NEIGHBOURHOOD RUCKUS WHEN THEY SCREENED THE ALAN ROBERTS ADULT MOVIE PANORAMA BLUE. RENE BOND HAD NEVER LOOKED BETTER THAN SHE DID PROJECTED JUST AFTER DUSK ON THAT FOUR STORY SCREEN.

OR HOW ABOUT WHEN BARBARELLA SCREENED AT SANTA MARIA'S HIWAY DRIVE-IN? MAN, BY THE TIME IT REACHED ITS 4TH NIGHT, A MASS OF 12 AND 13 YEAR-OLD BOYS HAD LINED UP ON THE ROOF OF THE KACHLER FAMILY HOUSE LIKE A FLOCK OF ROOSTING CROWS, ALL ACHING FOR A PEEK AT THE CURVES OF LOVELY MISS JANE FONDA.

THE SOUND COMING OUT OF THE METAL SPEAKER BOXES CLAMPED TO THE DRIVER'S SIDE WINDOW OF YOUR DAD'S CAR WAS FRANKLY TERRIBLE AND VERY TINNY COMPARED TO THE QUALITY WE'VE COME TO EXPECT TODAY, AND YET NO ONE IN YOUR FAMILY COMPLAINED. YOU DIDN'T EXPECT MORE THAN SIMPLY BEING ABLE TO HEAR THE DIALOGUE.

YOU STILL SMILE TODAY AS YOU REMEMBER HOW YOUR PARENTS FORBADE YOU FROM GOING ON DATES ALONE WITH BOYS AT THE OL' STARLITE DRIVE-IN, BUT YOU WOULD OFTEN GO ANYWAY. THE KIDS CALLED IT "THE PASSION PIT".

5 DERANGED FEATURES

DUSK to DAWN

ALL NITE · ALL HIT SHOW

"LISTEN TO KUPD FOR OTHER SURPRISES"

PLUS "LAST HOUSE ON THE LEFT PART II"

PLUS "NIGHT OF THE LIVING DEAD"

PLUS "MASSACRE AT CENTRAL HIGH"

PLUS "RATS ARE COMING, WEREWOLVES ARE HERE"

PLUS "FLESH GRINDERS"

(R) A nightmare of holy terror.

The Maniac Show Of The Century Comes To Your Town This Weekend

TOMORROW AT THE DRIVE-INS

ALL DRIVE-INS OPEN FRI. THRU. SUN. ONLY

1 How to SATISFY a Woman
2 TEENAGE PARTY GIRLS COLOR
3 "CARNAL CIRCUIT" RESTRICTED
DUFFERIN DRIVE-IN
S. OF HWY. 7 •
OPEN 7:00 P.M.
SHOW FROM 7:30

LOVE CLINIC
PLUS! "Sugar Daddy" IN SENSUOUS COLOR
PLUS! "MAN HUNGRY WOMEN" RESTRICTED
BAY RIDGES DRIVE-IN
HWY. 2 W OF BROCK
BOX OFFICE OPENS 7:00
SHOW STARTS AT 7:30

1 DIARY OF A SINNER
2 THE SENSUOUS STEWARDESSES
3 BIKINI BANDITS
PARKWAY DRIVE-IN
N. OF STEELES OFF WOODBINE •
OPENS 7:00 SHOW FROM 7:30

IT'S A TRIPLE FAR OUT TRIP SHOW

KATHY'S FRIENDS LOVED ACTION - ANY KIND!

BEST FRIENDS ①

in COLOR R

CATCH THE PINK ANGELS ②
...IF YOU CAN!

R COLOR

They took a trip on an escape machine without brakes!

...and ended up on the road to hell!

WILD RIDERS ③

COLOR R

CROWN INTERNATIONAL PICTURES

AND EVERY THEATRE HAD ONE. BUT HOW MANY HAD A "MONKEY PIT"? THE VALLEY DRIVE-IN THEATRE IN MONTCLAIR CALIFORNIA DID. THE OWNERS PUT THEIR COLLECTION OF PRIMATES ON DISPLAY IN CAGES NEXT TO THE PLAYGROUND. REMEMBER BEING TOLD BY YOUR PARENTS TO NOT STICK YOUR FINGERS IN THE CAGES, WHICH ONLY MADE YOU WANT TO DO IT ALL THE MORE? HA HA!

LIVING IN TULSA KINDA SUCKED, BUT REMEMBER HOW HAPPY YOU WERE TO GET THAT SUMMER JOB AT THE CONCESSION STAND OF THE ADMIRAL TWIN IN THE LATE '80S? HOW 'BOUT THAT NIGHT YOU WERE SENT OUT TO GET MORE BUTTER, AND YOU SPILLED AN ENTIRE BUCKET OF IT ALL OVER THE INSIDE OF THE CAR YOUR PARENTS GAVE YOU FOR GRADUATION? THAT CAR SMELLED LIKE POPCORN UNTIL THE DAY YOU SOLD IT. MAN, YOU WOULDN'T SOON FORGET THAT THEATRE, EVEN AFTER IT BURNT DOWN. AT LEAST YOU CAN STILL REVISIT THAT HISTORIC TEMPLE BY WATCHING THE OUTSIDERS FROM 1983. PARTS OF FRANCIS FORD COPPOLA'S FILM WERE SHOT IN AND AROUND THE ADMIRAL TWIN.

IT WASN'T JUST ABOUT THE MOVIE, AND AS APPARENT AS THAT IS IN RETROSPECT IT WAS ALSO APPARENT TO YOU THEN AS WELL. OFTEN, BEING AT THE DRIVE-IN WAS THE EQUIVALENT OF SITTING ON YOUR PORCH. IT WAS ABOUT BEING WITH THE PEOPLE YOU LOVE, OR IN THE CASE OF HORNY TEENS, THE PEOPLE YOU WANT TO LOVE.

AND THEN THERE WAS THAT TIME YOU WERE ELEVEN, BACK IN 1981. YOUR PARENTS TOOK YOU TO TARZAN THE APE MAN WITH BO DEREK, AND YOU WERE SUPPOSED TO GET INTO THE BACK SEAT AND FALL ASLEEP AFTER IT WAS OVER. YOU DID AS YOU WERE TOLD, BUT ALL THE BLOOD-CURDLING SCREAMING DURING AN AMERICAN WEREWOLF IN LONDON WOKE YOU UP, AND YOU SECRETLY PEEKED OVER THE LEATHER SEAT AND WATCHED YOUR FIRST HORROR MOVIE IN SILENT AWE. YOU WERE NEVER THE SAME.

THE DRIVE IN, MAAN! THAT WAS A THING WE **LOVED**. WHO WOULDN'T?

Presents

Ride 'Em Cowgirl!

By
D.J. Bryant & Robin Bougie

THE SEX FILM AND THE WESTERN ARE AS OLD AS CINEMA ITSELF. IT WASN'T UNTIL THE SEXPLOITATION BOOM OF THE '60s, HOWEVER, THAT THE SEX WESTERN SUBGENRE REALLY TOOK OFF.

WILD GALS of the NAKED WEST! (1962)

WAS ONE OF THE EARLIEST FILMS TO MELD THE TWO GENRES, DIRECTED BY THE SEXPLOITATION KING HIMSELF, RUSS MEYER. MEYER CREATED AN EXTREMELY STYLIZED AND CARTOONY VERSION OF THE WEST, COMPLETE WITH HAND-PAINTED BACKDROPS AND HIS SIGNATURE LARGE-BREASTED WOMEN.

BLAM! BLA

LEE FROST, WES BISHOP AND BOB CRESSE DEBUTED THE

HOT SPUR

(1968) SEVERAL YEARS LATER. MORE OF A REVENGE TALE THAN A SEX FILM, IT INCLUDED NUMEROUS RAPE SCENES (AN XXX FORMULA COPIED IN THE MOVIES THAT FOLLOWED). THE FILM IS NOTABLE FOR ITS GRITTY REALISM AND SOLID PERFORMANCES.

BRAND of SHAME

(1968) DEBUTED A MERE 6 MONTHS LATER. THIS SOFTCORE OUTING BENEFITTED GREATLY FROM ITS GORGEOUS FEMALE CAST, INCLUDING:

PAULA PLEASURE. MARSHA JORDAN LYNN HALL SAMANTHA SCOTT

WITHIN A YEAR, PRODUCER ED FORSYTH JOINED THE FILTHY RODEO OF SMUT WITH

The RAMRODDER

WHICH DEPICTED A COWPOKE GETTIN' BUSY WITH "TUWANA" (KATHY WILLIAMS), THE TRIBAL INDIAN CHIEF'S DAUGHTER.

AND CHARLIE'S RIGHT HAND MAN BOBBY BEAUSOLEIL IN AN APPROPRIATE ROLE AS A VENGEFUL CASTRATING WARRIOR!

THE FILM FEATURED NOT ONE MANSON FAMILY MEMBER BUT TWO: CATHERINE "GYPSY" SHARE AS A RAPED INDIAN MAIDEN,

THE "NUDIE" WESTERN SOON TRANSITIONED TO THE AGE OF HARDCORE PORNOGRAPHY.

A DIRTY WESTERN 1975

WAS AN EARLY CLASSIC OF THE GENRE. IT FEATURED THE LOVELY BARBARA BOURBON - WHO ONLY DID THREE PORN FILMS IN HER CAREER. AGAIN, THIS IS A HIDEOUS AND UNPLEASANT FILM FULL OF RAPE, SODOMY, AND SADISM PERPETRATED ON A TRIO OF YOUNG SISTERS BY THREE ESCAPED CONVICTS.

THE WINTER OF 1849 1976

IT WAS COWBOYS AND CUMSHOTS GALORE WHEN RIK TAZINER DIRECTED THIS DESPICABLE AND SCUMMY HIGH PLAINS PARADE OF SEX. THE RAPE OF A VERY VIRGINAL LOOKING YOUNG LADY BY AN EYEPATCH-ADORNED SCUZBALL (WHOSE SWEAT YOU CAN PRACTICALLY SMELL THROUGH YOUR TV SET) IS THE HIGHLIGHT IN THIS BOOT-SCOOTIN' SHITSCAB.

AFTER SEVEN YEARS OF FUCKING ASSHOLES, I WANNA FUCK ME A WOMEN!

DIRECTOR ANN PERRY TOOK HIM ON IN A STARRING NON-SEX ROLE IN THIS WELL MADE MOVIE, AND HE STRUTTED AROUND LIKE A PAUNCHY VERSION OF JOHN WAYNE. HIS OTHER CO-STARS WERE THORA BIRCH'S PORNO-STAR PARENTS!

JACK BIRCH

CAROL CONNORS

1978 SWEET SAVAGE

AN AMBITIOUS PRODUCTION THAT ONE CRITIC CALLED "SURELY THE BEST PORN-WESTERN EVER MADE." THIS WAS ONE OF THE ONLY XXX FILMS WHERE A WELL KNOWN, AGING MAINSTREAM ACTOR MADE THE DROP DOWN TO HARDCORE. THE GRUFF & GRAVELY-VOICED ACTOR, ALDO RAY, WAS TRYING TO KEEP HIS HEAD ABOVE WATER AND PAY HIS MEDICAL BILLS AFTER CONTRACTING THROAT CANCER.

ShowDown
(1985)

This modern day western by director Henri Pachard chronicled the adventures of an out-of-the-way dude ranch/whore house and starred Nina Hartley, Jamie Gillis, and Sharon Mitchell. Of particular interest was the chance of seeing the cast on horseback and Jamie Gillis trying to fuck a confused member of the pussy posse in a hammock.

Saddle Tramp
(1988)

This juicy Jack Remy western/comedy starring Hyapatia Lee, Peter North, and Nina Hartley is more renowned for its oddball lactation scene than any sort of interesting or accurate old-west storyline.

DO IT AGAIN! DO IT AGAIN!

WESTERN
NIGHTS
1994

This couples movie starring Kylie Ireland, Jordan Lee, Asia Carrera and Tera Heart was the third part in Wicked's "...Nights" series, and was well received by fans with its old-timey soundtrack and sexy set pieces taking place in a blacksmith shop and a stagecoach.

The most recent western porno is Adam and Eve Productions award winning (2004)

RAWHIDE

Director Nicholas Steel's old west fuck-fest featured popular contemporary porn actresses such as:

CARMEN LUVANA   OLIVIA DEL RIO   BROOKE BALENTYNE   TAYLOR RAIN

Set in 1875 against a scenic outdoor backdrop, and packed with anal sex, girl-on-girl, and various other sizzling hump scenes, the 3 disc special edition DVD came bound in a leather case and loaded with special features.

With the western having lost a lot of favor with mainstream Hollywood audiences, and the prohibitive cost of producing a frontier fuck feature, it's unlikely that we'll see porn producers dabbling in cowpoke poking in the near future. Good thing we've got all these classics to enjoy! Yeehaw!

THE END

FOR MORE, VISIT: DJBCARTOON.LIVEJOURNAL.COM

SUPER VIXENS (1975)

ALTHOUGH NOT AS WELL KNOWN AS HIS FASTER, PUSSYCAT! KILL! KILL! OR BEYOND THE VALLEY OF THE DOLLS, RUSS MEYER'S SUPERVIXENS REMAINS ONE OF THE MOST WATCHABLE AND OVER-THE-TOP ENTRIES IN HIS EXCELLENT SEX-MOVIE FILMOGRAPHY.

THE MOVIE GROSSED 18 MILLION DOLLARS AT A TIME WHEN MOVIE TICKETS ONLY COST $1.50, AND ALSO AT A TIME WHEN NO ONE WANTED TO SEE SOFTCORE ANYMORE -- WHAT WITH THE ADVENT OF DEEP THROAT AND PORNO CHIC. AND YET RUSS MEYER, THE KING OF SEXPLOITATION, PACKED MILLIONS OF BUTTS INTO SEATS ALL ACROSS THE CONTINENT. I RECENTLY GOT THE SUPERVIXENS REGION 2 ARROW DVD, WHICH PRESERVES THE LASERDISC COMMENTARY BY THE NOW DECEASED SMUT-KING, AND THE OLD CURMUDGEON REVEALS ALL KINDS OF TASTY MORSELS AS HE RAMBLES AND BLATHERS.

"THIS GUY WAS ALWAYS A PROBLEM", RUSS MUMBLES AS HE GRIPES ABOUT HIS HUNKY STAR (CHARLES

SHARI EUBANK · CHARLES NAPIER
CHRISTY HARTBURG · SHARON KELLY

NOW...

Russ Meyer's
Super VIXENS

Warning: Sex and Violence Can Be Dangerous to Your Health.

COLOR   106 MINS.

PITTS) WHO CAUSED UNREST ON SET WHILE CONSTANTLY TRYING TO WOO AN UNRECEPTIVE CO-STAR (SHARI EUBANK). "HE ALWAYS WANTED TO GET LAID."

IT'S ALSO PRETTY FUNNY TO HEAR HIM BRAG ABOUT NOT GETTING ANY FILMING PERMITS AND CHORTLE DURING THE DISTURBING AND HYPER VIOLENT SUPERANGEL DEATH SCENE AS A BRILLIANTLY PSYCHO CHARLES NAPIER STOMPS EUBANK'S CHARACTER TO DEATH IN A BLOOD-FILLED BATHTUB. RUSS SEEMS REALLY BEMUSED BY THE FACT THAT THE BATHROOM THEY DESTROYED BELONGED TO A CREW MEMBER, AND NONE OF THE PROPERTY DAMAGE WAS FAKED IN ORDER TO CREATE THE CARNAGE. ("IT'S A GOOD THING HIS WIFE WAS OUT OF TOWN WHEN WE SHOT THIS!")

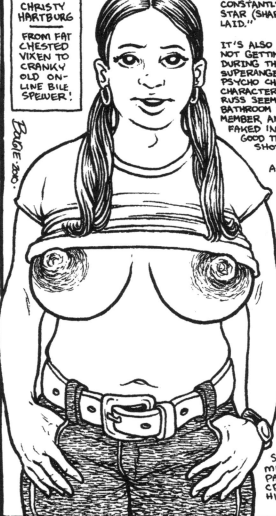

CHRISTY HARTBURG

— FROM FAT CHESTED VIXEN TO CRANKY OLD ON-LINE BILE SPEWER!

BAGGE 2000.

ALTHOUGH SHE IS USED THE LEAST OF THE SEVEN HEFTY-CHESTED FEMALE SPECIMENS IN THE FEATURE, PIG-TAILED PRINCESS CHRISTY HARTBURG IS SO VERY MEMORABLE AS HER HEAVING BOSOM GROANS AND THREATENS TO BURST FREE FROM HER TINY TOP. WHAT A GAL! BARELY 5 MINUTES ON THE SCREEN, AND YET SHE UNIFORMLY ADORNS EVERY SINGLE SCRAP OF PROMO PRINT FOR SUPERVIXENS, NOT TO MENTION THE VHS AND DVD COVERS.

ODDLY ENOUGH, AFTER 20 YEARS FULLY REMOVED FROM THE PUBLIC EYE, HARTBURG RE-EMERGED LAST YEAR AS THE POISON PEN BEHIND A CONSERVATIVE POLITICAL BLOG OUT OF SARASOTA FLORIDA CALLED THEODORESWORLD.NET. ONLY NOW SHE CALLS HERSELF "WILD THING", QUOTES RUSH LIMBAUGH, AND IS HYSTERICAL ABOUT MUSLIMS. YOU KNOW... IT'S ALWAYS THE CHRISTIAN GIRLS WHO GET INTO SEX FILMS TO PISS OFF DADDY, AND THEN SETTLE BACK INTO THEIR CONSERVATIVE ROOTS ONCE THEIR PARENTS ARE IN THE GROUND AND CAN'T GET OUTRAGED ANYMORE.

SUPERVIXENS IS SHOT IN THE SPLENDID MEYER STYLE HIS FANS ADORE (RUSS NEVER PANS, TILTS OR DOLLIES, INSTEAD CREATIVELY SUGGESTING MOVEMENT IN HIS EDITING), AND PACKED TO THE

RAFTERS WITH GORGEOUS WOMEN WITH MASSIVE BOOBS AND ROUND CURVY HIPS. I'M NOT GONNA SPEND ANY TIME HERE GOING INTO NEEDLESS DETAIL ABOUT THE PLOT, BUT I WILL SAY THAT SUPERVIXENS IS WILDLY ENTERTAINING FROM MINUTE ONE TO MINUTE ONE HUNDRED AND SIX, AND THAT CULT FILM ENTHUSIASTS SHOULD CONSIDER IT TO BE REQUIRED VIEWING.

—BOUGIE · 2010.

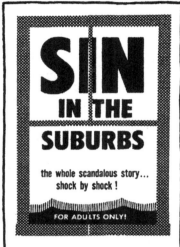

SIN IN THE SUBURBS
the whole scandalous story...
shock by shock!

FOR ADULTS ONLY!

WOW. WHAT A MOVIE! 1964'S SIN IN THE SUBURBS IS AS MATURE AND INTELLIGENT AS THE GENRE OF SEXPLOITATION GETS WITHOUT TOTALLY DROPPING THE SEXPLOITATION ANGLE AND GOING FULL ON CASSAVETES STYLE. DIRECTOR JOE SARNO HAD HIMSELF SOME KEEN CHOPS, AND TRIED TO DO MORE THAN JUST TITILLATE MASTURBATORS. HE STROVE -- WITHOUT SENTIMENTALITY -- TO GET THEM TO UNDERSTAND THE HUMAN CONDITION. HONESTLY, FOR A BLACK AND WHITE FILM THAT BARELY HAS ANY NUDITY, FEW SEX SCENES, AND NO SWEARING OR DIRTY TALK SIN IN THE SUBURBS SHOULD SIMPLY NOT BE AS RIDICULOUSLY HOT AS IT IS. BUT SUCH IS THE POWER OF SARNO, MY FRIENDS.

ONLY 15 PRINTS OF THIS FILM WERE EVER ACTUALLY STRUCK SO MODERN DAY AUDIENCES SHOULD FEEL BLESSED THAT ONE OF THEM SURVIVED AND SOMEHOW GOT INTO THE HANDS OF MIKE VRANEY AT SWV, WHO RELEASED S.I.T.S. IN A FINE EXTRAS-PACKED DVD EDITION FEATURING AN EDUCATIONAL COMMENTARY BY JOE (RIP) AND HIS WIFE/LEADING LADY PEGGY STEFFANS.
—BOUGIE

☆ RAPED BY A WEREWOLF ☆

IT HAS BEEN OPINED BY SOME CRITICS THAT THE FOLLOWING EXCHANGE FROM 1987'S THE HOWLING III IS SOME OF THE WORST DIALOGUE IN THE HISTORY OF MODERN FILM:

PRIEST: YOU SHOULD NOT RUN AWAY FROM HOME.
GIRL: I DON'T LIKE HOME.
PRIEST: WHY, CHILD?
GIRL: BECAUSE MY STEP FATHER TRIED TO RAPE ME. AND HE'S A WEREWOLF.

CLEARLY THESE FOOLS HAVE CONFUSED WORST WITH BEST. (A COMMON PROBLEM I'VE NOTICED) AND BESIDES, MY WEREWOLF STEP FATHER ONLY EVER CAME WHEN THERE WAS A FULL MOON (MINE). HAAAAAAAAA ;COUGH;

WHAT WITH THE DEPRESSING ADVENT IN POPULARITY OF THE TWILIGHT BOOKS AND FILMS, I'M HOPING WE'LL SEE A POSITIVE SPIN-OFF: A GLUT OF WEREWOLF SEXUAL ACTS CAPTURED ON CAMERA. MMMM-HMMM. THE GROWLING, THE SWEAT, THE SCREAMING, THE THRUSTING, AND THE GEYSERS OF LUPINE EJACULATE. ONLY A SCANT FEW FILMS HAVE DELIVERED THE GOODS AS OF THIS LATE DATE (1975'S LA BETE, 1982'S THE BEAST WITHIN AND 2006'S BIG BAD WOLF), BUT LET US LOOK AT THAT PATHETIC TURN OUT SIMPLY AS A CHALLENGE, NOT A DEFEAT. THE ORIFICE IS HALF FULL, NOT HALF EMPTY!

CONSIDER THIS YOUR CALL TO MATTED, HAIR-COVERED ARMS! GLUE FAKE FUR TO OVERSIZED ACTORS AND SEND THEM FLYING, DONGS ENGORGED! PUT ANY AND ALL NECESSARY FUNDS INTO THE COST OF FUR SUITS, PROSTHETIC BONERS, AND BUCKETS OF THICK ARTIFICIAL EJACULATE, AND SEXUALLY VIOLATE ANYONE WHO

WILL SIGN OF THE LINE WHICH IS DOTTED! WE CAN DO THIS THING, MY FILM MAKER FRIENDS! WE CAN MAKE DREAMS COME TRUE!

· 2010 · —BOUGIE ☆

IN A MODERN ERA WHEN BURLESQUE IS ONCE AGAIN HIP AND 1960S FASHION IS BACK WITH A VENGEANCE, I CAN ONLY HOPE THAT THE SAME COUNTERCULTURE ENTHUSIASM FOR THE MORE TAWDRY AESTHETICS OF THE ERA WILL TRICKLE DOWN TO THE MOVIES THAT ORIGINALLY POLLENATED AMERICA WITH THE JAZZY SEED OF BIG CITY SIN AND ECCENTRIC PERVERSITY: THE 1960S SEXPLOITATION MOVIE. VA-VA-VA-VOOM!

A KOO-KOO HEP-CAT AND HIS LIL' FOXY HEP-KITTEN COULD SCARCELY DO BETTER THAN A CERTAIN DVD TRIPLE FEATURE RELEASED BY SOMETHING WEIRD VIDEO IN 2003. AFTER WADING THROUGH OVER A HUNDRED SIMILAR RELEASES, I NOW FEEL SECURE IN DEEMING THIS PARTICULAR EXAMPLE AS ONE OF THE SINGLE GREATEST '60S SEXPLOITATION DVDS EVER PRESSED. I'M SPEAKING OF THE "TOTAL FULFILMENT TRIPLE FEATURE" OF **RENT-A-GIRL**, **AROUSED**, AND **HELP WANTED FEMALE**.

LOVELY LISA PETRUCCI ONE HALF OF THE AFOREMENTIONED SOMETHING WEIRD -- A COMPANY SOLELY RESPONSIBLE FOR KEEPING THE CLASSIC SEXPLOITATION GENRE ALIVE AND AVAILABLE TO AN ENTIRE GENERATION OF FILM FANS -- HAD THIS TO SAY WHEN I ASKED ABOUT THE FILMS IN QUESTION:

"THIS IS MORE BLACK BRAS, STOCKINGS, PANTIES, AND PERVERSITY THAN SHOULD EVER BE CAPTURED ON CELLULOID! AND RENT-A-GIRL FEATURES ALL MY FAVOURITE NEW YORK NUDIE STARLETS: DARLENE BENNETT, JUNE ROBERTS, GIGI DARLENE AND JUDY ADLER. DOESN'T GET BETTER THAN THAT!"

INDEED IT DOES NOT.

RENT A GIRL (1965) IS A 77 MINUTE BLACK-AND-WHITE MOOSE-KNUCKLE WHERE HOPELESSLY NAIVE COSMOPOLITAN KAREN (BARBARA WOOD) COLLECTS A CRUEL LIFE LESSON WHEN HER DREAM GIG AT A NEW YORK MODELLING AGENCY TRANSFORMS INTO A HATEPLOW OF FORCED PROSTITUTION. SHIT GOES FROM BAD TO NIGHTMARISH WHEN OUR INNOCENT GAL ENDS UP AT A KINKY MANHATTAN SOCIALITE ORGY THAT FEATURES HUSBAND-SWAPPING, WHIPPING, LESBIANISM, A GIDDY GAME OF STRIP-POOL, BRANDING, GO-GO DANCING, BODY-PAINTING, AND A PERVERT PHOTOGRAPHER IN A TOP HAT THAT GETS HIS JOLLIES SPRAYING BITCHES WITH A SELTZER BOTTLE! ONLY IN NEW YAWK, FOLKS! KEEP AN EAR OUT FOR THOSE AMAZING OL' UP-TEMPO MUSIC LIBRARY NUMBERS OF THE ERA, BECAUSE THEY'RE ON HEAVY ROTATION HERE.

THAT WOULD BE TERRIFIC ENOUGH, BUT THIS DISC STILL HAS TWO MORE POLITICALLY INCORRECT SWINGIN' SEX BOMBS FOR US TO DETONATE! WHOOPEE!

ONE OF THE BEST ROUGHIES EVER MADE, **AROUSED** (1966) OPERATES MORE AS AN EROTIC INDEPENDENT CRIME DRAMA THAN A SEXPLOITATION MOVIE. IT'S ALSO AN ODD CHOICE FOR A TITLE, SINCE AROUSED ACTUALLY CENTERS ON A PSYCHO WITH AN AVERSION TO SEXUAL FEELINGS AFTER A CHILDHOOD OF BEING LOCKED UP IN A CLOSET WHILST HIS HOOKER MOMMY COAXED MEN TO CRY FROM THEIR PENISES. IT'S THIS BACK STORY THAT PROVIDES FUEL FOR HIS HARMFUL

HATRED TOWARDS PROSTITUTES, AND SENDS THE MODERN JACK THE RIPPER TO PROWL THE RAIN-SLICKED MANHATTAN STREETS FOR VICTIMS. A HIGHLIGHT IS SULTRY BLACK BEAUTY FLEURETTE CARTER AS ANGELA, A GODDAMN KNOCKOUT OF A GIRL USED BY THE POLICE AS MANIAC-BAIT.

BRIEF, TWISTED, AND LOADED WITH FILM NOIR DIALOGUE AND DISSONANT JAZZ, AROUSED IS NOT ACTUALLY ALL THAT FAR OFF A SIMILAR NYC PRODUCTION CALLED **BLAST OF SILENCE** (1961 DIR: ALLEN BARON) WHICH HAS BEEN DEEMED NOTEWORTHY ENOUGH TO BE HONOURED WITH A PLACE IN THE CRITERION COLLECTION. I DOUBT WE'LL EVER LIVE TO SEE SIMILAR RESPECT FOR THIS, THE VERY FIRST EFFORT OF WRITER/DIRECTOR ANTON HOLDEN, WHO ENDED UP TOILING AWAY AS A DIALOGUE AND SOUND EDITOR IN THE TV INDUSTRY -- A JOB THAT HE DOES TO THIS VERY DAY. CINEMATOGRAPHER GIDEON ZUMBACH (WHO BOTH EXPLOITATION EXPERT CASEY SCOTT AND I CAN'T FUCKING BELIEVE DIDN'T GO ON TO DO ANYTHING ELSE)

ADULTS ONLY!

IS A BLOODY GENIUS. HIS BLACK-AND-WHITE 16MM PHOTOGRAPHY IN THIS FILM IS OFTEN JAW DROPPING, EMPLOYING JAGGED-ANGLES AND FREEZE FRAMES AT KEY MOMENTS, SUCH AS THE ANXIOUS ELEVATOR ATTACK AND THE WAVE OF RAGE THAT SENDS THE POSSE OF PROSTITUTES ON A VIGILANTE MANHUNT.

AROUSED AND RENT-A-GIRL ARE TWO OF THE VERY FEW LOCAL FLICKS PRODUCED BY NEW YORKS CAMBIST FILMS. HELMED BY LEE HESSEL, CAMBIST WAS ONE OF THE LONE COMPANIES THAT PUSHED FOR A MORE ART-HOUSE STYLE SEX FILM DESPITE THE MEAGRE BUDGETS AND GRINDHOUSE THEATRES THEY WERE BEHOLDEN TO. THE CAMBIST LINE UP WAS TINY COMPARED TO OTHER COMPANIES SUCH AS CHANCELLOR AND AMERICAN FILMS DISTRIBUTION, BUT WHAT THEY LACKED IN QUANTITY THEY MADE UP FOR IN QUALITY. MANY OF THEIR MOST MEMORABLE OFFERINGS WERE SUMPTUOUS FOREIGN TITTY PICTURES THEY WOULD GOBBLE UP FOR STATESIDE DISTRIBUTION, SUCH AS ARMANDO BO'S PUT OUT OR SHUT UP (1958), EMILIO VIEYRA'S FEAST OF FLESH (1967), DANIELLA BY NIGHT BY MAX PECAS, AND IGNACIO F. IQUINO'S NAKED MELODRAMA THE UNSATISFIED (1964) STARRING RITA CADILLAC.

IT'S ALSO WORTH MENTIONING THAT AROUSED WAS THE FOCUS OF A NOTEWORTHY OBSCENITY TRAIL IN JOLIET, ILLINOIS, WHEN THE MANAGER OF THE PRINCESS THEATER WAS ARRESTED AND A PRINT OF AROUSED WAS SEIZED BY THE WILL COUNTY SHERIFF. CAMBIST HAD THE BRASS ONES TO FILE AN ANTICENSORSHIP SUIT AGAINST THE STATE OF ILLINOIS. AMAZINGLY, THEY WON. THE PRECEDENT-SETTING 1968 RULING STATED THAT "NO FILM MAY BE SEIZED WITHOUT THE OPPORTUNITY TO DEFEND ITSELF IN A TRIAL PROCEEDING", AND SERVED AS A GREAT DETERRENT OF ON-THE-SPOT CENSORSHIP OF FILM, A PRACTICE THAT, UP UNTIL THAT POINT, WAS TRADITIONAL BEHAVIOUR BY POLICE IN MANY PARTS OF THE COUNTRY.

THE FINAL MULE-KICK ON THIS DISC IS CERTAINLY THE CRAZIEST. HELP WANTED FEMALE IS A FREAKY LITTLE MADE-IN-CALIFORNIA BEAN-BAGGER THAT RUNS BARELY OVER AN HOUR, BUT PACKS MORE WONKY THRILLS THAN A HALF DOZEN RUN-OF-THE-MILL SEXPLOITERS. ONE OF THE TRUE HIDDEN GEMS IN THE SOMETHING WEIRD CATALOGUE, THIS DEGENERATE OPUS DOES ABSOLUTELY NOTHING BY THE BOOK, WHICH MAKES FOR ONE OVERTLY UNPREDICTABLE MOVIE EXPERIENCE AND ONE HAPPY BOUG! ‿‿

JO-JO THE LESBIAN KUNG-FU GIRL AND HER DOWNRIGHT HOMELY JUNKIE GIRLFRIEND LUANA ARE NOT ONLY PATHETIC FUCKPUMPS, BUT THEY'RE DOWN IN THE DUMPS. WHEN THEY AREN'T OUT PICKING UP SALESMEN (THAT THEY SCREW AND THEN ROB) THEY'RE BA-DONK-DONK-DONKING THEIR WAY THROUGH PRIVATE STRIP SHOWS FOR SUBURBAN LOW-LIFES. ONE SUCH SKUZZBAGIO IS THE EVENLY-TANNED, ASCOT-SPORTING MR. GREGORY. NOW MR. GREGORY IS A REAL PIECE OF WORK, LET ME TELL YOU. THIS MIDDLE-AGED LOTHARIO LOVES TO OGLE WHORES SHAKING THEIR BREAD-WINNERS IN HIS LIVING ROOM WHILE HE REGALES THEM WITH WILD STORIES (TOLD IN FLASHBACK)

(CONTINUED FROM PREVIOUS PAGE)

ABOUT HOW HE AND HIS FORMER GAL-PAL CHOPPED UP NUBILE YOUNG HITCHHIKERS. SHOULD WORLD-WEARY KUNG-FU-HOOKERS RUN FOR THEIR LIVES WHEN WEIRD OL' MR. GREGORY STARTS TRIPPIN' BALLS AND BABBLING OF HIS CARNAGE-CAKED PAST, OR IS IT JUST THE DRUGS TALKING?

THIS WAY-OUT MASTERPIECE FEATURES HEAPING HELPINGS OF MARVELLOUS WIGS, OVERBEARING STRIPTEASES, GOOEY BLOODLETTING-AS-FOREPLAY, A BED THAT GETS MADE INTO A MAKESHIFT FORT, PIPE-SMOKING, FINGER-SUCKING, HAMMY OVERACTING -- AND I'D BE REMISS IF I DIDN'T MAKE ENTHUSIASTIC MENTION OF THE KUNG-FU AGAIN.

MR. GREGORY WAS TONY VORNO, AND HE PERFORMED IN NOT ONLY HELP WANTED FEMALE, BUT 8 OTHER MOVIES WITH DIRECTOR JOHN HAYES (AKA HAROLD PERKINS). CONSIDERING VORNO WAS ONLY IN 13 FILMS IN HIS ENTIRE CAREER -- ONE CAN SAFELY SUPPOSE THAT THE TWO WERE GOOD FRIENDS AND ENJOYED WORKING TOGETHER. I'M TOLD TONY WAS ALSO THE LOCATION MANAGER FOR DENNIS HOPPERS **EASY RIDER** AS WELL.

—BOUGIE '10

IT'S A CLAS-SICK
☆☆☆☆
DIR: JACK GARFEIN 1961

NOT TO BE CONFUSED WITH THE UNRELATED 1986 JONATHAN DEMME FILM STARRING JEFF DANIELS AND MELANIE GRIFFITH, THIS LESSER KNOWN (YET FAR SUPERIOR) BLACK AND WHITE EFFORT IS FROM DIRECTOR/WRITER JACK GARFEIN, WHO HIRED THE ALWAYS AWESOME SAUL BASS TO DESIGN THE OPENING CREDIT SEQUENCE. THIS TITLE ANIMATION (A GRAPHIK, ESOTERIC ODE TO THE HUSTLE-AND-BUSTLE OF A STEAMY NEW YORK CITY DAY) IS A GREAT FIT, PREPARING THE AUDIENCE FOR THE URBAN MADNESS TO COME. IT IS ARGUABLY ONE OF THE FINEST TITLE SEQUENCES BASS EVER DID.

CARROLL BAKER, STILL FRESH-FACED DESPITE BEING A FEW YEARS REMOVED FROM HER CAREER-DEFINING ROLL IN **BABY DOLL**, SKIPS AND SCAMPERS OUT OF THE ELEVATED KINGSBRIDGE SUBWAY STATION NEAR HER HOME AND FLITS RIGHT INTO THE FOUL GRASP OF A RAPIST WHO THROWS HER IN A BUSH AND PROCEEDS TO CRUELY FUCK THE INNOCENCE AND WHIMSY RIGHT OUT OF HER.

CARROLL BAKER WAS JUST ABOUT THE CUTEST THING GOING IN 1961.

THIS JARRING BEGINNING CONTINUES RIGHT INTO A 15 MINUTE WORDLESS MONTAGE OF ITS AFTERMATH. WE WITNESS BAKER CREEP HOME, PASS OUT, DESTROY ALL OF THE EVIDENCE OF HER ATTACK, QUIT SCHOOL, RUN AWAY FROM HOME, GET A DEPRESSING JOB AT A WOOLWORTH 5 AND DIME, RENT A ROOM IN A SCUMMY EAST HARLEM FLOPHOUSE, FLIP OUT WHEN ANYONE TOUCHES HER, AND TO SOME EXTENT -- LOSE HER MIND.

EVENTUALLY OUR VIOLENTLY DEFLOWERED HEROINE STROLLS ON OVER TO THE MANHATTAN BRIDGE WITH THE SOUR INTENT OF LEAPING TO HER DOOM, BUT IS PULLED TO SAFETY BY A MECHANIC PLAYED BY RALPH MEEKER. AT FIRST GLEAN, MEEKER SEEMS TO BE THE ONLY KIND-HEARTED HUMAN BEING REMAINING IN THIS DIRTY AND DEBAUCHED LANDSCAPE, AND THIS FIRST IMPRESSION PROMPTS THE BABY-FACED BLONDE TO LIFT HER GUARD AND FOLLOW HIM TO HIS DANK, GROUND-LEVEL CRAMPED APARTMENT ON THE LOWER EAST SIDE.

BUT CARROLL'S CHARACTER HAS NO LUCK, WHATSOEVER. THE MOMENT SHE ENTERS, SHE IS THE SOLE CAPTIVE OF A LOVE-STARVED MENTAL CASE WHO KIDNAPS HER AND FORBIDS HER TO LEAVE AS COMPENSATION FOR HAVING SAVED HER LIFE. A MOVIE THAT BEFORE

ENCOMPASSED LARGE PARTS OF SQUALID NYC (ALL SHOT ON LOCATION BY ESTEEMED GERMAN CINEMATOGRAPHER EUGEN SCHÜFFTAN IN SLUMS NOW TRANSFORMED INTO HIGH-PRICED REAL ESTATE), WILL BECOME A VIOLENT AND CLAUSTROPHOBIC SINGLE SET PLAY, A CINEMATIC TACTIC DESIGNED TO PUT ITS TWO MAIN CHARACTERS UNDER A MICROSCOPE.

STAR CARROLL BAKER WAS MARRIED TO THE DIRECTOR OF SOMETHING WILD, AND DURING THE COURSE OF HER FOURTEEN YEARS OF MATRIMONIAL UNION WITH JACK GARFEIN, THEY PRODUCED TWO CHILDREN AND THIS MOVIE -- ALL OF WHICH WERE INDEPENDENTLY FINANCED. RAISED CATHOLIC, BAKER CONVERTED TO JUDAISM AS A

CAROLL BAKER, EMBROILED IN PSYCHOLOGICAL TRAUMA.

ARTIST AL HIRSCHFELD CREATED THIS TENSE ILLUSTRATION TO HELP PROMOTE THE FILM FOR UNITED ARTISTS DURING ITS ORIGINAL THEATRICAL RUN.

PRONOUNCEMENT OF HER DEVOTION TO JACK.

BAKER HAD A SUCCESSFUL CAREER THROUGHOUT THE LATE FIFTIES AND ON INTO THE SIXTIES, AND WOULD ROUND OUT THAT DECADE BY DIVORCING GARFEIN, MOVING TO ITALY, AND STARRING IN SOME RAD GIALLO FILMS. WHILE ON LOCATION IN AFRICA FOR THE 1965 MOVIE MISTER MOSES, A MAASAI

CHIEF OFFERED 150 COWS, 200 GOATS, SHEEP, AND $750 FOR HER HAND IN MARRIAGE. SHE POLITELY TURNED THE CHIEF DOWN, BUT APPEARED WITH HIS WARRIORS ON THE COVER OF LIFE MAGAZINE'S 17 JULY 1964 ISSUE.

JACK WAS (LIKE MUCH OF THE REST OF THE CAST) A MEMBER OF LEE STRASBERG'S PRESTIGIOUS ACTOR'S STUDIO. UNFORTUNATELY, GARFEIN FELL OUT OF STRASBERG'S GOOD BOOKS WHILE DIRECTING A PLAY THAT FEATURED LEE'S DAUGHTER, SUSAN. THIS EGO-FUELED SHIT STORM RESULTED IN LEE TAKING OVER THE PLAY, AND HIS WIFE PAULA INFORMING THE PRESS THAT GARFEIN CONTRIBUTED FUCK-ALL TO THE CREATION OF THE PLAY, AND THAT HE'D INVENTED HIS PAST AS A TEENAGE AUSCHWITZ SURVIVOR TO GARNER SYMPATHY. NOW, TAKING INTO ACCOUNT THAT JACK AND CARROLL LIVED IN THE SAME APARTMENT BUILDING AS THE STRASBERGS, ONE CAN ONLY IMAGINE THE JUICY BEHIND-THE-SCENES DRAMA GOING ON IN THAT SITUATION!

BASED ON ALEX KARMEL'S NOVEL "MARY ANN", THIS FILM SURELY MUST HAVE SEEMED LIKE A SURE BET FOR INVESTORS

MMAAAANNN...
I LOVE THIS MOVIE!
SEE!?

WHO HAD JUST WITNESSED CARROLL NOMINATED FOR A BEST ACTRESS OSCAR FOR HER EXCELLENT AFOREMENTIONED ROLE IN THE SOUTHERN GOTHIC ODDITY, BABY DOLL, IT WAS NOT TO BE. ASIDE FOR A FEW IMPRESSED CRITICS IN FRANCE AND ITALY, SOMETHING WILD WAS PANNED, RESULTING IN A DOMESTIC BOX OFFICE BOMB, AND A JARRING HALT TO GARFEIN'S DIRECTORIAL CAREER. FURTHERMORE, THE MOVIE HAS VIRTUALLY VANISHED-- NOT ONLY FROM REPERTORY SCREENS, BUT FROM ANY HOME FORMAT RELEASE.

COMPLETELY UNAPPRECIATED IN ITS TIME (AND WOULD ASSUMEDLY BE EQUALLY AS GALLING TO MODERN DAY FEMINISTS), THIS INDIE ARTHOUSE-TRASH CLASSIC IS JUST ACHING TO BE REDISCOVERED BY CULT FILM FANS.

— BOUGIE 2010 ☆

THE GAUNTLET (1977. DIRECTED BY CLINT EASTWOOD)

THANKS TO THE JAW-DROPPING THEATRICAL POSTER PAINTED BY THE AMAZING FRANK FRAZETTA FOR YEARS BEFORE I ACTUALLY SAW THIS MOVIE, I ASSUMED IT WAS ABOUT SOME POST-APOCALYPTIC FUTURE WHERE CITIES LAY IN RUINS. TURNS OUT THE CONAN-STYLE MASS CARNAGE DEPICTED IS SIMPLY FRANK'S REPRESENTATION OF THE VIOLENT FINALE OF THE FILM IN WHICH CLINT EASTWOOD (AS AN UNRELIABLE, ALCOHOLIC COP) AND HIS REAL-LIFE GAL-PAL OF 25 YEARS, SANDRA LOCKE (A PROSTITUTE ON THE RUN FROM THE MOB) TAKE ON ALL COMERS IN A BULLET-RIDDLED GREYHOUND BUS.

IT ISN'T PARTICULARLY WELL-WRITTEN, BUT OVERALL THIS IS A WORTHWHILE '70S COP-THEMED ACTION FILM. CLINT IS ASSIGNED TO ESCORT LOCKE, WHOSE FOUL-MOUTHED LAS VEGAS WHORE

"Classic Eastwood...fast, furious and funny"
Roger Ebert, Chicago Sun-Times

CLINT EASTWOOD
THE GAUNTLET

CLINT EASTWOOD
"THE GAUNTLET" Starring SONDRA LOCKE

IS ALL SASS AND NO CLASS. IF HE CAN GET HER TO PHOENIX TO TESTIFY AGAINST A BIGWIG AUTHORITY FIGURE THE SHIT WILL HIT THE FAN, SO THE TWO ARE FORCED TO NAVIGATE A GAUNTLET OF DIRTY COPS, BIKERS, MOB HENCHMEN, AND HIGHLY TRAINED ASSASSINS WHO WANT THEM BOTH DEAD.

THE FUNNIEST TIDBIT OF UN-PC VIOLENCE TAKES PLACE WHEN LOCKE AND HER PROTECTOR ARE BEATEN UP AND NEARLY RAPED WHILE RIDING THE RAILS, HOBO-STYLE. THEY ARE ACCOSTED BY SOME BIKERS AND THEIR BIKER BITCH, THE LATTER OF WHOM CLINT PUNCHES RIGHT THE FUCK OFF THE TRAIN. NOW, THE ACT OF BEATING UP LADIES MAY SEEM MISOGYNISTIC AT FACE VALUE, BUT PUNCHING THE FACES OF PEOPLE WHO DESERVE IT, REGARDLESS OF THEIR GENITALS, IS A REWARDING VIEWING EXPERIENCE IN A GENRE WHERE STOIC HEROES OFTEN DON'T PRACTICE PUGILISTIC EQUALITY.

THE INGREDIENT LIST OF THIS ROAD MOVIE IS A MULTITUDE OF FAST-PACED SHOOTOUTS, AND CHAOTIC CHASE SCENES CAST ACROSS BARREN DESERT LANDSCAPES. I MEAN, I'M TALKING OVER-THE-TOP BULLET-RIDDLED SHOOT EM UPS; MORE THAN 8,000 ROUNDS WERE USED FOR THE FINALE. EASTWOOD DIRECTED, BUT INITIALLY SAM PECKINPAH WAS SLATED FOR THE JOB, AND HE HAD KRIS KRISTOFFERSON AND ALI MACGRAW IN MIND FOR THE LEAD ROLES. THE THREE OF THEM WOULD INSTEAD MAKE CONVOY (1978) TOGETHER. STEVE MCQUEEN AND BARBRA STREISAND WERE ALSO PENCILLED IN AS THE TWO MAIN CHARACTERS IN THE GAUNTLET BEFORE CLINT STEPPED IN, BUT REPORTS SAY THE TWO DID NOT GET ALONG, AND FOR THAT REASON BACKED OUT OF THE PROJECT.

IN RETROSPECT, WHAT IS ACTUALLY OUTSTANDING ABOUT THIS MOVIE COMES AROUND TO WHAT MY INITIAL RELATIONSHIP WAS WITH IT: ITS AMAZING PAINTED ONE-SHEET BY FRANK FRAZETTA. IT IS A POSTER THAT IS SO OUTSTANDING, IT ALMOST DOESN'T EVEN NEED A FILM.

☆ CONTINUED FROM PREVIOUS PAGE ☆

KEEP IN MIND THAT THIS WAS (AT THAT TIME) THE BIGGEST BUDGETED FILM EASTWOOD HAD EVER WORKED ON, AND SOMEONE AT WARNER BROS. HAD SHIT THE BED. THE MOVIE HAD BEEN BADLY MARKETED, EARLY SNEAK PREVIEWS WERE POORLY HANDLED, AND THE SHIP WAS SINKING BEFORE IT HAD EVEN GONE ON ITS MAIDEN VOYAGE.

CLINT NEEDED A SECRET WEAPON, AND TOOK IT UPON HIMSELF TO DO DAMAGE CONTROL. BEING BOTH A FAN AND A FRIEND OF FRAZETTA, EASTWOOD KNEW EXACTLY WHO TO CALL, AND WHEN HE AND LOCKE ARRIVED TOGETHER AT THE PAINTER'S HOME IN CONNECTICUT AND SAW HOW THE TWO OF THEM HAD BEEN DEPICTED, IT BECAME IMMEDIATELY APPARENT THAT ALL THE DRAMA AND FUSSING OVER THE MOVIE HAD BEEN FOR NOTHING. A SERIOUS (BUT UNDISCLOSED) AMOUNT OF MONEY HAD BEEN SPENT ON THE PAINTING, AND FRANK FRAZETTA HAD BROUGHT THE NOISE: THE GAUNTLET WOULD GO ON TO MAKE NEARLY $35 MILLION DOLLARS WORLD WIDE, AND FINISHED JUST OUTSIDE OF THE TOP 10 BOX OFFICE EARNERS OF THAT YEAR.

—BOUGIE·2010·

GENE SIMMONS PLAYS A KILLER TRANNY!

HUH HUH

NO, IT'S NOT JUST YOU, I WANT TO PUNCH THAT FACE AS HARD AS I CAN, TOO.

JOHN STAMOS IS: LANCE STARGROVE!

25 THINGS I LEARNED FROM: Never Too Young To Die

1) JOHN STAMOS HAS A MULLET, AND CAN CRY REAL TEARS.

2) LOS ANGELES HAS A PIPELINE THAT CAN EASILY SEND ENOUGH RADIOACTIVE WASTE INTO THEIR DRINKING SUPPLY TO RUIN IT FOR TEN THOUSAND YEARS.

3) IF GOLDFISH ARE EXPOSED TO RADIOACTIVE WASTE, THEY MUTATE INSTEAD OF DYING.

4) YOU CAN DIVERT NUCLEAR WASTE INTO LOS ANGELES' DRINKING SUPPLY WITH A PROGRAM ON ONE FLOPPY DISK AND NOTHING CAN EVER PREVENT THIS FROM HAPPENING UNLESS YOU STEAL SAID FLOPPY DISK.

5) BAD GUYS DON'T MAKE BACK-UP COPIES OF THEIR ALL-IMPORTANT FLOPPY DISKS.

6) IF YOU GET A BAD GUY'S ALL-IMPORTANT FLOPPY DISK, YOU SHOULD SEND IT TO YOUR SON, RATHER THAN DESTROYING IT.

7) IF YOU KNOW SOMEONE ON YOUR SIDE IS A TRAITOR, DON'T TELL ANYONE ELSE. IT'S PROBABLY NOT IMPORTANT.

8) PSYCHOTIC HERMAPHRODITE GANG LEADERS PLAYED BY GENE SIMMONS HAVE ENDLESS RESOURCES AT THEIR DISPOSAL, INCLUDING LIMITLESS WEAPONS, VEHICLES, AND POST-APOCALYPTIC GOONS.

9) HERMAPHRODITES ARE MALE AND FEMALE, SO THEY'RE BETTER THAN THE REST OF US, AND YET HERMAPHRODITES ARE ONLY HALF MAN, MAKING THEM LESS MANLY THAN JOHN STAMOS.

10) IF YOU SAY THE WORD "STARGROVE" TO A STRANGER, THEY WILL IMMEDIATELY RECOGNISE IT AS SOMEONE'S NAME AND ASK YOU WHY YOU SAID THAT NAME.

11) UNDERGROUND SECRET SPY LAIRS SHOULD ALWAYS GLOW BRIGHT RED WHEN THE KEY TO OPENING THEM IS NEARBY, IN CASE YOUR SON NEEDS TO FIND IT AFTER YOU'RE DEAD.

12) IT'S NOT SAFE TO LEAVE YOUR CRATE MARKED "GRENADES" IN YOUR BARN, UNDER THE FLAMMABLES.

13) IF KILLERS WANT TO TORTURE YOU FOR INFORMATION, THEY WILL KNOCK YOU OUT, TAKE YOU TO YOUR OWN HOME, AND LEAVE YOU ON THE FLOOR UNTIED. THAT WAY, WHEN YOU COME-TO, THERE WILL ONLY BE TWO BAD GUYS FOR YOU TO BEAT-UP.

14) INDUSTRIAL-GRADE FURNACES HAVE INTERCOM SYSTEMS INSIDE OF THEM, JUST IN CASE YOU DECIDE TO CHAT WITH WHATEVER IT IS THAT YOU'RE BURNING.

15) YOU CAN BE ALMOST BURNED ALIVE IN

☆ CONTINUED FROM PREVIOUS PAGE ☆

AN INDUSTRIAL-GRADE FURNACE, YET STILL NOT GET SWEATY.

16) ASIAN ROOMMATES ARE GOOD FOR ONLY TWO THINGS: IMPOSSIBLE INVENTIONS AND COMIC RELIEF.

17) IF YOU USE GUM TO STICK A MINIATURE LISTENING DEVICE TO SOMETHING, YOU SHOULD PUT THE LITTLE DEVICE IN THE GUM BEFORE YOU CHEW IT.

18) HOTSHOT GYMNASTS OFTEN PRACTICE BY SPASTICALLY WAVING THEIR HANDS AROUND WHILE JUMPING UP AND DOWN ON THEIR TRAMPOLINES.

19) WRESTLERS THINK THEY'RE MORE MANLY THAN GYMNASTS, BUT WILL STOP TRYING TO BULLY THEM AFTER THEY USE THE OL "WHAT'S THIS ON YOUR SHIRT" FINGER-INTO-CHIN TRICK.

20) IF SOMEONE IS USING A BULLET-PROOF UMBRELLA TO BLOCK YOUR BULLETS, JUST CONTINUE SHOOTING THE UMBRELLA MINDLESSLY.

21) JOHN STAMOS ISN'T INTO SUBTLE FLIRTATION. IF YOU WANT TO HAVE SEX WITH HIM, TRY GOING TOPLESS, OR SHOWERING NAKED WITH HIS GARDEN HOSE.

22) APPLES ARE NO SUBSTITUTE FOR SEX.

23) WHEN YOU'RE BEING USED AS BAIT FOR PSYCHOPATHIC KILLERS, AND KNOW THAT THEY WILL BE ATTACKING AT ANY SECOND, GET BORED AND HAVE SEX.

24) JOHN STAMOS CAN LIFT A MUCH LARGER MAN WITH HIS LEGS WHILE HANGING FROM A RAILING.

25) IN 1986, JOHN STAMOS WAS TOO YOUNG TO DIE. GENE SIMMONS, HOWEVER, WAS NOT.

BY: DOCTOR BIOBRAIN. VISIT HIM AT BIOBRAIN.BLOGSPOT.COM

BOUGIE SAYS: YEAH, YOU GUYS REALLY NEED TO CHECK OUT NEVER TOO YOUNG TO DIE! HOLY SHIT, IS THIS EVER A FORGOTTEN GEM OF TURD-ENCRUSTED RADNESS! IT'S ONE OF THOSE STUPID '80s ACTION MOVIES THAT NEEDS TO BE UNEARTHED AND GOBBLED UP BY A WHOLE NEW GENERATION OF MOVIE NERDS! GET IT.

THE BASEMENT OF HIS MANSION. BOUGIE LOOOOVE IT!

SADLY, CANDICE RIALSON GAVE UP ACTING IN 1979 AND PASSED AWAY (LIVER DISEASE) IN MARCH 2006 AT THE RELATIVELY YOUNG AGE OF 54. IT SUCKS THAT SHE IS NO LONGER WITH US, BUT ALSO UNFORTUNATE IS THAT SHE DIED UNAWARE OF HER FANS AND HOW IMPORTANT SHE WAS TO SO MANY OF US. NO ONE ASIDE FROM HER NEAREST N' DEAREST EVEN KNEW THAT SHE'D PASSED AWAY UNTIL FOUR MONTHS AFTER IT HAD HAPPENED.

 I WANT TO TURN THIS FILM INTO CHOCOLATE CAKE, AND THEN **FUCK IT!**

PETS

OUT OF PRINT SINCE ITS RELEASE ON HOME VIDEO 30 YEARS AGO, THE NOTORIOUS GRINDHOUSE EXPLOITATION CLASSIC PETS, WITH ITS THEMES OF PEEPSHOW SADOMASOCHISM AND DOMINANCE (THE FILM CONSTANTLY COMPARES HUMANS TO ANIMALS) IS ONCE AGAIN AVAILABLE ON A HOME FORMAT THANKS TO CODE RED DVD. A CULT DRIVE-IN CLASSIC, THE MOVIE IS LOADED WITH COPIOUS NUDITY, SCUZZY SITUATIONS, AND QUOTABLE DIALOGUE. ITS ORIGINAL 1974 AD CAMPAIGN IS THE DEFINITION OF LURID, INCLUDING A POSTER WITH BITCHES ON THEIR KNEES WHILE WEARING DOG COLLARS/LEASHES, AND A TRAILER BUILT AROUND IMAGES OF SCANTILY-CLAD CANDICE RIALSON CRAWLING ON ALL FOURS AND BEING WHIPPED.

DID I SAY CANDY RIALSON? OH SHIT, YES I DID. AND THOSE WHO ARE AWARE OF HER OTHER GRINDHOUSE EFFORTS SUCH AS **CANDY STRIPE NURSES, SUMMER SCHOOL TEACHERS,** AND **CHATTERBOX** KNOW SHE BE REASON TO STAND UP AND TAKE SOME NOTICE. THE PHYSICAL EMBODIMENT OF THE BLONDE '70S CALIFORNIA BEACH BUNNY AND THE DIRECT INSPIRATION FOR BRIDGET FONDA'S CHARACTER IN TARANTINO'S "**JACKIE BROWN**"), RIALSON RIPS IT UP AS BONNIE, AN INNOCENT TEENAGE DRIFTER WHO WANDERS FROM ONE INTENSE SCENARIO TO THE NEXT, WITH ONLY HER BEGUILING CHARM PROTECTING HER.

AT FIRST SHE IS TEAMED UP WITH PAT (A SASSY N' SEXY CHOCOLATE SISTER WHO KNOWS HOW TO GET STABBY WITH A KNIFE), AND THEN FINDS HERSELF MACKED UPON AND PICKED UP BY GERALDINE, AN OVERPROTECTIVE SEASIDE LESBO PAINTER WHO SPOTS HER STEALING FRUIT AND RECRUITS HER AS A MODEL AND SEX TOY. EVENTUALLY BONNIE FLEES INTO THE ARMS OF HER FINAL AND MOST TWISTED BENEFACTOR, A WEALTHY ART COLLECTOR PERVERT WHO KEEPS BOTH ANIMALS AND LADIES IN A PRIVATE ZOO IN

CANDICE RIALSON, ON A SHORT LEASH

SOUTHERN DISCOMFORT

BY: DON GUARISCO ☆ 2010 ☆ WWW.SCHLOCKMANIA.COM☆

"SOUTHERN DISCOMFORT". I WAS FIRST INTRODUCED TO THIS SUBGENRE DURING A VISIT TO CINEFILE VIDEO IN LOS ANGELES. THOSE TWO WORDS WERE USED TO HIGHLIGHT ONE OF MANY CREATIVELY NAMED SECTIONS WITHIN THE STORE. THE SPECIFIC TITLES LISTED UNDER THIS HEADER HAVE FADED FROM MEMORY BUT THE CONCEPT HAS TAKEN ON A LIFE OF ITS OWN IN MY PERSONAL CINEMATIC PANTHEON OVER THE YEARS.

TO THESE EYES, A SOUTHERN DISCOMFORT MOVIE IS A FILM WHERE CITY FOLK WANDER INTO THE BOONIES AND RUN AFOUL OF THE WRONG COUNTRY FOLK, THUS SETTING THE STAGE FOR SOME SORT OF TRAGIC MAYHEM. HOWEVER, MAYHEM ITSELF ISN'T THE RAISON D'ETRE OF THESE FILMS (THAT WOULD BE THE "RURAL TERROR" MOVIE WHICH ARE THE CINEMATIC CHILDREN OF THE TEXAS CHAIN SAW MASSACRE). INSTEAD, SOUTHERN DISCOMFORT FILMS USUALLY BLEND THRILLER AND DRAMA ELEMENTS TO CREATE A STORY THAT MANIPULATES THE AUDIENCE WITH LIFE-AND-DEATH THRILLS WHILE OFFERING SOME SORT OF SOCIAL COMMENTARY, USUALLY FOCUSING ON HOW EASILY THE LINE BETWEEN CIVILIZATION AND SAVAGERY CAN BE BLURRED.

THE ROSETTA STONE OF SOUTHERN DISCOMFORT IS DELIVERANCE, WHICH SET MANY OF THE GENRE'S KEY ELEMENTS IN PLACE FOR ALL ITS CINEMATIC OFFSPRING TO FOLLOW (MORE ON THAT BELOW). AS YOU WILL SEE, THIS SUBGENRE REMAINED POTENT OVER A LONG PERIOD OF TIME BECAUSE IT WAS SO EASY TO CROSSBREED IT WITH OTHER EXPLOITATION FILM STYLINGS. THE ROAD MOVIE, THE WOMEN-IN-PRISON FILM AND PARTICULARLY THE RAPE-REVENGE FILM HAVE ALL BEEN SUCCESSFULLY SPLICED WITH THE SOUTHERN DISCOMFORT FILM TO CREATE UNIQUE HYBRIDS.

THE FOLLOWING IS A CAPSULE GUIDE OF NOTEWORTHY SOUTHERN DISCOMFORT EPICS --HORROR FILMS HAVE MOSTLY BEEN AVOIDED, BUT A HANDFUL ARE INCLUDED BECAUSE OF HOW CLOSELY THEY FOLLOW THE GENRE'S TRAGEDY-DRIVEN PLOT STRUCTURE AND THEMATIC OBSESSIONS. WHAT YOU ARE ABOUT TO READ IS NOT JUST A RECOMMENDED VIEWING LIST, IT IS A SURVIVAL GUIDE. LEARN THE LESSONS OF THESE FILMS WELL SO YOU CAN REMAIN SAFE ON YOUR NEXT JOURNEY OUTSIDE THE CITY LIMITS.

DELIVERANCE (1972)

THE GENRE'S FATHER AND STILL AS POTENT AS IT WAS IN 1972. ADAPTED BY AUTHOR JAMES DICKEY FROM HIS POPULAR NOVEL, IT TELLS THE TALE OF FOUR CITY BOYS -- BURT REYNOLDS, JON VOIGHT, NED BEATTY, AND RONNY COX -- WHO TAKE A CANOEING EXCURSION DOWN A RURAL

87

PLEASE!
Do NOT See It With Someone You Love!

THANK HEAVENS, IT'S ONLY A MOVIE!
THANK HEAVENS, IT'S ONLY A MOVIE!
THANK HEAVENS, IT'S ONLY A MOVIE!
THANK HEAV   ONLY A MOVIE!
THANK HEA   ONLY A MOVIE!
THANK HEA   ONLY A MOVIE!
THANK HE   Y A MOVIE!
THANK HE   Y A MOVIE!

IT'S ONLY A MOVIE!

NIGHTMARE H♥NEYMOON

RIVER. WHEN HALF OF THE QUARTET IS VICTIMIZED BY A PAIR OF LUSTY, NASTY MOUNTAIN MEN, THUS BEGINS A HELLISH VISION QUEST THAT KILLS ONE MEMBER OF THE GROUP AND CAUSES TWO OF THE OTHERS TO BECOME KILLERS. DICKEY'S SCRIPT IS AN ARTFUL, FASCINATINGLY AMBIGUOUS MEDITATION ON WHAT IT MEANS TO BE A MAN AND JOHN BOORMAN DIRECTS IT WITH STYLE, BUT DOESN'T FLINCH FROM THE BRUTALITY WHEN IT COMES. THE RESULT IS AS SHOCKING AS IT IS THOUGHTFUL, AND NO MATTER HOW MANY TIMES IT GETS JOKED ABOUT, THE INFAMOUS "SQUEAL LIKE A PIG" SETPIECE REMAINS A WHITE-KNUCKLE HILLBILLY SQUIRMFEST OF THE HIGHEST ORDER.

NIGHTMARE HONEYMOON (1973) A YANKEE WAR VETERAN (DACK RAMBO) AND HIS SOUTHERN BRIDE (REBECCA DIANNA SMITH) DITCH THEIR WEDDING RECEPTION AND ARE CHASED BY THE WEDDING PARTY - IT'S HER FAMILY'S CRAZY TRADITION. THEY DO SUCCESSFULLY ESCAPE, BUT END UP IN TROUBLE WHEN THEY WITNESS A CONTRACT KILLING WHILE HIDING NEAR A FISHING CAMP, AND THE WIFE FINDS HERSELF RAPED BY ONE OF THE KILLERS (A REALLY SCARY JOHN BECK). THE HUSBAND TRACKS THE TWO TO NEW ORLEANS WHERE HE SPENDS THEIR HONEYMOON TRYING TO GET REVENGE. THIS IS A STUDIO FILM, SO IT'S LIGHT ON SLEAZE, BUT THE ACTING IS GOOD AND THE MOVIE DELIVERS A TENSE CHASE-AND-STANDOFF FINALE. DIRECTOR ELLIOT SILVERSTEIN (CAT BALLOU) TOOK OVER THE PRODUCTION WHEN NICOLAS ROEG QUIT AFTER FIVE DAYS OF SHOOTING.

MACON COUNTY LINE (1974) DELIVERANCE IS THE TOP DOG AMONG ENTRIES INTO THE SOUTHERN DISCOMFORT GENRE, BUT THIS IS A CLOSE SECOND. IT WAS INSPIRED BY A REAL-LIFE TRAGEDY AND WAS WRITTEN AND PRODUCED BY MAX BAER JR (JETHRO FROM THE BEVERLY HILLBILLIES), WHO ALSO STARS AS A SMALL-TOWN DEPUTY. IT STARTS OFF AS A ROAD MOVIE WITH AMERICAN GRAFFITI OVERTONES ABOUT BROTHERS (REAL BROS ALAN AND JESSE VINT) ENJOYING A LAST WEEKEND OF HIJINX BEFORE JOINING THE ARMY. THEY GET STRANDED IN THE TITLE COUNTY AT THE SAME TIME THAT A PAIR OF ESCAPED CONVICTS RAPE AND MURDER THE DEPUTY'S WIFE. BEING IN THE WRONG PLACE AT THE WRONG TIME LEADS TO TRAGEDY ON BOTH SIDES. IT'S REALLY AN INDIE DRAMA (WITH HUMOR) THAT OFFERS AN UNCOMPROMISING CRITIQUE OF SOUTHERN LIFE IN THE 1950S, BUT THE LAST 20 MINUTES STILL PACK A PUNCH.

RETURN TO MACON COUNTY (1975) THIS QUICKIE SEQUEL TO MACON COUNTY LINE IS A WHOLE DIFFERENT KETTLE OF CRAWFISH. THIS TIME, TWO HOTRODDERS (NICK NOLTE AND DON JOHNSON) ARE EN ROUTE TO CALIFORNIA TO TAKE PART IN A RACE. THEY PICK UP A HITCHHIKER (ROBIN MATTSON -- WHO IS AS CRAZY AS SHE IS

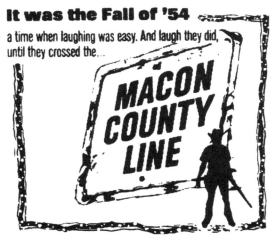

It was the Fall of '54

a time when laughing was easy. And laugh they did, until they crossed the...

MACON COUNTY LINE

SEXY) AND RUN AFOUL OF A DEPUTY (ROBERT VIHARO) WHO BECOMES OBSESSED WITH TRACKING THEM DOWN FOR THEIR PETTY CRIMES. REALLY, IT'S THE 1970S VERSION OF A 1950S DRAG-RACE FLICK THAT HAPPENS TO HAVE A SOUTHERN DISCOMFORT SUBPLOT FOR ADDED SPICE. IT LACKS THE WEIGHT OF ITS PREDECESSOR, BUT THE CAST AND RICHARD COMPTON'S CONFIDENT DIRECTION MAKE IT AN AGREEABLE PROGRAMMER.

THE HOUSE BY THE LAKE (A.K.A. DEATH WEEKEND 1975)
A MODEL (BRENDA VACCARO) ACCOMPANIES A WEALTHY DENTIST TO HIS LAVISH COUNTRY HOME. A GANG OF HOODS (LED BY AN INTENSE DON STROUD) HASSLE THEM ON THE DRIVE UP, BUT SHE SUCCEEDS IN DRIVING THEM OFF THE ROAD. UNFORTUNATELY, THE HOODS TRACK THEM DOWN AND KICK OFF A NIGHTMARISH HOME-INVASION SCENARIO THAT RESULTS IN MUCH DEATH AND DESTRUCTION. THE FIRST OF SEVERAL CANADIAN ENTRIES ON THIS LIST OWES MORE TO STRAW DOGS THAN IT DOES TO DELIVERANCE, BUT IT MIRRORS THE CLASS WARFARE ETHOS OF THE GENRE AND DIRECTOR WILLIAM FRUET OFFSETS THE EXPECTED SUSPENSE AND VIOLENCE WITH UNEXPECTED PSYCHOLOGICAL DEPTH. VACCARO AND STROUD REALLY GET INTO THEIR PERFORMANCES (AND WERE REPORTEDLY HAVING A TORRID AFFAIR OFFSCREEN). FUTURE HOLLYWOOD COMEDY AUTEUR IVAN REITMAN CO-PRODUCED AND DIRECTED THE 2ND UNIT.

POOR PRETTY EDDIE (1975)
OUTRAGEOUS BLEND OF SLEAZE, SURREALISTIC ARTSINESS AND BLACK HUMOR THAT STARS LESLIE UGGAMS AS A FAMOUS SINGER WHOSE CAR BREAKS DOWN IN A PODUNK TOWN. SHE'S SOON RAPED BY AN UNBALANCED ELVIS WANNA-BE (MICHAEL CHRISTIAN) - AND THAT'S ONLY THE

SO PRIVATE YOU CAN DO ANYTHING YOU WANT ...ANYTHING!

THE HOUSE BY THE LAKE

GRAND PRIZE WINNER "SITGES" INTERNATIONAL TERROR FILM FESTIVAL

BRENDA VACCARO in "The House by the Lake"
also starring
DON STROUD
Co-Starring
RICHARD AYRES
KYLE EDWARDS
DON GRANBERY
Executive Producers ANDRE LINK and JOHN DUNNING
Produced by IVAN REITMAN
Written and Directed by WILLIAM FRUET
Color prints by MOVIELAB
A REITMAN/DUNNING/LINK FILM
AN AMERICAN INTERNATIONAL RELEASE
R

LESLIE UGGAMS
SHELLEY WINTERS

POOR PRETTY EDDIE
HE DOES ALL THE THINGS YOU LIKE...TO FORGET! R
Plus! — "BLOOD OF THE DRAGON"

BEGINNING OF HER SORDID NIGHTMARE. THIS OBSCURITY PROBABLY HAS THE SLEAZIEST ATMOSPHERE OF ANY FILM ON THIS LIST. FOR INSTANCE, THE SLO-MO RAPE SCENE IS INTERCUT WITH TOWNIES WATCHING TWO DOGS HUMPING, AND WHEN UGGAMS REPORTS HER RAPE TO THE SHERIFF (SLIM PICKENS!) HE EXCITEDLY ASKS HER "DID HE BITE YA ON THE TITTIES?". THE DIRECTION IS STYLISH IN AN OFFBEAT WAY, AND A KILLER CAST (SHELLEY WINTERS, TED "LURCH" CASSIDY AND DUB TAYLOR) KEEP IT ENGAGING. THE WEDDING FINALE IS ONE OF THE ALL-TIME KILLER EXPLOITATION FILM ENDINGS.

RACE WITH THE DEVIL (1975)
A PAIR OF COUPLES (WARREN OATES, LORETTA SWIT, PETER FONDA, LARA PARKER) TAKE AN RV ON THE ROAD FOR A CAMPING TRIP. THE VACATION TURNS SOUR WHEN THEY ACCIDENTALLY WITNESS A SATANIC RITUAL KILLING AND BARELY ESCAPE THE SCENE OF THE CRIME WITH THEIR LIVES. THUS BEGINS A MUCH-LOVED FUSION OF CAR-

CHASE FILM, PARANOID THRILLER AND DEVIL-SCARE HORROR FLICK THAT BENEFITS FROM GAME PERFORMANCES BY ITS CAST AND MUSCULAR DIRECTION FROM B-MOVIE VET JACK STARRETT. THE SOUTHERN DISCOMFORT ELEMENT COMES FROM THE SUSPICIOUS TREATMENT THE COUPLES GET WHEN THEY TRY TO REPORT THE CRIME (AND THE WAY THE FACELESS CULTISTS EASILY BLEND IN AMONG THE SMALL TOWN CITIZENS). LOOK OUT FOR SEVERAL KILLER CAR STUNTS AND A GENUINELY SCARY SURPRISE ATTACK BY A SNAKE. TRIVIA: THIS WAS CO-WRITTEN AND SUPPOSED TO BE DIRECTED BY LEE FROST, WHO ALSO MADE THE INFAMOUS PORN ROUGHIE "A CLIMAX OF BLUE POWER."

NIGHTMARE IN BADHAM COUNTY (1976)
DESPITE ITS T.V. MOVIE ORIGINS, THIS IS AS NASTY AS ANY OTHER MOVIE ON THIS LIST. THE STORY HAS TWO COEDS (LYNNE MOODY, DEBORAH RAFFIN) ON A CROSS-COUNTRY TRIP GETTING BUSTED ON PHONY CHARGES BY A NASTY SHERIFF (CHUCK CONNORS), WHO RAPES ONE OF THEM BEFORE SENDING THEM TO A COUNTY WORK-FARM. THE STORY BECOMES A SOUTHERN-FRIED MIDNIGHT EXPRESS AS THEY SUFFER ENDLESS INDIGNITIES AND PLOT AN ESCAPE. THE END RESULT IS PACKED WITH GREAT GUEST STARS (ROBERT "BRADY BUNCH" REED AS A DUDE WHO LIKES THE YOUNG STUFF AND TINA LOUISE AS A NASTY GUARD) HOWEVER IT'S DELLA REESE WHO STEALS THE SHOW WITH A SOULFUL TURN AS A VETERAN PRISONER. BE SURE TO CHECK OUT THE RARE VHS VERSION, WHICH HAS A LONGER CUT OF THE FILM USED FOR FOREIGN THEATRICAL DISTRIBUTION, AND INCLUDES NUDE SCENES (INCLUDING ONE WHERE A BUTCH FEMALE GUARD GETS A CON IN A NAKED CLINCH IN EXCHANGE FOR A PLATE OF FRIED CHICKEN). TRIVIA NOTE: ODDLY, THIS MOVIE BECAME ONE OF THE ALL-TIME BOX OFFICE CHAMPS IN CHINA.

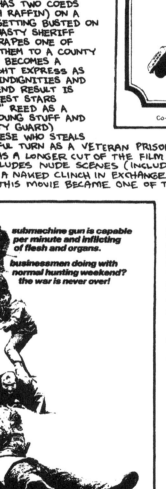

SHOOT (1976)
ARTSY CANADIAN DRAMA STARS CLIFF ROBERTSON AS THE LEADER OF A GROUP OF SUBURBAN MEN (INCLUDING ERNEST BORGNINE) WHO GO ON HUNTING TRIPS TO FEEL MACHO. ON ONE SUCH TRIP, THEY RUN AFOUL OF ANOTHER GROUP OF MEN ON THE OTHER SIDE OF A RIVER AND EXCHANGE SHOTS. WHEN THEY RETURN TO TOWN, ROBERTSON ASSEMBLES A GROUP OF MEN FOR A RETURN ENGAGEMENT WITH THEIR FOES. THE SCRIPT MEANDERS A BIT IN THE MIDSECTION, BUT THIS IS A MOSTLY EFFECTIVE ARTHOUSE OFFERING WITH A FABLE-LIKE STORYLINE THAT OFFERS PLENTY OF COMMENTARY ON GUN CONTROL, MILITARISTIC IMPULSES AND THE DARK SIDE OF MACHISMO. ROBERTSON AND BORGNINE ARE BOTH VERY GOOD, AND THE FILM OFTEN HAS THE FEEL OF A LUCID NIGHTMARE.

JACKSON COUNTY JAIL (1976)
THIS DOWNBEAT ROAD MOVIE FEATURES THE FORMER TIME MACHINE STAR YVETTE MIMIEUX AS AN L.A. CAREER WOMAN WHO LEAVES HER LOUSY JOB AND UNFAITHFUL LOVER TO TAKE A GIG IN NYC. ON THE ROAD TRIP THERE, SHE SUFFERS A STRING OF MISFORTUNES THAT LAND HER IN A JAIL CELL WHERE SHE IS RAPED BY AN UNHINGED NIGHT JAILER. SHE KILLS HIM IN SELF-DEFENSE AND ESCAPES WITH A FELLOW PRISONER (TOMMY LEE JONES) AS THE POLICE GIVE CHASE. AN AMBITIOUS GENRE ENTRY THAT IS ALSO A CULT FAVORITE THANKS TO EXCELLENT PERFORMANCES FROM MIMIEUX AND JONES, AND UNUSUALLY DEFT DIRECTION BY MICHAEL MILLER (WHO ENDED UP BECOMING A PROLIFIC T.V.

DIRECTOR). IT ALSO OFFERS A SAVAGE COMMENTARY ON HYPOCRISY AND SEXISM IN AMERICAN SOCIETY, WITH A DAZZLINGLY BLEAK FINALE THAT DRIVES ITS MESSAGES HOME. ONE OF THE BEST NEW WORLD PICTURES PRODUCTIONS. REMADE TWICE BY MILLER AND MIMIEUX AS A T.V. FILM CALLED OUTSIDE CHANCE, AND YEARS LATER AS MACON COUNTY JAIL.

THE HILLS HAVE EYES (1977)
A CITY FAMILY HEADED TO CALIFORNIA RUNS INTO TROUBLE WHEN THEIR R.V. BREAKS DOWN IN THE DESERT AND THEY ARE ATTACKED BY AN ANIMALISTIC, INBRED FAMILY THAT LIVES IN THE NEARBY HILLS. AFTER LOSING A FEW OF ITS MEMBERS, THE CITY FAMILY IS FORCED TO GET IN TOUCH WITH THEIR COLLECTIVE INNER SAVAGE TO FIGHT BACK. WES CRAVEN'S SURVIVAL-HORROR CLASSIC MAKES THE SOUTHERN DISCOMFORT ROLLCALL BECAUSE IT EXPLICITLY FOCUSES ON THE "THIN LINE BETWEEN CIVILIZED AND SAVAGE" THEME, AND HAMMERS IT HOME WITH BLUNT

What they do to her in Jackson County Jail is a crime!

The cops are there to protect her.
But who will protect her from the cops?

JACKSON COUNTY JAIL
The way out is murder!

Starring **YVETTE MIMIEUX**
Co-Starring TOMMY LEE JONES · ROBERT CARRADINE · NANCY NOBLE
Directed by MICHAEL MILLER Produced by JEFF BEGUN Written by DONALD STEWART · A NEW WORLD PICTURE
PRODUCTION SERVICES BY TBC PRODUCTIONS I METROCOLOR [R] RESTRICTED

EFFECTIVENESS (THE NOCTURNAL ATTACK ON THE R.V. IS THE STUFF OF NIGHTMARES). IT ALSO PROVIDED AN EARLY ROLE FOR DEE WALLACE-STONE, AND MADE A HORROR ICON OUT OF MICHAEL BERRYMAN. CRAVEN WOULD LATER PRODUCE A SLICKER YET INFERIOR REMAKE OF THE FILM WITH ALEXANDRE AJA AT THE HELM.

I SPIT ON YOUR GRAVE (1978)
THIS CROSS-OVER BETWEEN THE SOUTHERN DISCOMFORT AND RAPE-REVENGE GENRES FOCUSES ON A NEW YORK CITY WRITER (CAMILLE KEATON) WHO RENTS A HOUSE IN A SMALL TOWN TO WORK ON HER FIRST NOVEL. SHE RUNS AFOUL OF A QUARTET OF MISOGYNIST CREEPS WHO SUBJECT HER TO A BRUTAL GANG-RAPE. WHEN THE PATSY OF THE GANG FAILS TO FOLLOW INSTRUCTIONS TO KILL HER, SHE NURSES HERSELF BACK TO HEALTH AND TAKES REVENGE. ORIGINALLY RELEASED AS DAY OF THE WOMAN, MEIR ZARCHI'S FILM IS EXPLICIT (THE THIRTY MINUTE, MULTI-PART GANG-RAPE SEQUENCE IS TRULY UNNERVING) BUT NOT AS EXPLOITATIVE AS ITS LEGEND SUGGESTS. IT SUFFERS FROM CRUDE FILMMAKING AND WEAK PERFORMANCES FROM THE MEN, BUT KEATON GIVES A FANTASTIC, DARING PERFORMANCE AS THE VENGEFUL HEROINE AND THE FINISHED PRODUCT HAS A RAW, UNCOMPROMISING SENSIBILITY THAT MAKES IT WORK.

RITUALS (1978)
IN THIS EFFECTIVE CANADIAN HORROR RIFF ON DELIVERANCE, A QUARTET OF DOCTORS (INCLUDING HAL HOLBROOK AND CANUCK STALWART LAWRENCE DANE, WHO ALSO PRODUCED) GO TO A REMOTE ISLAND FOR A FISHING TRIP. AN UNSEEN ATTACKER TOYS WITH THEM - STEALING THEIR BOOTS, LEAVING A DEER'S SEVERED HEAD NEAR THEIR CAMP - AND STARTS PICKING THEM OFF ONE BY ONE. THE SURVIVORS QUICKLY LOSE THEIR CIVILITY AND DIGNITY AS THEY TRY TO SURVIVE. IT'S A SLOW-BURNER BUT DOES A GREAT JOB OF CONVEYING THE PARANOIA OF ITS TRAPPED, PANICKY HEROES. THE END RESULT IS BLEAK TO THE POINT OF NIHILISM AND DELIVERS AN UNFORGETTABLY BRUTAL PAYOFF. HOLBROOK AND DANE GIVE BRAVE, TOP-SHELF PERFORMANCES THAT SHOULD HAVE WON AWARDS. RELEASED IN THE U.S. AS THE CREEPER AND VOTED "DOG OF THE WEEK" BY SISKEL AND EBERT, WHO OFTEN MISSED THE BOAT ON FILMS LIKE THIS.

Not since Deliverance...

Rituals

ASTRAL FILMS presents 'RITUALS'

STARRING **HAL HOLBROOK** CO-STARRING
LAWRENCE DANE ROBIN GAMMELL • KEN JAMES • GARY REINEKE

MOTHER'S DAY (1980)
A TRIO OF FEMALE FRIENDS CELEBRATE THEIR ANNUAL REUNION WITH A CAMPING TRIP. UNFORTUNATELY, THIS PUTS THEM IN THE CROSSHAIRS OF A TWISTED MATRIARCH WHO HAS RAISED HER TWO BOYS TO RAPE AND KILL. WHEN ONE OF THE WOMEN DIES, THE OTHER TWO STRIKE BACK WITH A FEROCITY THAT THE KILLER TRIO DOESN'T SEE COMING. THIS HIGHLY EFFECTIVE BLEND OF SHOCK-HORROR AND DARK SATIRE IS A BIG FAN FAVORITE THANKS TO ITS ECCENTRIC SENSE OF HUMOR (THE TWO SONS ARGUE ABOUT THE MERITS OF PUNK MUSIC VS. DISCO) AND A HARD HITTING FINALE THAT UTILIZES SOME UNFORGETTABLY TWISTED CHOICES OF WEAPONRY. IT WAS DIRECTED

BY CHARLES KAUFMAN, BROTHER OF TROMA FOUNDER LLOYD KAUFMAN, AND A REMAKE WAS MADE BY DARREN BOUSMAN OF **SAW** SEQUELS INFAMY AT THE HELM.

SOUTHERN COMFORT (1980)
LOUISIANA, 1973 -- A GROUP OF NATIONAL GAURDSMEN ON A TRAINING MANEUVER IN THE SWAMP GET LOST AND FIND THEMSELVES IN A SKIRMISH WITH SOME CAJUNS. WHEN ONE SOLDIER PRANKISHLY SHOOTS OFF SOME BLANKS, AND THE CAJUNS SHOOT BACK --KILLING THEIR TROOP LEADER -- THE TRAINING EXERCISE QUICKLY DEGENERATES INTO PARANOIA AND SQUABBLING AS THE WEEKEND WARRIORS TRY AND FIND THEIR WAY OUT WHILE THEIR MOSTLY UNSEEN ENEMIES CALMLY PICK AWAY AT THEIR RANKS. WALTER HILL'S NERVE-JANGLING ENTRY INTO THIS GENRE WORKS BEAUTIFULLY BOTH AS A THRILLER AND AS A COMMENTARY ABOUT THE FOLLY OF THE VIETNAM WAR. IT ALSO BOASTS A MARVELOUS CAST -- KEITH CARRADINE AND POWERS BOOTHE ARE THE LEADS, BUT THERE ARE ALSO STANDOUT TURNS FROM FRED WARD, PETER COYOTE, AND BRION JAMES. THE FINALE SET IN A CAJUN VILLAGE DURING A PARTY WILL HAVE YOU ON THE EDGE OF YOUR SEAT.

HUMAN EXPERIMENTS (1980)
LOUNGE SINGER RACHEL (LINDA

REDNECK RAPE ON THE ROCKS IN "I SPIT ON YOUR GRAVE"

CHARLES KAUFMAN'S
MOTHER'S DAY

HAYNES OF **ROLLING THUNDER** FAME)
IS ACCUSED OF A MURDER SHE DID NOT COMMIT WHILE ON A RURAL BAR TOUR, AND GETS SENT TO PRISON. WACKO SHRINK (GEOFFREY LEWIS) TARGETS HER FOR HIS HIGHLY UNORTHODOX "REHABILITATION" PROGRAM, AND SHOCKS ENSUE. THIS IS AN AMBITIOUS AND UNDERRATED LITTLE FLICK THAT BLENDS A SOUTHERN DISCOMFORT SET-UP WITH WOMEN-IN-PRISON AND PSYCHOLOGICAL THRILLER MOTIFS. DIRECTOR GREG GOODELL ALSO WROTE A WELL-LIKED BOOK ABOUT LOW BUDGET FILM PRODUCTION, AND ENJOYED A LONG CAREER WRITING AND PRODUCING T.V. MOVIES WHILE WRITER RICHARD

SOUTHERN COMFORT

DISCOMFORT NAIL-BITER THAT MODELS ITSELF UPON DELIVERANCE, AND PILES ON THE "CITY VS. COUNTRY" BAGGAGE IN A BIG WAY. THE FILM SCORES POINTS BY FOCUSING ON PSYCHOLOGY OVER GORE AND SHOWING A DARK SENSE OF HUMOR. IT'S ALSO WORTH NOTING THAT THE FINALE INVOLVES ONE OF THE MOST CREATIVE METHODS OF DISPATCHING A VILLAIN EVER SHOWN IN A MOVIE. YOU CERTAINLY WON'T SEE IT COMING, THAT'S FOR SURE.

ROTHSTEIN ALSO WROTE FOR THE HITCHHIKER PAY-CABLE SERIES.

JUST BEFORE DAWN (1980)
FIVE ADVENTURE-SEEKING CITY TYPES (INCLUDING BRIAN DE PALMA FAVORITE GREGG HENRY) WANDER INTO THE WOODS TO CHECK OUT OF A PIECE OF LAND OWNED BY ONE OF THE GROUP. SOON ENOUGH, THEY ARE GETTING MORE ADVENTURE THAN THEY WANTED THANKS TO A MACHETE-WIELDING MENACE. GEORGE KENNEDY ALSO SHOWS UP AS A FOREST RANGER WHOSE EARLY WARNINGS ARE IGNORED. JEFF LIEBERMAN'S FILM IS USUALLY LUMPED IN THE SLASHER GENRE, BUT IT'S ACTUALLY A SOUTHERN

HUMAN EXPERIMENTS

The victims: young female inmates

The nightmare has begun—

JUST BEFORE DAWN

Released by Picturmedia, Ltd.
© MCMLXXI Oakland Productions Ltd.

MIDNIGHT (1982)
THIS BACKWOODS SHOCKER WAS MADE BY JOHN RUSSO, CO-WRITER OF NIGHT OF THE LIVING DEAD. A TEEN GIRL RUNS AWAY FROM HOME AFTER KNOCKING OUT HER LECHEROUS ALKIE STEPFATHER (LAWRENCE TIERNEY) AND FALLS IN WITH A PAIR OF SHOPLIFTING TRAVELERS. WHEN THEY CAMP OUT IN THE WRONG SMALL TOWN, THEY ARE ACCOSTED BY A FAMILY OF SATAN WORSHIPPERS COLLECTING SACRIFICIAL VICTIMS FOR THEIR NEXT CEREMONY. THE SCRIPT, DIRECTION AND MOST OF THE PERFORMANCES ARE AMATEURISH AT BEST, BUT THE MOVIE HAS A GRITTY DOWNBEAT FEEL, AN INTERESTING CATHOLIC INFLUENCE AND A RAW BUT EFFECTIVE LAST HALF-HOUR. TIERNEY FARES WELL AND JOHN AMPLAS TURNS UP AS A MEMBER OF THE SATANIC FAMILY. THERE'S ALSO SOME FLEETING FX WORK BY TOM SAVINI. WARNING: THE FILM'S CHINTZY YET CATCHY SOFT-ROCK THEME SONG WILL REMAIN STUCK IN YOUR HEAD LONG AFTER YOU SEE IT.

TRAPPED (A.K.A. BAKER COUNTY U.S.A. 1982)
A PACIFIST COLLEGE KID (NICHOLAS CAMPBELL) TAKES A TRIO OF YOUNG PALS INTO THE BACKWOODS FOR A CAMPING GET-AWAY WHERE THEY WITNESS A MURDER BY A PSYCHO HILLBILLY (HENRY SILVA) WHO DOMINATES HIS SMALL TOWN WITH AN IRON FIST. THIS EFFECTIVE CANADIAN SUSPENSE FLICK WAS PENNED BY MY BLOODY VALENTINE SCREENWRITER JOHN BEAIRD, AND DIRECTED BY WILLIAM FRUET, WHO ALSO HELMED DEATH WEEKEND. SOLID FILMMAKING AND A MEMORABLY WILD TURN FROM SILVA HELP IT RISE ABOVE ITS DERIVATIVE ORIGINS AND THE FINALE IS WORTH THE WAIT. IT WAS ALSO SHOT IN GEORGIA, WHICH AIDS THE ATMOSPHERE QUITE A BIT.

CHILDREN OF THE CORN (1984)
THIS ADAPTATION OF A STEPHEN KING SHORT STORY FOLLOWS A COLLEGE-AGE COUPLE WHO DISCOVER THAT A SMALL NEBRASKA TOWN HAS BEEN OVERTAKEN BY CHILDREN WHO HAVE KILLED THE TOWN'S ADULTS. THE BRATS WORSHIP A DEITY WHO LURKS IN THE

CORNFIELDS, AND COMMIT SUICIDE AT AGE 19 TO APPEASE IT. UP THERE WITH MAXIMUM OVERDRIVE AND THE MANGLER AS ONE OF THE WORST KING ADAPTATIONS. IT HAS A FEW EFFECTIVE SEQUENCES BUT PADS OUT ITS SOURCE MATERIAL INSTEAD OF EXPANDING IT, AND DOESN'T MAKE THE MOST OF ITS CRITIQUE OF FUNDAMENTALIST CHRISTIANITY. THE BEST SCENE HAS THE HERO DECRYING ANY RELIGION DRIVEN BY HATE, AND A PRE-TERMINATOR LINDA HAMILTON STARS WITH PETER HORTON AS THE COUPLE. STILL, IT HAS A FOLLOWING DESPITE ITS MANY FLAWS AND SPAWNED AN AMAZING SIX SEQUELS PLUS A T.V. MOVIE REMAKE.

裸の復讐

NAKED VENGEANCE

THE NEW KIDS (1985)

TWO RECENTLY ORPHANED ARMY BRATS (SHANNON PRESBY AND A PRE-FULL HOUSE LORI LOUGHLIN) MOVE TO FLORIDA TO LIVE WITH THEIR UNCLE, WHO OWNS A RUNDOWN TOURIST ATTRACTION CALLED SANTA'S VILLAGE. THEY SOON LOCK HORNS WITH A GANG OF EVIL HICKS LED BY DRUG-DEALER DUTRA (JAMES SPADER!), WITH SKIRMISHES ULTIMATELY ERUPTING INTO A BATTLE ROYALE FINALE AT SANTA'S VILLAGE. THIS IS PROBABLY THE BEST MOVIE THAT SEAN "FRIDAY THE 13TH" CUNNINGHAM EVER MADE, AND YET IS ONE OF HIS LESSER-KNOWN EFFORTS. THE MOVIE IS EXCITING, TIGHTLY-PACED, HAS A NICE SENSE OF DARK HUMOR AND OVERFLOWS WITH ENDLESSLY QUOTABLE WHITE-TRASH DIALOGUE (ADDED BY NOVELIST HARRY CREWS DURING REWRITES). EVEN BETTER SPADER'S PERFORMANCE AS THE VILLAIN IS A HIGH-CAMP THING OF WONDER (HE'S LIKE THE SLEAZE MOVIE VERSION OF A TENNESSEE WILLIAMS VILLAIN) AND THE FINAL SETPIECE IS ONE FOR THE EXPLOITATION RECORD BOOKS.

NAKED VENGEANCE (1985)

AFTER HER HUBBY IS SHOT TO DEATH IN A RANDOM CRIME, CARLY (DEBORAH TRANELLI FROM DALLAS) MOVES BACK TO HER SMALL-TOWN HOME TO STAY WITH HER PARENTS. UNFORTUNATELY, EVERY GUY IN THIS TOWN IS A HORNY MISOGYNIST AND A GROUP OF THEM GANG-RAPE HER AND THEN SHOOT HER PARENTS WHEN THEY WALK IN ON THE CRIME. SHE FAKES A CATATONIC STATE, AND USING A MENTAL HOSPITAL AS A BASE OF OPERATIONS, SHE PLOTS HER REVENGE. FILIPINO SCHLOCK-AUTEUR CIRIO SANTIAGO CLEARLY HAD I SPIT ON YOUR GRAVE IN HIS SIGHTS WHEN HE CRAFTED THIS HARD-HITTING EXPLOITATION RIFF. THE RESULTS ARE VERY ENTERTAINING, AND LUDICROUSLY UNSUBTLE. TRANELLI GIVES A GUTSY, COMMITTED PERFORMANCE, AND ALSO SINGS THE FILM'S ENDEARINGLY KITSCHY POWER-BALLAD THEME SONG.

Keep telling yourself — It's only a Nightmare!

THE BACKWOODS MASSACRE

IN COLOR [R]

an Independent-International release

copyright MCMLXXXV Independent-International Pictures Corp.

"BACKWOODS MASSACRE" -- ALSO KNOWN AS "MIDNIGHT"

BULLIES (1986)

WHEN THE MORRISES MOVE TO A SMALL TOWN TO RUN A GROCERY STORE, THEY QUICKLY RUN AFOUL OF THE CULLEN CLAN. THIS NASTY BUNCH USES INTIMIDATION AND VIOLENCE TO KEEP THE ENTIRE TOWN IN CHECK. MATT (JONATHAN CROMBIE), THE DISAFFECTED SON OF THE MORRISES, FALLS IN LOVE WITH THE CULLENS' OUTCAST DAUGHTER (OLIVIA D'ABO) AND IS ULTIMATELY GOADED INTO FIGHTING BACK IN A STRAW DOGS-ESQUE FINALE. THIS IS A QUITE STRAIGHTFORWARD BUT WELL-CRAFTED THRILLER WITH STURDY DIRECTION BY CANADIAN EXPLOITATION VET, PAUL LYNCH (PROM NIGHT). KEEP AN EYE PEELED FOR DEHL BERTI, WHO PROVIDES A STRONG PERFORMANCE AS A RECLUSIVE INDIAN WHO BEFRIENDS THE YOUNGEST MORRIS KID AND TEACHES HIM THE MANLY SKILLS HIS REAL FATHER DOESN'T KNOW.

ABDUCTED (1986)

A COED JOGGER (ROBERTA WEISS) GETS KIDNAPPED BY A CRAZED MOUNTAIN MAN WHILE JOGGING NEAR THE EDGE OF THE WILDERNESS. HE'S DETERMINED TO MAKE HER HIS SUBSERVIENT BITCH, AND SHE'S DETERMINED TO ESCAPE. THERE'S A TWIST AT THE MIDWAY POINT THAT ALTERS THE DYNAMICS, BUT THAT'S BEST LEFT UNSPOILED. THIS MINIMALIST CAT-AND-MOUSE TALE FROM BOON COLLINS IS UNIQUE BECAUSE IT DOWNPLAYS SLEAZE IN FAVOR OF CHARACTER STUDY AND PSYCHOLOGICAL THRILLER ELEMENTS. THE GAMBIT WORKS BECAUSE WEISS IS LIKEABLY COOL UNDER PRESSURE, AND KING-PHILLIPS IS MEMORABLY CREEPY AS HER CAPTOR. THE FILM ALSO USES ITS CANADIAN MOUNTAIN AND FOREST LOCATIONS TO SUPERB EFFECT. LATER FOLLOWED BY A SEQUEL THAT PIT KING-PHILLIPS AGAINST A TRIO OF FEMMES.

HUNTER'S BLOOD (1987)

A CITY-BRED FIVESOME GO ON A HUNTING TRIP IN A WILDERNESS AREA THAT ONE OF THE GROUP OWNS. THEY SOON DISCOVER SAID LAND IS INHABITED BY A FAMILY OF POACHERS WHO SELL PURLOINED GAME TO BURGER JOINTS AND END UP IN A LIFE-AND-DEATH STRUGGLE AS THEY TRY TO ESCAPE THE WOODS. THIS LATE-PERIOD DELIVERANCE THROWBACK ISN'T NEARLY AS GOOD AS ITS CULT REP SUGGESTS BECAUSE THE PACE IS TOO SLUGGISH AND THE SECOND HALF MAYHEM TOO WEAKLY ORCHESTRATED. DESPITE THE SLACK SPOTS, IT'S AN ACCEPTABLE TIME-KILLER.

A CLOSING NOTE FROM YOUR HUMBLE REVIEWER: PLEASE DROP BY MY BLOG -- WWW.SCHLOCKMANIA.COM -- AND YOU WILL FIND FULL-LENGTH REVIEWS OF ALL THE FILMS COVERED IN THIS ARTICLE. HAPPY READING AND BE CAREFUL IN SMALL TOWNS.

DON GUARISCO .2010.

AFTER DELIVERANCE COMES...

HUNTERS BLOOD

18

THE ULTIMATE TEST OF SURVIVAL

FURTHER PROOF OF THE ENDURING FASCINATION WITH INCARCERATED BABES, THE MOST POPULAR EPISODE OF *CHARLIE'S ANGELS* IS THE ONE WHERE THEY ALL GO TO PRISON,

ANGELS IN CHAINS

OUR HIGHEST RATED SHOW EVER. THE NETWORK WOULD RUN IT *EVERY* WEEK IF YOU'D ALLOW THEM TO.

LEONARD GOLDBERG
EXECUTIVE PRODUCER

AND WHY NOT? THIS ONE HAS IT ALL.

BARK
WOOF

MERELY THE FOURTH ANGELS EPISODE EVER, THE SHOW OPENS LIKE A CLASSIC B-GRADE DRIVE-IN FEATURE, WITH A BUXOM PRISONER TRYING TO ESCAPE.

LAUREN TEWES (FROM *THE LOVE BOAT*) PLAYS THE MISSING CONVICT'S HALF-SISTER WHO HIRES THE ANGELS TO FIND HER.

FARRAH FAWCETT'S NIPPLES REMAIN VERY ERECT THROUGHOUT THIS EPISODE. IN THE FIRST SCENE WE SEE HER, SHE IS LOOKING DOWN AT HER OWN HARD NIPPLES. REALLY!

THE ANGELS DRIVE TO PINE PARISH COUNTY AND SPEED DOWN A LOCAL HIGHWAY IN ORDER TO BE ARRESTED.

THE SHERIFF PLANTS A BAG OF PILLS *AND* POT IN THE ANGELS' CAR AND THEY ARE SENT TO PRISON.

HEAD GUARD MAXINE IS PLAYED BY MARY WORONOV WHO WAS ALSO THE PRINCIPAL IN *ROCK N' ROLL HIGH SCHOOL*.

A YOUNG KIM BASINGER PLAYS ONE OF THE OTHER INMATES.

MAXINE SMIRKS SADISTICALLY AS SHE DEMANDS *THE* ANGELS OPEN THEIR TOWELS TO BE SPRAYED WITH DISINFECTANT.

THE SUBJUGATION & HUMILIATION OF THE ANGELS IS INTENSE & SUSTAINED.

ARE THERE DRESSING ROOMS?

WHAT DO YOU THINK THIS IS? SAKS FIFTH AVENUE? NOW *DROP* THE TOWELS & GET TO IT.

THE GIRLS ARE MADE TO DRESS UP FOR A 'PARTY' AT 'THE HOUSE'

THEY AND OTHER INMATES ARE FORCED TO ACT AS 'ESCORTS' FOR WEALTHY PARTY GOERS.

FARRAH ACTING

GRAB THE WHEEL!

THE ANGELS ESCAPE BY CHOKING TWO COPS WITH THEIR MANACLES.

STILL ACTING HARD

NEXT THEY FLEE ON FOOT, CHAINED TOGETHER LIKE THREE SIDNEY POITIERS IN 'THE DEFIANT ONES'. THEY SPLASH SEXILY THROUGH THE SWAMP IN THEIR FLARED PRISON DENIM.

IN THE END, BOSLEY HIRES KIM BASINGER AS A RECEPTIONIST! WAY TO GO, BOSLEY!

TED DAVE/006

96

I Want More

(1970, B&W) aka Sock It to Me with Flesh
Directed and produced by Jack Beap

"THEY ALL WANT MORE. THAT'S WHAT OUR STORY IS ABOUT... HOW THEY GET IT."

MAN, THOSE PSEUDO-MONDO SEXPLOITATION 'DOCUMENTARIES' OF THE LATE '60S AND EARLY '70S REALLY CRACK ME UP. YOU KNOW THE KIND; WHERE VIEWERS ARE INTRODUCED TO "WAY OUT" SEX SCENES AND SWINGERS VIA STAGED INTERVIEWS AND OBVIOUSLY FAKED HIDDEN CAMERA FOOTAGE? WELL JACK BEAP'S **I WANT MORE**, MAY WELL BE MY FAVORITE OF THE BUNCH, DESPITE BEING A LESSER KNOWN EFFORT IN AN ODD SUBGENRE OF SEXY PRE-HARDCORE FILMIC DECEPTION.

WE ARE INTRODUCED TO THE SKYLINE OF HOLLYWOOD BY A 'DOCUMENTARIAN', WHO IS PROBABLY BEAP HIMSELF. OUR GUIDE STUMBLES OVER HIS DELIVERY AND REPEATS HIMSELF A FEW TIMES, EITHER THROUGH INCOMPETENCE, OR AS A SLY METHOD OF CONVINCING THE VIEWER OF THE RAW REALITY OF WHAT IS TO COME. HE EXPLAINS THAT THE SUNSET STRIP IS JUST THE PLACE FOR ANYONE TO GET THEIR "SEXUAL KICKS" FULFILED BY ANSWERING AN AD IN A 50 CENT UNDERGROUND SEX PAPER, AND THAT EVEN THOUGH "THE BIG HOLLYWOOD PRODUCERS ARE TOO SCARED", HE'LL BE WITH US EVERY STEP OF THE WAY - GIVING AN UNEROTIC AUDIO EXPLANATION OF EVERYTHING WE'RE ABOUT TO SEE... AS WE'RE SEEING IT.

THE FIRST EXPOSE DISHES THE DIRT ON A SEXY YOUNG REDNECK COUPLE FROM NORTH CAROLINA WHO COLLECT $100 PAYCHEQUES FOR DRYHUMPING EACH OTHER IN THE NUDE AT UPSCALE PARTIES. HAROLD AND SALLY JO EVEN HAVE SEX WITH SALLY'S COUSIN IN PUBLIC "CUZ SHE'S KIN AND WE LIKE EACH OTHER". OUR GUIDE VOICES HIS BREATHLESS AMAZEMENT AT THE SITUATION, AND WE MOVE ON.

THE NEXT PIECE IS PERHAPS THE MOST ASTONISHING, IF ONLY FOR THE JAW-DROPPING LOCATION BEAP AND HIS BOYS FOUND TO SHOOT IN. WE'RE INTRODUCED TO WHAT HAS GOTTA BE ONE OF THE COOLEST LOOKING ABANDONED HOMES I'VE EVER SEEN, AND IT'S CLEAR THAT THE RUNDOWN AND GRAFFITTI-ED SQUAT SUPPOSEDLY BELONGING TO A TOUGH BIKER GANG CALLED 'THE DEVIL'S DISCIPLES', IS NOT A CHEAP SET, BUT AN ABANDONED MANSION IN THE HEART OF L.A. WHEN THE NARRATOR ASKS A GANG MEMBER WHY A NUDE GIRL IS RIDING A MOTORCYCLE AROUND THE OVAL TWO TIERED FOYER HALLWAY, HIS FLIPPANT RESPONSE OF "HEY MAN, SHE'S JUST PRACTICING!" IS ALONE WORTH THE PRICE OF ADMISSION.

INTERESTINGLY, THERE WAS AT THE TIME A NOTORIOUS BIKERGANG (WHO WERE RESPONSIBLE FOR AS MANY AS 63 MURDERS) UNDER THE SAME NAME IN MONTREAL, QUEBEC - BUT I DOUBT THAT EVEN THEY SCREWED THEIR GIRLS WHILE IN BED WITH THEIR HARLEYS, PORKED STONED GROUPIES WHILE SITTING IN THE KITCHEN SINK, AND ADMITTED FREELY TO GRAVEROBBING - ALL OF WHICH THESE LEATHER CLAD GREASEBALLS DO.

OTHER VIGNETTES INCLUDE: A BLONDE NYMPHOMANIAC HITCHHIKER WHO TAKES ON 4 DUDES WHILE A VERY UNHIDDEN "HIDDEN CAMERA" CAPTURES THE ACTION, THE FAKE FRENCHMAN WHO CALLS HIMSELF "THE BEAVER BARBER" AND TRIMS HIS CLIENTS PUSSIES INTO HEART SHAPED DESIGNS, THE NAKED SHENANIGANS OF "THE LARGEST SHOWER IN CALIFORNIA", AND A DISTURBING FAT PERVERT WHO EATS "NOTHING BUT CHOPPED MEAT AND COTTAGE CHEESE" AND PAYS CUTE HIPPY CHICKS TO MAKE OUT IN A COFFIN THAT FLOATS IN HIS SWIMMING POOL (!??!)

AND JUST WHEN YOU THOUGHT IT COULDN'T GET ANY MORE HILARIOUS, THE BIG FINISH FEATURES A CAMERAMAN WHO MAGICALLY FILMS BOTH HIMSELF AND HIS CAMERA PEEKING IN ON A BEVERLY HILLS SWINGERS PARTY FEATURING MARSHA JORDAN OF **RAMRODDER** AND **THE TOY BOX** FAME. THE FOUR SECOND AUDIO LOOP OF DEMENTED SPED UP CROWD RHUBARB GIVES THIS QUIRKY PEEPING TOM SCENE A SICKENING, NIGHTMARISH ACID TRIP FEEL THAT MAKES FOR A PERFECT CAPPER TO A VERY ENJOYABLE SLEAZY VIEWING EXPERIENCE.

DVD FROM SOMETHING WEIRD.

HEY -- I JUST WANT TO PIMP MY WIFE FOR A SECOND HERE: REBECCA DART IS AN ANIMATOR + SHE WORKED ON **MISSION HILL** AND **PUCCA**! YAY!

PEOPLE DON'T NEED TO KNOW THIS!

CINEMA SEWER INTERVIEWS: JODY MAXWELL

Jody Maxwell, legendary erotic film and stage star, began her career in porn after being discovered at a University morality symposium by one of the speakers, Deep Throat director -- Gerard Damiano. As well as enjoying a career as a fuck-film star through the '70s, Jody had a sexy, stand-up, comedic stage show in her repertoire, and was a writer and columnist for national men's magazines like Cheri, Escapade, Capers, Partner, and Adult Cinema Review.

After many years plying her trade as a phone sex cum-queen, Jody has written a book detailing the hi-lights and lo-lights of the trade in her book 'My Private Calls', and is now working on a sequel to the book. Jody was also recently inducted to the Legends of Erotica Hall of Fame in Las Vegas. I caught up with the busy Miss Maxwell recently, and this was the shit that was slung:

Cinema Sewer: Hi Jody! Thanks for talking with me. So, you were one of the stars of this bizarre little satanic XXX roughie called THE DEVIL INSIDE HER, which was a nasty, scuzzy, little ass-blaster directed by Zebedy Colt back in the 1970s. For those not familiar with Zebedy Colt, can you give us a little rundown on who he was?

Burning with satanic lust, she had
THE DEVIL INSIDE HER

starring TERRI HALL
JODI MAXWELL
and ROD DUMONT as the "DEVIL"

co-starring
DEAN TATE • ZEBEDY COLT • NANCY DARE
with a special appearance by ANNIE SPRINKLES

X RATED   COLOR

produced by LEON DeLEON directed by HOWARD NORTH

JODY MAXWELL: ZEBEDY COLT, WHO BOTH WROTE AND DIRECTED THE MOVIE, AS WELL AS ACTED IN IT, IS A TERRIFIC GUY. HE IS SO VERY TALENTED IN ALL ASPECTS OF THEATER BECAUSE OF HIS OWN LEGITIMATE THEATER AND OFF BROADWAY BACKGROUND. HE ENJOYED SURROUNDING HIMSELF WITH TRAINED ACTORS AS MUCH AS POSSIBLE, AND SEVERAL OF US IN THE MOVIE CAME FROM LEGITIMATE THEATER BACKGROUNDS AS WELL. ZEB WAS PRETTY PERSUASIVE, TALKING TO THE PRODUCER AND GETTING HIM TO SPEND MORE THAN HE WANTED. ULTIMATELY, IT WAS A PRETTY GOOD SIZED CAST.

I ENJOYED WORKING WITH ZEBEDY. HE HAD A LOVELY HOME HE SHARED WITH HIS COMPANION VAL - WHO WAS PRETTY COOL TOO. SHE WORKED BEHIND THE SCENES, COOKING AND SUCH. A GREAT COOK! ZEBEDY HAD A PROPENSITY TO WRITE ON THE DARK SIDE. HE JUST LIKED TO STRETCH HIMSELF THAT WAY, HOWEVER, HE WASN'T REALLY DARK LIKE THAT. SINCE WE WERE DOING 35 MM STILL, NOT ALL THEATERS IN THE COUNTRY WERE WILLING TO RUN HIS MOVIES, BECAUSE HE WOULD GO RIGHT TO THE EDGE IF HE COULD. SOME THEATERS WERE JUST AFRAID OF TESTING THE WATERS. I RECENTLY HEARD THAT HE'S ACTING IN OFF BROADWAY PLAYS AGAIN.

CS: And you worked together as well in **UNWILLING LOVERS**... that was a freaky little deranged turd of a movie too. I loved it!

JM: UNWILLING LOVERS WAS ANOTHER MOVIE I LOVED WHEN I READ THE SCRIPT, AND IT WAS ONE OF THE MOST CHALLENGING MOVIES I DID. WE SHOT ON LOCATION IN THE POCONOS AND NEW YORK, AND I LOVED GETTING TO WORK WITH ROD DUMONT AGAIN. HE WAS SO DAMN NICE AND SO **HOT** TOO. HE COULD GIVE JOHN HOLMES A RUN FOR HIS MONEY, AND WAS MORE ATTRACTIVE IN EVERY WHICH WAY.

WE HAD A THREESOME, ZEB, ROD, AND ME IN THE FILM, WHICH INTRODUCED SOME MALE-ON-MALE EROTICA INTO A HETROSEXUAL MOVIE, WHICH WAS CONSIDERED A NO-NO UP TO THAT POINT. IT WAS AN INCREDIBLY HOT SCENE WHERE ZEB PLAYED A MENTALLY CHALLENGED PERSON WHO MIMICS PEOPLE THROUGHOUT THE MOVIE. ROD AND I ARE MAKING LOVE, AND HE COMES IN AND WATCHES US, WHICH INITIALLY BOTHERS MY CHARACTER. EVENTUALLY, AS A LARK, ROD'S CHARACTER LETS HIM JOIN US, AS ROD FIGURES HE CAN SHOW HIM HOW TO PLEASURE A WOMAN. HOWEVER, ZEB'S CHARACTER SEES ME SUCKING ROD AND HE ATTEMPTS TO COPY ME. ROD'S CHARACTER IS CLEARLY HETRO, AND ZEB'S CHARACTER DOESN'T KNOW ANY BETTER.

I FOUND THE WHOLE SCENE ACTUALLY QUITE EROTIC, AND I SERIOUSLY LIKE THIS
MOVIE A LOT. OF THE THREE OF US, I WAS THE ONLY ONE NOT NERVOUS
ABOUT THE SCENE! I GUESS WE KNOW WHY. THAT 3-WAY
CAUSED SOME THEATERS TO NOT RUN THE MOVIE, BUT
I SLIPPED INTO A THEATER IN SAN DIEGO AND
WATCHED THE AUDIENCE WATCH THAT
SCENE, AND THEY **LOVED** IT! OF
COURSE, I WAS DOING SOME PRETTY
HOT THINGS MYSELF!

YOU KNOW, I NEARLY DIED FOR
REAL MAKING UNWILLING LOVERS.
WE HAVE A CHASE SCENE WHERE I'M
RUNNING FOR MY LIFE, AND THEY
GIVE ME THESE LITTLE BALLET-TYPE
SLICK FLATS TO WEAR WHILE
RUNNING THROUGH A FOREST, ENDING
UP ON SOME ROCKS ABOVE A
WATERFALL OVER THE DELAWARE.
I HAD WARNED ZEBEDY AND THE
COSTUMER THAT ANYONE, ESPECIALLY
ME, RUNNING IN THESE SHOES
THROUGH THE FOREST AND ACROSS
WET ROCKS WAS AN ACCIDENT
WAITING TO HAPPEN. THEY JUST
LAUGHED, NOT TAKING ME SERIOUSLY.
WELL, BEING A PROFESSIONAL, I
SAID OKAY. THEY SAID "BE CAREFUL".
YEAH... RIGHT.

THE DAY THE SCENE IS TO BE SHOT
COMES, AND I HAVE ON STOCKINGS,
A DRESS, AND THESE DAMN SHOES.
I RUN FOR MY LIFE. I TRIPPED AS I RAN, BUT I KEPT RUNNING. SO FAR, SO GOOD... THEN I HIT
THE FIRST BOULDER, AND **ZOOM!** DOWN I WENT, AND SLID ALL THE WAY OVER TO THE EDGE
OF THE CLIFF - ABOUT TO GO OVER. THE CAMERAS ARE STILL RUNNING AND SOMEHOW I STILL
STAYED IN CHARACTER. MY CLOTHING WAS TORN. I WAS BRUISED AND BATTERED AND EVEN
A LITTLE BLOODY. I REMEMBER TO THIS DAY WHAT I WAS THINKING. "THEY HAD BETTER GET
ALL THIS ON CAMERA, BECAUSE I AM EITHER
GOING TO DIE, OR IF I DON'T DIE I AM **NOT**
DOING A SECOND TAKE ON THIS!"

ANYWAY, THEN HERE COMES THE KILLER WHO
DIDN'T REALIZE WHAT HAD HAPPENED TO ME
BECAUSE HE WAS STILL BEHIND THE TREES.
HE HAD **NO** IDEA THAT I BODY SKIDDED PARTLY
OVER THE EDGE, FIGHTING NOT TO GO OVER.
BUT THEN MY HERO COMES AND RESCUES ME,
AND HE KNEW I WAS REALLY INJURED. SO,
HE RESOLVES THE KILLER AND **CAREFULLY**
RESCUES ME. BOTH OF THESE MEN WERE
PROFESSIONAL ACTORS BEFORE PORN, AND
KEPT IN CHARACTER. CHUCK, THE HEAD
CAMERAMAN, WAS VERY HAPPY WITH US. ROD
DUMONT GAVE ME A MARVELOUS MASSAGE
AFTERWARDS AND CLEANED ALL MY WOUNDS TOO.

JODY SLUTS
IT UP!

JODY, ON NYC'S INFAMOUS "SHOW WORLD":

"I WAS THE FIRST TRUE PORN STAR TO DO
A STAGE SHOW AT SHOW WORLD. I USED
TO BE AMAZED TO STEP OUTSIDE
AND SEE ME SITTING
ON JAMIE GILLIS,
FUCKING, WITH MY
BREASTS BOUNCING UP
AND DOWN AS I WAS
RIDING HIM. I WAS
ALWAYS AMAZED THAT
PEOPLE WALKING DOWN
THE STREET COULD SEE
THAT. IT ALSO MADE ME
WEAR A HAT AND
SUNGLASSES. LOL!"

CS: Fuck... and that all shows up on screen too,
doesn't it? I remember seeing that rocky cliff in the
movie. That must have been pretty freaky. It's too
bad that UNWILLING LOVERS is so damn hard to
find. You don't see a lot of porn movies about retard
killers. Heh.. maybe that's why no one has made it
available. Zebedy is STILL too racy for America.

JM: MOST OF IT SHOWS UP IN THE MOVIE, BUT
NOT ALL. I REMEMBER THINKING AT THE TIME
THAT IT WOULD BE ONE HELL OF A HEADLINE.
DYING IN THE DELAWARE RIVER, DOING MY OWN
STUNTWORK IN A PORN MOVIE!

THE MOVIE'S WORKING TITLE WAS "MAMA'S BOY"
BY THE WAY. IT WAS ORIGINALLY RELEASED
UNDER THAT NAME. THE MOVIE HAS A STRONG
STORYLINE, A GOOD PLOT, AND A LOT OF SEX.
I LOVED THE SCRIPT, AND I LOVED THE ROLE.
IT WAS STRONG AND INTERESTING. IT WAS AN
ACTING ROLE WITH GOOD SEX. THIS MOVIE
COULD HAVE BEEN A BOOK OR AN R-RATED
MOVIE. TAKE OUT THE HARDCORE SEX, AND IT
WOULD HAVE HELD UP WELL. THERE IS A LOT
OF EXCELLENT SEX THOUGH, AND SOME
NECROPHILIA. THE PRODUCERS HAD HOPED THE
STORYLINE AND MOVIE WAS SO STRONG THAT
THE HOMOSEXUALITY WOULDN'T MATTER. OF
COURSE, IT DID MATTER IN SOME THEATERS,
ESPECIALLY IN THE SOUTH.

CS: Yeah, they hates them there faggots in the
south. He-yuk.

99

JM: WELL, FOR ZEBEDY THERE WEREN'T ANY RESTRICTIONS. OF COURSE, WE HAD ALL KINDS OF GREAT SEX IN THE MOVIE. ROD AND I HAD AN OUTSIDE SEX SCENE I REALLY LIKED A LOT! HE COULD GIVE HOLMES COMPETITION IN SIZE, ONLY ROD GOT A DEFINITE ERECTION. HE ALSO HAD INTERESTING TESTICLES, WHICH IS SOMETHING I HAVE NEVER SAID IN AN INTERVIEW BEFORE. HE HAD DELIBERATELY STRETCHED THEM OVER THE YEARS AND THEY HUNG DOWN ABOUT 5 AND A HALF INCHES. I HAD NEVER SEEN ANYTHING LIKE THAT PREVIOUSLY. I WAS AMAZED THE FIRST TIME I SAW THEM WHEN WE WERE FILMING **THE DEVIL INSIDE HER.**

CS: I'm always hearing from older porn stars that Holmes had problems staying hard. Actually, everything I've heard about Holmes says that in real life he was pretty pathetic. Have you seen WONDERLAND yet? It's pretty great, and got overlooked by a lot of critics and movie goers when it came out last year.

JM: I HAVEN'T SEEN **WONDERLAND**, SO I CANNOT COMMENT ON IT. IN FACT, YOU ARE THE FIRST PERSON TO TELL ME YOU HAVE SEEN IT. MY EXPERIENCES WITH JOHN ARE PRETTY LIMITED. I MET HIM ON THE EAST COAST IN THE '70s. HE HAD SOUGHT ME OUT AND SAID HE WOULD LIKE VERY MUCH TO WORK WITH ME. HE TOLD ME HE HAD WATCHED MY SUCKING ABILITIES IN SOME MOVIES AND HE THOUGHT THEY WERE THE GREATEST HE HAD EVER SEEN. HE SAID HE HAD EXPERIENCED LINDA LOVELACE, BUT HE WAS CONVINCED WATCHING ME THAT I WAS BETTER, AND WANTED TO EXPERIENCE IT FIRST HAND. HE ALSO ASKED ME OUT TO DINNER, BUT I VERY NICELY TURNED HIM DOWN, SO THAT WASN'T A PROBLEM. ANYWAY, WE DISCUSSED MAKING A ROBERTA FINDLAY MOVIE TOGETHER. JOHN ABSOLUTELY BEGGED ME TO CO-STAR WITH HIM, AND I WAS SERIOUSLY CONSIDERING IT. HOWEVER, JOHN AND I WERE BOTH EXPENSIVE, AND THE TWO OF US WERE MORE THAN THEY COULD AFFORD, ALTHOUGH THEY REALLY DID TRY. JOHN WAS VERY DISAPPOINTED.

JODY'S SENIOR CLASS PICTURE

CS: I would be too! Roberta Findlay was awesome! I love her old porn movies. **A WOMAN'S TORMENT** is fucking dope. I've seen it mentioned that you have one of the biggest clits in classic porn, but I never noticed that it was particularly huge or anything. Was I not paying attention?

JM: MANY HAVE FALLEN IN LOVE WITH MY CLIT. I WAS BORN WITH IT, AND CAME BY IT NATURALLY. THE FIRST TIME I SAW MY CLIT ON THE BIG SCREEN WAS AT THE WORLD PREMIERE OF **PORTRAIT** IN PHILADELPHIA, AND I COULDN'T BELIEVE IT! I KNEW IT WAS BIGGER THAN OTHERS, BUT THAT DROVE THE POINT HOME TO ME.

CS: Well shit, now I feel bad that I haven't been looking at your clit close enough.

JM: IT WAS ALWAYS AN ADVANTAGE BECAUSE IT WAS RIGHT OUT THERE, AND SO EASILY ACCESSIBLE! I HAVE NEVER HEARD ANY COMPLAINTS, AND I CAN ASSURE YOU I HAVE NEVER COMPLAINED! I THINK I WAS VERY LUCKY TO HAVE SUCH A WONDERFUL CLIT. I FOUND IT TO BE WAY MORE SENSITIVE TO TURN ON THAN THE AVERAGE WOMAN'S, BY MY OWN OBSERVATIONS, AS WELL AS FROM CONVERSATIONS WITH OTHER WOMEN TOO. LICKERS NEVER HAVE TO "DIG" TO FIND IT. MY CLIT WAS NEVER INTO HIDE AND SEEK.

CS: You did a couple double anal penetration scenes back during a time when it was pretty rare to see that. You didn't use a stand-in, did you? Was it painful to get double-stuffed in the poopchute?

YOU HEAR THAT, REBECCA?! 2 COCKS IN THE PUSSY, AND ONE IN THE ASS AT THE **SAME TIME!!** DO YOU THINK Y—

DREAM ON LITTLE MAN.

—DAMMIT!

JM: ACTUALLY, I HAVE A DOUBLE PENETRATION OF THE PUSSY WHILE AT THE EXACT SAME TIME I HAVE AN ANAL PENETRATION IN **THE DEVIL INSIDE HER.** THE GUYS WERE SO WELL ENDOWED, AND I'VE ALWAYS BEEN NOTED FOR HAVING VERY TIGHT ORIFICES. SO IT WAS INTERESTING.... TO PUT IT MILDLY. IT WAS ALSO THE MOST DIFFICULT SEX SCENE, LOGISTICALLY, THAT I DID. IT'S ON THE ALTAR, OUTSIDE, IN THE MIDDLE OF THE NIGHT IN THE WOODS, AND IT WAS DIFFICULT TO GET ALL THE BODIES IN PLACE. COINCIDENTALLY, I RECEIVED A FAN LETTER ONLY YESTERDAY ABOUT THAT SPECIFIC SCENE. MY FAN SAID IT WAS FAR AND AWAY THE MOST FASCINATING SCENE

HE'S EVER SEEN IN AN EROTIC FILM.

I DID A DOUBLE ANAL PENETRATION IN **SATISFIERS OF ALPHA BLUE**. I NEVER USED A BUTT-DOUBLE OR A STAND IN FOR ANYTHING. THAT WOULD HAVE BEEN AGAINST MY OWN SELF SET RULES! I FELT MY OWN SEXUAL ABILITIES WERE CERTAINLY WHAT PEOPLE WERE EXPECTING AND WHAT THEY SHOULD GET, OR I SIMPLY WOULDN'T DO THE SCENE.

You were telling me earlier about doing a movie called **EXPOSE ME LOVELY**, which was like some Raymond Chandler porn noir or something? I gotta see that one, it sounds freakin' amazing.

"A high speed trip to adventure and solid sexual high-jinks! Combines hard-boiled detective lingo with hard-core sex that never lets down."
— Al Goldstein

EXPOSE ME, LOVELY ...if you dare!

STARRING
JENNIFER WELLES
INTRODUCING
CARY LACY

Due to the shocking ending of this unusual film, no one will be admitted during the last 10 minutes.
DO NOT REVEAL THE ENDING

ADULTS ONLY ⓧ IN COLOR

WORLD 49th ST.
49th St. Bet. 6th & 7th Ave. • Opens 9:45 A.M. • C17-5747

SHOW TIMES: 10, 11:35, 1:05, 2:40, 4:15, 5:45, 7:20, 8:50, 10:30, 12 am

J.M: **EXPOSE ME LOVELY** WAS AN ARMAND WESTON MOVIE. UNFORTUNATELY, ARMAND WAS FILLED WITH TALENT AND DIED TOO YOUNG. I STAR IN THIS MOVIE WITH RAS KEAN AND OTHERS, AND IT'S A REALLY GOOD MYSTERY OF THE RAYMOND CHANDLER TYPE WITH MANY TWISTS AND TURNS. I PLAY AN ARTIST NAMED TERRY LAWFORD WHO DOES SCULPTURES OF MENS PENISES.

CS: You had a good time making it?

JM: OH, IT WAS WONDERFUL! THIS MOVIE HAS TO BE ON THE LIST OF ALL TIME GREAT XXX FILMS. IT'S AN EXCELLENT STORY, AND HAS GREAT SEX SCENES. SPEAKING FOR MYSELF, I FEEL I HAD ONE OF THE HOTTEST SEX SCENES EVER. I RECENTLY RE-WATCHED IT AND WAS BLOWN AWAY ALL OVER AGAIN. RAS AND I WERE REALLY HOT AND VERSATILE, AND WE GOT SO INTO IT THAT ARMAND STOPPED BREAKING INTO THE SEX AND LET US CONTINUE ON. I'M HAPPY TO SEE IT'S OUT ON DVD NOW. YOU CAN BUY IT ALL OVER THE NET.

CS: The guy credited as "Brother Theodore" who you co-starred with in **GUMS** from 1976... is that the same Brother Theodore who was infamous in New York for his spoken word performances?

JM: THERE WAS ONLY ONE BROTHER THEODORE, AND YES, HE WAS INFAMOUS FOR HIS SPOKEN WORD IN NEW YORK AND ALL OVER THE COUNTRY! HE WAS IN **GUMS**, AS WERE A LOT OF COMEDIC PEOPLE. IT WAS A VERY EXPENSIVE MOVIE, MADE BY A HOLLYWOOD GROUP THAT HAD ONLY BEEN INVOLVED IN NON-X FILMS, PREVIOUSLY. THE MOVIE WAS

A SATIRE OF **JAWS**, AND IS TOTALLY OUTRAGEOUS BEYOND YOUR WILDEST IMAGINATION. THE LATE TERRI HALL PLAYED THE MERMAID THAT 'ATE' HER VICTIMS TO DEATH. ROBIN, I KNOW THAT YOU WOULD LOVE THIS MOVIE!

CS: I believe it, girlfriend! It sounds nuts from what I've heard. It's too bad it's nearly impossible to find.
I once saw this old photo of you with Warren Beatty at the Democratic national convention. What were you doing there? Which election was that?

JM: OH, WARREN BEATTY AND ME! THAT WAS TAKEN AT THE DEMOCRATIC CONVENTION IN 1976. THAT'S WHEN I WAS A BABY IN THE BUSINESS. I WAS ON THE STAFF AT CHERI MAGAZINE AT THE TIME AND I COVERED BOTH NATIONAL POLITICAL CONVENTIONS AS FEATURE STORIES FOR THE MAGAZINE. WITH MY OWN PERSONAL BACKGROUND IN POLITICS SINCE I WAS LITERALLY A KID, IT WAS A THRILL FOR ME! STRANGELY, I DISCOVERED THE DEMOCRATS LIKED TO PARTY, BUT WHEN IT CAME TO SEX, IT WAS THE REPUBLICANS, HANDS DOWN.

CS: So, how connected with the adult industry are you now?

JM: WHEN I LEFT THE ADULT INDUSTRY, I STAYED PERIPHERALLY CONNECTED FOR YEARS BY THE FACT THAT I BEGAN DOING FANTASY PHONE SEX CALLS AS AN EROTIC FILM STAR FOR A COMPANY THAT HAD A FEW OTHER STARS. I HAD CALLS FOR 12 YEARS, WHICH HAS TO BE SOME KIND OF RECORD! THE STARS DID THE CALLS FROM WHEREVER WE PLEASED, NOT FROM SOME OFFICE — SO IT WAS EASY TO KEEP IT UP, NO PUN INTENDED. OF COURSE SINCE I HAVE COME OUT WITH MY BOOK "MY PRIVATE CALLS", I FIND MYSELF SOMEWHAT MORE CONNECTED TO THE ADULT INDUSTRY AGAIN. IT'S A STRANGE FEELING.

CS: Well, Your new book sounds pretty cool! And you've got a website?

JM: MY WEBSITE IS WWW.JODYMAXWELL.COM WHERE PEOPLE CAN ORDER MY BOOK OR CONTACT ME. I'M VERY PROUD OF "MY PRIVATE CALLS". I KEPT DETAILED NOTES OF ALL MY CALLS THAT I HAD, WHICH FILLED OVER 60 LARGE JOURNALS. I WROTE IN TOTAL DETAIL ABOUT SOME OF THOSE CALLS, WITH NOTHING CENSORED OR LEFT OUT, EXCEPT THE CALLERS REAL NAMES. THEN THERE'S THE SEX! I DEFINITELY TELL WHAT THE CALLS

ARE REALLY LIKE, NOT WHAT PEOPLE ASSUME THEY ARE. I ALSO WROTE SOME AUTOBIO MATERIAL IN EVERY CHAPTER, IN BETWEEN CALLS, EXPOSING SOME OF MY PROFESSIONAL LIFE AND SOME OF MY PERSONAL LIFE.

CS: That sounds pretty cool. Honestly, I've never done the phone sex thing myself, but I'm totally curious what it would be like to have these dudes calling you and expecting you to make them cum. Is it pretty easy to gauge what a stranger wants just from the way he talks to you?

JM: IN THE BOOK I TALK ABOUT GETTING FAMILIAR WITH THE GUY AT THE BEGINNING OF THE CALL, IF POSSIBLE, SO THAT WOULD HELP ME FIGURE OUT WHERE TO GO WITH HIM. GAUGING WHEN A STRANGER WOULD CUM TAKES PRACTICE.

CS: I'll bet. I can't even tell when I'm gonna cum sometimes. It's just like - BLAM!

JM: MOST MEN WOULD SAY SOMETHING, OR GROAN, OR BREATHE AUDIBLY OVER THE PHONE LINE AND I COULD JUST TELL WHAT WAS HAPPENING. THERE WERE THOSE, OF COURSE, WHO NEVER UTTERED A SOUND OR BREATH DURING THE SEX PART AND I HAD TO TRY AND FIGURE IT OUT WITHOUT THE FEEDBACK. THEY WERE TOUGHEST. I GOT REALLY GOOD AT GAUGING WHAT MEN WANTED BY THE WAY THEY TALKED TO ME. OF COURSE, MANY, MANY MEN (AND I ENCOURAGED THEM TO DO SO) TOLD ME WHAT THEY WANTED IN DETAIL. ONE OF MY MOST FACINATING GUYS WAS THE CALLER I NICKNAMED "PECAN PIE". HIS CALLS BECAME MORE INVOLVED AND COMPLICATED OVER THE YEARS. IN HIS CASE, HE GAVE ME ALL THE PLAYERS AND I WOULD CREATE A TALE FOR HIM INVOLVING THE PEOPLE. HE HAD SPECIFIC PEOPLE, PLACES, AND TIMES.

AGAIN, READERS CAN GET "MY PRIVATE CALLS" THROUGH MY SITE: WWW.JODYMAXWELL.COM

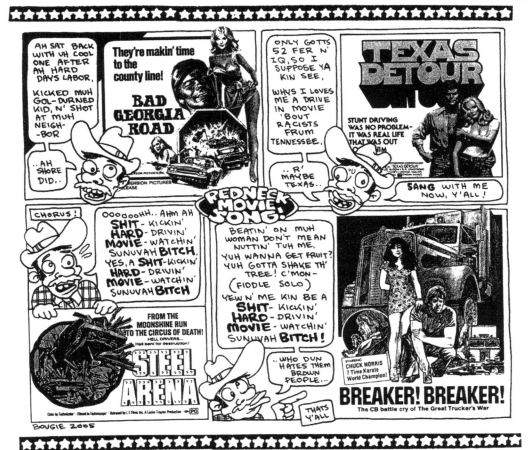

RANDOM TRIVIA !!!

* THE RED FONT USED FOR THE OPENING TITLE SEQUENCE OF PULP FICTION (1994) IS THE SAME USED IN LEE FROST'S POLICEWOMEN (1974).
* ACCORDING TO ROSIE PEREZ, THE REASON YOU DON'T SEE HER FACE DURING HER NUDE SCENE IN DO THE RIGHT THING (1989) IS BECAUSE SHE FELT EXPLOITED AND WAS SOBBING.
* WHEN CAVEMAN (1981) PLAYED AT DRIVE-INS IN AUSTRALIA, EVERY CAR WAS GIVEN A PAMPHLET WITH JUST OVER 30 "CAVEMAN WORDS" AND THE ENGLISH LANGUAGE TRANSLATION FOR EACH.

CHICKS IN CHAINS

THE FILIPINO W.I.P. CINEMA OF ROGER CORMAN

...JUST ANOTHER DAY ON THE INSIDE, DOING HEROIN AND PAINTING YOUR NAILS...

IN THE EARLY '70S, ROGER CORMAN GREW WEARY OF MAKING BIKER GANG FILMS AND FIGURED THAT SHOOTING WOMEN IN PRISON MOVIES IN THE PHILIPPINES COULD ALLOW HIM TO MAKE FILMS CHEAPER, IN BETTER WEATHER, MORE EXOTIC LOCATIONS, AND WITH A CAST AND CREW WILLING TO WORK FOR PEANUTS IN HOPES OF MAKING IT BIG IN THE INTERNATIONAL MARKET. AND AFTER HE HIRED A YOUNG U OF C FILM STUDENT NAMED JACK HILL (A CLASSMATE OF FRANCIS FORD COPPOLA), AND LOCAL FILIPINO DIRECTORS EDDIE ROMERO AND GERRY DE LEON TO WORK FOR AMERICAN INTERNATIONAL PICTURES, CORMAN WOULDN'T EVEN HAVE TO DO ANY WORK TO REAP THE REWARDS.

CORMAN'S PLAN (NOW CALLED "OFFSHORING") WAS REVOLUTIONARY, AND HIS THINKING WAS THAT IF US PRISONS WERE BAD, THEN THOSE IN THE PHILIPPINES MUST BE TRULY SHOCKING AND SICKENING IN THE TREATMENT OF THEIR INMATES. TRUE, GRINDHOUSE THEATER-GOERS WERE QUITE ACCUSTOMED TO POORLY LIT FILMS -- THE KIND THAT CAMOUFLAGE ALL THE HORRID PRODUCTION VALUES AND VISUAL LAMENESS SO COMMON IN LOW BUDGET GENRE FARE. BUT CORMAN'S FILIPINO SHIT? MAN, IT IS UNSUPPRESSED AND VOLUMINOUS IN COMPARISON! LOVELY TROPICAL SETTINGS, NATIVE ACTORS -- IT ALL LOOKED **SO** LEGIT.

AND STUNTS N' MASSIVE EXPLOSIONS? NOT A PROBLEM. AS JACK HILL ONCE TOLD FANGORIA MAGAZINE, "IF THEY WANT TO HAVE A MAN ON FIRE, THEY JUST SET A GUY ON FIRE WHO'LL TRY AND JUMP INTO THE THE WATER AS QUICK AS HE CAN." SOUTHEAST ASIA, BABY... WHERE LIFE IS CHEAP!

IT WAS AN IDEA TOO GOOD TO FAIL. WITHIN 300 DAYS IN A MONEYMAKING FLOOD OF LOW BROW EXCELLENCE, CORMAN HAD 4 OF THESE FUNKPIES COOKED UP -- WHICH ARE SOME OF THE MOST ENTERTAINING WIP FEATURES TO EVER BE MADE BY AN AMERICAN PRODUCTION COMPANY.

THE BIG DOLL HOUSE (1971)

QUENTIN TARANTINO ONCE DEEMED JACK HILL "THE HOWARD HAWKS OF EXPLOITATION," CITING THE DIRECTOR'S ABILITY TO WORK IN SEEMINGLY ANY GENRE AND DELIVER A MIND BOGGLING WAD OF THRILLS EACH TIME. JACK IS IN MY TOP 5 FAVORITE DIRECTORS OF ALL TIME, AND IT'S BECAUSE OF FILMS LIKE THIS WHICH JUST EFFORTLESSLY BRING JOY-- AND NOT JUST BECAUSE OF ALL THE SKIN AND SLEAZE EITHER. THESE FILMS HAVE A NUANCED BRILLIANCE ABOUT THEM.

SOME OF THE SKIN IN QUESTION BELONGED TO SOON-TO-BE WIP QUEEN ROBERTA COLLINS,

they caged their bodies but not their desires

BIG DOLL HOUSE

COLOR

HERE IN HER ROOKIE OUTING. SHE'D LATER GO ON TO APPEAR IN NO LESS THAN THREE OTHER CLASSIC WIP FLICKS, BUT HERE SHE PLAYS ALCOTT, ONE OF THE PRISONERS JUDITH BROWN MEETS AFTER SHE'S TAKEN TO THE PRISON IN A LARGE, OBVIOUSLY HANDMADE, BAMBOO CAGE MOUNTED ON THE BACK OF A TRUCK. MMM HMM. LOVE THAT WHITE SLAVERY.

BUT IT'S BLAXPLOITATION SUPERSTAR PAM GRIER (IN HER FIRST SPEAKING FILM ROLE) WHO CLEARLY RULES THE ROOST AS SHE SINGS THE POWERFUL TITLE SONG, "LONG TIME WOMAN", (LATER REUSED IN JACKIE BROWN) AND PORTRAYS A RAW, TOUGH

LESBIAN PROSTITUTE WHO DESPISES MEN ("YOU'RE ROTTEN, HARRY. YOU KNOW WHY? 'CAUSE YOU'RE A MAN. ALL MEN ARE FILTHY.")

BROOKE MILLS PLAYS A REDHEAD JUNKIE CELLMATE, WHO, IN THE MIDDLE OF THE NIGHT SUDDENLY GETS UP AND TRIES TO SET OUR NEW FISH ON FIRE. WHEN JUDITH OBJECTS TO BEING SET ALIGHT, THE REST OF THE GALS JUMP HER AND STUFF HER HEAD DOWN THE TOILET WHILE ACCUSING HER OF BEING A SPY. JACK HILL REGULAR SID HAIG HEIGHTENS THE WEIRDNESS PLAYING A HORNY GOOF WHO BRINGS THE PRISONERS FOOD N' OTHER TREATS FOR THE PROMISE OF UNLOADING SOME NUTGLUE.

HEAD GUARD, LUCIAN (KATHRYN LODER) IS EERILY SCRAWNY WITH HER TOOTHPICK ARMS AND EXISTS MOSTLY TO REMIND US THAT ANOREXIA IS A HORRIBLE DISEASE, AND TO CHAIN N' TORTURE THE PRISONERS WITH SNAKES AND WHIPS. OH, AND TO WEAR SHORT SKIRTS. ALL OF THE STERN POWERFUL FEMALE GUARDS WEAR THESE REALLY TIGHT SKIRTS, BROWN KNEE HIGHS, CUTE LITTLE HATS, AND CARRY SUBMACHINE GUNS. IT'S QUITE AN IMPRESSIVE DISPLAY, ACTUALLY.

HILL LENSED THIS FAST PACED EXPLOITATION QUICKIE FOR $125,000 WHICH WAS QUICKLY RELEASED IN THE U.S. ALONG WITH FILIPINO DIRECTOR GERARDO DE LEON'S **WOMEN IN CAGES** -- BOTH SPEEDILY EARNING BACK THEIR PALTRY INITIAL INVESTMENTS MANY TIMES OVER FOR CORMAN'S NEW WORLD PICTURES COMPANY.

PROBLEMS WITH THE CENSOR BOARD FOR A FILM LIKE **THE BIG DOLL HOUSE** WERE TO BE EXPECTED, BUT IT REPORTEDLY DISMAYED EVEN THE HARDENED CORMAN WHEN HE SAT DOWN TO WATCH THE DAILIES, WITH DEPICTIONS OF VIOLENT SADISM, DEATH, HEROIN INJECTION, AND MALE RAPE ("GET IT UP, OR I'LL **CUT** IT OFF!!"). DESPITE THIS, THE FILM HAS A MARVELOUS CAMPINESS THAT NEVER SEEMS TOO HEAVY -- MAKING IT A PERFECT MOVIE TO PUT ON AT A PARTY. PROVIDING YOU'RE NOT THROWING A PARTY FOR A BUNCH OF WOMEN WHO WERE BRUTALLY MISTREATED IN JAIL, THAT IS.

WOMEN IN CAGES (1971)

WOW. LOOK AT THIS CAST AND CREW. I CAN ONLY ASSUME THAT THIS AND ~~THE BIG DOLL HOUSE~~ WERE FILMED BACK TO BACK, BEING AS THE ONLY DIFFERENCE IS THAT GERRY DE LEON NESTLES HIS BUMCHEEKS INTO THE DIRECTORS CHAIR THIS TIME OUT. PAM GRIER TAKES OFF THE INMATE GOWN AND SINKS HER TEETH INTO THE ROLE OF THE EVIL PRISON GUARD "ALABAMA". JUDY BROWN IS NO LONGER THE NEW FISH (INSTEAD PLAYING A MORE SEASONED INMATE) AND ROBERTA COLLINS BY CONTRAST NOW PLAYS THE ROLE OF THE EDGY JUNKIE. THE ONLY NEW PLAYER IN THIS ONE IS JENNIFER GAN WHOSE ONLY OTHER IMPORTANT CREDIT WAS AS MARLENE IN **NAKED ANGELS** (1969).

GRIER'S SADISTIC WARDEN IS AN EMBITTERED EX-CRACK WHORE FROM DETROIT, WHO IS NOW A POT-LOVING LESBIAN WITH A FULLY-EQUIPPED MEDIEVAL TORTURE CHAMBER... INCLUDING A GUILLOTINE!! THE FILM PLACES HER EVIL BLACK ASS IN THE POSITION OF SLAVE DRIVER, GLEEFULLY WATCHING OVER HER "WHITE BITCHES" TOILING AWAY IN THE PLANTATION UNDER A SCORCHING HOT JUNGLE SUN. ROLE REVERSALS LIKE THIS JUST MAKE ME GIDDY!

TWO OF THE JAIL BIRDS ATTRACT HER ATTENTION, HOT BLOODED REDHEAD GAN, AND "SANDY," AN EVEN REDDER-HEADED REDHEAD PLAYED BY JUDY BROWN. THE TWO GIRLS DON'T GET ALONG, SO PAM UTILISES HER DISTINCT FORM OF CONFLICT RESOLUTION ("SEND THEM TO THE PLAYROOM!") WHEN THEY GET INTO A KNIFE FIGHT.

NOW, LET ME DESCRIBE THIS TORTURE SCENE, 'CAUSE IT'S A GEM! (TRULY, TRULY, TRULY OUTRAGEOUS). FIRST, BROWN IS STRIPPED DOWN AND HAS HER BOUND ARMS YANKED OVER HER HEAD. SHE'S THEN LOCKED INTO SOME IRON BOOTS WHICH ARE THEN SLOWLY AND AGONIZINGLY SPREAD APART... AND THAT'S NOT EVEN THE TORTURE PART YET AS ALABAMA THEN ADVANCES ON SANDY'S **VERY** EXPOSED HONEY POT WITH A GLOWING HOT BRAZIER! HOLY CRAPTAXI!!

WITH THAT KINDA TREATMENT BEING DISHED, THE LADIES DESPERATELY WANNA ESCAPE WORKIN' DEM CANE FIELDS. BUT 'BAMA KEEPS HERSELF A GROUP OF SWEATY FILIPINO BANTITOS ON CALL; VILE DOUCHEBAGS -- SENT OUT LIKE A PACK OF LECHEROUS DOGS TO

ROUND UP ANY SISTERS DUMB ENOUGH TO TRY 'N MAKE A BREAK FOR IT. THE THING IS...
SHE PAYS THE SAME WHETHER THEIR VICTIMS COME BACK ALIVE OR DECEASED, RAPED OR
UNRAPED. YES, THINGS GET UGLY.

DESPITE THIS, AFTER ROBERTA COLLINS IS TORTURED VIA BEING STRAPPED NAKED TO A
GIANT SPINNING WHEEL AND STABBED WITH AN INTIMIDATING 4-PRONGED SPEAR (!?!?), OUR
GIRLS EVENTUALLY HATCH AN
ESCAPE PLAN AND GET WHILE THE
GETTING'S GOOD. THIS IS A REALLY
FUCKING **FUN** MOVIE, WITH THE OVER-
THE-TOP VIOLENCE PLAYED NOT FOR
SHOCKS, BUT FOR OUTLANDISH CAMP
EFFECT, AND ALABAMA'S WILD
COMEUPPANCE WHILE TIED TO A ROCK AND
SPOUTING RACIAL POLITICS ("A WHITE MAN
RAPED ME, A WHITE BITCH CAN   KILL ME!")
IS ONE OF THE MOST ENTERTAINING
SCENES OF GRIER'S CAREER.

THE HOT BOX (1972)
THIS HAS THE HONOUR OF BEING THE 1ST
FILM TO COMBINE THE NURSE AND WIP
PICTURE FORMULAS, ALTHOUGH IT'S ONE
OF THE LESS REMEMBERED FILMS
FROM EITHER GENRE. ONE WOULD
THINK THE PICTURE WOULD GET
SOME SORT OF REVIVAL SINCE
JONATHAN DEMME WAS CO-WRITER
AND 2ND UNIT DIRECTOR, BUT IT
REMAINS SOMEWHAT UNKNOWN.

DIRECTOR JOE VIOLA AND DEMME
HAD ALREADY WORKED FOR
CORMAN ON THE LOW BUDGET
BIKER FLICK **ANGELS HARD AS
THEY COME**, AND HERE DISH US
4 DELIBERATELY VACANT U.S.
PEACE CORPS NURSES (PLAYED
BY MARGARET MARKOV AND 3
NOBODIES) KIDNAPPED BY "THE
PEOPLES ARMY", WHICH IS JUST
ANOTHER NAME FOR "INDIGENT
POSSE OF INEBRIATED NITWITS IN
SOME GENERIC BANANA REPUBLIC". THE
NURSES ARE FORCED TO SPEND MOST OF
THEIR INCARCERATION TOPLESS, AND
SLOWLY BECOME DANGEROUS GUN
TOTING RADICALS ONCE THEY ARE
HIPPED TO THE SIMILARITIES BETWEEN THE
CORRUPT LOCAL GOVERNMENT AND THE
NIXON ADMINISTRATION BACK HOME.

THE HOT BOX

A tropical torture chamber where anything can happen.

THEIR GUNS ARE HOT AND THEIR BODIES HARD.

Starring
ANDREA CAGAN · MARGARET MARKOV
RICKEY RICHARDSON · LAURIE ROSE
CARMEN ARGENZIANO · CHARLES DIERKOP
METROCOLOR

SUFFICIENTLY CONVINCED OF THE
RIGHTEOUSNESS IN BLOODLETTING FOR THE CAUSE OF REVOLUTION, OUR BITCHES BUST
SOME ASS! THE AIR-HEADS UNLEASH ALL HELL ON THOSE WHO WOULD STAND IN THE
WAY OF THEIR RADICAL LEFT WING POLITICS, AS THEY STOMP THROUGH THE JUNGLE, GUNS
IN HAND. OH, DID I MENTION THE NURSES TAKE OFF THEIR SHIRTS A LOT? THIS IS
A TON OF FUN, ESPECIALLY WATCHING THE FILM CHURN OUT PREACHY 1960s STYLE
LIBERAL PROPAGANDA WHILE BLATANTLY EXPLOITING FEMALE FLESH AND
GLORIFYING VIOLENCE. I ♡ **THE HOT BOX** AND ALL OF ITS ECCENTRICITIES!

PAM GRIER

THE BIG BIRD CAGE (1972)
ONCE AGAIN, JACK HILL PULLS OUT ALL THE STOPS AS WRITER
AND DIRECTOR FOR THE FILM WITH THE AWESOME POSTER
TAGLINE: "WOMEN SO HOT WITH DESIRE THEY MELT THE CHAINS
THAT ENSLAVE THEM!"

OUR HEROINE, TERRY (ANITRA FORD, WHO WAS A PRIZE
SHOWGIRL ON "THE PRICE IS RIGHT" AND HERE MAKES HER
FILM DEBUT), IS AN ACTRESS WHO IS BOINKING THE PRIME
MINISTER OF SOME SHITTY LITTLE JUNGLE-INFESTED COUNTRY,
AND THE TWO GO OUT ONE NIGHT CLUBBING WHERE THE ON
STAGE MUSIC IS BEING PROVIDED BY MISS PAM GRIER AND
THE SCENE-CHEWING MR. SID HAIG!

THEY'RE LOUNGE SINGERS!? FUCK NO! GRIER AND HAIG
ARE SCUMMY REVOLUTIONARIES NAMED BLOSSOM AND DJANGO,
WHO BRANDISH WEAPONS AND PROCEED TO ROB THE PUBLIC
TO FINANCE UPROAR + TUMULT. DJANGO HAS THE BRILLIANT
IDEA OF SNATCHING TERRY FOR RANSOM (DOES KIDNAPPING EVER
WORK?) BUT THE PLAN TURNS TO SHIT WHEN THE COPPERS
MOVE ON IN -- POLICE WHO BLAME THE WHOLE ROTTEN
DEBACLE ON THE KIDNAPPING VICTIM -- TERRY!

THUS ANITRA FINDS HERSELF IN A RUSTIC JUNGLE PRISON OVERSEEN BY WARDEN ZAPPA, A VILLAIN **SO** EVIL, THE FIRST ACT WE SEE HIM COMMIT IS THE KICKING OF A PUPPY WHILE SCREAMING "NO FIGHTING! NO FORNICATION! WORK WORK! PUNISHMENT, PUNISHMENT!!" THIS IS A GUY WHO LOVES HIS JOB. ODDLY ENOUGH, ALL HIS FEMALE INMATES ARE IN THE AGE RANGE OF 17-23, WITH A DRESS CODE COMPRISED OF CUT-OFFS AND BRALESS TANK TOPS.

THE BIG BIRD CAGE ITSELF IS WORTHY OF AWE. THE DAMN THING IS THREE STORIES TALL, AND IS USED TO MILL SUGAR. THIS FORMIDABLE STRUCTURE WAS DESIGNED BY HILL'S FATHER, A BRILLIANT GENTLEMAN WHO ALSO DESIGNED THE DISNEY LAND CASTLE, AND WORKED FOR WARNER BROS. THE CAGE, WITH ITS DESTRUCTIVE CRUSHING GEARS, IS ACTUALLY USED AS PUNISHMENT FOR BACK TALKERS. DON'CHA JUST LOVE THE NAMES FOR THE PLACES OF PUNISHMENT IN THESE MOVIES? THE PLAYPEN. THE OVEN. THE BIRD CAGE. THE MADHOUSE. THE HOTBOX. THE MEAT LOCKER. THE SAUNA. THE HOLE? **AWESOME**.

I DON'T WANNA BLAB TOO MUCH MORE ABOUT THIS ONE -- SINCE IT'S BEST ENJOYED WITH A FAIRLY EMPTY SLATE -- EXCEPT TO SAY THAT IT'S LITTERED WITH EXPLOITATION GREATS SUCH AS FOXY MARISSA DELGADO, FUNKY CAROL SPEED, SWEATY VIC DIAZ (THE PETER LORRE OF THE PHILIPPINES), AND OF COURSE, THE AFOREMENT-IONED FORD, GRIER AND HAIG -- WHO STEALS ALL HIS SCENES IN TYPICAL HAIG-IAN FASHION. (LOOK FOR HIM AS "CAPTAIN SPAULDING" IN **THE DEVIL'S REJECTS**)

ALSO TAKE NOTE THAT AT THE BEGINNING OF THE FILM, WHEN ANITRA IS TAKEN TO THE PRISON BY BOAT, THE COVE THAT SHE'S DROPPED OFF AT IS THE SAME ONE SUBSEQUENTLY USED FOR THE KURTZ COMPOUND IN **APOCALYPSE NOW** (1979). THE DVD HAS JACK HILL AUDIO COMMENTARY. CHECK IT OUT.

BLACK MAMA, WHITE MAMA DESPITE WIDESPREAD BELIEF IN MOVIE GEEK CIRCLES, THIS AIP RELEASE WAS NOT, IN FACT, PRODUCED BY ROGER CORMAN — EVEN THOUGH AMERICAN INTNL. PICTURES FOLLOWED HIS FORMULA FLAWLESSLY. CORMAN, AFTER A LONG ASSOCIATION WITH THE COMPANY, ANGRILY CUT TIES AND STARTED A RIVAL PRODUCTION COMPANY CALLED NEW WORLD AFTER AIP PRESIDENT JIM NICHOLSON RE-EDITED 4 OF HIS MOVIES WITHOUT PERMISSION.

BUT AIP CONTINUED TO FLOURISH WITHOUT CORMAN'S INPUT, AND BLACK MAMA, WHITE MAMA -- WITH DIRECTOR EDDIE ROMERO AND A STORY BY JONATHAN DEMME (WHO WOULD MAKE HIS OWN WIP FEATURE, **CAGED HEAT**, TWO YEARS LATER) MARKS BLAXPLOITATION GIANT PAM

GRIER'S TRIUMPHANT RETURN TO AIP. SHE'D BEEN A TELEPHONE SWITCHBOARD OPERATOR FOR THE COMPANY PREVIOUSLY, BUT HERE GRIER IS A SOUL SISTAH IN FOR PROSTITUTION WHILE HER WHITE-AS-DRIVEN-SNOW COUNTERPART (MARGARET MARKOV IN HER BEST ROLE) IS A PATTY HEARST-STYLE POLITICAL REVOLUTIONARY.

MARKOV IS THE NEW FISH, AND OBVIOUSLY THE FIRST THING A NEW FISH WOULD DO BEHIND BARS IS GIT NEKKID AND HIT THE COMMUNAL SHOWERS -- WHICH YOU MIGHT EXPECT TO BE AN UNCOMFORTABLE AND SOMBRE EVENT FOR SOMEONE WHO HAD JUST LOST THEIR FREEDOM -- BUT HERE IT'S A TIME FOR FUN AND GIGGLES. ALL WHILE LESBIAN GUARD DENSMORE (PLAYED BY LYNN BORDEN, WHO CONTRACTED TYPHOID DURING THE CHOLERA AND TYPHOID EPIDEMIC THAT WAS SWEEPING THE AREA DURING FILMING) MASTURBATES AS SHE SPIES ON THE GOOFING SOAPED UP PRISONERS.

DENSMORE INSTANTLY TAKES A SHINE TO PAM, AND SUMMONS HER AFTER LIGHTS OUT FOR SOME SWEATY RUG MUNCHING. PAM REFUSES, AND LOOKS TO BE FACING THE WRONG END OF A SEVERE BEATING, BUT EVENTUALLY SHE AND MARKOV ARE SENT TO "THE OVEN", WHICH IS A LARGE METAL CLOSET IN THE MIDDLE OF A FIELD -- JUST BIG ENOUGH FOR TWO GIRLS TO STAND BACK TO BACK. IN THE SEARING TROPICAL HEAT THE WALLS GET RED HOT,

AND THE TWO NAKED BEAUTIES MUST STRUGGLE TO AVOID TOUCHING THEM (BURNT NIPPLES) WHILE WITHSTANDING THE SOARING TEMPERATURES.

THE EARLY '70s STREET SLANG, THE WILLINGNESS OF OUR GIRLS TO EXPOSE SWEATER PUPPIES, AND THE LIBERAL AMOUNTS OF JUICY BLOOD-LETTING MAKE THIS A CLASSIC, AND WHEN THE TWO ESCAPE -- SHACKLED AT THE WRIST, B.M.W.M. SUDDENLY TURNS INTO A VIOLENT REMAKE OF 1958's **THE DEFIANT ONES!** YAY!

GRIER'S IMPOVERISHED HOOKER CONSTANTLY QUARRELS WITH MARKOV'S REVOLUTIONARY RICH BITCH, AND CHAINED TOGETHER THE TWO MAKE THEIR WAY THROUGH A DANGEROUS JUNGLE WITH A PACK OF DOGS HOT ON THEIR HEELS. AND WHILE THIS WAS THE ROLE THAT CONVINCED GRIER TO TURN TO ACTING AS A SERIOUS CAREER (SHE WENT ON TO CULT STARDOM AND EVENTUAL POP-CULTURE ICON STATUS) MARKOV, AMID **NO** ACCLAIM, SADLY DROPPED OUT OF THE MOVIE BUSINESS IN THE MID-SEVENTIES. IT'S A SHAME, BECAUSE SHE WAS PRETTY FUCKIN' COOL.

IF ANYONE OF YOU KNOW MARGARET NOW, YOU CAN TELL HER I SAID SO.
—BOUGIE. 2006.

MARGARET MARKOV

GOTTA GET UP

GOTTA KEEP WATCHIN' WIP MOVIES!

MILES TO GO B-FOR I REST... GUH

STACK OF DVDS

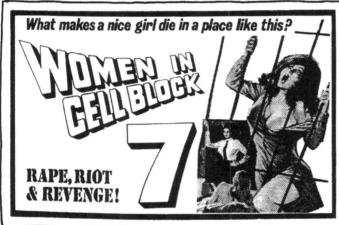

What makes a nice girl die in a place like this?

WOMEN IN CELL BLOCK 7

RAPE, RIOT & REVENGE!

WOMEN IN CELL BLOCK 7 (1973) PRETTY AVERAGE WIP OLDIE THAT DOES HAVE IT'S FINER POINTS -- SUCH AS SOME REALLY AMAZING CAR CHASE SCENES WHERE DUDES ARE DRIVING AT BREAKNECK SPEEDS THROUGH EUROPEAN BACK ALLEYS, CAVITY SEARCHES, PISSED OFF N' PROTESTING INMATES WHO GET HOSED DOWN BY THE GUARDS, AND DIALOGUE LIKE "TELL THAT BITCH SHE OWES ME A PILE OF DOPE. AND I BETTER GET IT, OR I'LL CUT HER TITS OFF." STARRING SWEDISH HOTTIE ANITA STRINDBERG.

Too Much Information STARRING: ME!

OK, I'VE ALREADY MENTIONED IT IN A COUPLE INTERVIEWS (ALWAYS AS THE ANSWER TO "WHAT ARE YOU MASTURBATING TO THESE DAYS?") BUT I WOULD LIKE TO STATE IT AGAIN SO THAT MY FAMILY, FRIENDS, AND MY POSTHUMOUS BIOGRAPHER ARE ALL AWARE: I TOTALLY GET OFF ON LESBIAN FACE-FARTING PORN.

WHAT IS LESBIAN FACE FARTING PORN, AND WHY WOULD SOMEONE BEAT OFF TO IT? WELL, I DOUBT YOU'D ASK, BUT I'M GONNA PRETEND THAT YOU'RE **DYING** TO KNOW. THAT'S HOW THIS GAME WORKS!

THIS OBSCURE GENRE OF XXX FIRST APPEARED ON THE SMUT SCENE IN THE EARLY 2000s, VIA A BRAZILIAN PORN COMPANY CALLED MFXMEDIA.COM. THEY ALSO SPECIALISE

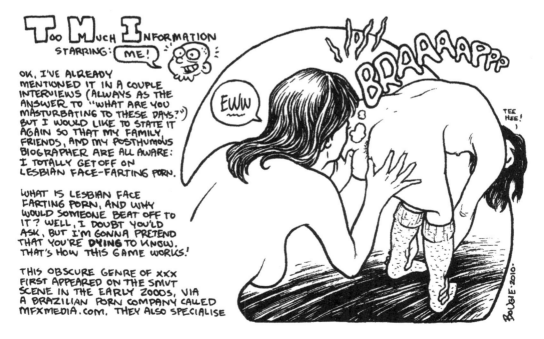

IN SCAT (EWWWWW!!), VOMIT (GROSS), AND SPIT (KINDA HOT), BUT NONE OF THAT DOES IT FOR ME LIKE THE FARTING DOES. WHO KNOWS WHAT IT'S ALL ABOUT, BUT THIS IS CERTAINLY ONE OF THOSE ODD MODERN SITUATIONS WHERE YOU HAD NO CLUE YOU FOUND SOMETHING TITILLATING UNTIL YOU HAPPENED ACROSS IT ONLINE.

IT CAN'T JUST BE ANY OL' DYKE FARTING INTO ANOTHERS MUG, THOUGH. THERE ARE SPECIFICS, PEOPLE. **ALWAYS** SPECIFICS. FOR WHATEVER REASON, IT HAS TO BE HUMILIATING AND FEATURE FORCED FACE-SITTING AND OTHER DEGRADING ASPECTS. THATS THE STUFF. THE VICTIM HAS TO WINCE AND GROAN IN DISGUST AS EACH FLATULENT ANAL BLAST ERUPTS IN HER FACE, OR ON HER QUIVERING OUTSTRETCHED TONGUE. THAT ADORABLE PINK PUCKER NEEDS TO INVERT AND VIOLENTLY BELCH ITS FURY AN INCH FROM HER KISSER, OTHERWISE THE BOUG CAN'T CUM.

JESUS, IS THIS WHAT IT'S COME TO? (MOPS FOREHEAD WITH HANDKERCHIEF) OK, ENOUGH OF THAT. LET US GET BACK TO IT. TALLY HO! MANY MORE MOVIES TO WATCH!

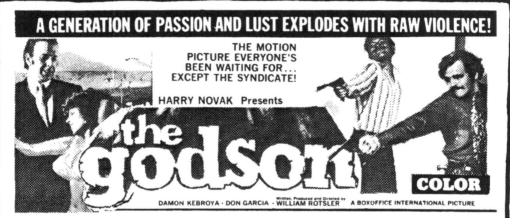

WILLIAM ROTSLER IS MY KIND OF PORNOGRAPHER. IN THE LATE '60S AND '70S HE WROTE BOOKS ON SMUT, EDITED THE INFAMOUS ADAM FILM WORLD MAGAZINE, AND DIRECTED 12 SOFTCORE MOVIES WITH TITLES SUCH AS **MANTIS IN LACE**, ~~AGONY OF LOVE~~, AND **STREET OF A THOUSAND PLEASURES**. HE EVEN HAULED HIS FAT BEARDED ASS OUT IN FRONT OF THE CAMERA AND GRABBED TIT ONCE AND AWHILE.

HUMOROUS AND HUMBLE ABOUT HIS PLACE IN SEX FILM HISTORY, ROTSLER SEEMS IN DISBELIEF THAT A YOUNGER GENERATION COULD FIND ANYTHING TO ENJOY ABOUT THE SKINFLICKS HE MADE. "THEY MUST BE BORED. LOOK AT WHAT TURNED YOUR FATHERS AND GRANDFATHERS ON! BORRRRRIIIING".

"REMEMBER WHEN I STARTED, THEY WEREN'T ALL THAT SURE YOU COULD ACTUALLY SHOW A NAKED FEMALE BREAST. EVERYONE WAS WALKING ON EGGS, UNSURE, UNCERTAIN. EVERYONE A PIONEER. NUDITY ON FILM AFTER ALL, BROUGHT ON THE SELF-CENSORSHIP BY HOLLYWOOD. THERE HAD ONLY BEEN THE UNDER-THE-COUNTER PORNOGRAPHY. THERE WAS NOTHING TO GO BY. IT SEEMS SILLY NOW, BUT NOT THEN."

IN MY OPINION, ROTSLER'S STANDOUT EFFORT IS A CRUNCHY LITTLE GUNS N' WHORES POT-BOILER CALLED **THE GODSON** WHICH WAS PRODUCED BY DRIVE-IN MAVEN HARRY NOVAK, AND RELEASED ON DVD BY SWV IN 2003. BEATING COPPOLA'S **THE GODFATHER** TO THE SCREEN BY A FULL YEAR, THE GODSON FEATURES JASON YUKON (WHO DID HARDCORE A YEAR LATER IN **SEX AS YOU LIKE IT**) AS AN UP N' COMING MOBSTER WHO PUTS A TARGET ON HIS CHEST BY TURNING ONE OF THE FAMILY'S MEAGRE BROTHELS INTO A HUGE SUCCESS. WHEN A DRUGGED OUT HOOKER OFFERS OUR BOY INSIDER INFO IN RETURN FOR KEEPING HER LITTLE SISTER OUT OF THE BIZ, AN OPPORTUNITY FOR ADVANCEMENT IS SEIZED WITH BLOOD-CAKED FISTS.

A BULLET-RIDDLED FINALE GORGEOUSLY SHOT IN AN ABANDONED DESERT TRAILER PARK IS A HIGHLIGHT, BUT FOR SCI-FI NERDS (ROTSLER IS ONE HIMSELF) THE STANDOUT SEQUENCE TAKES PLACE IN THE HOME OF AUTHOR HARLAN ELLISON, WHO APPEARS BRIEFLY STRADDLED ON A CHAIR BY TWO BUCK-NAKED SLUTS. THIS ORGY WAS SHOT IN ELLISON'S ABODE (WHICH IS NOTEWORTHY FOR ITS FUNKY DECOR) AFTER HARLAN AND ROTSLER TOOK IN A SCIENCE FICTION CONVENTION. YOU CAN BET I WAS SQUINTING MY EYES TRYING TO READ THE TITLES ON THE SPINES OF HIS VAST BOOK COLLECTION!

THERE IS A LOT TO LIKE HERE (JASON YUKON'S AMAZING WHITE MAN 'FRO AND MUTTON CHOPS FOR STARTERS) BUT THE GODSON IS A FRUSTRATING WATCH AT TIMES, AND REQUIRES PATIENCE. THERE IS A REALLY GRUNGY STORY ABOUT GANGLAND WHORING SOMEWHERE IN HERE, AND YET THERE APPEARS TO BE BITS MISSING. IT WAS CLEAR THERE HAD BEEN SOME MEDDLING GOING ON, BUT I WASN'T SURE WHERE IT HAD ORIGINATED. HAD SOMETHING WEIRD CUT SCENES OR USED AN OLD EDITED PRINT TO MAKE THEIR DVD, OR HAD NOVAK'S BOXOFFICE PICTURES FUCKED WITH THE MOVIE IN THE

EDITING STAGES? MAYBE ROTSLER HAD JUST RUN OUT OF MONEY OR WAS SIMPLY A TARD IN THE EDITING ROOM? I GOT MY ANSWER WHEN I READ A LISTING FOR THE MOVIE IN AN OBSCURE GUIDE TO SEX FILMS WRITTEN BY ROTSLER HIMSELF.

"FAST PACED MOVIE ABOUT AN AMBITIOUS HOOD, RUINED BY DISTRIBUTOR'S RECUTTING. ONE STAR OUT OF FOUR."
 -CONTEMPORARY EROTIC CINEMA (1973. BALLENTINE)

ONE COULD SENSE ROTSLER'S EMBITTERED STANCE WITH EVEN JUST THOSE FEW WORDS TO GO ON. FURTHER LIGHT WAS SHED ON THE MATTER IN 1994 WHEN MICHAEL WELDON RAN A PROFILE ON ROTSLER WRITTEN BY BILL WARREN IN PSYCHOTRONIC VIDEO, ISSUE 18.

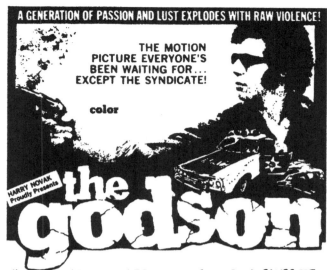

A GENERATION OF PASSION AND LUST EXPLODES WITH RAW VIOLENCE!

THE MOTION PICTURE EVERYONE'S BEEN WAITING FOR... EXCEPT THE SYNDICATE!

color

HARRY NOVAK Proudly Presents

the godson

"I WAS PROUDEST OF THE GODSON", HE TOLD WARREN. "I WAS TO DO A GANGSTER MOVIE FOR BOXOFFICE -- AND BY THAT I MEAN ONE WITH NAKED LADIES. 'THE GODFATHER IS COMING OUT SOON,' PETER PERRY TOLD ME. 'COULD YOUR STORY FIT THAT TITLE?' 'NO', I SAID, 'BUT I'LL WRITE YOU ONE THAT WILL.' PETER RUINED THAT PICTURE. I HAD EVERYTHING MOTIVATED, EVERYTHING COVERED, VERY NEATLY DONE. I DID MY CUT, GAVE IT TO PETE TO HAVE THE NEG CUT, AND TOOK A BUNCH OF MY FRIENDS TO SEE IT IN A THEATER. I ENDED UP WITH MY HEAD ON THE SEAT IN FRONT OF ME. HE HAD MOVED NAKED LADIES AROUND SO IT MADE NO SENSE, LEFT OUT STUFF, GRRRR! YOU WOULD BE WATCHING THE STORY, THEN CUT TO TWO PEOPLE SIMULATING SEX, THEN TO THREE, THEN BACK TO THE STORY. MADE NO SENSE."

I FOUND ROTSLER'S COMPLAINT VERY INTERESTING. TOO OFTEN WE SEE A FILM LIKE THIS AND JUDGE QUITE THE FILM IN SOME REALLY THE DIRECTOR HARSHLY IF IS LACKING WAY. I DO

EEOWTCH!! JASON YUKON TWISTS WHORE BOOBIES TO MAKE HIS POINT.

l'enfer des filles Soumises

Starring JASON YUKON · ORITA de CHADWICK · DAMON KEBROYA · DON GARCIA
Director of Photography PHILLIP DAKOTA · Music SOUTHERN AND HENSLEY · Written Produced and Directed by WILLIAM ROTSLER
A BOXOFFICE INTERNATIONAL PICTURE

THINK WE TEND TO FORGET HOW MANY COOKS ARE IN THESE KITCHENS, ANY ONE OF WHOM CAN FUCK UP A FINE FILM WITH A POOR DECISION.
·2010·
 -BOUGIE

CINCI-NAUGHTY

ART BY COLIN UPTON · WORDS BY ROBIN BOUGIE

WHEN A JURY IN CINCINNATI FOUND 30 YEAR OLD "TIP-TOP MAGAZINES" STORE OWNER SHAWN JENKINS GUILTY OF OBSCENITY FOR SELLING A COPY OF **MAX HARDCORE EXTREME VOL. 7** TO AN UNDERCOVER COP -- AND HANDED A 3 YEAR JAIL SENTENCE TO A MAN SELLING A DIRTY VIDEO THAT IS LEGALLY AVAILABLE FROM THOUSANDS OF RETAILERS AND ONLINE SOURCES, IT WAS BUT ONE OF MANY SUCH INCIDENTS IN THE CITY'S HISTORY.

WORST SALE EVER!

SHAWN JENKINS: (ARTISTS INTERPRETATION)

SO WHAT'S ON THE TAPE THAT'S SO HORRIBLE? WELL, IT'S THE FIRST EVER APPEARANCE OF THE "ASS-STRAW", A LONG CLEAR TUBE THAT MAX STICKS IN THE POOP-HOLE OF HIS CO-STARS SO THEY CAN SUCK A BALL-LOAD OF HIS CUM PLUS THE GLASS OF MILK HE POURS IN THEIR GAPING SHITHOLES.

DOOK DOOK DOOK

THE GIRLS HAPPILY SUCK THE CHUNKY BILE AND GIGGLE AS MAX GIRLS ARE WONT TO DO. IT'S ALL VERY PERVERSE YET CONSENSUAL -- JUST LIKE A GOOD FILTHY PORNO IS SUPPOSED TO BE.

"REAL CUTE!"

SHLURP

THE ACCUSED PREVIOUSLY SAW A MISTRIAL HANDED DOWN BECAUSE A JUROR COULDN'T MANAGE TO ACTUALLY STAY AWAKE WHILE HAVING TO SIT THROUGH A VIEWING OF THE MAX VIDEO, DESPITE ASSISTANT PROSECUTOR BRAD GREENBERG OPENLY PRONOUNCING IT:

"FLAT OUT VILE"

Z

HOURS BEFORE THE RULING WAS HANDED DOWN, A POLL WAS RELEASED THAT STATED THAT 70 PERCENT OF THE REGISTERED VOTERS IN CINCINNATI CONSIDERED ENFORCING OBSCENITY LAWS AS "IMPORTANT", AND AN ALARMING 44 PERCENT CONSIDERED IT "THE HIGHEST PRIORITY", ABOVE EDUCATION. ABOVE FEEDING THE HUNGRY. ABOVE STOPPING VIOLENT CRIME.

THE CITY IS PROUD OF IT'S PAYROLL OF CONSERVATIVE BULLIES, AND CINCINNATI SHERIFF SIMON LEIS HAS BEEN AT IT FOR YEARS. HE INSTIGATED THE PROSECUTION OF ROBERT MAPPLETHORPE IN 1990, ARRESTED DENNIS BARRIE (THE DIRECTOR OF THE OHIO CONTEMPORARY ARTS CENTER) AND MOST RECENTLY SPEARHEADED THE TRIAL OF SHAWN JENKINS.

MY EYES! MY EYES!

THE CITY'S PROUD ANTI-PORN HISTORY GOES BACK EVEN FURTHER TO THE INFAMOUS 1977 HUSTLER OBSCENITY TRIAL RECREATED IN 1996'S **THE PEOPLE VS LARRY FLYNT.** LARRY'S CONVICTION WAS OVERTURNED, BUT THAT DIDN'T STOP THE CITY FROM CONSTANTLY BRINGING FLYNT IN ON CHARGES, THE MOST RECENT BEING THE TRIAL IN WHICH A HUSTLER--OWNED RETAILER PLED GUILTY FOR SELLING XXX SMUT IN 1999.

SIR, IT'S CINCINNATI AGAIN...

OH, FOR FUCK'S SAKE!

THEN THERE WAS THE 1994 BUST OF "THE PINK PYRAMID" (THE CITY'S ONLY GAY AND LESBIAN BOOKSTORE) FOR ITS SALE TO UNDERCOVER COPS OF PIER PAOLO PASOLINI'S CLASSIC **SALO: 120 DAYS OF SODOM.** "SALO" IS A BITTER, GRUELLING POLITICAL ALLEGORY - NOT A HARDCORE PORNO. THE CITY NEVERTHELESS CHARGED THE OWNER WITH THREE COUNTS OF PANDERING OBSCENITY.

HMM

WELL, IT'S GOT "SODOM" IN THE TITLE!

?

ELYSE METCALF, OWNER OF "ELYSE'S PASSION" ON SYCAMORE ST, WAS TARRED AND FEATHERED IN 2001 FOR RENTING **AIR TIGHT GRANNY, JEFF STRYKER'S UNDERGROUND,** AND **KITTY FOXX'S AGED TO PERFECTION VOL. 15.** SHE FACED UP TO 3 YEARS IN PRISON, BUT THANKFULLY WAS ACQUITTED.

IN JULY 2002, "CITIZENS FOR COMMUNITY VALUES" MEMBERS CHECKED INTO ROOMS AT THE MARRIOTT NORTH IN WEST CHESTER TOWNSHIP, AND THE CINCINNATI MARRIOTT NORTHEAST. THEY WATCHED ADULT MOVIES TOGETHER AT EACH ONE, THEN FORWARDED THE TAPES TO COUNTY PROSECUTORS' OFFICES. FOLLOWING THIS, LOCAL HOTELS WERE FORCED TO BAN ADULT MATERIAL.

AND LET'S NOT FORGET JENNIFER DUTE WHO LOST HER 2003 OBSCENITY CASE FOR SELLING HOMEMADE TAPES OF HER SELF HAVING BORING-LOOKING SEX WITH VARIOUS PARTNERS. SHE WAS JAILED FOR A YEAR MAINLY BECAUSE THE JUDGE WAS MORALLY OPPOSED TO THE IDEA THAT A YOUNG WHITE MOTHER WOULD FUCK BLACK MEN AND FILM IT.

CINCINNATI IS A LITIGIOUS, NIGHTMARE TURDHOLE OF MADDENING CONTRADICTIONS, BUT PERHAPS TRIAL LAWYER AND FREE SPEECH ADVOCATE H. LOUIS SIRKIN RECENTLY PUT IT BEST:

"WHEN YOU WRITE ABOUT CINCINNATI AND CENSORSHIP, YOU CAN PUT THAT WE MAY NOT HAVE ANY ADULT BOOK STORES HERE, BUT WE ARE ALREADY AHEAD OF LAST YEAR IN MURDERS, AND WE ARE ALSO KEEPING OUR RANKING IN BANK ROBBERIES, BEING FOURTH IN THE NATION."

DOWN WITH SMUT!

COLIN UPTON 06

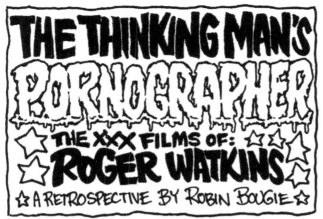

THE THINKING MAN'S PORNOGRAPHER

THE XXX FILMS OF: ROGER WATKINS

☆ A RETROSPECTIVE BY ROBIN BOUGIE ☆

CINEMA HISTORY IS LITTERED WITH A VAST ARRAY OF FILMMAKERS CREATING SMUT UNDER ALIASES IN ORDER TO HIDE THEIR PORNOGRAPHIC OUTPUT FROM THE MAINSTREAM PUBLIC. WITH SEX BEING SUCH A FROWNED UPON ACT, I SUPPOSE IT'S NO SURPRISE THAT THE VAST INDUSTRY OF XXX HAS BEEN A BREEDING GROUND FOR THESE TYPE OF NOM DE PLUME SHENANIGANS.

PORN DIRECTOR RICHARD MAHLER, FOR INSTANCE, IS BETTER KNOWN NOWADAYS UNDER HIS REAL NAME, ROGER WATKINS -- AND AS THE DIRECTOR OF THE GORY CULT HORROR FILM **LAST HOUSE ON DEAD END STREET**, WHICH HE MADE UNDER ANOTHER MONIKER AS WELL -- VICTOR JANOS.

LHODES IS A CLASSIC EXAMPLE OF A SUPPOSEDLY LOST FILM THAT WAS TREATED AS SOMETHING OF AN URBAN LEGEND FOR YEARS, AND BLOWN OUT OF PROPORTION THROUGH WORD OF MOUTH. WHEN IT COMES TO MOVIE DORKS, THE RARER SOMETHING IS, THE COOLER IT IS -- AND FOR DECADES AFTER ITS EARLY 1970S RELEASE, NO ONE KNEW WHO "VICTOR JANOS" REALLY WAS.

ONCE THE FILM AND ITS CREATOR WERE TRACKED DOWN IN UPSTATE NEW YORK IN THE EARLY '90s, THE LEGEND BECAME FACT. MANY GENRE CRITICS, ASSUMEDLY DRAWN IN BY THE NOTION OF THE MYSTERY OF THE FILM BEING SOLVED, SOMEHOW FOUND THE SNUFF-THEMED MOVIE ITSELF TO BE TERRIFYING. (A SWEET-ASS SPECIAL EDITION DVD WITH LOTS OF EXTRA FEATURES WAS EVEN MADE) I'M SAD TO SAY THAT BESIDES FOR THE UNSETTLING SCENE OF THE NAKED WRITHING GIRL IN AL JOLSON BLACKFACE, AND THE WONDERFULLY REPULSIVE GORY FINALE, I FOUND **LHODES** TO BE SLOPPY AND MOSTLY FORGETTABLE, AND CLEARLY NOT UP TO PAR WITH WATKINS FAR LESS APPRECIATED HARDCORE FILMS.

ROGER WATKINS... I WANNA HAVE YOUR BABY!!

EEW →

"I APPLIED MY VISION BUT FOR THE MONEY" WATKINS TOLD ANDY COPP IN AN INTERVIEW FOR NEON MADNESS ZINE, "BUT I TOOK A LOT OF RISKS IN DOING SO. I WENT INTO PORN BECAUSE I WAS BROKE, MY WIFE WAS PREGNANT, AND I WAS OFFERED A DEAL I COULD NOT REFUSE. ODDLY ENOUGH THE PARTICULAR PEOPLE I DEALT WITH IN THAT PECULIAR INDUSTRY WERE FAR MORE HONEST THAN THE SO CALLED 'LEGIT' SCUM BAGS."

WATKINS ONLY DIRECTED 8 PORN FILMS BETWEEN 1979 AND THE MID 1980S, BUT HE'S ONE OF MY ALL TIME FAVOURITE PORNOGRAPHERS SIMPLY BECAUSE HE MADE AN EFFORT TO MAKE HIS MOVIES WORK ON SEVERAL OTHER LEVELS ASIDE FROM JUST MEAT BEATING FODDER. HE WASN'T AFRAID TO DEPRESS THE FUCK OUT AUDIENCES, A TRAIT NEARLY UNHEARD OF IN AN INDUSTRY THAT HAS ALWAYS BEEN ABOUT SIMPLY MAKING VIEWERS HORNY TO THE EXCLUSION OF ALL ELSE.

IRONICALLY, THE REASON STORY, CHARACTERISATION, AND MOOD WERE GIVEN SUCH FOND ATTENTION BY WATKINS IN HIS PORN FILMOGRAPHY IS BECAUSE HE DISLIKED THE SEXUAL ASPECTS OF PORN CINEMA EVEN WHILE HE WAS MAKING IT, AND ONLY DIRECTED AND WROTE XXX BECAUSE THE NON PORN WORLD WOULDN'T HAVE HIM. HE ONCE CALLED **PINK LADIES** "AN EXERCISE IN STUPIDITY", REFUSED ON PRINCIPAL TO SHOOT ANY OF THE HUMPY PUMPY IN **HER NAME WAS LISA**, AND DISOWNED **COSMOPOLITAN GIRLS**, LABELLING IT AS "FUCKING GARBAGE".

ALL OF THIS PUTS AN INTERESTING CONCEPT IN MY HEAD THAT WAS NOT THERE PRIOR TO LEARNING OF WATKINS' TOTAL DISDAIN FOR PORN. PERHAPS WHAT THE MEDIUM HAS ALWAYS LACKED IS MORE DIRECTORS WHO DON'T CARE ABOUT PORN WHATSOEVER. ARTISTS WHO INCLUDE SLOPPY, SLEAZY TRIPLE-X FUCKING AS A REQUIREMENT, BUT WHO ARE FAR MORE INTERESTED IN THE MOVIE GOING ON BETWEEN THE SEX SCENES. SOMETIMES

"100%! HIGHEST RATING! Finally a film I can rave about... Erotically Stupendous!"
—Hustler

"100%! The best sex film you'll see this year! Vanessa is DYNAMITE!!"
—Al Goldstein's Mag.

HER NAME WAS *Lisa*

Starring **VANESSA DEL RIO SAMANTHA FOX** COLOR Ⓧ

IT TAKES A TOURIST'S VIEWPOINT TO MAKE YOU REALLY SEE YOUR OWN STOMPING GROUNDS.

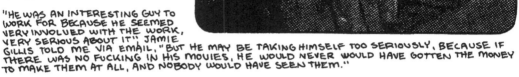
GILLIS GETS GOBBLED IN 'MIDNIGHT HEAT'

ROGER WATKINS HAS, FROM TIME TO TIME, BEGRUDGINGLY ADMITTED THAT HE LIKES HIS FILMS **MIDNIGHT HEAT** AND **CORRUPTION** (BOTH STARRING CLASSIC PORN LEGEND JAMIE GILLIS) BUT THAT HE'S STILL NOT ENTHUSED ABOUT THE COPULATION THAT TAKES UP MUCH OF THEIR RUNTIME. "I'VE MADE COPIES OF THEM, WHERE I GOT RID OF ALL THE PORNOGRAPHY, AND THEY'RE ONLY LIKE THIRTY MINUTE MOVIES BUT THEY'RE GOOD." HE TOLD ART ETTINGER IN AN INTERVIEW FOR ULTRA VIOLENT MAGAZINE.

"HE WAS AN INTERESTING GUY TO WORK FOR BECAUSE HE SEEMED VERY INVOLVED WITH THE WORK, VERY SERIOUS ABOUT IT" JAMIE GILLIS TOLD ME VIA EMAIL, "BUT HE MAY BE TAKING HIMSELF TOO SERIOUSLY, BECAUSE IF THERE WAS NO FUCKING IN HIS MOVIES, HE WOULD NEVER WOULD HAVE GOTTEN THE MONEY TO MAKE THEM AT ALL, AND NOBODY WOULD HAVE SEEN THEM."

CLASSIC PORN DIRECTOR SHAUN COSTELLO CONCURS. "PEOPLE PAID HIM GOOD MONEY TO MAKE THOSE SEX FILMS, AND IF THEY HAD NO SEX IN THEM THEY WOULD NEVER HAVE BEEN MADE. SO INSTEAD OF MAKING MOVIES HE COULD HAVE BEEN TENDING BAR OR WAITING TABLES SOMEWHERE. WOULD HE HAVE PREFERRED WAITING TABLES TO MAKING MOVIES, REGARDLESS OF THEIR CONTENT? I THINK WE CAN PREDICT THE ANSWER."

FROM: 'MIDNIGHT HEAT'

EVENTUALLY WATKINS CHILLED A LITTLE AND SHOT ALL THE HARDCORE IN HIS OWN FILMS, SEEMINGLY REALISING THAT LIKE IT OR NOT, THE LIFE OF A XXX DIRECTOR IS GOING TO IMBED YOU ASS-DEEP WITH FREAKY PEOPLE AND SITUATIONS. "I'M NOT OFFENDED BY PORNOGRAPHY," SAID WATKINS. "I DON'T FIND IT AS EROTIC AS I WOULD R-RATED STUFF. THE CLOSE UPS OF PENETRATION AND STUFF LIKE THAT, FOR ME JUST ISN'T THAT SEXY."

"I'M IN DAVE DARBY'S OFFICE, WE WERE GOING TO DO MIDNIGHT HEAT, AND SHE COMES IN", WATKINS SAID OF HIS FIRST MEETING (AND SEVERAL MORE OF HIS FILMS, FOR THAT MATTER). "HE ALWAYS SAYS TO THEM, 'IS THERE ANYTHING YOU LIKE TO DO ESPECIALLY, SEXUALLY?'. I'LL NEVER FORGET, SHE GOES 'WELL YEAH, A LITTLE BIT OF SHIT AND A LITTLE BIT OF PISS, YOU KNOW... I'LL EAT IT.' (LAUGHS) AND I'M LIKE, 'OH GOD'. BUT YEAH, MOST OF THESE PEOPLE WERE LIKE SEXUAL OUTLAWS".

I FIRST DISCOVERED **MIDNIGHT HEAT** (1983) ON THE BIG SCREEN ONE NIGHT OVER 5 YEARS AGO DURING A VISIT TO THE FOX THEATER HERE IN VANCOUVER (BACK WHEN IT WAS STILL THE LAST 35mm PORN HOUSE ON THE CONTINENT) AND THE MEMORY OF THAT NIGHT IS STILL FRESH. AFTER I GINGERLY STEPPED AROUND THE CRUISING GAY THEATER PATRONS AND WANDERED OUT OF THAT CUM AND PISS STAINED TEMPLE OF DEPRAVITY OUT INTO THE THICK FOG FILLED NIGHT AIR, I WAS ACUTELY AWARE OF THE FACT I'D SEEN ONE OF MY MOST BELOVED PORN FILMS -- #4 ON MY ALL TIME LIST TO BE PRECISE. (GOD, I'M SUCH A GEEK)

PERENNIAL C.S. FAVOURITE JAMIE GILLIS STARS AS A LONELY NEW YORK HITMAN IN THIS SLEAZY FILM NOIR TRIPLE X FEATURE THAT TREATS PLOT AND ATMOSPHERE WITH THE SAME RESPECT THAT IT GIVES TO THE HARDCORE COUPLING ON DISPLAY. JAMIE OPENS THINGS UP BY ASSASSINATING A VICTIM IN A SUIT AND THEN HEADS OVER TO HIS BOSS'S PLACE TO GO BALLS DEEP INTO THE MOBSTER'S HORNY WIFE. UNLUCKILY FOR THEM, THE CAPPO WALKS IN AND GIVES GILLIS THE INFAMOUS KISS OF DEATH. SWEATING IT, JAMIE HOLES UP IN A BOWERY FLOPHOUSE (ACTUALLY PRODUCER DAVE DARBY'S RUNDOWN OFFICE) WHERE HE SPENDS MUCH OF HIS TIME PONDERING HIS SAD EXISTENCE AND PHONING ESCORT SERVICES.

TISH AMBROSE IN 'AMERICAN BABYLON'

TWO HOOKERS ARRIVE TO PERFORM A LESBO FLOOR SHOW AND KEEP THE KILLER COMPANY WHILE HE DECIDES HIS NEXT MOVE. HE SPENDS THE BETTER PART OF THE DAY FUCKING ONE PROSTITUTE (AVON PRODUCTIONS REGULAR CHERI CHAMPAGNE) WHILE HE MAKES THE OTHER ONE WATCH, ONLY TAKING TIME OUT TO SMOKE UP AND STARE OUT THE WINDOW WHILE RECITING EXISTENTIAL MUSINGS ABOUT THE SHIT-STAINED WINOS DOWN ON THE PAVEMENT.

"WHAT SEPARATES THEM FROM US? ONE DAY THEY WOKE UP AND SAID FUCK IT", HE COLDLY INTONES AS REPEATED HYPNOTIC SLOW-MO LOCATION SHOTS OF GRIM, COLD, RAINY STREETS PUNCTUATE THE MOVIE LIKE SAMPLINGS OF A RAYMOND CHANDLER NOVEL.

JAMIE TELLS CHERI TO STAY FOR THE NIGHT, AND AFTER EXAMINING HIS REVOLVER, SHE ASKS HIM, "DO YOU EVER THINK ABOUT THE PEOPLE YOU KILL?". HE TELLS HER HE DOES, AND SHE ADMITS THAT, AS A WHORE, SHE CRAVES AFFECTION FAR MORE THAN SEX. "SOMEONE WHO REALLY LIKES ME", SHE LAMENTS. LATER ON HE CONFIDES IN HER THAT "ONLY A PERSON IN CONSTANT TERROR OF ANNIHILATION CAN EXPERIENCE LIFE THE WAY IT SHOULD BE EXPERIENCED", AND ASKS HER, "WOULD YOU KILL ME IF I ASKED YOU TO?". NEEDLESS TO SAY, THINGS RAPIDLY GET BLEAKER IN THAT COLD GREY HOTEL ROOM, AND IT ISN'T LONG BEFORE DEATH COMES KNOCKING AND THE HITMAN HAS TO PUT HIS MORBID SKILLS TO THE TEST.

MIDNIGHT HEAT IS A HEAVY, MISANTHROPIC, DOWNBEAT MANHATTAN OFFERING FROM WATKINS UNDER HIS MAHLER MONIKER, BUT IT WAS WITH **HER NAME WAS LISA**, WATKINS' FIRST PORN FILM (WHICH APPEARED IN NYC PORNO GRINDHOUSES IN 1979) THAT THE DIRECTOR BEGAN TO HONE HIS CRAFT.

THIS DEPRESSING SPIRAL INTO SEXUAL SADNESS INTRODUCES TO US A MASSAGE GIRL NAMED LISA (SAMANTHA FOX) WHO BECOMES AN OVERNIGHT SENSATION AS A MODEL, THEN SLIPS INTO A BIZARRE WORLD OF KINKY SEX AND DRUGS. FIXATED WITH THE MELANCHOLIC ASPECTS OF SEXUALITY, THIS SCARY TALE OF LISA'S SHORT, SQUALID LIFE BEGINS WITH HER NUDE CORPSE IN A CELLOPHANE BAG IN THE MORGUE. THIS IS CLASSIC BIG APPLE PORN, AND IT DOES NOT SHY AWAY FROM MIXING DEATH OR GENDER POLITICS WITH SEX. CHECK OUT FOX REAMING OUT A WEALTHY RAPISTS BUNGHOLE WITH A STRAP-ON DILDO FOR EVIDENCE OF THE LATTER.

THIS ENTIRE SHIT-SCAB OF A MOVIE IS FASCINATINGLY TOLD IN FLASHBACKS, AND DURING THE NEXT 70 MINUTES, SAMANTHA FOX PROVES THAT SHE WAS AN ACTRESS THAT COULD HAVE MADE A LIVING IN MAINSTREAM CINEMA. AS A TOUGH, COLD-HEARTED WOMAN WHO DOESN'T MUCH CARE FOR MEN, SHE PLAYS A DOMINATRIX WHO IS CONSTANTLY INGESTING QUAALUDES, AND EVENTUALLY GETS HOOKED ON HEROIN AND DISINTEGRATES INTO THE HUMAN EQUIVALENT OF DOGSHIT. BACK IN THE DAY SCREW MAGAZINE CITED IT AS THE BEST XXX MOVIE OF 1979.

WHEN ASKED BY ART ETTINGER WHY **HER NAME WAS LISA** WAS SO DARK AND NIHILISTIC, WATKINS AGAIN SPOKE OF DAVE DARBY WHO PRODUCED HIS FILMS: "HE SAYS 'ROGER, WE GOTTA DO SOMETHING LIGHT, MAN! THIS IS TOO HEAVY!'. BUT THE WAY THAT CAME ABOUT WAS THE SAME DAY WE WERE WITH DANNY CANTON (ASSISTANT CAMERAMAN ON **LHODES**), WERE UP IN HIS OFFICE AND I THOUGHT THIS WAS SLIGHTLY PERVERSE – IT TURNED OUT HE HAD A DAUGHTER NAMED LISA. SO (DARBY) SAYS TO ME, 'I WANT OUR MOVIE TO START OUT WITH A GIRL NAMED LISA... IT STARTS OUT AND THIS GIRL IS IN A COFFIN. NOW I DON'T KNOW HOW SHE GOT IN THE COFFIN...' SO THATS HOW IT STARTED. HE MORE OR LESS BEGGED FOR THAT ONE."

PINK LADIES APPEARED IN 1980, AND IT STUPEFIED REVIEWERS AND AUDIENCES ALIKE. "CAN ANYONE PRODUCE AN ADULT FILM WITH ALMOST CONTINUOUS SEX AND ALMOST NO STORY LINE, BUT SO OUTRAGEOUS AND FAR OUT THAT MOST MEN AND WOMEN WHO WATCH IT CAN'T STOP LAUGHING -- OR EVEN OCCASIONALLY IDENTIFYING WITH THE CHARACTERS? RICHARD MAHLER HAS IN THIS ONE." SAID BOB RIMMER, IN HIS "X-RATED VIDEOTAPE GUIDE" REVIEW.

CORRUPTION (1983) IS A STORY ABOUT A BUSINESSMAN (JAMIE GILLIS AGAIN, BLESS HIS HEART) THAT "SELLS HIS SOUL" FOR POWER. HOWEVER, HE'S BETRAYED BY HIS DASTARDLY

COURIER (THE WONDERFULLY EVIL GEORGE PAYNE) AND FINDS HIMSELF
IN SERIOUS TROUBLE. THE DESPERATE GILLIS MUST THEN
CALL UPON HIS SLEAZEBALL HALF-BROTHER (THE CLOWN PRINCE
OF PORN, THE LATE BOBBY ASTYR) TO HELP HIM SET THINGS
STRAIGHT.

ASTYR RUNS A DECREPIT BAR WITH UNDERGROUND ROOMS
AROUND WHICH JAMIE WANDERS AND WATCHES PEOPLE
INDULGE IN WILD, UNCOMMITTED, END-OF-THE-WORLD
TYPE SEX. HE PEEPS ON TWO WOMEN LATHERING EACH
OTHERS BOOBS AND GETTING ALL LEZZED OUT IN
THE SHOWER, THEN A MAN ACTING LIKE A DOG
BEFORE A WOMAN BRANDISHING A WHIP. TO
JAMIE'S HORROR, THE MAN LOOKS **JUST** LIKE
HIM. NEXT, HE SPOTS A DEAD WOMAN IN A ROOM
WITH CREEPY ORGAN MUSIC PLAYING, WHERE A
CLOWN WEARING A TOP HAT STRIPS HER AND
SCREWS HER CORPSE WILDLY. BELIEVE IT OR
NOT, IT GETS WEIRDER FROM THERE!

BEING AS THIS IS WATKINS IN FULL EFFECT, THE
HARDCORE SEX IS ALMOST INCIDENTAL TO THE PATHOS,
WITH ZERO CUM FACIALS OR ANAL SEX, AND SOME
OF THE GIRLS DON'T EVEN HAVE SEX AT ALL. THAT'S
NOT TO SAY THIS ISN'T **HOT AS FUCKIN' HELL**. TIFFANY
CLARK SLOWLY LICKING JAMIE'S VIENY SHAFT,
VANESSA DEL RIO BEING THE USUALLY-INSATIABLE
VANESSA DEL RIO, AND MALISSA STRONG FORCING
JAMIE TO LICK HER BOOTS WILL DO PLENTY TO KEEP
YOUR ATTENTION.

"THE SEX IS EQUALLY DARK AND BIZARRE IN THIS
STRAINED STAB AT EXISTENTIALISM." WROTE ADULT FILM
WORLD, AND FILTH HISTORIAN JIM HOLLIDAY, WHO CALLED
CORRUPTION "A THINKING PERSON'S PORNO WITH GREAT
CLASSICAL MUSIC". PERHAPS MOST MEMORABLY, THE
LATE DAN SHOCKET DECLARED IT "THE MOST SPLENDID
FAILURE EVER MADE."

WATKINS ALSO DIRECTED
AMERICAN BABYLON (1985),
DECADENCE (1987) (NEITHER
OF WHICH I'VE SEEN), WROTE **MYSTIQUE** (1974) AND PENNED THE
EXCELLENT **NEON NIGHTS** (1981) FOR CECIL HOWARD, ALTHOUGH HE
WENT UNCREDITED FOR HIS EFFORT.

NEON NIGHTS HAS JAMIE GILLIS AS A CREEPY INCESTUAL DAD, THE
NUBILE LYSA THATCHER STARRING AS A TEENAGE RUNAWAY, AND
KANDI BARBOUR AS HER TENNIS-LOVIN' FREAKISH-NIPPLED (YOU
HAVE TO SEE KANDI'S NIPS TO BELIEVE THEM) FRIEND. AND
PEOPLE, THE STUNNINGLY GORGOUS VERONICA HART GETS IT IN THE
ASSHOLE... UM, MEOW MEOW MEOW? THIS IS A DARK, OFFBEAT, EROTIC
ROAD-MOVIE-FAIRY-TALE THAT IS QUITE OBVIOUS TO ME AS ONE
OF THE BEST EROTIC FILMS EVER MADE.

UPDATE: IN 2007, A YEAR AFTER I RAN THIS ARTICLE ABOUT HIS
SHORT-LIVED AND UNDER APPRECIATED PORN DIRECTING CAREER,
ROGER DIED OF HEART FAILURE IN APALACHIN, NEW YORK. R.I.P.
— BOUGIE

VIRGINIA (1983)

WHILE UNFAIRLY IGNORED BY MOST PORN
CRITICS, SHAUNA GRANT'S ROLE IN THE
EXCELLENT "VIRGINIA" WAS LAUDED BY AT
LEAST ONE REVIEWER -- DRIES VERMEULEN,
WHO WROTE THAT SHE "... ACCOMPLISHES A
PERFORMANCE THAT IS SO EMOTIONALLY
NAKED IT IS AT TIMES PAINFUL, EVEN
EMBARRASSING TO WITNESS". PLAYING A TEEN
COMING TO TERMS WITH HER DESIRE TO FUCK
HER OWN FATHER, GRANT WAS NEVER BETTER
THAN SHE WAS HERE, AND WOULD BE DEAD
ONLY A YEAR LATER -- HER HEAD BLOWN
APART BY A SHOTGUN BLAST AS SHE LAY IN BED
IN PALM SPRINGS, CALIFORNIA. THE OFFICIAL
METHOD OF DEATH WAS DETERMINED TO BE
SUICIDE, BUT SOME FRIENDS AND INDUSTRY
INSIDERS BELIEVE TO THIS DAY THAT FOUL PLAY
WAS INVOLVED. R.I.P. SHAUNA. YOU ARE NOT
FORGOTTEN.

— BOUGIE '10

THE UGLIEST CLASSIC ADULT MOVIE ADVERTISING EVER MADE

I'VE BEEN COLLECTING MOVIE ADVERTISING AND PRESSBOOKS FOR YEARS NOW, AND EVERY ONCE AND A WHILE I'M JUST MORTIFIED AT HOW POORLY DRAWN AND DESIGNED SOME OF THE X RATED STUFF WAS. HERE ARE SOME OF MY ALL TIME FAVORITES!

YOUNG FOXES

SUSANNE WAS 19. VIVIAN AND ROSEMARY WERE 16. JETTE AND KATE WEREN'T

Eros
WORLD FILM GROUP

UUGAHGGH!! SOOOO UGLY! THAT FLOATING DISEMBODIED HEAD DRAWN WITH PENCIL CRAYONS BY AN 11 YEAR OLD GIRL IS AN AFFRONT TO MY SENSES!

ENJOY!!

HA HA HA HA! OOH MAN, HOW FUCKIN' LAME IS THIS ONE? FROM THE "NEW NEW NEW" HASTILY DRAWN BY A RETARD WITH A MARKER, TO THE... WELL... WTF IS IT THAT SHE'S HOLDING?! THIS IS SO POORLY DONE, THE ONLY THING YOU CAN DO IS LAUGH... OR GO INSANE...

Color
ADULTS

IF MOTHER COULD SEE ME NOW
Starring: JOAN SHELL

IF THIS ARTIST'S MOTHER COULD SEE HIM NOW! THIS INTER-RACIAL XXX SLEAZE FEST SPORTS SOME JIVE ASS PATHETIC ART WORK! I MEAN, WHAT'S THE DEAL WITH THOSE TWO BLACK DUDES?! THEY LOOK LIKE INBRED MUPPETS! THE FONT IS HARD TO READ, THE LAYOUT IS HEINOUS, AND THE ART IS GROUNDS FOR DISMISSAL! OVERALL, IT'S PROOF THAT THEY JUST DIDN'T CARE.

NEW-NEW-NEW "NORMA'S GIRLS"
-Plus-
"Weekend Roulette"
8 MM Film For Sale
FLICK

OOOOHHH...DARK AND SCARY! BUT EVEN MORE SCARY IS THAT THEY EXPECTED THIS CRAP TO ENTICE AN AUDIENCE! THE POEM PENNED BY SOME SIMPLETON IS ALSO QUITE UPSETTING. ·BARF·

SINS OF RACHEL
COLOR by Eastman

"OH RACHEL, MY LOVE, THE LIVES YOU SHATTER.... IF YOU SHOULD DIE.... would it really matter...?"

Starring
Ann Noble
Jerome Scott
Brett Morrell
and
Chase Cordell
as Earl Thomas

Produced & Directed by
RICHARD FONTAINE

GEORGINA SPELVIN in
ALL THE WAY
in EASTMAN COLOR
RATED X
MECCA TWIN
711 Pike St. 622-7711

WA-HOO! YOU KNEW I HAD TO SAVE "THE BEST" FOR LAST. THIS UN-NAMED ARTIST'S RAD RENDITION OF MISS GEORGINA SPELVIN SHOULD BE THE STUFF THAT BAD ADVERTISING ART LEGENDS ARE MADE OF! HA HA! FEAST YOUR EYES, MY FRIENDS!

BOUGIE'S 9 LEAST FAVORITE THINGS ABOUT PORN MOVIES
(AN OPEN LETTER TO THE INDUSTRY)

1. FORMULA DRIVEN SCENES: DON'T YOU REALIZE THAT GIVING THE AUDIENCE EXACTLY WHAT THEY EXPECT ISN'T SEXY? ACTUALLY, IT'S FUCKING BORING.
2. FAKE TITS: EVERY GUY I EVER TALK TO ABOUT THIS THINKS THEY ARE GROSS. LADIES, PLEASE STOP DOING THIS TO YOURSELVES! SMALL NATURAL BOOBS ARE GREAT!
3. CENSORSHIP: I'M SICK OF SEEING OLDER FILMS BEING RELEASED ON DVD ALL EDITED.
4. A LACK OF FUN AND STORYTELLING: SO MANY OF THE OLDER FILMS REALLY HAD FUN WITH THE STORY, CHARACTERS, AND WEIRD PLOT DEVICES. THAT'S ALL BUT TOTALLY GONE IN MODERN SMUT.

- CONTINUED ON NEXT PAGE

PLACE
J.J.'S
AT
UP

STARRING
FHAROH AMOS as J.J.

Presented by
Eros
WORLD FILM GROUP

SHARON THORPE   CHARLES MORE

MARA JONES   SHELL KUGLER

and   SYLVESTER COPELAND

COLOR·

WELCOME TO MORE OF THE BEST EXAMPLES OF SHITTY AD ART FROM PORN'S EARLY DAYS!

OH FOR CHRIST'S SAKE! THEY JUST SHAMELESSLY SNAGGED SOME COPY FREE IMAGES OF FACES THAT WERE DESIGNED TO USE IN CATALOGS! INCREDIBLY LAME! AND THAT TITLE GRAPHIC IS SOOO POORLY REPRESENTED FROM A VISUAL STANDPOINT. I WONDER HOW MANY TIMES IT WAS READ AS "PLACE J.J.'S AT UP"? JUST AN INTENSELY UGLY AD MAT ALL AROUND. I LOVE IT!

NOOOOOO! WHAT'S WRONG WITH THIS ARTIST!? LOOK AT THE ARM OF THE GIRL HOLDING THE GUN!! HER UPPER ARM IS THREE TIMES TOO LONG! BUT THAT'S NOT THE ONLY THING, BECAUSE THE WOOD LETTER FONT IS TERRIBLE AND NEARLY UNREADABLE. THIS MOVIE AD IS SUCH A PILE OF WONDEROUSLY STINKY SHIT!

AND NOW AVAILABLE IN COMBO BOOKINGS:

MOONSHINE GIRLS

An Adult Film That Will Make You

Leave The City Lights For The Glamour Of The Hills!

In Sexy Color XXX Rated

SHE CAN HANDLE HIS PROBLEM HE WAS ...

Born Erect

CRISTINE ROBERTS · ERIC BRAUN
also Starring VICKI WEST · PETER STRAUS
MONIKA METZGER · BARBRA PETERSON
Directed by JON SANDERSON
Color by Technicolor   X Adults Only

ALSO AVAILABLE WITH TITLE: BORN READY

OK, SOMEBODY EXPLAIN THIS TO ME: HAS THIS GIRL BEEN BEATEN ABOUT THE FACE AND HEAD?! SHE'S GOT A BLEEDING NOSE! AND THE TITLE "BORN ERECT" MAKES ME THINK ABOUT NEWBORNS WITH HARD ONS! THAT'S NOT A GOOD THING! THIS GETS AN F-!!

CONTINUED FROM PREVIOUS PAGE –

5. MUSIC DROWNING OUT THE VOCAL TRACK: THE SOUNDS OF SEX ARE ONE OF THE HOTTEST THINGS ABOUT IT. TAKING THAT AWAY AND REPLACING IT WITH SHITTY TECHNO IS NEARLY CRIMINAL. STOP FUCKING DOING IT.

6. EXAGGERATED FAKE GROANING AND MOANING: GIRLS, IF YOU'RE NOT INTO IT, PLEASE DON'T BOTHER TRYING TO FAKE WITH THE STUPID MOANING. YOU'RE KILLING MY BONER, KILLING IT, DO YOU UNDERSTAND?

7. SO FEW FULL-BODIED WOMEN: I WANT TO SEE SOME WOMEN WITH ACTUAL CURVES IN MAINSTREAM PORN. I CAN'T BURP THE WORM TO SOME SKRAWNY ASS LIVING SKELETON. HAMBURGERS FOR EVERYONE! FEED THE PORN SLUTS!

8. DISHONEST COVERS: SHOWING A SCENE OR PERFORMER ON THE PACKAGING THAT ISN'T ANYWHERE TO BE SEEN ONCE YOU START WATCHING IT

9. IDENTICAL MASS PRODUCED "STARS" THAT LACK ANYTHING TO MAKE THEM AT ALL MEMORABLE. INDIVIDUALISM IS SEXY.

OH MY GOD, IT'S...

WOMEN IN FURY

(1985)

WRITTEN AND DIRECTED BY MICHELE MASSIMO TARANTINI, WOMEN IN FURY (AKA FEMMINE IN FUGA) IS AN ITALIAN-BRAZILIAN CO-PRODUCTION, WHICH KNOWS THE BEST PARTS OF THE GIRLS IN PRISON BLUEPRINT, AND COMFORTABLY FOLLOWS THEM TO A TEE. IF THE IDEA OF SWEATY, CATFIGHTING LESBIANS IN A SOUTH AMERICAN PRISON SOUNDS TO YOU LIKE AN APPEALING CUP OF SLEAZE, LOOK NO FURTHER!

LA CUNHA

SUZANE CARVALHO IS ANGELA, WHO IS SENTENCED TO 18 YEARS IN THE SAN ANTONIO LIBERTE WOMEN'S PRISON IN BRAZIL AFTER COVERING FOR HER HEROIN ADDICTED BROTHER (PAULO GUARNIERI) WHO MURDERS A LOCAL DRUG LORD.

AS THE FRESH MEAT IN THE RUSTED METAL AND CONCRETE HOT HOUSE, SHE IS THE IMMEDIATE PREY OF THE RESIDENT CELLBLOCK LESBIAN NAMED JOANNA.

"IN THIS CELL YOU'RE MINE -- AND YOU'LL LOVE IT!"

I MUST ADMIT THAT CARVALHO'S TURN AS THE INNOCENT-YET-VICTIMIZED NEW FISH IS ONE OF MY FAVORITES IN WIP HISTORY, AS SHE IS ROUTINELY RAPED, MOLESTED, BEATEN WITH WET TOWELS, AND HUNG BY A NOOSE.

ANGELA IS THE PRISON BICYCLE, AND EVERYONE GETS A RIDE!

THE ONLY PERSON THAT SHOWS THE UNJUSTLY JAILED ANGELA ANY TRUE COURTESY, IS DENISE, A COOL/CRAZY 300-POUND BLACK INMATE WHO DOESN'T TAKE ANY SHIT FROM ANYBODY, AND AT ONE POINT BEHEADS SOME MEAN CUNT WHO TRIES TO STAB ANGELA!

"EES OK, I LOOK AFTER YOO..."*

* ODDLY HIGH PITCHED VOICE.

ANGELA'S FORCED LESBIANISM SESSION AT THE HANDS OF THE HORNY MATRON IS ESPECIALLY NOTEWORTHY, AS IT'S PACKED WITH UNCOMFORTABLE TENSION, SENSUAL NIPPLE SUCKING, AND GLORIOUS FULL FRONTAL NUDITY.

BUT, OH CRUEL FATE, JUST MOMENTS BEFORE ANGELA IS GRANTED A FULL PARDON, CHAOS VIA A MASSIVE PRISON RIOT BREAKS OUT, AND SHE, JOANNA, AND 3 OTHER GIRLS ESCAPE INTO THE JUNGLE. JOANNA HUMOROUSLY SCREAMS AT THEIR PURSUERS:

COME N' GET US YOU FAG-LICKING BASTARDS!

WOMEN IN FURY IS A FUCKING BLAST, AND WON'T DISAPPOINT. IT'S OUT ON A DECENT DVD BY SHRIEK SHOW, EXCEPT FOR A REALLY FUCKING WEIRD ANOMALY THAT OCCURS FOR A BRIEF PERIOD DURING CHAPTER 8, WHEN THE ESCAPING GALS HAVE BEEN TIED UP BY SOME HORNY JUNGLE-DWELLING-JERKS ABOUT TO RAPE THEM.
FOR ABOUT A MINUTE YOU CAN CLEARLY HEAR BACKWARDS AUDIO FROM CHAPTER 1 BLEEDING THROUGH, COMPRISED OF GARBLED VOICES AND WAILING POLICE SIRENS!

Art by Bergin III, words by Robin Bougie

119

NIGHT OF THE JUGGLER (aka "New York Killer", aka "Pursued") 1980

HOT BALLS, WHAT WAS IT WITH 1980 BEING SUCH AN AMAZING YEAR FOR MOVIES? SO MANY OF MY FAVOURITE FILMS OF THE ERA COINCIDENTALLY CAME OUT THAT YEAR, AND THIS UNDERRATED HEART-STOPPING THRILLER FROM DIRECTOR ROBERT BUTLER IS ONE OF 'EM.

I DON'T KNOW WHAT THE USUALLY RESERVED SUITS AT COLUMBIA PICTURES WERE THINKING WHEN THEY GREEN LIGHTED THIS BIG BUDGET GRINDHOUSE EXPLOITATION BARN BURNER, BUT I SURE AM GLAD THEY DID. **NIGHT OF THE JUGGLER** COULD WELL BE THE GRUNGIEST AND TRASHIEST MOVIE EVER RELEASED BY A MAJOR HOLLYWOOD STUDIO. FROM BEGINNING TO END, IT JUST OOZES STREET LEVEL SLEAZINESS, WITH THE NASTIER PARTS OF NEW YORK PROVIDING A BACK DROP FOR A NON-STOP CHASE PICTURE ABOUT A FATHER WHOSE 16 YEAR OLD TOMBOY DAUGHTER IS NABBED OFF A CROWDED STREET RIGHT FROM UNDER HIS NOSE.

JAMES BROLIN IS ODDLY CAST AS THE TRUCK DRIVER DAD WHO IS IN CONSTANT HOT PURSUIT OF HIS DAUGHTER (ABBY BLUESTONE, WHO ALSO APPEARED IN **LITTLE DARLINGS** THAT SAME YEAR) AND HER KIDNAPPER, THE CREEPY CLIFF GORMAN WHO IS KNOWN TO THE POLICE AS "THE MOLE MAN". BUT THE BIG APPLE IS THE REAL STAR OF THIS FILM, AND EVERYONE IN IT IS PORTRAYED AS BEING UTTERLY CRAZY.

DURING THE NON-STOP CHASE, BROLIN ENCOUNTERS THE VARIOUS SINFUL DELIGHTS (NOW NO MORE) OF TIMES SQUARE, DERANGED LOW-LIFES, KNIFE WIELDING PIMPS (TITO GOYA, WHO AMAZED ME IN 1977'S **SHORT EYES**), PROSTITUTES (CLASSIC PORN VIXEN SHARON MITCHELL), A VICIOUS DOG MAULING, A PSYCHO CAB DRIVER (MANDY PATINKIN), A CROOKED COP (A YOUNG DAN "**BLOOD SIMPLE**" HEDAYA), MULTICULTURAL YOUTH GANGS STRAIGHT OUTTA **THE WARRIORS** (WHO HILARIOUSLY RISK THEIR LIVES TO PURSUE HIM FOR THE MOST TRIVIAL OF PERCEIVED AFFRONTS), AND EVEN HIS LOUD OBNOXIOUS EX WIFE!

JUGGLER'S RAPID FIRE PACING IS COMPLIMENTED BY THE FACT THAT EMMY WINNING **HILL STREET BLUES** DIRECTOR ROBERT BUTLER INJECTS THE SAME STREET SMART GRITTY NUTBAG REALISM TO EVEN THE MOST MINOR CHARACTERS. MY FRIENDS, DESPITE ITS TOTALLY UNAPPEALING TITLE, THIS IS THE KIND OF MOVIE THAT CINEMA SEWER WAS CREATED FOR.

> HA HA HA HA GO, BROLIN GO!!

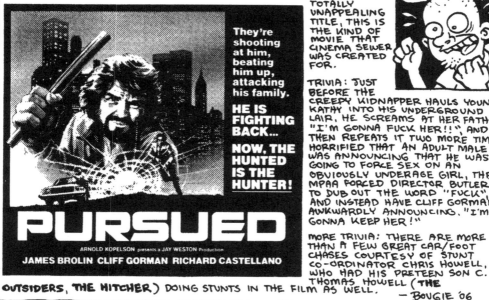

They're shooting at him, beating him up, attacking his family.

HE IS FIGHTING BACK...

NOW, THE HUNTED IS THE HUNTER!

PURSUED

ARNOLD KOPELSON presents a JAY WESTON Production

JAMES BROLIN CLIFF GORMAN RICHARD CASTELLANO

TRIVIA: JUST BEFORE THE CREEPY KIDNAPPER HAULS YOUNG KATHY INTO HIS UNDERGROUND LAIR, HE SCREAMS AT HER FATHER "I'M GONNA FUCK HER!!", AND THEN REPEATS IT TWO MORE TIMES. HORRIFIED THAT AN ADULT MALE WAS ANNOUNCING THAT HE WAS GOING TO FORCE SEX ON AN OBVIOUSLY UNDERAGE GIRL, THE MPAA FORCED DIRECTOR BUTLER TO DUB OUT THE WORD "FUCK" AND INSTEAD HAVE CLIFF GORMAN AWKWARDLY ANNOUNCING, "I'M GONNA KEEP HER!"

MORE TRIVIA: THERE ARE MORE THAN A FEW GREAT CAR/FOOT CHASES COURTESY OF STUNT CO-ORDINATOR CHRIS HOWELL, WHO HAD HIS PRETEEN SON C. THOMAS HOWELL (**THE OUTSIDERS, THE HITCHER**) DOING STUNTS IN THE FILM AS WELL.

— BOUGIE '06

JAPANESE ENEMAGEDDON!!!

TWO BIZARRE JAPANESE ENEMA DVDS (FROM PORN PRODUCTION COMPANY "NATURAL HIGH") ARRIVED IN MY MAIL THIS MORNING. **FOUNTAIN ENEMA** (NDHT-518.2010) IS MY FAVE OF THE TWO. IF YOU CAN IMAGINE A BUSBY BERKELEY-STYLE CHOREOGRAPHED MONTAGE OF ODDLY BEAUTIFUL ASS-PROPELLED LIQUID GLORIOUSLY ARCING THROUGH THE AIR, YOU'LL HAVE THE RIGHT IDEA.

ALSO, THERE IS **ENEMAGEDDON** 1 AND 2 (DOUBLE BILL! NHDT-056.2008) WHICH IS MORE COMPETITION AND LESS ARTISTRY. GIRLS LIFT WEIGHTS WHILE MILK IS PUMPED INTO THEIR BOWELS, AND THE ONE WHO CAN HOLD IT LONGEST, WINS!

BY: ROBIN BOUGIE '07
ART BY: TIMOTEO

OVER THE DECADES RUMOURS ABOUT THE EXISTENCE OF SNUFF MOVIES HAVE RUN RAMPANT DESPITE THE FACT THAT NO COLD HARD EVIDENCE EXISTS TO SUPPORT THESE DARK CLAIMS. AFTER A LARGE AMOUNT OF MY OWN RESEARCH INTO THE TOPIC, I'VE COME UP WITH NUTTIN' BUT A LOT OF DEAD ENDS AND GOOFY URBAN LEGENDS... WITH ONE EXCEPTION.

IN AUGUST 1989, COLUMBIA PICTURES UNLEASHED ON AMERICA THE ONE TRUE SNUFF MOVIE EVER RELEASED -- A CHILDREN'S MOVIE CALLED **THE ADVENTURES OF MILO AND OTIS**, WHICH WAS A REVAMPED VERSION OF A POPULAR JAPANESE FILM NAMED **KONEKO MONOGATARI** (A KITTEN'S STORY) **THE ADVENTURES OF CHATRAN**.

DEBUTING IN JAPAN THREE YEARS EARLIER, **KONEKO MONOGATARI** WAS AN ARTY FILM NOT GEARED TOWARDS KIDS AT ALL, BUT ADULTS, AND AS EARLY AS OCTOBER 1986, MERE MONTHS AFTER CHATRAN DEBUTED IN JAPAN, REPORTS OF ANIMAL CRUELTY SURFACED NOT ONLY IN JAPAN, BUT ELSEWHERE.

"CHATRAN'S LIFE IS FULL OF TRIALS AND TRIBULATIONS" THE UK'S ECONOMIST POINTED OUT. "MANY OF THEM TO DO WITH BEING SOAKED TO THE SKIN, LIKE FALLING OVER A WATERFALL IN A WOODEN BOX OR PLUMMETING FROM A CLIFF INTO THE SEA. IT IS HARD TO SEE HOW HE SURVIVED. INDEED, ACCORDING TO JAPAN'S BIGGEST ANIMAL-RIGHTS GROUP, HE DID NOT. OR, TO BE ACCURATE, A THIRD OF THE 30 CHATRANS USED DID NOT."

COLUMBIA PICTURES IGNORED REPORTS OF ABUSE AND KITTY/PUPPY KILLING BY THE JAPANESE PRODUCTION UNHINDERED BY ANIMAL RIGHTS LAWS, AND NOTED INSTEAD THAT THE FILM WAS MAKING HUGE PROFITS IN JAPAN. MONEY TALKS MY FRIENDS, AND EXECUTIVES AT COLUMBIA PICKED IT UP WITH A MIND TO OVERHAUL AND AMERICANISE THE FEATURE AS IS COMMON FOR MOST FOREIGN FILMS MARKETED IN THE USA. "IT NEEDED TO BE TAILORED TO AMERICAN KIDS WHO WATCH TEENAGE MUTANT NINJA TURTLES," SAID BRANDT REITER, AN ACCOUNT EXECUTIVE AT FUJISANKEI, THE JAPANESE OWNERS OF THE FILM.

SUSHI

FUJI SUPPLIED COLUMBIA WITH ALMOST 70 HOURS OF EXTRA FOOTAGE FROM WHICH TO MAKE THEIR OWN EDIT OF THE MOVIE. THE SUCCESSION OF ABUSES WOULD NOW BE LABELLED AS MILO AND OTIS'S "ADVENTURES", AND DESIGNED TO BABYSIT AMERICAN KIDS.

"SOME MIGHT SAY WE VULGARISED IT," SAID JIM CLARK (THE MAN IN CHARGE OF OVERHAULING THE MOVIE), "BUT WE FELT IT WAS ON THE ARTY SIDE."

JIM QUICKENED THE PACE, ADDED A LONG, EXHAUSTING SEQUENCE WHERE THE FURRY FRIENDS ADOPT A NEW-BORN CHICK, BROUGHT IN "NUTTY" BRIT DUDLEY MOORE TO NARRATE AND DO STUPID ANIMAL VOICES, AND FINALLY REMOVED MANY GRAPHIC SCENES OF ANIMALS FIGHTING AND OTHER ATROCITIES.

ASTONISHINGLY, SOME OF THE VIOLENCE AND OBVIOUSLY SNUFFY FOOTAGE IS STILL CLEARLY VISIBLE DESPITE COLUMBIA RECUTTING FOR A GRADE SCHOOL AUDIENCE. THE CAT, RENAMED MILO, STILL TAKES A LONG PLUNGE OFF A CLIFF INTO THE OCEAN (HARROWING SCENES OF HIM TRYING TO CLIMB BACK UP WERE CUT), IS ATTACKED VICIOUSLY BY ANGRY BIRDS, ENCOUNTERS A PISSED OFF SNAKE, IS PAINFULLY PINCHED ON THE LIP BY A CRAB, IS SENT WHITE WATER RAFTING DOWN A RIVER IN A FLIMSY LITTLE BOX -- AND ALL WHILE DUDLEY MOORE BABY TALKS STUPID SHIT LIKE "OH DEAR ME! OH MY GOODNESS!"

DESPITE ITS HAPPY-GO-LUCKY KIDS MOVIE MARKETING, THE ACTUAL CONTENT OF MILO AND OTIS IS TROUBLING, SHOWS ANIMALS IN OBVIOUS PAIN AND DISTRESS, AND IN A COUPLE CASES, IN THE MIDST OF A HORRIFIC DEATH. ACCORDING TO THE AMERICAN HUMANE SOCIETY, IT'S RUMOURED THAT AS MANY AS 27 KITTYCATS WERE KILLED DURING

PRODUCTION OF THE PICTURE.

DESPITE COLUMBIA PICTURES POSITION THAT THERE WAS NO BASIS TO THE ALLEGATIONS OF ABUSE, RUMOURS SWELLED AND WERE QUELLED IMMEDIATELY FOLLOWING REVIEWS BY THE TORONTO STAR AND A NEWSPAPER IN NEW JERSEY THAT BOTH NOTED:

"ALL [THE SCENES IN WHICH THE ANIMALS APPEAR TO BE IN DANGER] MAY BE MOMENTARILY UNSETTLING FOR YOUNG VIEWERS, BUT IT'S COMFORTING TO SEE IN THE CLOSING CREDITS THAT 'THE ANIMALS USED WERE FILMED UNDER STRICT SUPERVISION WITH THE UTMOST CARE FOR THEIR SAFETY AND WELL-BEING.'"

BUT WHAT THOSE REVIEWERS FAILED TO NOTICE WAS THAT COLUMBIA TOOK GREAT PAINS NOT TO STATE "NO ANIMALS WERE HARMED", WHICH HAS BEEN BOILERPLATE LANGUAGE ON MOVIE ANIMAL DISCLAIMERS FOR AS LONG AS ANYONE CAN REMEMBER. ODDLY, THE AMERICAN HUMANE SOCIETY ITSELF HAS DONE ITS BIT TO KEEP COLUMBIA PICTURES DIRTY LITTLE FURRY SECRET BY SUSPICIOUSLY NOT INCLUDING THE ADVENTURES OF MILO AND OTIS IN ITS EXHAUSTIVE "CURRENT INDEX OF FILM RATINGS". DO I SMELL A COVER UP?

MILO THE KITTY ISN'T THE ONLY ONE FUCKED WITH, ALTHOUGH HE DOES THE BEAR THE BRUNT. OTIS THE DOG, IS SENT NAKED-PAWED THROUGH DRIFTS OF DEEP SNOW, FORCED TO SWIM TO THE POINT WHERE THE DOG IS OBVIOUSLY BEGINNING TO DROWN, AND IN ONE VERY MEMORABLE SCENE, IS PITTED AGAINST A VERY HUNGRY BEAR.

MOST OF THE PEOPLE COMMENTING ON THE MOVIE'S LISTING ON THE INTERNET MOVIE DATABASE ARE BLISSFULLY UNAWARE OF THE BEHIND-THE-SCENES STORY, CALLING IT "WHOLESOME" AND "PERFECT FOR THE WHOLE FAMILY", TO THE POINT WHERE ONE HORRIFIED MOTHER'S TAKE ON THE FILM STICKS OUT LIKE A SORE THUMB:

"I'M SO UPSET, I PURCHASED THIS MOVIE FOR MY SON FOR VALENTINES DAY. I READ THE BACK OF THE MOVIE BEFORE PURCHASE. RATED 'G', CUTE LITTLE STORY, MADE BY COLUMBIA PICTURES, ENDORSED BY THE WASHINGTON POST, PURCHASED AT WALMART FOR $5. HOW CAN THIS BE WRONG? WRONG IS WHEN MY LITTLE SON CAME RUNNING "THEY'RE TORTURING THE ANIMALS!", I COULD NOT BELIEVE MY EYES! KITTENS SCREECHING FOR THEIR LIVES, ANIMALS YELPING, A DOG GETTING WHACKED BY A BEAR WITH A SUDDEN CUT AWAY AS IF THE DOG WAS KILLED. ANIMALS DON'T JUMP OFF 100 FOOT CLIFFS ON THEIR OWN. DON'T SHOW THIS MOVIE TO ANY CHILD!"

ANOTHER VIEWER CLUES IN AS WELL LATER ON DOWN THE LIST OF COMMENTS:

"CHATRAN HAS THE MERIT TO SHOW YOU HOW FAR YOU CAN GO TO EARN A FISTFUL OF MISERABLE BUCKS. SACRIFICING A DOZEN CATS WHO NEVER ASKED FOR ANYTHING DOES NOT REPRESENT MY CONCEPTION OF BRINGING FANTASY AND ENTERTAIN- -MENT TO AN AUDIENCE. THERE IS A DIFFERENCE BETWEEN A HORSE WITH A BROKEN LEG AND FIVE CATS THROWN FROM A CLIFF UNTIL ONE SURVIVES AND THE SEQUENCE IS WRAPPED UP. WATCHING CHATRAN IS LIKE WITNESSING SCIENTIFIC EXPERIMENTS ON ANIMALS, EXCEPT HERE THE ONLY GOAL IS TO MAKE MONEY."

BUT NOT EVERYONE AGREES. ONE REVIEWER ON AMAZON.COM POINTED OUT THAT "ANIMALS WERE CREATED FOR OUR ENJOYMENT, BIBLICALLY SPEAKING" AND FINISHES HIS ARGUMENT BY CHIDING THOSE WHO DISAGREE WITH HIS STANCE; "THE LATE DUDLEY MOORE WOULD NEVER HAVE LENT HIS NARRATIVE VOICE TO A MOVIE HE DIDN'T BELIEVE IN AND YOU SHOULD BE ASHAMED OF YOURSELVES FOR THINKING YOU'RE ABOVE THIS HIGHLY ENTERTAINING AND ANIMAL FRIENDLY FILM."

ASHAMED? FUCK YEAH. THERE IS SOME SHAME TO BE HANDED OUT IN THIS SITUATION, BUT IT SHOULDN'T BE DIRECTED AT THE AUDIENCE. THE PEOPLE RESPONSIBLE FOR THE MAKING AND DISTRIBUTION OF MILO AND OTIS KNOW WHO THEY ARE, AND THEY KNOW WHAT THEY PACKAGED AND SOLD TO THE KITTY N' PUPPY LOVIN' YOUTH MARKET.

Robin Bougie 2007

WOW!

LETTERS TO THE BOUGIEMAN

YIPPIE!!

THERE WAS AN OUTPOURING OF RESPONSE TO THE MILO AND OTIS ARTICLE FROM THE PREVIOUS PAGE THAT I FELT COMPELLED TO USE AN ENTIRE LETTERS PAGE TO SHARE THEM w/ READERS.

Robin, you really blew the fucking lid off with the MIlo and Otis article. Incredible, and some of your best reporting yet. I have a feeling though that people aren't going to want to buy what you're peddling. It may all be true, but that movie is seriously beloved. Have you been getting hate mail about this one? I really wouldn't doubt it. You've got some balls, man. First the Bianca Trump thing (have white racists tracked you down and cut off your cock yet, by chance?) and now this. You have more guts than most journalists working in the mainstream, Boug, and I mean that in all honesty. Keep it up, and don't forget to lock your door at night. My girlfriend and I think you're amazing.
-Jason S. _____

Re: "Is Milo in heaven, mommy?"
Although I agree that the scene where Milo is being pecked by birds and then jumps (is thrown) off a cliff, it is irresponsible for you to perpetuate an urban legend without backing it up with facts.
- J. P. Cline _____

I want to write to you and let you know THAT I KNOW that what you wrote about Milo and Otis is obviously a sick joke, and you are a sick, sad person for writing it. I grew up with that movie, and my daughter is growing up with it too. You should be ashamed of yourself, saying these things about something good that people really care about. I feel sorry for you and wish you would admit what you wrote was made up.

-Laura B. _____

You are a very dramatic and ignorant person. I seriously do not know how you can prove or find evidence to back up what you said. About 75 people worked daily on the set of "Milo & Otis". To think not one of the workers did anything to prevent the death or exploit hurt or dying animals is ridiculous. In the movie the director and crew were under supervision by government officials (especially during the critically endangered sea turtle scene). Please stop pretending you care about animals. I am an active animals right activist for 23 years and a vegan for 19 years. I have done my fair share of research in the flesh especially for this movie to the point of making contact with the producers and owners of the cat and dog. I would like you to think about how ridiculous you sound in this article. NOBODY GETS AWAY WITH ANIMAL CRUELTY. PERIOD.
—r _____

Here's what I have to say. I don't care if you believe me. My grandmother has told me this story so many times now and each time I can see how hard it is for her (even now, years after) to recount what she saw. My grandmother (as an Australian woman living in Japan, and a keen animal lover) was thrilled when her troubles paid off. She had sent in her application to a particular film producer after hearing word of an upcoming movie that's cast would be made up of entirely animals and nine weeks later her application was accepted.

On her first day at work she was handed a sick seal point kitten and told to make sure it would be ready for filming the next day. Sadly, the little kitten wasn't strong enough and it passed away in the middle of the night despite my gran's best efforts. Because she had spent the whole day looking after this poor sweetie, she hadn't had much time to ask around and view the other animals.

So, the next day she went looking for her boss, preparing herself to tell him of the loss. Only he didn't seem to care. Instead he told her to go see one of the handlers and see if there was a double. There was, and you can still see this little kitten appearing in the movie. He appears not long after the chicken scene.

One situation which she finds particularly distressing was on her 20th day on the job. She had gotten Milo#4 bathed and ready for a scene he was needed to appear in and then given him over to his handler who would take care of him on scene. Milo never returned. She says she was frantic and remembers tracking down his handler and asking what had happened. Apparently, there had been an 'accident' on set and Milo hadn't lived through it. It turns out there were many accidents on set, and during her four years of work on the set she was told many grisly tales. One was of a tiny nestling bird dying due to shock after a scene with a kitten. Nobody blames the lil' kitten, because as any cat lover knows, kitten are naturally curious, who they did blame was the director for even allowing such a thing to transpire.

My grandmother tells of a young Japanese girl who she became close friends with (and still keeps in touch today with) coming to her in tears saying that her charge Milo#2 had been injured after a seen with a hedgepig (she meant hedgehog) The poor kitty had received a open wound to his paw and was refused treatment. Milo's mother didn't have much luck either, she lost four of her kittens due to poor condition. Otis' wife#2 had been bred too young and later contracted a disease in her vagina, it was fatal.

Okay, that's all I really have to say. I know there is much more but I have to stop now so I don't sound unbelievable, and because a hot coat of tears are streaming down my face as I write these words. Please take what I have heard into consideration.
—Amy White

DART

ONE OF THE ALL-TIME BEST BAD MOVIES IS THE LAUGHABLE 1977 FEATURE, VIVA KNIEVEL, STARRING EVEL KNIEVEL AS HIS POMPOUS SELF.

THE FIRST FIVE MINUTES OF THE MOVIE QUICKLY SET THE TONE OF RIDICULOUS SELF-AGGRANDIZEMENT THAT IS TO FOLLOW. EVEL'S PORTRAYAL OF HIMSELF GIVES US SAD INSIGHT TO HIS WARPED AND EMBARRASSING SELF-IMAGE. EVEL PLAYED HIMSELF AGAIN IN THE 1980S ON T.V.'S 'THE BIONIC WOMAN'.

ONE OF THE HIGHLIGHTS OF THIS FEATURE IS THE GLOSSY OPENING THEME SONG AS SUNG BY CHARLES BERNSTEIN. DON'T MISS IT!

ONE FINE DAY, A MAN CAME HELMET FOR A CROWN, A

TO TOWN, A KING OF THE ROAD WITH A MOTORCYCLE BIRD, WHO'S NEVER COMING DOWN.

SHORTLY AFTER THE MOVIE'S RELEASE, EVEL WAS SENTENCED TO PRISON FOR A VIOLENT ASSAULT ON HIS FORMER PUBLICIST WITH A BASEBALL BAT. HE SERVED NEARLY SIX MONTHS IN JAIL EVEN THOUGH IT TURNED OUT HE HADN'T ACTUALLY COMMITTED THE BEATING HIMSELF BUT HIRED SOMEONE TO DO IT SINCE HIS OWN ARMS WERE IN CASTS!

WHAT AN ASSHOLE.

THE MOVIE BEGINS WITH A LONE FIGURE CARRYING A LARGE BOX DOWN A DARK HALLWAY.

THIS PRETTY MUCH DESTROYED HIS PERSONA AS A ROLE MODEL FOR CHILDREN. IDEAL STOPPED MAKING THE TOYS AND HIS CAREER NEVER FULLY RECOVERED.

THE FIGURE TURNS OUT TO BE KNIEVEL BRINGING A BOX OF KNIEVEL BRAND TOYS TO AN ORPHANAGE IN THE MIDDLE OF THE NIGHT. THIS IS CLEARLY SO THE AUDIENCE CAN SEE HOW SELFLESS AND GENEROUS HE'S SUPPOSED TO BE, SOMETHING THAT COULD NEVER BE CONVEYED BY HIS ACTING.

THE FIRST WE SEE OF EVEL IS HIS RING-COVERED, WISHES-HE-WAS-ELVIS HAND SHAKING THE SHOULDER OF A SLEEPING ORPHAN. WHEN THE KID TURNS OUT TO BE THE WRONG ONE, KNIEVEL GOES TO THE CHILD HE WAS LOOKING FOR AND SLAPS HIS FACE REPEATEDLY

IN ORDER TO WAKE HIM UP. THEN HE GIVES OUT TOY EVEL KNIEVELS TO ALL THE KIDS.

AS IF THAT WASN'T SAINTLY ENOUGH, ANOTHER ORPHAN BOY SUDDENLY THROWS DOWN HIS CRUTCHES AND STAGGERS TOWARD EVEL, SAYING:

YOU'RE THE REASON I'M WALKIN', EVEL!

WALKIN' EVEL?!

KNIEVEL IS THEN SCOLDED BY THE HEAD NUN FOR WAKING THE ORPHANS, SO HE CHARMS HER BY GIVING HER SOME CHOCOLATE FUDGE.

YOU'RE WICKED! YOU KNOW I'LL GET FAT.

LEISURE SUIT

NOBODY WILL NOTICE.

GENE KELLY, RED BUTTONS, LAUREN HUTTON, LESLIE NIELSON & MARJOE GORTNER ALL APPEAR IN THE FILM, BUT EVEN THE STAR-STUDDED CAST CAN'T LIFT THIS STINKER BEYOND THE PACE OF AN EPISODE OF QUINCY.

IT'S ALSO A SOUND SAMPLER'S PARADISE, WITH NUMEROUS DIALOGUE REFERENCES TO EVEL, MAKING THE CAST SOUND LIKE DEVOUT SATANISTS.

RED BUTTONS

EVEL IS MY PAL TOO!

EVEL NEEDS MORE ROOM!

GENE KELLY

THIS SCENE BETWEEN RED BUTTONS & GENE KELLY IS PROBABLY THE HIGH POINT OF THE FILM. RED BUTTONS MAKES A SENSIBLY HASTY RETREAT SOON AFTERWARD, LEAVING HIS ROLE AS THE SHIFTY AND JITTERY PROMOTER THE LEAST LOUSY PERFORMANCE IN THE MOVIE, AND THE MOST DIGNIFIED.

GENE KELLY, ON THE OTHER HAND, IS REQUIRED TO PLAY THE WASHED-UP DRUNKEN MECHANIC WHOSE WIFE DIED GIVING BIRTH TO THEIR ONLY SON. TO GO FROM SINGIN' IN THE RAIN TO THIS DARNED SEEMS A SHAME.

IT IS WORTH MENTIONING THAT ALL OF THE CRASH FOOTAGE IN VIVA KNIEVEL IS TAKEN FROM KNIEVEL'S REAL LIFE.

BUT CONSIDERING THE MOVIE CAME OUT THE SAME YEAR AS STAR WARS AND ANNIE HALL, WHAT CHANCE DID IT REALLY HAVE?

MARJOE GORTNER'S CHARACTER, JESSIE, EXPLAINS THE WHOLE PLOT IN A SINGLE SENTENCE.

HE ONLY BROUGHT YOU DOWN HERE FOR ONE PURPOSE, & THAT'S TO TAKE YOUR BODY BACK TO THE UNITED STATES AS COVER FOR ABOUT FIFTY MILLION DOLLARS OF COCAINE!

GORTNER WAS THE 1972 SUBJECT OF AN OSCAR WINNING DOCUMENTARY ABOUT HIS EXPERIENCE AS A CHILD EVANGELIST.

THERE IS AT LEAST ONE VERY NOTICEABLE CONTINUITY FLAW WHEN EVEL BUSTS GENE KELLY OUT OF THE MENTAL HOSPITAL. THE FIN OR WING OF

HIS FANCY MOTORCYCLE BREAKS OFF WHEN HE DRIVES THROUGH A DOOR, BUT THEN IT'S BACK ON BEFORE HE REACHES THE END OF THE HALLWAY!

I GUESS THE FILM MAKERS REALLY THOUGHT WE WOULDN'T NOTICE, SINCE THEY CHOSE THE PREVIOUS CHEAP SCENE AS THE FIRST THING WE SEE IN THE PROMO TRAILER FOR THE MOVIE!

THE BAD GUYS

AFTER THE INEVITABLE CAR CHASE & EXPLOSION, THINGS WIND UP PRETTY MUCH AS YOU'D EXPECT.

GENE KELLY IS REUNITED WITH HIS KID, EVEL GETS THE GIRL, LAUREN HUTTON, DESPITE ASKING HER IN AN EARLIER SCENE: "ARE YOU A WOMAN ... OR A MS.?"

IF THE MOVIE LEAVES YOU FEELING NOSTALGIC FOR THE CHAUVINISTIC GLORY DAYS OF EVEL KNIEVEL, DON'T FORGET, EVEL WAS ARRESTED FOR ASSAULTING HIS THEN 22-YEAR-OLD GIRLFRIEND AS RECENTLY AS 1994. ROBERT CRAIG 'EVEL' KNIEVEL WAS BORN IN 1938...

FOR MORE VISIT: WWW.TEDDAVE.COM

MESSAGE BOARD GANG-BANG:
SHAUN COSTELLO!

The following is an online message board conversation with Shaun Costello (aka Warren Evans) that took place over the span of two weeks on a movie message board I frequent called www.AVmaniacs.com in April of 2005. The "Shaun Costello Collection" dvd box set had just been released by Alpha Blue Archives, and we were in the middle of chatting about the pros and cons of the classic XXX films contained in the massive set, when all of a sudden, out of fucking nowhere, the director himself pops out from whatever rock he had been hiding under for the last 20 years, and introduces himself to the dozen or so movie-dorks taking part in the convo.

It was a bit of a shock, but he was indeed who he claimed to be. Most people in the industry had assumed this guy was either dead, or didn't want to be found. One can only assume that he had finally joined the digital age and had just googled himself and had previously simply not realized that anyone out there really remembered him or wanted to pick his brain about the films he made. But we certainly did, and the questions began almost immediately. Later, AV Maniacs moderator Ian Jane and I would go on to interview him privately, but I liked the way this little gang-interview played out, so I present that to you instead. The interview has been edited for clarity, and thanks to all those involved.

Gunnar Jonnson (Iceland): How did you start in this business and how did you get the idea for Forced Entry -- let alone being able to make such an incredibly grim film.

Shaun Costello: Forced Entry was shot in 1971, at various Queens and Manhattan locations. It was my first film and I really had no idea what I was doing. I was an actor, or fucker is more like it, in a few porno loops and sort of knew what was required. I also had spent a great deal of time jerking off in porno theaters, and thought that I had a complete understanding of what a guy wants to see in a xxx flick. Forced Entry was not a very good sex movie. I was having too much fun with the gore to pay much attention to the sex. When you see bloody scenes in a movie they can be traumatic, but when you're on the set trying to make mechanical devices seem like slit throats, it can be serious fun. It was 1971, peak Viet Nam time, and it seemed natural to make the rapist a deranged Viet Nam vet. The editing process was the most difficult, because I didn't know a thing about editing, and I couldn't afford a real film editor. Somehow I did it. The bottom line is this. I finished the film. The cast, crew, and lab all got paid. And the whole thing cost about $6,200. Of course I didn't make a dime, but 34 years later 80 minutes of film shot for $6,200 is still around and freaking people out.

Ian Jane (Portland): Long live the enema bandit! You have many fans on this board.

Waterpower was shot in the Fall of 1976. The elderly Jewish distributor, who was the XXX front man for the boys downtown, called and asked me to come and see him. I sit

down in his office and he says, "Look, I'm a grandfather, and I'm ashamed to have to say this, but they told me they need an enema picture". He had an audio tape of something called "The Enema Bandit". Since the boys who paid for it were too embarrassed to look at it, I was able to take great liberties, and have a lot of fun with it. It was an enormous cult hit in Germany, where it was released under the title "SCHPRITZ". It

was shot for next to nothing and to this day I think it's the funniest film I ever made.

William R (North Carolina): I need to re-label my WATERPOWER dvd as SCHPRITZ, if only to make me smile everytime I glance at it. Ian is correct, you have many a fan here. I'm glad these films were made, but I wonder how distributors (or whoever makes the decisions) would come to the conclusion that there was a market for such movies. Especially WATERPOWER.

SC: The pictures in this collection, with the exceptions of Forced Entry and Waterpower, were what was known in the business as "One Day Wonders". It was a simple formula: shoot in 12 to 14 hours, usually with a cast of six (3 males each of whom had to come twice, and 3 females) edit in two days, and deliver the answer print to the boys downtown. I was in most of the early films because I could do four come shots a day, and because I was free. The total budget for each picture was $5,000. I made a thousand and so did my partner, who was the shooter. The cast all made $100 each. We had one full time editor, one full time negative cutter, and did three pictures a week when we were at it full time, in between LSD binges and travel. Between 1973, when the bulk of these pictures were made, and 1977 we probably did about 120 of them. Why was Waterpower made? The money to make it came from a bunch of goons, who were the porno end of the Gambino crime family. Their leader, who was known by his initials, and whose name was only whispered, was shot by Sammy the Bull Gravano in the late eighties. You have to understand that these guys were not rocket scientists. Someone told one of them that there was a guy in the State Prison in Illinois who was giving college coeds enemas on the Urbana campus of the State U. (True story, by the way) When we were in pre production on this picture, Jamie Gillis actually wanted me to pay his air fare to Illinois to visit this guy in prison. I have not seen a print of Waterpower in 25 years. The goons that payed for it later put Gerry Damiano's name on it thinking that would make a difference.

Scott Favarelle (San Francisco): What was the print run/distribution pattern for most of these films? I know that Sherpix picked up Forced Entry, which did get a wider release than most of the films in the set. In the case of Waterpower, the fact that the mob was involved in distributing the films of Damiano, a "name" amongst the porn film community was likely why this was "commissioned" by them for a wider issue. These two films likely had a higher print count than the others.

SC: You're right on both films. Other than Waterpower and Forced Entry, all the others were "one day wonders" with little or no story line, cranked out by my factory in the early to mid seventies. Forced Entry had no mob connection at all. It was my first film of any kind and was funded by a childhood friend who had a few extra bucks and a fascination with porno. I needed to get him his money back, so when it was finally finished, I sold it to a porno producer named Jerry Entrator for a cash buyout, and he made the deal with Sherpix. I didn't make anything, but my friend got his money back, and I had actually made a feature length movie that people paid money to see in theaters. I was a happy camper. On the Waterpower/Gerry Damiano thing, Gerry was a wholly owned mafia slug with a really bad hair piece who did what he was told. Before he made Deep Throat he was a wig stylist in Corona, Queens. They certainly didn't have to ask his permission to put his name on anything.

Mark Savage: Hands-down, I think HOT DREAMS is one of the ten best porno films ever made. Terrific use of Mike Oldfield's music, great scene in the health spa, spectacular threesome on the boat. Very classy. Joanna Storm is amazing, as is Ms. Mitchell. You referenced DRESSED TO KILL very nicely in the opening in the shower.

SC: All my better films are re-makes, in whole or in part of films that I really liked. Waterpower was, of course, Taxi Driver. Hot Dreams was my last xxx film, and probably the last of the big budget 35mm porno films. From '79 to '83 I made Pandora's Mirror, Beauty, Heaven's Touch, and Hot Dreams. They all had six figure budgets, and were the last of their kind.

Mark Savage: Do you have a favourite film that you made?

SC: I don't really have a favorite film. But I have to say that I had more fun making and cutting Waterpower than any of the others. The boys down at Baddabing central were too macho to look at an enema movie so I could take an alleged porno flick, and turn it into a parody of itself. The scene where Jamie first sees an enema being administered in a weird theater to a gagged girl by a doctor and nurse is the funniest thing I ever put on film. They had to cleanse her of vile humors because she refused to share her toys. The Doctor reminds his patient, "Remember, Pamela.....you can always take more than you think you can". The girl had only one leg, something they told me not to show, and later made films under the name Long Jean Silver. I truly think that even if the boys who paid for it actually saw the film, they would not get it. These guys were the Gambino crime family porno unit. Their leader was shot in the late eighties by Sammy the Bull Gravano.

Chris Jeffreys: (Niagra Falls, Canada) The only cuts I could readily determine in WATERPOWER were enema expulsion scenes.

SC: There actually were enema expulsion close ups, which worried the cast and crew in terms of working in a disgusting atmophere. Strangely enough, all that came out was water, which was fine with all concerned. I never knew that the idiots cut them out. It makes no sense. Why go through the trouble of making a movie to satisfy enema freaks if you're not going to show the real thing. Actually an amazing thing happens in the last scene between Jamie and C. J. Lang. He's tied her up and given her the enema in a bath tub. Jamie is kneeling behind her and we cut to a close up of

JAMIE GILLIS GETTIN' CRAZEE

Jamie jerking his cock and C. J.'s asshole about to expell the water. Suddenly a stream of water shoots out and the second it hits the head of Jamie's cock he comes. What a pro. Actually, what a sick fuck, but he did gain the admiration of the crew.

John Ellsworth: I'm glad to see you're alive! Sleazoid Express had said that you were "sleeping with the fishes". Did you ever work with Bob Wolfe or know Phil Prince?

SC: Bob Wolfe.....Yikes.......He had a little studio on West 14th street, where he shot loops. I answered an ad in the East Village Other for xxx film actors. An hour after I showed up at Wolfe's studio I was doing my first loop. I couldn't believe they were paying me to do this. The girl was a really cute runaway. Anyway after we were done and she had left, Bob propositions me to fuck his wife. He had a small apartment on Perry Street, and she was nice enough and had no idea what I was there for. Bob leaves us alone for a bit and I tell her. So we do it while he watches. I wondered which one of us he was watching. On Phil Prinz.....He was involved with the Avon people. An old guy named Murray something owned the theater and Phil was his stooge. I never really worked for the Avon people. They were just too freaky. I worked for the boys downtown who supplied them with pictures.

Tim Meyer (Philadelphia): It sounds like you ought to be writing a history of the porn business.

SC: I have no interest in writing anything about porn history. I was there at the beginning, and probably played an

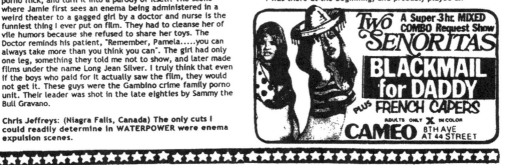

important role, but I'd rather leave it there. I'm just amazed that you guys are still watching this shit after all these years, and I'm happy to share anything I know about those days with all of you.

John Ellsworth: You get several mentions in Legs Mcneil's book (The Other Hollywood). Harry Reems, Gillis and Fred Lincoln all mention you. Btw. Gerard Damiano was just on the front page of my local Paper, He looks like he's still wearing the same hairpiece he had in Devil in Miss Jones.

SC: I knew Harry Reems (Herb Streicher), Fred Lincoln (Fred Perna), and Jamie Gillis (Jamie Gurman). We were actors together in the early days of both soft and hard core porn. I probably knew Herb best. We did a lot of LSD and mushrooms together. Jamie showed up a year or two after Herb and Fred. He was driving a cab in Brooklyn at the time. Fred screwed me out of some money when I sold a Porno documentary I had made called, "LOOPS" to Sean Cunningham. He worked for one day. I worked on it for three months, and he wound up making more than I did because he held out on signing a release, and Cunningham insisted that I pay the blackmail or there would be no deal. Fred moved to California, grew weird hair, wore platform shoes, and looked like he was trick or treating. On Gerry Damiano: Remember that he was a wig designer in Queens before he made Deep Throat, so it shouldn't surprise you that his hair piece was so ridiculous. But then, have you ever seen a good one?

Ian Jane (Portland): I watched the ABA (Alpha Blue Archives) release of WaterPower from the set and that

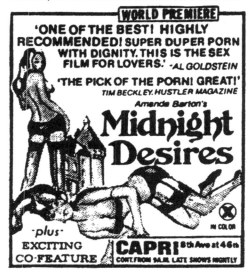

scene looks to be intact because, boy howdy, is there an expulsion scene. When she says 'There's shit everywhere' she's not lying. I'd never seen it with the expulsion scenes intact until last night, and I wasn't expecting it nor was I ready for it -- and it freaked me out to see it, especially when Jamie cleans them off with his mighty wizz.

William R (N. Carolina): He had this disturbing look of extreme joyous release on his face. As if he drank two gallons of water and was saving that piss all day.

John Ellsworth: I like the '70s porn stuff because of the high cost of film, and plus the fact it was so illegal at the time that it needed some sort of plot in case it got busted. It forced the makers to be a little more ambitious. I lost interest after it switched to video in 80's and that court case out in california that said they couldn't charge them with pandering or prostitution anymore. They no longer had to try. It's now like watching someone's vacation video.

SC: The modern porn/70's porn thing is tricky. If you're just looking for something to jerk off to, today's porn has beautiful girls who will do anything, and guys with huge dicks

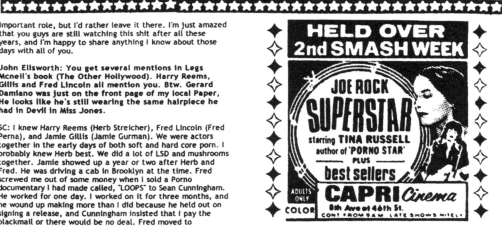

that stay hard. '70s porn was not as sexy, but it had a funky personality all its own. Back when we were doing the one day wonders, which were of course thinly improvised, I could not count the number of times that I had to do four out of the six required come shots. The guys were not reliable. Little dick fatsos like Bob Kerman were everywhere, and why anyone hired them was beyond me. I tried to stick with a small group of reliable guys who I knew would show up and perform. In those days there was only one black guy, and he had a medium sized dick that seldom maintained an erection. Very different times. Parts of Waterpower were scripted. Marlene W, Rob E, with the bound and gagged Long Jean Silver for instance. As the budgets went up the boys started demanding scripts. I resisted because the actors were so bad (with some obvious exceptions) that I thought they were better off being given a situation, and then allowed to improvise dialogue. The first real screenplay I did was for "PASSIONS OF CAROL", my Dickens' Cistmass Carol movie. This was the first hard core (the sex was awful) porno film to ever open in a regular theater, the Quad Cinemas, on East 13th Street in Manhattan.

John Ellsworth: Did you do Prisoner of Pleasure with Jean Silver or was that Mal Worob aka. Carter Stevens? Also: Mr 10 and 1/2. What do you remember about him?

SC: I really don't remember whether I made Prisoner of Pleasure or not. It sounds familiar, and I made a few pics with Jean Silver at around that time. My guess is that I did. So you know about Mal Worab? Where do you guys find out about this stuff? Mal was a character. He had an enormous loft/studio in the West 20's, which was a haven for underage runaways. Mal used to hang out at the Port Authority bus station trolling for the young stuff. This guy was a serious perv. At any given time there might be 5 or 6 runaway girls hanging out at his place. Bored porno actors might say to each other, "Hey, lets see who's at Mal's".
And by "Mr 10 and 1/2", I assume you mean Marc Stevens (Marc Kutner). During the one-day-wonder-years I used him

often. He was funny, reliable, and well endowed. In the mid seventies his mother found out that her only son was running a brothel in the West Village (true story) and she jumped out the window of the apartment building where he grew up. I bumped into him several years later at an after hours club and he was very friendly and happy to see me, and seriously coked out. I was told that he died of a cocaine overdose in the late eighties. The last time I saw him was at the Pyramid, on Avenue A. The Pyramid was my favorite dance bar. They had transvestite GO GO dancers on the bar, and a downstairs section that was off limits to all but the bravest.

John Ellsworth: That afterhours place you mentioned, was it the Mineshaft or The Hellfire Club?

SC: THE HELLFIRE CLUB was built as a interior set for the Al Pacino film "Cruising". The producers made a deal with the building's owner that they would build the set, an elaborate sex club, and leave it intact when they were finished shooting. This became the Hellfire Club, a location in which I shot several films, and a club at which I spent some serious personal time. It was open for about three years, 1979 to 1982. After that the name was used at many different locations. Only those who actually spent time in the original HFC truly understand how unique it was. It was gay, it was straight, it was tough, it was gentle, it was riddled with fashion models and celebs, not to mention myself and Jamie Gillis, and everyone got along. This was NOT a place for couples from the burbs, like Plato's Retreat, where most people kept their clothes on and were there only to watch, not to participate. The problem with places like Plato's, was that the people who DID participate were not worth watching. At HFC you'd see recognizable supermodels strutting through the maze, stroking hard cocks, sometimes as many as 15 to 20, that were pertruding through glory holes in the walls on either side. Jamie would watch action like this and turn and say to me, as he did so many times, "Ahhh, yes".

Wade Parker: Thanks for discussing shooting these movies, glad to know they weren't as horrendous to shoot as they appeared on screen. And since DOMINATRIX WITHOUT MERCY is so nasty, I guess it served its purpose so congrats. Do you remember who the girl was who shared the scene with Vanessa Del Rio? She's not credited on the film but she sure took a lot of abuse, or at least her character did.

SC: I really don't remember who was in the scene with Vanessa, but there WAS a girl named Sharon White who did some films and was truly masochistic. She would sometimes show up on the set with bruises from her boyfriend. She liked to be bound at the wrists and ankles, and left in a heap on the floor while the cast and crew broke for lunch. I caught a few crew members verbally abusing her (Which she enjoyed enormously) and put a stop to this by not hiring her again. This was a line that I never wanted to cross. Creating a blood curdling scene was fine with me as long as everything was make believe. Filming anyone actually being abused in any way was something that I had no interest in doing.

John Ellsworth: Do you have any stories about Jamie Gillis and Serena? Do you remember anything about them or their show at Show World?

SC: Serena was a trip. Jamie and I DP'd her a few times in his apartment. I think she did a DP scene in Afternoon

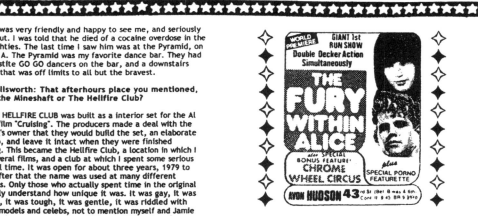

Delights.....very hot girl. She was involved in a custody battle with her ex, who lived in Marin County, north of San Francisco, and the story goes that she hired a helicopter and strafed his farm with a shotgun. Jamie told me this so it's probably true.

William R. (North Carolina): I just saw PANDORA'S MIRROR for the first time tonight. It's a very entertaining film. The Hellfire Club scene was great. I also couldn't help but laugh at Ron Jeremy. I love the guy, but seeing him in that mask made me chuckle.

SC: Ron Jeremy (Ronnie Hyatt) was just ridiculous. I used him because he had a big dick, it was always hard, and he showed up. But the girls hated working with him. He was always making eye contact with the crew while he was doing a sex scene, as though he was doing it for them. Like "Hey fellas, watch me fuck the shit out of this bitch". He had a big dick and he enjoyed hurting girls with it. He would hurt them intentionally, and after a while no one wanted to work with him.

John Ellsworth: Vanessa Del Rio, I know she was involved for awhile with that George Payne, Do you remember him? I heard that he was a massive speed freak and that he ripped her off big time before she wised up and kicked him to the curve.

SC: John E, leave it to you to know weird stuff. Yes, Vanessa let George Payne live with her, until he stole cash and a mink coat from her and took off for somewhere. George was basically gay. I realized early on with him that he couldn't function in a scene where there were no other guys. The next time you see him in a scene notice how he spends most of his time jerking off, and also notice that he is really looking at the other guy while he's doing whatever he's doing with the girl. I used George often. He was good looking, and easy to get along with, although pretty strange.

Robin Bougie: Ohhh man, I don't come around here for a couple weeks and LOOK what I miss! It's incredible to hear from you Warren! SOOO glad that you are still around and happy to share these stories with us! Do you mind if I quote some of what you've said in Cinema Sewer?

SC: Go ahead! This all happened a long time ago, in a galaxy far, far away, but it's an interesting exercise for me to relive some of this stuff, which I would not be doing without your curiosity. So, I guess we both benefit.

Robin Bougie: You've often got "Something of" the girl's name, like "The Summer of Suzanne". Did you title all your movies? Was there a conscious effort to make a shitload of films with a girl's name in the title?

SC: Good question about the "of" titles. This came from the boys downtown. They made title requests like The Pimples of Pamela. This morphed into "Teenage". Teenage anything was what they wanted. I can remember Sid Levine, who was the amiable grandfather type, the front man for the Gambino boys, after screening some "Teenage" title I made for him saying to me,"Teenage _____ . Are you guys kidding? You should call that 'Life Begins at Forty'!". Well, sometimes casting was difficult. Anyway, Sid was pretty forgiving.

John Ellsworth: How did the "one day wonder factory" operate?

SC: Here's how it worked: The middle man between the film maker and the boys was an elderly guy named Sid Levine, an amiable, likable man, who you would never guess was really a pornographer on a huge scale. At the height of production, I would guess that we were grinding out three pictures a week. My partner was the cameraman. I directed, and created the stories. We had a full time negative editor and a full time negative cutter. I would go down to Sid's office, on Broadway, one block south of Canal. I would give him three story lines (usually made up on the subway ride downtown). He would then give me a check for half. That would come out to $7,500 on three pics, since each pic had a total budget of $5,000. There was a banking scandal in the early seventies, when it was found that the Italian Corporation that had purchased European American Bank (formerly Franklin National Bank) was wholly owned by the Sicilian Mafia. This was about 2 years before the scandal broke, but I knew that something was odd about the bank that Sid used. I would take the check to the EAB branch about a block from Sid's office. I was taken into a room where two or three people were busy, sitting at tables, counting and wrapping stacks of cash and putting them in corrugated cardboard boxes. A pretty amazing sight. The branch manager, who knew me by now, would take the check from me, reach into one of the boxes, and hand me the cash. It turned out that this branch was controlled by the Gambino crime family who used it as a Laundromat. Each week a set of three films, shot two weeks ago, was delivered, while the three films from last week were being edited, and the three films to be shot this week were being thought up. I don't know what gave me the energy.

Peter Bliss: Did your paths ever cross with such actress stalwarts as Annette Haven and Seka?

SC: I met Annette Haven, but never worked with her. She was pretty, and she was nice, but she just had no cooze. At some point I was asked by the guys I worked for to use this new girl named Seka. She was a pain in the ass from day one. She refused to come to my office or apartment for an interview (no one ever did that). But the guys were pestering me so I made arrangements to visit a film set where she was working. This was normally taboo, but I knew the

director, and he agreed to it. When I got there I was sickened by what I saw. The lights were on, the crew was standing around. Seka, who looked like a tired stripper, was sitting in the middle of it all barely touching the genitals of the guy she was working with while some pimp/boyfriend type (he never left her side) was yelling at the poor guy who was trying to get hard. This was pitiful. The deal was that when you hired Seka you had to hire the boyfriend who would direct her sex scene. I took one look at this and told the boys downtown what the drill was, and that I passed on Seka forever. To their credit they said OK. My sets were the only ones without hard on problems because my sets were happy sets. I tried to create an environment where these actors could perform without any distractions.

I TRIED MY BEST WITH SHAUN'S HELP TO COMPLETE A FILMOGRAPHY FOR THE MAN. EVEN THOUGH IT'S FAR MORE COMPLETE THAN ANY LISTING MADE UP TO NOW, THERE ARE STILL MANY MOVIES MISSING FROM IT.

Heaven's Touch (1983)
Hot Dreams (1983)
Mistress Electra (1983) (uncredited)
... aka My Mistress Electra
Beauty (1982)
Dracula Exotica (1981)
... aka Love at First Gulp
Pandora's Mirror (1981)
Prisoner of Pleasure (1981) (as Jack Hammer)

Sunny (1981)
...aka Sunny Blue
Afternoon Delights (1981)
Slave of Pleasure (1981) (as Russ Carlson)
Sensual Encounters of Every Kind (1979)
Dirty Mind of Deborah (1979)
Two Lives of Jennifer (1978)
Fiona on Fire (1978) (as Kenneth Schwartz)
... aka White Flesh Is Weak
More Than Sisters (1978) (as Russ Carlson)
Lady on the Couch (1978)
A Taste of Bette (1978)
Art School (1978)
... aka School for the Sexual Arts
Dirty Susan (1977) (as Russ Carlson)
The Fire in Francesca (1977) (uncredited)
Women in Uniform (1977)
She's No Angel (1977) (as Russ Carlson)
Water Power (1977) (uncredited)
... aka Enema Bandit (reissue title)
... aka The Enema Killer
... aka Schpritz
Girl Scout Cookies (1976)
That Lady from Rio (1976) (as Amanda Barton)
Dominatrix Without Mercy (1976)
Midnight Desires (1976)
Summer of Suzanne (1976)
The Travails of June (1976)
Venture Into the Bizarre (1976)
Dark Side of Dannielle (1976)
The Fury Within Alice (1976)
Cheryl Surrenders (1976)
Head Nurse (1975)
Tycoon's Daughter (1975)
Go Fly a Kite (1975)
Schoolgirl Reunion (1975)
Two Senoritas (1975)
The Passions of Carol (1975) (as Amanda Barton)
Daughters of Discipline (1975)
Anger in Jenny (1975)
Tina Makes a Deal (1975)
Sexual Freedom in the Ozarks (1975)
Betrayed Teens (1975)
... aka Depraved Teens
Come Fly with Us (1974)
Love Bus (1974)
Teenage Nurses (1973)
Joe Rock SuperStar (1973)
Forced Entry (1972) (as Helmuth Richler)

YAY! IT'S TIME FOR A FILTHY COMIC FROM JOSH SIMMONS!

FOR THE PEOPLE
CELEBRITIES FUCKING

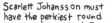
BENICIO del TORO & SCARLETT JOHANSSON

Scarlett Johansson must have the perkiest round breasts in movie-land. They cry out "Squeeze Me," while her unbelievable young bubble butt begs for you to stick your business up in dat-- The voluptuous curviness of her bod contrasts with and nicely compliments the vaguely muppet-ish beauty of her face-flesh. --Ms. Johansson claims to've fucked Benicio del Toro in an elevator--which, when queried in an interview, del Toro seemed barely to remember. Let's give the tall, brown ladies' man/guys' guy and Scandinavian Scarlett an epic view--

Bring back pubic hair!!

The public tires of the shaven nethers--Celebrities; Let the fur burst free once more!!

VA-VOOM!

SLAP-N- SLAP-

SHIFF-A-SHIFF-

HORG!

SPORK!

I LOVE YOU, SIS.

JAKE GYLLENHAAL is only allowed to fukk MAGGIE GYLLENHAAL in the ass. We don't want this ultra-cutey brother/sister team popping out one-eyed kiddies, now do we?--- That's some sexy incestin'!

GARFIELD totally nails SAMANTHA MORTON
-TAIL FUCK-

131

COULD THERE POSSIBLY BE A FUNNIER/HOTTER NERDLY CELEBRITY COUPLING THAN--

STEPHEN COLBERT & ILLEANA DOUGLAS?

One can certainly imagine Douglas to be an accommodating, generous, "anything goes"-kinda lover-- While Colbert clearly would have a stiff, straight, thick, milk-white, cut, Republican-American prick-- at a solid inch or 2 above the 5-6 inch average- And he would know just how to use that thing. Oh yessir. He would pump his junk straight up inside Douglas's sexy Olive Oyl frame. Star Power!!

EVERYMAN SCOTTISH ACTOR EWAN McGREGOR CARRIES HIMSELF WITH THE EASE OF A MAN WHO IS COMFORTABLE WITH THE SIZE OF HIS PENIS, WHILE MONICA BELLUCCI IS PRETTY MUCH SEX INCARNATE. THEY SHOULD DO IT FOR WE THE PEOPLES' ENLIGHTENMENT AND EDIFICATION.

But probably even more requested by the people-- MONICA BELLUCCI sexing up MONICA BELLUCCI

BY JOSH SIMMONS - 2006 - WITH SUGGESTIONS FROM A. STINSON, R. FRENCH + D. WEBB--

132

CHEN PING

SHAW'S SEDUCTIVE SIREN OF SEX AND SLAUGHTER

WORDS BY: DON GUARISCO '06
ART BY: JOSEPH BERGIN THE 3rd

WHEN I GOT MY FIRST REGION-FREE DVD PLAYER IN THE SUMMER OF 2004, I INVESTED HEAVILY IN A STRING OF CHINESE SHAW BROTHERS DVDs THAT HAD HIT THE R3 MARKET. I SOON DISCOVERED THAT THIS PRODUCTION COMPANY HAD MADE SO MUCH MORE THAN THE KUNGFU CHOPSOCKY I'D ALWAYS ASSOCIATED WITH THEIR NAME. INDEED, THEIR OUTPUT COVERED THE SPECTRUM OF VIEWING INTERESTS AND OFFERED COMEDIES, DRAMAS, ROMANCES, MODERN-DAY ACTION FARE, AND EVEN MUSICALS.

BEST OF ALL, THEY CRANKED OUT A TON OF SLEAZE EPICS IN BETWEEN THEIR MORE RESPECTABLE PRODUCTIONS. A GLANCE THROUGH THEIR 1970s CATALOG WILL TURN UP NASTY HORROR GUT-CHURNERS, CHEEKY SEX COMEDIES, AND SHAW'S OWN DELIRIOUSLY OVER-THE-TOP VERSIONS OF OTHER COUNTRIES' EXPLOITATION FARE. UNLIKE THEIR AMERICAN COUNTERPARTS, THESE HONG KONG SCHLOCK EPICS ALMOST ALWAYS HAD DECENT BUDGETS AND INSPIRED DIRECTION AND SET DECORATION FROM SHAW'S SQUAD OF TALENTED FILMMAKERS. THEY DELIVERED THE GRINDHOUSE GOODS, AND DID SO WITH SUPRISING, ARTFUL FLAIR.

THESE TRASHY FAVORITES ALSO PRODUCED SOME INTERESTING STARS OF THEIR OWN AND A VOCAL UNDERGROUND CONTINGENT HAS RISEN IN RECENT YEARS TO PRAISE THE FILMS OF CHEN PING. SHE ONLY HAD A HANDFUL OF STAR VEHICLES DURING THE MID-1970s, BUT THEY'VE LEFT A LIFETIME-SIZED IMPRESSION ON THE PSYCHES (AND LIBIDOS) OF MANY A CULT FILM FANATIC.

CHEN PING WAS BORN IN TAIWAN IN 1946. SHE BEGAN ACTING AT AGE 16, BUILDING HER CHOPS BY STARRING IN A VARIETY OF FILMS AND TV SHOWS IN HER HOMELAND. SHE SIGNED ON WITH THE SHAW BROS. STUDIO IN 1972, KICK-STARTING HER CAREER AS AN EXPLOITATION GODDESS WITH THE RAPE-REVENGE MELODRAMA **KISS OF DEATH**. BY THIS TIME, SHE'D DEVELOPED ENOUGH RANGE AS AN ACTRESS TO PERFORM IN COMEDIES, DRAMAS AND ACTION FARE WITH EQUAL SKILL. THIS VERSATILITY ALLOWED HER TO PLAY A WIDE ASSORTMENT OF ROLES DURING HER TIME AT SHAW BROTHERS. SHE SPENT THE REMAINDER OF THE 1970s CRANKING OUT SEVERAL FILMS A YEAR FOR THE STUDIO.

THE APPEAL OF CHEN PING IS THE FACT THAT SHE DID IT ALL WITH HER OWN UNIQUE STYLE AND WAS NOT YOUR CONVENTIONAL SEXBOMB. WITH HER ROUND FACE AND SLIM BUSTLINE, SHE LACKED THE MOVIE STARLET LOOKS AND BUXOM FIGURE USUALLY ASSOCIATED WITH A SEX SYMBOL.

HOWEVER, ATTITUDE IS THE MOST CRUCIAL PART OF BEING SEXY -- AND CHEN PING HAD ATTITUDE TO BURN. LIKE PAM GRIER OR CLAUDIA JENNINGS, SHE WAS THE KIND OF STAND ALONE EXPLOITATION FILM STARLET WHO CARRIED HERSELF WITH NATURAL GRACE NO MATTER WHAT SITUATION HER CHARACTER WAS PLACED IN. WHETHER SHE WAS DOFFING HER CLOTHES OR KICKING SOME ASS, SHE CAME ON LIKE A NO-BULLSHIT, STONE-COLD FOX.

THE FOLLOWING IS A QUICK OVERVIEW OF HER MOST MEMORABLE FILMS FROM THE BELLBOTTOM ERA. THEY'RE ALL WELL WORTH THE TIME FOR AN ADVENTUROUS EXPLOITATION FILM FAN...

CHEN IN "THE SEXY KILLER"

KISS OF DEATH (1972)

IN THIS GRIM YET STYLISH REVENGE OPUS, CHEN PING TOPLINES AS AN INNOCENT FACTORY GIRL WHO IS RAPED BY A GANG OF STREET CROOKS AS SHE'S COMING HOME FROM WORK. THE POOR GIRL IS NOT ONLY LEFT TRAUMATIZED, BUT SOON DISCOVERS SHE'S BEEN LEFT WITH AN INCURABLE VENEREAL DISEASE WITH THE POETIC NAME OF "VIETNAM ROSE".

SHE LANDS A JOB AS A BAR HOSTESS, WHERE SHE TRACKS HER FOES AND LEARNS DEADLY KUNG FU FROM ITS OWNER (LO LIEH) WHO HAS A BUM LEG AND A HEART OF GOLD. IN NO TIME FLAT SHE'S PAINTING THE NIGHTCLUBS RED WITH RAPIST BLOOD. THE END RESULT IS A BLAST OF RAZZLE-DAZZLE SHAWSPLOITATION AS THE BOOTY-KICKING SCRIPT KEEPS THE REVENGE SCENARIO TIGHTLY PLOTTED WHILE ALSO WORKING IN SOME FASCINATING SLEAZY DETOURS -- LIKE THE BASTARD WHO DRUGS GIRLS, SHOOTS PORNOS WITH THEM WHILE THEY'RE HIGH, AND THEN USES THE FILMS TO BLACKMAIL THEM INTO PROSTITUTION.

HO MENG-HUA DIRECTS THE MAYHEM WITH FLAIR, HANDLING THE RAPE SEQUENCE WITH SURPRISING SUBTLETY, USING WORDLESS IMAGES THAT PLAY LIKE COMIC BOOK PANELS BROUGHT TO LIFE. HE ALSO NEVER SHIES AWAY FROM GIVING THE VIEWER PLENTY OF ACTION AND SHOCKS; THE FINALE BEING ONE STAGGERINGLY BRUTAL BRAWL. BEST OF ALL THOUGH, IS CHEN PING'S PHYSICAL TRANSFORMATION FROM GREENHORN FACTORY GIRL TO AVENGING ANGEL IN GO-GO BOOTS. IT'S TOTALLY BELIEVABLE BECAUSE SHE THROWS HERSELF INTO THE ROLE WITH THE KIND OF UNBRIDLED EMOTION AND TOTAL SINCERITY THAT FEW WESTERN ACTRESSES WOULD DEVOTE TO SUCH A MOVIE. IT'S A LARGER THAN LIFE PERFORMANCE, AND SET THE TONE FOR HER CAREER BEAUTIFULLY.

CHEN-LICIOUS MOMENT: CHEN'S REACTION AFTER SHE CLAIMS HER FIRST BAD-GUY VICTIM IS REPRESENTED BY A WAVE OF EMOTIONS THAT RIPPLE ACROSS HER FACE. EXHAUSTION, SATISFACTION, SHOCK, RAGE, FEAR. IT PERFECTLY ENCAPSULATES THE ALL-SYSTEMS-GO GUSTO OF HER PERFORMANCE.

THE SEXY KILLER (1976)

REMEMBER THE PAM GRIER EARLY '70s CLASSIC **COFFY**? THIS IS A VIRTUAL SCENE-FOR-SCENE REMAKE, WITH CHEN PING ESSAYING THE ROLE OF A POLITICIAN-DATING HOTTIE WHOSE SISTER IS DRUGGED AND SEDUCED BY A DEALER WORKING WITHIN A BIG DRUG RING. HEARTBROKEN AND OUTRAGED, SHE VOWS REVENGE AND WORKS HER WAY THROUGH THE ORGANIZATION LIKE A BLACK WIDOW, SEDUCING AND DESTROYING HER WAY TO THE TOP.

SEXY KILLER SUCCEEDS DESPITE ITS COPYIST ORIGINS BECAUSE IT ADDS ITS OWN UNIQUE STYLE. FOR ONE THING, THE SCRIPT WILDLY AMPS UP THE BASE EXPLOITATION ELEMENTS OF THE SCENARIO. CASE IN POINT: THE KINGPIN IN **COFFY** LIKED A LITTLE LIGHT S+M AND TRASH TALK -- BUT THE KINGPIN HERE IS A FULL-ON B+D FREAK WITH A

PERSONAL TORTURE CHAMBER IN HIS MANSION! THE FILM IS ALSO DIRECTED WITH GRINDHOUSE ELAN BY SUN CHUNG, AN UNDERRATED SHAW STAFFER WHOSE STYLE CAN BEST BE DESCRIBED AS FEVERISH -- THE OPENING SEQUENCE (DEPICTING THE DRUGGING AND RAPE OF THE LITTLE SISTER CHARACTER IN A SWINGIN' NIGHTCLUB) HAS GOT TO BE ONE OF THE MOST FRENETIC OPENING SCENES IN '70s EXPLOITATION CINEMA HISTORY!

FINALLY, CHEN'S INTENSE PERFORMANCE AS THE TITLE ATTRACTION SEALS THE FILM'S APPEAL. BY TURNS SEDUCTIVE AND BRUTAL, SHE FACES UP TO THE EVER-DEEPENING WEB OF CORRUPTION AROUND HER WITH A TAKE-NO-PRISONERS SENSE OF FURY THAT IS GALVANIZING -- AND VERY HOT, TOO! SHE ALSO HAS SEVERAL SCENES WHERE SHE FIGHTS KUNG-FU BATTLES WHILE TOPLESS. "HUBBA HUBBA" IS THE ONLY LOGICAL DESCRIPTION.

CHEN-LICIOUS MOMENT: IT ARRIVES DURING HER FINAL JUGGERNAUT-LIKE ASSAULT ON THE DOMAIN OF THE VILLIANS. THERE'S A FEW SECONDS BEFORE SHE GOES AFTER THE KINGPIN'S MEN WITH A PUMP ACTION SHOTGUN WHERE SHE'S GOT AN ICY SCOWL ON HER FACE AS SHE CALMLY, EFFORTLESSLY, LOCKS AND LOADS HER WEAPON. HOT.

CRAZY SEX (1976)

WHEN SHE WASN'T TEARING IT UP IN SEXY ACTION/EXPLOITATION ITEMS, CHEN SPENT HER TIME ACTING IN SHAW'S EROTIC COMEDIES. SHE FREQUENTLY TEAMED UP WITH LI HAN-HSIANG, THE TWO FORMING AN ACTRESS DIRECTOR PARTNERSHIP THAT MADE FOR CONSISTENTLY ENGAGING SMUT. CRAZY SEX IS A GREAT EXAMPLE -- A TWO PART ANTHOLOGY WITH STORIES DEPICTING MARITAL INFIDELITY GOING TO COMIC EXTREMES. MS. CHEN PLAYS TWO PARTS IN THIS, A RARE SEX-COMEDY THAT WORKS -- THE HUMOR GENUINELY FUNNY AND NEATLY INTERWOVEN WITH THE FILM'S THEMES OF INFIDELITY AND SEXUAL FRUSTRATION. LI HAN-HSIANG ALSO HAS AN EYE FOR SEDUCTIVE IMAGERY -- LOOK OUT FOR A DAZZLING EPIC-LENGTH DOLLY THAT PANS PAST THE GOINGS-ON IN A SERIES OF BROTHEL ROOMS.

PING HANDLES HER DUAL ROLES BEAUTIFULLY: SHE EXTERNALIZES THE REAWAKENED PASSION OF A GANGSTER'S WIFE BY TRANSFORMING FROM DOUR LUMP INTO LUSTY SEX KITTEN. SHE ALSO HANDLES THE ROLE OF A MADAM WITH THE SLY, UNFLAPPABLE ATTITUDE OF A WOMAN WHO HAS SEEN EVERY KINK UNDER THE SUN BUT STILL LOVES THE CHALLENGE OF SATISFYING THEM.

CHEN-LICIOUS MOMENT: DURING THE BROTHEL STORY, THERE'S A MOMENT WHERE SHE LIES DOWN ON A BED BEFORE HER PROSTITUTE STUDENTS AND DEMONSTRATES THE PROPER WAY TO GYRATE ONE'S HIPS ON THE BED TO GIVE THE CLIENT MAXIMUM SATISFACTION. DON'T BE SURPRISED IF THIS SCENE GIVES YOU WOOD/GETS YOU WET.

BIG BAD SIS (1976)

MS. CHEN RETURNS TO THE MEAN STREETS OF HONG KONG IN THIS FEMINIST-PLOITATION TAKE ON THE URBAN ACTION GENRE. SHE PLAYS A TOUGH, LONE-WOLF TYPE WHO WORKS IN A GARMENT FACTORY AND ACTS AS PROTECTOR TO HER FELLOW (MOSTLY SINGLE) FEMALE CO-WORKERS. WHEN THE LOCAL CASINO OWNER BEGINS PREYING UPON HER CO-WORKERS AND HER BOSS, SHE TEAMS UP WITH LOCAL TEAHOUSE OWNER CHENG (THE GREAT CHEN KUAN TAI) TO FIGHT BACK. THIS IS SORT OF A SEQUEL TO THE CHEN KUAN TAI VEHICLES **THE TEAHOUSE** AND **BIG BROTHER CHENG**, AND THE END RESULT IS A CHINESE ANSWER TO JAPAN'S "PINKY VIOLENCE" MOVIES.

THE SCRIPT HITS ALL THE RIGHT MELODRA--MATIC NOTES, AS ALL THE FEMALE HEROINES HAVE SOME SORT OF KILLER TRAGIC BACK STORY -- AND IT SPICES UP THE EPISODIC PLOTLINE. DIRECTOR SUN CHUNG CAPTURES THE ACTION WITH SUPER-CHARGED FUNKY VIGOR, WITH THE FINALE (ATMOSPHERICALLY STAGED IN A ROCK QUARRY AT NIGHT) AS AN AUDIOVISUAL BLITZKRIEG OF BASHING AND BLOODSHED.

HOWEVER, IT'S PING'S PERFORMANCE THAT CEMENTS IT ALL TOGETHER. SHE GIVES A STAR TURN WORTHY OF A DOUGLAS SIRK HEROINE, GRADUALLY REVEALING THE SAD, VULNERABLE EX-SINNER BENEATH HER ICY-COOL GUARDIAN ANGEL EXTERIOR. SHE ALSO LOOKS RATHER BUTCH IN THIS FILM (FAVORING PANTSUITS

III

FOR MORE J.B.3, VISIT: SAYUNCLECOMICS.COM

135

AND SHORT HAIR) WHICH ADDS A CERTAIN KINK TO HER USUAL SEXINESS. YOWZA!

CHEN-LICIOUS MOMENT: A FLASHBACK SEQUENCE WHERE CHEN REVEALS HER BACKGROUND AS A FORMER CASINO DEALER--THE CONTRAST BETWEEN HER REMORSEFUL BUTCH MODERN DAY IDENTITY AND HER TATTOOED, SEXED UP WILD PAST SELF GENERATING AN ELECTRIC CHARGE FOR VIEWERS.

THE VENGEFUL BEAUTY (1977)

SHAW BROS. HAD HIT IT BIG A FEW YEARS PREVIOUS WITH **THE FLYING GUILLOTINE** AND ITS SEQUEL SO THEY DECIDED TO SQUEEZE A LITTLE MORE PROFIT OUT OF THE FRANCHISE WITH THE VENGEFUL BEAUTY. THE PLOT IS SIMPLE ENOUGH: CHEN PING PLAYS THE PREGNANT WIFE OF A ROYAL COURT MEMBER WHO GOES ON THE RUN WHEN THE POWER-MAD EMPEROR KILLS HER HUSBAND AND SENDS AN ARRAY OF FLYING GUILLOTINE-TOTING GOONS TO GET HER. THANK--FULLY, SHE'S WELL VERSED IN THE MARTIAL ARTS, AND TEAMS UP WITH A COUPLE FELLOW OUTCASTS WHO HELP HER FIGHT BACK.

HO MENG-HUA DIRECTED THIS ONE, AND HE GIVES IT A BREATHLESS, KINETIC PACE, PAIRING CHEN WITH SOME TOP FLIGHT SHAW CO-STARS HERE. LO-LIEH IS AMUSINGLY NASTY AS THE EMPEROR'S RIGHT HAND MAN, WHILE YUEH HUA AND NORMAN CHU MAKE EXCELLENT KICKASS FIGHTERS/ROMANTIC FOILS FOR OUR HEROINE. SHAW YIN-YIN STEALS A SCENE AS AN UNDERCOVER ASSASSIN WHO HAS A DRAMATIC SWORDFIGHT WITH PING WHILE TOPLESS.

THE COOLEST ASPECT OF THIS MOVIE HOWEVER, IS THAT IT ALLOWS US TO EXPERIENCE CHEN PING AS AN ACTION STAR. SHE PULLS THIS OFF WITHOUT A HITCH, POURING HER NATURALLY TOUGH, SEXY, INTENSE PERSONA INTO THE CHARACTERIZATION WHILE ALSO EXCELLING AT ALL THE PHYSICAL AND ACROBATIC RIGORS OF THE FILM'S NEAR-CONSTANT FIGHT SEQUENCES.

CHEN-LICIOUS MOMENT: WHEN CONFRONTED WITH A GANG OF BADDIES IN A BAMBOO FOREST, CHEN LEAPS, SLASHES, AND BACKFLIPS HER WAY THROUGH THEM WITHOUT EVEN BREAKIN' A SWEAT! GOTTA LOVE A WOMAN WHO CAN HANDLE HERSELF IN A FIGHT.

GOTTA LOVE CHEN PING.

OTHER CHEN PING FILMS TO LOOK OUT FOR:

MINISKIRT GANG (1974)
THE HOOKER AND THE HUSTLER (1975)
BLACK MAGIC (1975)
THE BEAUTIFUL VIXEN (1976)
MIGHTY PEKING MAN (1977)
LADY EXTERMINATOR (1977)
THE CALL GIRLS (1977)
THE SENSUAL PLEASURES (1978)
PSYCHOPATH (1978)
GAMBLER'S DELIGHT (1981)

UNDERAPPRECIATED FUCK STARS: FAITH

COLLECT 'EM ALL!

OK, SO MAYBE THE STAR OF THE VERY POPULAR WWW.INBEDWITHFAITH.COM SITE CAN'T **REALLY** BE CATAGORIZED AS "UNDERAPPRECIATED" THE WAY SOME GIRLS IN THIS BIZ CAN, BUT SHE HAS YET TO BE ON A PORNO DVD, AND SHE'S SO FREAKIN' **HAWT**, I FIGURE SHE'S WORTHY OF SOME ATTENTION. THIS YOUNG BRIT INTERNET PRINCESS HAS STARTLING **32G TITS** THAT ARE **ALL REAL**. NORMALLY I'M NOT A BOOB MAN, **BUT THEM SHITS IS DOPE**!

—BOUGIE

THE LOVELY MISS SYLVA KOSCINA

3 ACTION CLASSICS
BY SPANISH DIRECTOR
ANTONIO ISASI

✧◆✧◆✧◆✧◆✧◆✧

BORN IN MARCH 1927 IN MADRID, SPANISH DIRECTOR ANTONIO ISASI MOVED TO BARCELONA IN HIS EARLY TWENTIES AND FOUND WORK AS A BEST BOY WITH EMISORA FILMS. DURING HIS TENURE THERE, HE'D EVENTUALLY BE MOVED UP TO EDITOR, AND BEGAN TO FIND SOME SUCCESS IN THE SPANISH FILM INDUSTRY. IN 1955 HE'D LEAVE EMISORA TO ESTABLISH HIS OWN PRODUCTION COMPANY CALLED "PRODUCCIONES ISASI".

ISASI DIRECTED MOVIES FROM 1950 TO 1988, BUT IT WAS WITH THREE ACTION THRILLERS MADE CONSECUTIVELY IN THE MIDDLE OF HIS CAREER THAT HE FINALLY BROKE THROUGH WITH CREATIVE WORK THAT NOT ONLY MADE MONEY AT THE BOX OFFICE BOTH DOMESTICALLY AND ABROAD, BUT ALSO GRABBED THE ATTENTION OF CRITICS AND ACCOLADE-GIVERS.

PRESENTED WITH THE BEST DIRECTOR AWARD FOR EACH OF THESE THREE MOVIES FROM THE LAUDED SPANISH CINEMA WRITERS CIRCLE AWARDS (AS WELL AS THE BEST FILM AWARD FOR ALL THREE FROM THE BARCELONA-BASED SANT JORDI AWARDS), ISASI WAS ONE OF THE TOP DOGS OF THE SPANISH FILM INDUSTRY FROM 1966 TO 1973. SHOT BY THE TALENTED CINEMATOGRAPHER JAUN GELPI, ALL THREE MOVIES DESERVE TO BE BETTER KNOWN TODAY THAN THEY ARE.

THAT MAN IN ISTANBUL (1965)
THE FIRST OF THE THREE FILMS IS THIS B-MOVIE SPY THRILLER. FAST-PACED, QUICK-WITTED, AND SLIGHTLY SATIRICAL, THE MOVIE ENERGETICALLY WHIPS THROUGH THE PLOT, WHICH CONCERNS A MILLION DOLLAR RANSOM THAT HAS BEEN DOLED OUT TO SOME BAD GUYS IN RETURN

SLYVA KOSCINA AND GOOD OL' HORST BUCHHOLZ

GARY
LOCKWOOD
ELKE
SOMMER
LEE J.
COBB
AND JACK
PALANCE

THEY CAME TO ROB LAS VEGAS

FOR THE SAFE RETURN OF AN AMERICAN NUCLEAR SCIENTIST, WHEN HE ISN'T RETURNED AS PROMISED, SECRET AGENT KENNY (SYLVA KOSCINA) JETS TO TURKEY AND TEAMS UP WITH A PLAYBOY-GAMBLER NAMED TONY (HORST BUCHHOLZ) TO HELP HER FIND THE SCIENTIST -- WITH THE PROMISE THAT HE CAN POCKET THE MILLION SMACKERS RANSOM.

A BEAUTIFUL CURVY HEROINE, TREACHERY, NARROW ESCAPES, EXOTIC SETTINGS, KLAUS KINSKI SIDEKICKS NAMED BOGO AND BRAIN, FABULOUS 1960s EURO AESTHETICS AND ATMOSPHERE, AND BOND-INSPIRED SPY ADVENTURE. IT STARTS OUT VERY STRONG, OVERSTAYS ITS WELCOME AFTER THE FIRST HOUR, BUT THIS IS STILL REALLY FUN STUFF.

THEY CAME TO ROB LAS VEGAS (1968)
IT BE HEIST TIME, BABY! I LOVE A GOOD HEIST MOVIE, AND THIS IS ONE OF THE BEST THAT I HAVE PEEPED. OK, AS OF THIS WRITING I HAVEN'T ACTUALLY SEEN THAT MANY -- BUT LAY OFF, OK?! I'M WORKIN' ON IT! THERE ARE ONLY SO MANY HOURS IN A DAY.

THE SETTING IS (DUH) LAS VEGAS, AND THE CAPER INVOLVES THE SEVEN MILLION DOLLAR ROBBERY OF A HIGH TECH ARMOURED CAR WHILE IT ROLLS THROUGH THE DESERT BETWEEN VEGAS AND LOS ANGELES. THE CAST (GARY LOCKWOOD, THE LOVELY ELKE SOMMER LEE J. COBB AND JACK PALANCE) ARE TERRIFIC ACROSS THE BOARD, AND THE FASCINATING AND CREATIVE CHOICE TO SHOOT THE ACTION WITH VIRTUALLY NO CAMERA MOVEMENT (EVEN THE ACTION SCENES ARE EDITED BETWEEN QUICKLY CUT SHOTS FROM FIXED POSITIONS) MAKES THIS A MEMORABLE ISASI OFFERING.

UNPREDICTABLE AND NERVE WRACKING DESPITE THE SLOW DELIBERATE PACING, THE TENSION BETWEEN THE THIEVES IS QUITE PALATABLE WHEN THINGS DON'T GO ACCORDING TO THE PLAN. (DO THEY EVER?) THIS IS YET ANOTHER MOVIE THAT DESERVES TO BE BETTER KNOWN THAN IT IS.

SUMMERTIME KILLER (1972).
CHRIS MITCHUM MAKES IT HIS MISSION TO KILL THE FOUR GANGSTERS WHO DID HIS DAD IN.

BUT WHEN THE LAST OF THE FOUR IS ONLY WOUNDED AFTER HIS ASSASSINATION ATTEMPT, HIS ELEMENT OF SURPRISE IS RUINED. WITH THE BAD GUY NOW ON HIGH ALERT, MITCHUM INSTEAD KIDNAPS THE MAN'S SEXY 19 YEAR OLD DAUGHTER (OLIVIA HUSSEY) AND KEEPS HER CAGED IN A HOUSEBOAT.

THIS ITALO-SPANISH-FRENCH CO-PRODUCTION IS A PRIME EXAMPLE OF EARLY '70s EURO-ACTION EXPLOITATION FARE, IT ISN'T AS SLEAZY OR AS VIOLENT AS SOME OF THE OTHER FILMS IN ITS GENRE, BUT IT MAKES UP FOR THAT WITH PLENTY OF ENTERTAINMENT VALUE IN THE SAME VEIN AS THE GREAT CHARLES BRONSON MOVIE FROM THE SAME YEAR: **THE MECHANIC.**

IN KEEPING WITH THE SPANISH/ITALIAN SPAGHETTI WESTERNS THAT PRECEDED IT, THE MAIN CHARACTER SEEKS HIS VENGEANCE WITH A SENSE OF FOCUS AND GRITTY EMOTION-FREE BRAVADO, AND HE'S PRESENTED WITH STYLE VIA GELPI'S CRISP CINEMATOGRAPHY AND ISASI'S STYLISH DIRECTION.

THE HIGHLIGHT IS THE EXHILARATING MOTORCYCLE STUNT WORK AND CAR CHASES! THIS SHIT IS SERIOUSLY UNDER RATED!

·2010· BOUGIE

OLIVIA HUSSEY · CHRIS MITCHUM

EASTMANCOLOR

why does a nice young man who likes girls, dogs and motorcycles... have to go around killing people?

SHOT ON LOCATION IN NEW YORK, LISBON, BARCELONA, ROME,

A film of **ANTONIO ISASI**

the summertime killer

THE PASSIONS OF CAROL (1975)

SHOT ON 16MM FILM WITH A BUDGET OF $18,000, THIS HARDCORE PORN PRODUCTION FROM SHAUN COSTELLO WAS THE VERY FIRST XXX ADULT FILM TO OPEN IN A REGULAR THEATRE. BUT THE OCCASION WASN'T ALL THAT LEGENDARY. IN FACT, WHEN IT OPENED AT NEW YORK'S QUAD CINEMAS ON MONDAY, MARCH 24TH 1975, IT WAS TO AN EMPTY THEATRE.

PORN HISTORIANS ARE IN NEAR UNANIMOUS AGREEMENT ABOUT ITS QUALITIES, BUT IN HINDSIGHT, DIRECTOR SHAUN COSTELLO HAS CALLED THE EFFORT "ODD", AND ALSO CATEGORISED IT AS HIS FIRST FLOP. "IT WAS BIG, IT WAS NOISY, IT WAS COLOURFUL, IT WAS FUNNY, BUT THERE WAS ONE THING IT WASN'T; IT WASN'T SEXY."

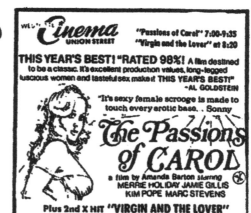

PERHAPS NOT, BUT SOMETIMES BEING ENTERTAINING IS ENOUGH. THE MOVIE CASTS MARY STUART IN THE TITLE ROLE AND EXISTS AS AN UNUSUAL PORN VERSION OF CHARLES DICKENS'S TIMELESS A CHRISTMAS CAROL. MR. 10 1/2 HIMSELF, MARC STEVENS, PLAYS A GHOSTLY COBWEB-COVERED JACOB MARLEY, AND JAMIE GILLIS IS CAST AGAINST TYPE AS THE HARRIED BOB CRATCHET -- ALTHOUGH INSTEAD OF A DISABLED SON, HE'S GOT A CUTE CRIPPLED WIFE NAMED TINY KIM (PLAYED BY KIM POPE).

"I HAD NEVER WORKED ON A SOUND STAGE BEFORE", ADMITTED COSTELLO, "I HAD TO KEEP THE PRODUCTION GOING 24 HOURS A DAY TO COMPLETE IT ANYWHERE NEAR ITS ORIGINAL BUDGET. IT WAS SHOT AT WHAT BECAME MOTHER'S SOUND STAGE IN NEW YORK'S EAST VILLAGE. MY WONDERFUL NEIGHBOURS, WHO LIVED IN MY RENT CONTROLLED APARTMENT BUILDING ON EAST 21ST STREET, BUILT THE SETS, SEWED THE COSTUMES, AND IN GENERAL JUST MADE IT ALL HAPPEN. MY FRIEND DAVID WOOL CREATED THE SKYLINE OF MANHATTAN THAT IS SEEN FROM CAROL SCROOGE'S WINDOW, AND BUILT IT OUT OF CORRUGATED CARDBOARD."

OTHER HIGHLIGHTS: DIRTY RAGGY ANNE AND ANDY NEEDLEWORK, ECLECTIC MUSIC CHOICES SUCH AS 'KONTAKTE' BY STOCKHAUSEN AND 'TUBULAR BELLS' BY MIKE OLDFIELD, A FLESH-PACKED THREE WAY IN A ROOM MADE OF MIRRORS, ADULTS PLAYING CHILDREN IN A ROOM FULL OF OVERSIZED PROPS, AND THE FACT THAT YOU CAN GET NAKED WITH SOMEONE YOU LIKE AND WATCH THE FILM ON X-MAS EVE WITH A COUPLE OF MUGS OF EGG NOG!
—BOUGIE

LOVE
BONE
before he LOVES you

Bone (1972. Dir: Larry Cohen)

AS A DIRECTOR, LARRY COHEN TENDED TOWARDS CULT-FAVE HORROR AND THRILLER GENRE OFFERINGS, BUT IT WAS WITH HIS MOSTLY UNKNOWN DEBUT THAT HE WAS AT HIS UNINHIBITED BEST. LARRY IS AN EXCEPTIONAL SCREENWRITER AS WELL, AND THIS SATIRICAL PSYCHODRAMA IS A GLORIOUS EXAMPLE OF THAT, AS TALENTED ACTORS ARE PROVIDED WITH SOME VERY UNUSUAL AND MEMORABLE MATERIAL TO WORK WITH.

IT'S 1970, AND A RICH WHITE COUPLE (ANDREW DUGGAN, JOYCE VAN PATTEN) ARE CONFRONTED RIGHT IN THEIR OWN HOME BY A THREATENING BLACK MAN WHO LEERS AND SNEERS HIS WAY INTO A HOSTAGE SITUATION. THE KIDNAPPER IS BONE (YAPHET KOTTO) AND HE SENDS THE HUSBAND OFF TO A LOCAL BANK TO MAKE A HUGE WITHDRAWAL ON HIS BEHALF, WHILE HE STAYS BACK AT THE RANCH GETTING HIS DICK HARD WITH SOME MIDDLE AGED POON. BUT WHAT BONE DOESN'T REALISE IS THAT THERE IS NO MONEY, AND THE MARRIAGE IN QUESTION IS IN THE CRAPPER. THIS IS EVIDENCED BY OL' HUBBY LEISURELY GOING TO A BAR AND BANGING AN ODDBALL FLOWER-CHILD SLUT (YOUNG ENOUGH TO BE HIS KID) INSTEAD OF RACING BACK WITH A BAG OF CASH TO SAVE THE MISSUS.

THAT'S JUST THE TIP OF THE ICEBURG IN THIS INEXPLICABLY OVERLOOKED BLACK (REALLY BLACK) COMEDY/SHOCKER ABOUT CLASS WARFARE, RACE RELATIONS, AND THE WAYS IN WHICH MEN AND WOMEN RELATE IN OUR MODERN WORLD.

KINGDOM OF THE SPIDERS (1977)

THE MYSTERIOUS DEATH OF COLBY'S (WOODY STRODE) PRIZE CALF HAS STUDLY VERDE VALLEY VETERINARIAN "RACK HANSEN" (WILLIAM SHATNER) CONCERNED AND EMOTING, AS ALL SHATNERS ARE WONT TO DO WHEN A CAMERA GETS IN FRONT OF THEM.

SHIT-HOT ENTOMOLOGIST DR. ASHLEY (TIFFANY BOLLING) KICKS OUT THE BLOOD TESTS AND DISCOVERS THAT MASSIVE DOSES OF SPIDER VENOM WERE THE CAUSE OF DEATH. TIFF (WHO WAS ALSO ADORABLE IN **THE CANDY SNATCHERS**) FIGURES THAT DDT HAS SO DEPLETED THE LOCAL TARANTULAS' FOOD SUPPLY THAT, IN ORDER TO SURVIVE, THE ARMIES OF EIGHT LEGGED KILLERS ARE HUNTING DIFFERENT PREY: LOCAL LIVESTOCK, PETS.... AND HUMANS! SHOCK!! THEN SHE GETS NAKED AND HAS A SHOWER.

KINGDOM OF THE SPIDERS FEATURES AN - AS THEY SAY - "INTOXICATING BLEND" OF ADEQUATE ACTING, DECENT WRITING, AND SKILLFUL DIRECTION. THE RESULT IS A SEMI-SOLID ATMOSPHERIC LOW BUDGET THRILLER THAT HAS BECOME BELOVED AMONGST NATURE-ON-THE - RAMPAGE FILM DEVOTEES, AND DESPITE THE FACT THAT IT LOOKS A LITTLE LIKE A MADE FOR TV MOVIE, EVEN B-MOVIE HATERS MUST ADMIT THE MAYHEM IN THE LAST HALF HOUR IS PRETTY DAMN COOL.

ONE OF THE REAL THRILLS FOR VIEWERS IS GETTING TO SEE WHAT WILLIAM SHATNER HAS TO ENDURE AS AN ACTOR WHILE BEING ALMOST COMPLETELY COVERED IN REAL SPIDERS. OL' SHATS' VERY CONVINCING REACTIONS TO THE ARACHNID INVASIONS ON HIS TERRITORIAL BUBBLE ARE AWESOME! ANOTHER ROUND OF KNEE SLAPPING OCCURS AS A PILOT IS ENGULFED BY THE HAIRY BEASTIES IN HIS PLANE. HE CAREENS OUT OF CONTROL, ALL THE WHILE SCREAMING AT THE TOP OF HIS LUNGS LIKE A TOTAL PUSSY.

THE MAIN FLAWS HERE ARE ONLY REALLY NOTICEABLE TO THOSE WHO LOOK FOR SILLY CONTINUITY ERRORS AND SCIENTIFIC FLUBS INSTEAD OF JUST SHUTTING THE FUCK UP AND BEING ENTERTAINED BY A BRAINLESS SPIDER-ATTACK FILM. ANYONE WHO KNOWS POOP ABOUT TARANTULAS KNOWS THEY DON'T SPIN WEBS, AND THAT THEIR VENOM PRE-DIGESTS VICTIMS INSTEAD OF POISONING THEM INTO IMMOBILITY. YOU KNOW, FOR EASY STORAGE AND LEISURELY DRINKING OF FLESH N' ALL THAT. YEAH, DESPITE THEIR BAD REP, TARANTULAS ARE BASICALLY HARMLESS TO PEOPLE - SO YOU GOTTA BELIEVE THAT THE HIGH RATE OF SPIDER SMASHING VIA BOOTS AND MOVING VEHICLES WILL UNDOUBTEDLY UPSET SPIDER OWNERS.

DIRECTOR JOHN "BUD" CARDOS HAS HAD SOMETHING OF AN ECLECTIC AND KOOKY CAREER IN EXPLOITATION CINEMA SINCE THE 1960s, INCLUDING STINTS AS A 2ND UNIT DIRECTOR, STUNTMAN, SPECIAL EFFECTS CO-ORDINATOR AND EVEN SOME ACTING DUTIES. ONE OF HIS EARLIEST JOBS WAS AS AN ASSISTANT TO THE BIRD WRANGLERS ON ALFRED HITCHCOCK'S 1963 CLASSIC, **THE BIRDS.**

WITH **KINGDOM OF THE SPIDERS**, CARDOS SHOWS A HIGH DEGREE OF PROMISE AS A DIRECTOR, AND IT'S KINDA SAD KNOWING HIS CAREER WENT AND DIED FOLLOWING THIS CREATURE FEATURE. TWICE (1ST FOR **THE DARK** (1979) AND THEN FOR **MUTANT** IN 1984) HE WAS BROUGHT IN TO CLEAN UP CHAOTIC, MANGLED PRODUCTIONS AFTER THE ORIGINAL DIRECTORS HAD BEEN SHIT-CANNED. TAINTED BY FAILURE, CARDOS QUICKLY FOUND HIS CAREER IN RUINS.

THE SCORE, ALTHOUGH RECYCLED, HAS SOME OF THE BEST USE OF STOCK MUSIC CUES (SEVERAL FROM CLASSIC **TWILIGHT ZONE** EPISODES) TO BE HEARD OUTSIDE OF A GEORGE A. ROMERO MOVIE. IT LATER TURNED UP IN THE HEAVILY CENSORED VERSION OF JOE D'AMATO'S GORY ZOMBIE-CANNIBAL CHUNK-BLOWER **ANTHROPOPHAGOUS** (1980) WHICH SAW RELEASE IN THE US AS **THE GRIM REAPER.**

THE CREEPY SPECIAL EFFECTS COURTESY OF GREG AUER (**THE HILLS HAVE EYES** - 1977) ARE IMPRESSIVE CONSIDERING THE LOW BUDGET, MAINLY CONSISTING OF NASTY-LOOKIN' CADAVERS COCOONED IN SPIDER SPOOGE AND COVERED IN BITE MARKS. REPORTEDLY GENERATING OVER $17 MILLION IN ITS INITIAL RELEASE, SHATNER WAS SAID TO BE WORKING ON A SEQUEL THROUGHOUT THE '80s, WITH HIMSELF ATTACHED AS DIRECTOR AND THE PLOT DESCRIBED AS A "CONSPIRACY-THRILLER"(??) THE WHOLE PROJECT FIZZLED WHEN STUDIO HEADS GOT A PEEP AT HOW BAD SHATNER FUCKED UP MAKING **STAR TREK 5: THE FINAL FRONTIER** (1989.) K.O.T.S CO-PRODUCER IGO KANTOR HAS RECENTLY ANNOUNCED PLANS TO MOUNT A SEQUEL/REMAKE OF HIS OWN. WE'LL SEE.

SPIDERS IS SCAREEE

FART FOR LIFE

FEMALE CONVICT SCORPION
女囚701号

SIGH... MAYBE IT'S THE FILM GEEK IN ME, BUT I SHORE DO LUVS ME A DAME THAT FUCKS SHIT UP IN A MOVIE. THERE IS JUST SOMETHING SO SATISFYING ABOUT A CONFIDENT WOMAN WHO TAKES NO DUNG, AND HANDS OUT PAIN AND SUFFERING TO ANYONE WHO GETS ALL UP IN HER GRILL AND DESERVES TO TASTE A SLICE OF PUMMEL PIE.

IT'S OBVIOUS THAT I'M NOT THE ONLY ONE WHO GETS OFF ON THIS WHEN I SEE MOVIES LIKE **KILL BILL** ACHIEVE CRITICAL AND BOX OFFICE SUCCESS.

BUT IT'S IMPORTANT TO NOTE THAT SUCH MOVIES OWE SOMETHING TO THOSE THAT WENT BEFORE THEM. DIRECTORS LIKE QUENTIN TARANTINO ARE STEEPED IN REFERENTIAL PROPS TO THE FILMS THEY ADORE, AN' OL Q.T. HAS STATED THROUGH BOTH DEED AND WORD THAT HE WAS INSPIRED BY THE FILMS OF STOIC JAPANESE HEADTURNER MEIKO KAJI.

WHILE NOT A MARTIAL ARTS OR WEAPON EXPERT, THE QUIET RAGE FILLED CHARACTER OF SASORI (SCORPION) PLAYED BY THE RAVEN HAIRED KAJI IN THE **FEMALE CONVICT SCORPION** MOVIES FROM THE EARLY '70S IS POSSIBLY THE TOUGHEST, NO-NONSENSE WOMAN I'VE EVER HAD THE PLEASURE OF SEEING IMMORTALISED ON FILM. SHE'S JUST A REGULAR GAL WHO'S BEEN DRIVEN DEMONIC BY A BROKEN HEART, AND IF YOU CROSS HER (AND PEOPLE OFTEN SEEM TO MAKE THE MISTAKE OF DOING SO), YOU WILL UNDOUBTEDLY FIND YOUR ASS EITHER DEAD, OR IN SOME EXCRUCIATING AGONY. SHIT, JUST TRYING TO GUESS HOW SCORPION WILL GO ABOUT HANDIN' OUT THAT REVENGE-THEMED PUNISHMENT IS ALMOST AS FULFILLING AS SEEING IT EXACTED. SHE'S A MIXTURE OF FELINE FEROCITY AND K-9 CRAZY, AND HER HATRED OF MEN AND THE ESTABLISHMENT THAT WRONGED HER COOKS BENEATH THE COLD STEEL GLARE OF HER EYES -- AND YET, SHE IS A MYSTERY.

MEIKO KAJI WAS BORN MASAKO OTA ON MARCH 24th 1947 AND STARTED HER MOVIE CAREER IN 1967 DURING A TIME WHEN JAPAN'S MAJOR PRODUCTION COMPANIES WERE IN THE MIDST OF FINANCIAL STRUGGLES. AUDIENCES WERE SLIGHT, MONEY WAS BEING LOST, AND ONLY SEVERAL INDY COMPANIES WERE EVEN PROFITING AT ALL. IN THE EARLY '70S, A COMPANY CALLED NIKKATSU DESPERATELY CAME UP WITH A NEW STATEGY - AND WOULD LAUNCH THIS NEW GENRE WITH MEIKO IN THEIR **ALLEYCAT ROCK** SERIES (AKA **STRAY CAT ROCK**). THE STAGE WAS SET FOR KAJI AND FOR JAPANESE TRASH CINEMA FANS EVERYWHERE.

THE FILMS WERE GEARED TOWARDS A YOUTH MARKET, AND FEATURED STORY LINES IN WHICH JUVENILE GANGS VIOLENTLY CONFRONTED EACH OTHER FOR VARIOUS REASONS-USUALLY INVOLVING HONOR OR PUSSY. MEIKO APPEARED IN 5 OF THESE FILMS SHOT AT A BREAKNECK PACE UP UNTIL LATE 1971, SOME OF WHICH

FEMALE PRISONER #701: SCORPION (1972)

FULL SIZE ILLUSTRATIONS ON THIS AND FOLLOWING PAGES BY JOSEPH BERGIN THE THIRD

SLID OFF INTO KITSCHY MUSICAL COMEDY (**ALLEYCAT ROCK: BEAT '71**) AND OTHERS WHICH BRAZENLY DISPLAYED ANTI-AMERICAN ALLEGORIES (**ALLEYCAT ROCK: SEX HUNTER**). WHILE WELL MADE, THE SERIES NEVER REALLY REALISED ITS TRUE POTENTIAL AS SLEAZY SEXPLOITATION, INSTEAD FALTERING AS SOMEWHAT TEPID SOAP OPERA.

A YEAR LATER IN 1972, NIKKATSU RESTRUCTURED AGAIN WITH A DIRECT FOCUS ON LOWER BUDGET EROTIC FILM -- MANY OF WHICH ARE NONETHELESS OF CONSIDERABLE ARTISTIC VALUE AND DISPLAY COCKLOADS OF AWESOMENESS. THESE FILMS WERE USUALLY HUGE BOX OFFICE EARNERS, AND THE GENRE BECAME KNOWN AS "ROMAN PORNO", OR "PINK FILM", AND MEIKO SUDDENLY FOUND HERSELF AT GROUND ZERO. UNINTERESTED IN BECOMING A TYPICAL SOFTCORE PINKU-EIGA STARLET, KAJI BROKE CONTRACT AND JOINED TOEI STUDIOS, WHO HAD BEGUN THEIR OWN LINE OF GRITTY SEX THEMED SLEAZEPOTS THEY CALLED "PINKY VIOLENCE". TOEI WOOED HER WITH THE CHOICE ROLE OF "MATSU" (AKA SASORI) WITH FIRST TIME DIRECTOR SHUNYA ITO -- AND THE STORY AND VISUALS ADAPTED IN A DARK GORGEOUS COMIC BOOK STYLE FROM A MANGA CREATED BY TOORU SHINOHARA.

SASORI AS SHE APPEARED IN THE ORIGINAL JAPANESE MANGA.

FEMALE PRISONER #701: SCORPION HIT THEATERS THE SAME YEAR TO CONSIDERABLE SUCCESS. AN OFFBEAT MIX OF SLY EROTICISM, PATHOS, AND BLOODY ACTION, THE FILM BRILLIANTLY BLENDED ART-CINEMA AND EXPLOITATION-PACKED WOMEN-IN-PRISON MOVIES EFFORTLESSLY, WITH ONLY ITS SEQUEL BESTING ITS NEAR FLAWLESS AMALGAMAT--ION OF THE TWO UNLIKELY GENRES. IN ACADEMIC TERMS: ITO'S IDEOLOGICAL STANCE MANAGES -- THROUGH THE PORTRAIT OF A FEMALE BROUGHT TO THE BRINK OF SAVAGE SUBMISSION BY SOCIETY -- TO CONJURE AN ASIAN BROAD'S HEROIC EMANCIPATORY TRAVAIL. TITTY HUNTERS SHOULD ALSO TOTALLY FUCKING NOTE THAT F.P.#701:S REMAINS, TO THIS DAY, THE ONE FILM CONTAINING LUSCIOUS NUDE SEX SCENES VIA MISS KAJI. COMMENCE DROOLING, BOYS.

THE FOLLOW UP, **FEMALE CONVICT SCORPION: JAILHOUSE 41** (SEE CINEMA SEWER #14) CAME OUT THE SAME YEAR. (HOW THE HELL DID THEY MAKE THESE AMAZING MOVIES SO _FAST_?!) THANKS TO PART ONE'S SUCCESS, SULTRY MEIKO MADE FULL USE OF HER NEW STAR STATUS TO ESCAPE MOST OF THE OBLIGATORY NUDITY, ALTHOUGH HER JAILED CHARACTER STILL GETS HOGTIED, HOSED DOWN, TORTURED, AND GANG-RAPED BY FIENDISH PRISON GUARDS.

ASTONISHINGLY BEAUTIFUL IN ITS VISUAL AND NARRATIVE ABSTRACTION AND ASS SLAPPINGLY NASTY IN ITS MIXTURE OF FETISHISM AND BRUTALITY, PART TWO IS THE TRUE GEM IN THESE 4 FILMS WHICH I UNRESERVEDLY CONSIDER TO BE MY ALL TIME FAVORITE SERIES IN FILM HISTORY (YES, YOU READ THAT RIGHT). MATSU SPEAKS EVEN LESS, (TWO LINES IN 90 MINUTES) EMOTES MORE, AND THE ENTIRE THING IS JUST PEPPERED WITH AMAZING SURREALIST INTERLUDES THAT NEVER OVERSTAY THEIR WELCOME.

THE TORTURE-HARDENED VIXEN OF FEW WORDS TEARS IT UP WHILE ON THE LAM IN THE SUBLIME THIRD FILM IN THE SERIES **FEMALE CONVICT SCORPION: BEAST STABLE** WHICH WAS RELEASED A SHORT TIME LATER IN '73.

DIRECTOR ITO DELIVERS ANOTHER QUASI-

FEMALE CONVICT SCORPION: JAILHOUSE #41 (1972)

EXPERIMENTAL PIECE IN WHICH SCORPION HAS BROKEN OUT OF JAIL, IS ON THE RUN FROM THE COPS, AND AT ONE POINT RUNS WILDLY THROUGH THE STREETS HANDCUFFED TO A POLICEMAN'S SEVERED ARM! SHACKING UP WITH A MEEK GIRL WHO ALLOWS HER RETARDED BROTHER TO SCREW HER SO HE'LL LEAVE OTHER GIRLS ALONE, MATSU EVADES THE FUZZ AND ENDS UP GOING TOE TO TOE WITH YAKUZA GANGSTERS HELMED BY ONE OF THE QUEEN BEES FROM HER TIME ON THE INSIDE. BUT HER EXACTED REVENGE ONLY FUELS THE FIRE OF A HATRED-FILLED PUGNACIOUS COP (SANS ARM!) WHO WANTS TO BRING SCORPION DOWN IN A FIERY SHOWDOWN.

DESPITE RIPPING ME A NEW ANUS, ITO'S BUNUEL-ESQUE MASTERPIECE ENDED UP FAILING TO PLEASE   TOEI, WHO DECIDED TO REPLACE HIM WITH YASUHARU HASEBE FOR THE 4th MOVIE. **FEMALE CONVICT SCORPION: GRUDGE SONG.** ALTHOUGH PRESERVING THE ORIGINAL W.I.P. TONE OF THE SERIES, HASEBE AVOIDED THE OBVIOUS OPTION OF EXTENDING MATSU'S CHARACTER ARC AND INSTEAD HAD HER UNCHARACTERISTICALLY LIFT HER DEFENCES AND FALL IN LOVE WITH A MAN -- ONLY TO HAVE HER HEART BROKEN AGAIN BY HIS PATHETIC INTERMINABLE MALE WEAKNESS. WHILE THE LEAST IMPRESSIVE OF THE KAJI SASORI FILMS, **GRUDGE SONG** IS FAR FROM BEING MEDIOCRE, AND STILL RULES THE FUCKIN' SCHOOL IN COMPARISON TO MANY OF THE W.I.P. OFFERINGS OF THE ERA.

DISAPPOINTED BY THE LOSS OF ITO AS DIRECTOR, KAJI JUMPED SHIP AFTER COMPLETION OF **GRUDGE SONG**, AND WAS REPLACED FOR THE FIFTH INSTALMENT BY YUMI TAKIGAWA, WHO WAS DISCOVERED A FEW MONTHS EARLIER IN THE KICKASS **SCHOOL OF THE HOLY BEAST** (SEE CINEMA SEWER #15) BY BONDAGE-KING NORIFUMI SUZUKI. ANOTHER 6 SEQUELS WOULD BE BIRTHED, ENDING WITH THE SO-SO YAWNER **SCORPION'S REVENGE** (AKA SASORI IN USA) IN 1998.

MEIKO KAJI WOULD GO ON TO STAR IN OTHER STAND OUT JAPANESE FILMS SUCH AS THE UNFORGETABLE **LADY SNOWBLOOD**, KINJI FUKASAKU'S **YAKUZA GRAVE YARD** (1976) AND A FINE CO-STARRING ROLE WITH SONNY CHIBA IN **SISTER STREETFIGHTER** (1978), BEFORE BOWING OUT OF FILM TO EXCLUSIVELY RESTRICT HERSELF TO TV WORK IN TOKYO, WHERE IN HER 50s SHE IS STILL ACTIVE TODAY.

FEMALE CONVICT SCORPION: BEAST STABLE (1973)

The story of FEMALE CONVICT SCORPION
- as told by series director Shunya Ito

"AT THE TIME, THERE WAS A COMIC DRAWN FOR ADULTS THAT WAS PUBLISHED IN A WEEKLY MAGAZINE. IT WAS VERY SUCCESSFUL, AND I READ IT FROM TIME TO TIME. THE IDEA TO ADAPT IT CAME WHEN A PRODUCTION COMPANY ASKED ME WHETHER THE PROJECT INTERESTED ME, AND SUGGESTED ACTRESS MEIKO KAJI IN THE LEAD. AS THE PRINCIPAL CHARACTER OF THE SERIES, SHE WAS REALLY INTERESTING, AND I INVESTED MYSELF IN THIS PROJECT."

"IT WAS MY FIRST FILM, AND I WANTED TO BENEFIT FROM THIS OCCASION TO LOOK FURTHER INTO THE IDEAS THE PRODUCERS HAD ON THE SERIES. I MADE A POINT OF WRITING THE CHARACTER IN AN ORIGINAL WAY, AND WISHED FOR THE CHARACTER OF SCORPION TO BE AT THE SAME TIME SPIRITUAL AND PHYSICAL. AND I WANTED TO ACCENTUATE THAT AND MAKE THE FILM SOPHISTICATED."

"AFTER THE FIRST FILM WENT SO WELL, I WAS ENTRUSTED WITH THE REALISATION OF THE SECOND. IN THE FIRST MOVIE, THE HEROINE IS JUSTIFIED BY THE IDEA TO EXERT HER PERSONAL REVENGE, IT IS SOMETHING OF A SIMPLE MOTIVATION, AND FEELINGS PUSH HER TO ACT. SCORPION IS A CHARACTER WHO IS DEFINED THROUGH HER ACTS. BUT FOR THE 2ND MOVIE, THE CHARACTER PASSES TO A HIGHER STAGE. SCORPION IS A CRIMINAL WHO RADICALISES HERSELF AND IS NOT LIMITED TO A PERSONAL REVENGE, BUT GOES UNTIL BEING OPPOSED TO THE STATE ITSELF."

"SHE'S A VICTIM HUNTING FOR THE VICTIMISERS. FROM THIS IDEA, I REALLY

WANTED SCORPION TO TAKE ON A MULTIDIMENSIONAL SYMBOLIC ROLE, THE ROLE OF AN IDOL WHO BECOMES A LEGEND WHILE UNDERGOING MANY HUMILIATIONS. HER IMPRISONMENT AND HUMILIATIONS DO NOTHING BUT REINFORCE THE FEELING OF REVOLT SHE HAS. SO SCORPION IS SET UP AS A LEADER OF THE PRISONERS, AND TAKES A GROUP ON AN ESCAPE MISSION, THUS THE HISTORY OF THE MANGA SHAPES THE 2ND FILM, AND THE PROJECT WAS MUCH CLOSER TO THE ORIGINAL WORK."

"IN JAPAN, WE HAVE A SELF CENSORSHIP COMMITTEE FOUNDED BY A FEDERATION OF PRODUCERS. IT IS A SYSTEM COMPROMISED TO PREVENT THE INTERVENTION OF OUTSIDE FORCES, AND THE CENSOR HAS THE ROLE OF LIMITING ALL THAT COULD BE TOO EXCESSIVE. WE MUST PRESENT OUR IDEAS, AND IT IS A QUESTION OF NEGOTIATING WITH THE CENSOR. THANKS TO THE WAY THE SYSTEM IS SET UP, I COULD IN FACT IMPOSE MY IDEAS FOR THIS FILM. I PROFITED FROM A CERTAIN FREEDOM."

"FROM THE BEGINNING, THE 1ST FILM 'FEMALE PRISONER 701: SCORPION' WAS A PROJECT ANSWERING TO A HIGHER ORDER. IT SEEMED TO ME THAT MEIKO KAJI WAS NOT MADE FOR THE ROLE OF SASORI. THIS IS THE IMPRESSION WHICH I HAD AT THE BEGINNING, BUT THEN I ASKED HER TO BREAK WITH THE IMAGE THAT SHE HAD FORGED UP TO THAT POINT. I WAS RATHER HARD WITH HER ABOUT THIS TOPIC, AS I FELT THE SUCCESS OF THE FILM HINGED ON IT. SHE WAS A STUBBORN WOMAN, BUT ANSWERED MY REQUEST AND EVENTUALLY I FELT THAT OUR COLLABORATION WENT GRADUALLY. MEIKO RESPONDED TO MY DIRECTION WELL, ALTHOUGH SHE DID NOT LIKE IT WHEN I COMMENTED THAT SHE WAS SO GOOD IN THE ROLE OF SASORI NOT BECAUSE OF HER FEMININITY, BUT RATHER BECAUSE SHE HAS A REAL TOMBOY QUALITY. BUT IT'S TRUE, IF THE SUCCESS OF THE FILMS MADE MEIKO A STAR, IT IS NOT SO MUCH THANKS TO HER FEMALE CHARMS, BUT RATHER THANKS TO A LITTLE MALE SIDE OF HER WHICH GIVES HER THE AIR OF A BOY."

I DON'T KNOW IF I REALLY AGREE WITH ITO HERE...

A TOMBOY? AS IF A FEMALE CHARACTER CAN'T BE STRONG AN' BE FEMININE? BULL!

"I WAS VERY LUCKY TO HAVE MET AND WORKED WITH MEIKO KAJI, AND IT IS THIS WHICH BROUGHT SUCCESS TO THE FILM. AFTER WE COMPLETED THE FIRST MOVIE, WE KNEW THE SECOND ONE HAD TO STAND ON ITS OWN. TO ME, THE 2ND FILM WAS A WONDERFUL OCCASION OF TALENTED PEOPLE COMING TOGETHER. WE WERE IN OSMOSIS."

"FROM MY POINT OF VIEW, IT WOULD BE TOO SIMPLISTIC TO SUMMARISE THE DEBATE OF FEMINISM WITH ONLY ONE IDEA OR OPINION. FEMINISM IS A REVOLT AGAISNT THE OLD WAYS, A REVOLT AGAINST A WORN OUT REGIME. BUT YOU SHOULD KNOW THAT IT IS ONLY BY CHANCE THAT I CHOSE A WOMAN FOR THE CHARACTER OF A REBEL. SINCE I CHOSE A FEMALE CHARACTER, THE QUESTION OF SEX AND VIOLENCE AROSE OBVIOUSLY, SO I COULD NOT IGNORE THE DEBATE ABOUT FEMINISM, BUT UNDERSTAND THAT IT WAS NOT A DEBATE WHICH I SOUGHT."

FEMALE CONVICT SCORPION: GRUDGE SONG (1974)

SCORPION

女番長ブルース

牝蜂の挑戦

"IN MY FILM, I WANTED TO EXPLOIT THE TOPIC OF A REBELLION FALLING UNDER A RADICAL ACTION. ALL WHAT MAKES MY SCORPION TRILOGY INTERESTING IS IN THAT CONCEPT. AT THE BEGINNING, AN ORDINARY GIRL IS USED WITHIN THE FRAMEWORK OF AN INVESTIGATION WHERE THE POLICE FORCE INFILTRATES THE YAKUZA. AFTER THE INVESTIGATION, SHE IS USED AND THROWN AWAY. CONSEQUENTLY, THIS GIRL THINKS OF NOTHING BUT BEING AVENGED FOR WHAT WRONG WAS DONE TO HER. I BELIEVE THAT FOR MY PART, PASSION AND THE EXTREME ACTS WHICH RESULT FROM IT PUTS FORWARD THIS QUESTION: 'TO WHAT LENGTHS WILL YOU GO?'"

IF A CHARACTER IS DEFINED BY HER ACTIONS, THEN HOW DOES ONE GO ABOUT DEPICTING THESE ACTS? IT IS THIS STEP WHICH INTERESTED ME, AND THIS WAS WHEN I REALISED THAT FOR THIS CHARACTER, WORDS HAD BECOME USELESS. I CUT ALL THE DIALOG THAT I HAD WRITTEN FOR SASORI, AND IN THE 2ND FILM THE PRINCIPAL CHARACTER PRONOUNCES HARDLY TWO SENTENCES -- TWO VERY SHORT SENTENCES. THE DIALOG WAS SUPERFLOUS IN THIS FILM. ONLY THE ACTS COUNTED. THIS IS THE ONLY WAY WHICH I CAN EXPLAIN THE DESIGN OF THE FILMS.

"WITH THESE FILMS, I TRIED TO IMPOSE AS MUCH AS POSSIBLE MY VISION OF THE CINEMA AND TO APPLY IT TO THE SCREEN. FOR ME, A FILM IS PROJECTED AS A LUMINOUS RAY OF LIGHT IN THE DARKNESS. IT IS TO SOME EXTENT A MAGIC WORLD. I WANTED TO PRESERVE THAT MAGIC ASPECT IN MY FILMS. DURING THE PROJECTION OF A FILM, I WANT TO BRING THE AUDIENCE INTO A FANTASTIC UNIVERSE. I WANT THAT AUDIENCE TO TRAVEL THROUGH A WORLD COMPLETELY CUT FROM REALITY. THAT IS MY OBJECTIVE, AND IT IS WITH THESE CONVICTIONS THAT I BEGAN MY CAREER. THE SET OF THEMES DEVELOPED AROUND THIS HEROINE TAKE THEIR FORM IN THE WAY THE STORY IS TOLD, AND THE STORY WAS THE SUBJECT WHICH I WANTED TO INTRODUCE. I TRIED TO REMAIN FAITHFUL TO MY IDEAS IN ALL OF THE FILMS WHICH I MADE. PERHAPS I DID NOT ACHIEVE MY GOAL."

"CERTAIN WORKS INFLUENCED ME. THINKING ABOUT IT TODAY, THERE ARE FILMS THAT I SAW IN MY YOUTH WHICH PARTICULARLY TOUCHED ME. I REALLY LIKED THE FILMS OF FEDERIKO FELLINI, AND ALSO INGMAR BERGMAN... AND BUNUEL. I VERY MUCH ENJOYED THEIR FILMS. SOME HAVE SAID THAT MY FILMS CAN OCCASION- ALLY BE JUVENILE. TO AVOID FALLING INTO THE CURSE OF BEING JUVENILE, I TRIED TO GIVE A SURREALIST COLOR TO MY WORKS. ACCORDINGLY, I FOUGHT TO KEEP FROM TURNING THE SASORI MOVIES INTO A SERIES OF EVENTS FROM THE DAILY NEWSPAPER. SCORPION HAD TO BE FANTASTIC, AND CERTAIN SCENES ARE COARSE. WHILE RETAINING THIS COARSENESS, THE PLAN WAS TO REACH A HIGHER LEVEL. I HOPE I SUCCEEDED."

THANKS TO THE NOW DEFUNCT: www.meiko-kaji.com
FOR THE USE OF THIS INTERVIEW!

— ROBIN BOUGIE '05

EASY (1979. DIR. BY ANTHONY SPINELLI)

IF YOU COULD ADD UP THE AMOUNT OF GENTLEMAN'S RELISH GENERATED BY VIEWERS FOR JESSIE ST. JAMES THROUGHOUT HER TEN YEAR (1978-1988) PORN CAREER, I WOULDN'T BE SURPRISED TO FIND OUT THAT IT EQUALLED AT LEAST A COUPLE OLYMPIC-SIZED SWIMMING POOLS. SHE WAS JUST **THAT** HOT. IN "EASY", THE SMALL CHESTED BLONDE GODDESS STARS AS KATE, A HIGH SCHOOL TEACHER WHO IS MANIPULATED INTO SUCKING OFF ONE OF HER HORNY MALE STUDENTS ONE DAY AFTER CLASS. ARRIVING HOME LATER, SHE'S RAPED AT KNIFEPOINT BY ONE OF HIS PALS, AN EXPERIENCE THAT PROVES TO BE HER LAST STRAW. WITH THE TASTE OF THE AGGRESSIVE YOUNG MAN'S BUTTHOLE STILL ON HER LIPS, KATE QUITS HER JOB AND MOVES TO A NEW TOWN -- ONLY TO DISCOVER THAT SHIT FLOATS DOWNSTREAM. THE NEXT TIME SHE'S FORCED TO SUBMIT IS AT THE HANDS OF ANOTHER WOMAN (GEORGINA SPELVIN), WITH THE GIRL-ON-GIRL RAPE TRIUMPHING AS THE STANDOUT SEXING IN THE PRODUCTION.

It's More Than Her Name, It's Her Way of Life!

EASY

TABOO

BY: MIKE MYHRE. 2006

THE FIRST PORN MOVIE I EVER SAW WAS "TABOO" DIRECTED BY KIRDY STEVENS, AND STARRING KAY PARKER & MIKE RANGER. IT RANKS WITH "DEEP THROAT" AS ONE OF THE MOST SUCCESSFUL PORN MOVIES EVER.

THE STORY IS TYPICAL '70s PORNO CHEESE. BARBARA'S HUSBAND LEAVES HER CAUSE SHE WON'T DO IT WITH THE LIGHTS ON.

HER SON PAUL IS IN LOVE WITH HER, DESPITE HAVING A HOT, ALBEIT DUCK-LIPPED GIRLFRIEND.

BARBARA'S NYMPHO FRIEND HOOKS HER UP ON A DATE WITH A CREEP WHO TAKES HER TO AN ORGY.

SHE DOESN'T JOIN IN, INSTEAD SHE GOES HOME AND ENDS UP BEGINNING A SEXUAL RELATIONSHIP WITH HER SON.

THERE'S A BUNCH OF OTHER STUFF, LIKE HOW HER NYMPHO FRIEND RESEMBLES A YOUNG ANGELA LANSBURY, AND BARBARA ENDS UP WITH HER FAT, UGLY, MYSOGINIST BOSS, BUT THAT'S THE GIST.

THE VIDEO WAS PASSED AROUND BETWEEN MYSELF AND 2 FRIENDS, EACH OF US OWNING IT FOR A COUPLE OF WEEKS.

HOWEVER, MY FRIEND WHO HAD ORIGINALLY FOUND IT HAD AN ATTACK OF CONSCIENCE DURING HIS SECOND TURN WITH IT...

CRUNCH!
CRACK!

...AND HE CRUSHED IT IN A **VICE**.

QUALITY NUDITY WAS SCARCE FOR US IN THOSE DAYS BEFORE THE INTERNET, CONSEQUENTLY, WE DIDN'T FORGIVE HIM UNTIL WE WERE EIGHTEEN.

2 FROM ANDY

FROM WHAT I'VE SEEN OF THE FILMS OF ANDY SIDARIS, WHICH RANGE FROM HIS FIRST MOVIE STACEY IN 1973, TO HIS LAST FILM L.E.T.HAL LADIES: RETURN TO SAVAGE BEACH IN 1998, THE EARLIER THEY DATE IN HIS FILMOGRAPHY, THE HIGHER THE BUDGET THEY WILL HAVE, THE SEXIER THE BITCHES WILL BE, AND THE BETTER THE OVERALL PRODUCT WILL STAND. PERHAPS MATT FARKAS SAID IT BEST:

"CONSIDER THE TALENT ON DISPLAY IN SIDARIS'S EARLIER FILMS - ANNE RANDALL (PLAYBOY PLAYMATE OF THE MONTH MAY 1967), THE DELECTABLE ANITRA FORD, BARBARA LEIGH AND SUSAN KIGER (PLAYBOY PLAYMATE OF THE MONTH JANUARY 1977) - PLUS THE THESPIC EFFORTS OF WILLIAM SMITH, JOHN ALDERMAN AND REGGIE NALDER. AS MUCH AS I ENJOY THE NATURAL CURVES OF DONNA SPEIR AND HOPE MARIE CARLTON, THEY CAN'T HOLD A CANDLE TO THEIR PREDECESSORS IN THE SIDARIS CANON."

WITH THAT STATEMENT IN MIND, I'D LIKE TO INTRODUCE YA'LL TO STACEY AND SEVEN, ANDY'S FIRST TWO CINEMATIC EFFORTS. UNAVAILABLE ON DVD (AS OF THIS WRITING), THESE EXPLOITATION RARITIES ARE WELL WORTH CHASING, ROPING, AND DRAGGING INTO THE EARTHY MUD WHERE THEY DESERVE TO BE.

ANNE

RANDALL

A PIONEERING EMMY-AWARD WINNING DIRECTOR OF TV SPORTS SHOWS (SUCH AS NFL MONDAY NIGHT FOOTBALL ON ABC) AND TV COMMERCIALS (HE CREATED NEARLY 300 OF THEM), ANDY ALSO PIONEERED WHAT HE CALLED THE "HONEY SHOT" (CLOSE-UPS OF CHEERLEADERS AND PRETTY GIRLS IN THE STANDS AT SPORTING EVENTS). EVENTUALLY SIDARIS GOT AWAY FROM THE CONFINES OF THE IDIOT BOX AND BRANCHED OUT INTO DRIVE IN MOVIES, INCLUDING HIS SAVVY WIFE ARLENE AS HIS PRODUCTION PARTNER.

BUT IT WAS PARTNERING UP WITH ROGER CORMAN ON STACEY THAT ANDY FIGURED (CORRECTLY) THAT A SMART CASH-IN WOULD BE TO GET AN EX-PLAYBOY PLAYMATE AS THEIR LEAD ACTRESS. LOVELY MISS ANNE RANDALL FIT THE BILL AS BLONDE BOMBSHELL STACEY PERFECTLY, CAUSING WOMB WEASLES TO SQUIRM ACROSS THE COUNTRY. IN THE FILM, HER CHARACTER IS EMPLOYED BY A WELL-TO-DO MATRIARCH TO UNRAVEL A WEB OF DECEIT SPUN BY SCUZZY SERVANTS AND REPUGNANT RELATIVES WHO ARE ALL IN LINE FOR THEIR INHERITANCE. MATCHED WITH HER SIDEKICK (ALAN LANDERS) OUR SNOOPING GAL ON THE GO DISCOVERS A BEFUDDLING FRAMEJOB/BLACKMAIL MURDER PLOT AND IS FORCED TO KICK SOME BOOTY. DID I MENTION THERE WAS A LOT OF FAST CARS AND BARE TITS, TOO? YOU CAN BET YOUR BIPPY THERE IS.

MEDIA ORCHARD SPOKE TO
SIDARIS ABOUT HIS FILM IN 2006:
"WITH MY FILM PRODUCTION
COMPANY, I HOOKED UP WITH
ROGER CORMAN. WE EACH PUT UP
$37,500 FOR A TOTAL OF $75,000.
I DIRECTED AND PRODUCED AND
CO-OWNED STACEY. THIS FILM HAD
OVER 3,000 THEATRICAL PLAY
DATES IN THE US. IT ALSO DID
VERY WELL IN THE INTERNATIONAL
MARKET. THE FILM DID QUITE
WELL FOR ME AND FOR ROGER
OBVIOUSLY. STACEY WAS A 'GUNS
'N BABES' FLICK. IT SET ME ON
THE PATH TO DO 13 MORE FILMS
IN THAT GENRE."

SIDARIS CERTAINLY LOVED THE
GENRE ALL RIGHT, AND WOULD GO
ON TO REMAKE STACEY 12 YEARS
LATER AS MALIBU EXPRESS (1985),
BUT THIS TIME WITH A MALE LEAD
(DARBY HINTON). GIVE ME ANNE
RANDALL OVER THAT ANY DAY.
RAISED IN SAN FRANCISCO, ANNE
BROKE INTO THE SHOW BIZ
RACKET IN THE EARLY '60S AT
THE AGE OF 13 AS A REGULAR
DANCER (ALONG WITH ACTRESS
BARBARA BOUCHET!) ON DICK
STEWART'S TEENYBOPPER KPIX
DANCE PARTY. SOON AFTER THAT
SHE DEVELOPED A LOVELY SET OF
SUCK-SACKS, BARED THEM FOR
PLAYBOY'S CAMERAS, AND ENDED
UP MARRYING DICK YEARS LATER.
SADLY, ANNE HAD NO MEMORY OF
MAKING STACEY WHEN I RECENTLY
ASKED HER ABOUT IT. EITHER
THAT, OR SHE WAS PRACTICING THE
TIMELESS ART OF 'SAYIN' NUTTIN'
IF YA GOT NUTTIN' NICE TO SAY.

**Death
is their way of life!**

When
the
going
gets
rough,
send for
SEVANO'S
Playmates.

SEVEN

MELVIN SIMON PRODUCTIONS presents
An **ANDY SIDARIS** Film
WILLIAM SMITH in "SEVEN"
Executive Producer **MELVIN SIMON**
Screenplay by **WILLIAM DRISKILL** and **ROBERT BAIRD**
Story by **ANDY SIDARIS** Produced and Directed by **ANDY SIDARIS**
AN AMERICAN INTERNATIONAL RELEASE
© 1979 SIDAN PRODUCTIONS, INC.

R RESTRICTED
UNDER 17 REQUIRES ACCOMPANYING PARENT OR ADULT GUARDIAN

FOLLOWING THAT UP, ANDY MADE SEVEN (1979) WITH THE
ALWAYS AWESOME WILLIAM SMITH. "STRICTLY FOR THE
BRAIN-DAMAGED", WROTE TIMEOUT FILM GUIDE, AND YOU
WILL INDEED BE BRAIN DAMAGED WHEN THIS SCROTUM-
WAGGING CLASSIC SLAPS YOU UPSIDE YOUR STUPID HEAD.
RIGHT OUT OF THE STARTING GATE WE WITNESS TWO
HITMEN GUNNING DOWN AN UNDERCOVER GOVERNMENT
AGENT AND HIS INNOCENT WIFE, AN ASSASSIN PERFORMING
A HAWAIIAN DANCE IN FRONT OF A CROWD, THEN
THROWING A FUCKING BURNING SPEAR RIGHT INTO A
GUY'S CHEST, AND THEN -- HIGHLIGHT OF HIGHLIGHTS -- A
THIRD KILLER ON ROLLER SKATES SKATING DOWN A
HIGHWAY, NAILING MOTHERFUCKERS WITH A CROSSBOW !

AND THAT WAS JUST THE FIRST 8 MINUTES. SHIT MAN,
EVEN IF THIS MOVIE DIDN'T HAVE ANYTHING ELSE HAPPEN
IN THE REMAINING HOUR AND A HALF, IT WOULD STILL
FUCKIN' SLAY. ON TOP OF THAT, HOWEVER, WE HAVE A
HANG-GLIDING BLACK DUDE DROPPIN' BOMBS, AND THE
ORIGINATION OF THE "GUN VS SWORD" GAG THAT WAS
POPULARISED IN RAIDERS OF THE LOST ARK AND THE
AFOREMENTIONED WILLIAM SMITH PLAYING THE HEAD OF A
HIGHLY TRAINED A-TEAM-STYLE GROUP HEADQUARTERED
IN HAWAII. HE AND HIS FACE-GRINDERS ARE OFFERED A
MILLION BUCKS A HEAD ON SEVEN MARTIAL ARTS HITMEN
WHO ARE RUNNING AMOK ON THE ISLAND.

"IN MAKING A MOVIE," EXPLAINED SIDARIS WHEN ASKED ABOUT THE SECRET TO ENTERTAINING FILMS, "THE MOST IMPORTANT THING YOU CAN DO IS TO KEEP THE ACTION MOVING AS YOU TELL THE STORY. WE DON'T DO LONG, DRAWN OUT SCENES WITH UNDERLYING PSYCHOLOGICAL BS. WE SET THE STORY, SET THE PACE AND MOVE ON. WE KNOW PEOPLE LIKE OUR STYLE. AND, YES, WE THROW IN NUDITY WHENEVER POSSIBLE AND AUGMENT IT WITH A WHOLE BUNCH OF CHASES, EXPLOSIONS AND GUNSHOTS."

ANDY SIDARIS LOST HIS BATTLE WITH THROAT CANCER AND PASSED AWAY ON MARCH 7TH, 2007 IN BEVERLY HILLS, CALIFORNIA.

"(ANDY SIDARIS) WILL ALWAYS BE REMEMBERED AS ONE OF THE GREATEST WRITERS/DIRECTORS OF 'GUY FLICKS' THE FREE WORLD HAS EVER KNOWN."
- KEN KNIGHT (AUTHOR OF "THE NAKED DIARIES")

REMEMBMR BACK IN CINEMA SEWER BOOK ONE WHEN I TATTLED ABOUT HOW YOUNG HOLLYWOOD ACTRESS THORA BIRCH'S PARENTS WERE 1970s PORN PERFORMERS CAROL CONNORS AND JACK BIRCH? REMEMBER HOW THAT FACT CAUSED ME TO BABBLE FOR PAGES ABOUT THE RIPE POSSIBILITIES OF THORA NOT ONLY FOLLOWING IN THOSE XXX FOOTSTEPS, BUT ENTICING SOME OF HER LOVELY CO-STARS TO DO SO AS WELL?

WELL NOT ANYMORE. I'M GONNA GIVE THE STAR OF GHOST WORLD THE RESPECT SHE DESERVES. NO LONGER SHALL I BELITTLE HER TALENTS BY WRITING ABOUT HER AS IF SHE WERE A SLAB OF BEEF, TO BE HELD TO THE GROUND NAKED, LIKE A DOG IN HEAT. THE WAY SHE'D BE JACK-KNIFED AND MOANING AS HER ELASTIC POOP PASSAGE IS POUNDED AND PRIED OPEN WITH A BIG PINK DILDO....

I WON'T. CINEMA SEWER IS TOO GOOD FOR THAT.

THORA BIRCH
FUCK YEAH

GHOST WORLD

BOUGIE. 2010.

THIS DRAWING IS DEDICATED TO MY PAL, CHRIS ENG!

CHRISTINA LINDBERG RULES THE UNIVERSE!

YEAH, I'M AN UBER-FAN OF THIS SWEDISH GAL. SHE'S BEEN IN SO MANY DOPE MOVIES! LOOK HER UP, Y'ALL! SHE'S SO CHOICE.

I SEE HER IN MY MIIIND !!!!!

OOHH, CHRISTIINA... MMM ♡ MM ♡ YOU DON'T HAVE TO SHOOT AT ♡... THORA.. NO, ♡ SHE'S OF NO THREAT TO YOUU...

BAKA

KISSY KISSY SMOOTCH

SHEESH

ZENRA!

SOFT ON DEMAND — JAPAN'S BIGGEST ADULT MOVIE COMPANY — IS PREPARING FOR OLYMPIC-SIZED THRILLS WITH ITS FORTHCOMING RELEASE OF "ZENRA SUPOTSU SENSHUKEN (ALL NUDE SPORTS CHAMPIONSHIPS)", THE LATEST IN ITS LARGE CATALOG OF DVDS FEATURING PEOPLE CARRYING OUT A VARIETY OF ACTS AND TASKS NAKED. "ZENRA" AFTER ALL, MEANS "COMPLETLY NUDE."

THANKS TO THE BRILLIANT PORN GURUS AT S.O.D. JAPANESE ATHLETES ARE BARING MORE THAN THEIR SOULS IN THE QUEST FOR ATHLETIC GREATNESS. AND WHEN THERE IS NO LEOTARD OR ANNOYING UNIFORM TO COVER THEIR GOODIES, WATCHING THE MUSCLES RIPPLE AND SWEAT FLY AS THEY GO ABOUT THEIR ASTONISHING FEATS IS 10X BETTER THAN OL' G-RATED OLYMPICS.

THIS NEWEST ZENRA TITLE FEATURES NAKED SPORTS WOMEN DISPLAYING THEIR SKILLS AT VOLLEY BALL, FENCING, SOCCER, AND JUDO.

IN EARLIER SPORTS-RELATED TITLES, S.O.D. PAID LITTLE ATTENTION TO THE GIRLS ACTUAL ATHLETIC ABILITIES, NOW THAT'S CHANGED, WITH THE LADIES REQUIRED TO HAVE BEEN RANKED WITHIN THE TOP JAPANESE ATHLETES IN THEIR SPORT, OR TO BE THE HOT TARGET OF SPORTS TALENT SCOUTS.

ZENRA SPORTS SERIES 1 (5 IN 1): FEATURING 4½ HOURS OF THE BEST MOMENTS IN ALL NUDE SWIMMING AND ALL NUDE WEIGHT TRAINING! – FUCK YEAH!

ZENRA BASKETBALL: BEAUTIFUL ASIAN HONIES DRAIN BASKETS AND DO ALL KINDS OF JUMPING, BLOCKING, AND THROWING. STARRING 'RINA USUI' AND 23 OTHER TALENTED BALLERS.

ZENRA CHALLENGER - 108 GIRLS EDITION: THIS ONE PITS 108 NAKED GALS AGAINST EACH OTHER COMPETING FOR $600,000 IN CASH! WITH BOWLING, CYCLING, AND THE ANSWER TO HOW MANY NAKED GIRLS WILL FIT IN A PHONE BOOTH,

FIGHT LIKE ATHENA: WITH A BLACKBELT IN KARATE, ERIKA NAGAI PREVIOUSLY STARRED IN "BALL BREAKER ERIKA". IN THIS ONE SHE AGAIN USES A MAN'S PENDULOUS SCROTUM LIKE A PUNCHING BAG! INCLUDES BUKKAKES AND COSPLAY!

WOW! THANK YOU, JAPAN!!!

ART BY TIM GRANT • LETTERING AND WRITING BY ROBIN BOUGIE '05

MISS NUDE AMERICA (AKA "THE CONTEST") 1976. DIRECTED BY JAMES BLAKE

IF YOU LIKE ME, SAW NIGHTMARE ON ELM STREET AND WONDERED WHAT JOHNNY DEPP'S CHARACTER WAS REFERRING TO WHEN HE STATES "I'M GOING TO WATCH MISS NUDE AMERICA AND THEN GO TO SLEEP", THEN WONDER NO LONGER MY PERVERTED PALS.

SURELY ONE OF THE STRANGEST SLICES OF AMERICANA EVER CAPTURED ON FILM BEGAN AS A PROJECT INITIATED BY STUDENTS AND INSTRUCTORS AT TWO IVY LEAGUE CAMPUSES IN THE EARLY SEVENTIES. MODELLED AFTER THE "NEW JOURNALISM" STYLE OF AUTHOR HUNTER S. THOMPSON AND THE CINEMA VERITE EFFORTS OF THE AMAZING MAYSLES BROTHERS, THE FILM DEPOSITS US IN A PLACE CALLED 'NAKED CITY' UNDER THE WATCHFUL EYE OF THE MAN WHO RUNS IT, CREEPY WHEELCHAIR-BOUND MULTIPLE SCLEROSIS SUFFERER DICK DROST.

WHO THE FUCK WAS DICK DROST? ALL BUT FORGOTTEN TODAY SAVE FOR HIS MEMORABLE TURN IN THIS RARE AND RELATIVELY UNKNOWN DOCUMENTARY, DICK VIEWED HIMSELF AS A WHEELED SVENGALI, AND WOULD DO EVERYTHING HE COULD TO FLAUNT THIS IMAGE BY HAVING NAKED YOUNG WOMEN (SOME OF WHOM WERE RUNAWAYS HE HAD TAKEN IN) TEND TO HIS EVERY NEED WHILE PUSHING HIM AROUND IN HIS WHEELCHAIR. SEEING HIM IN MISS NUDE AMERICA, IT BECOMES QUITE CLEAR THAT HE WAS UNARGUABLY GIFTED WITH A MANSON-ESQUE HOLD OVER PRETTY AND IMPRESSIONABLE FOLLOWERS WHO HUNG ON HIS EVERY WORD.

DROST INHERITED A RELATIVELY BENIGN AND INNOCENT CAMP FOR SUN-LOVERS (PREVIOUSLY THE CLUB ZORRO NUDIST RESORT JUST OUTSIDE ROSELAWN INDIANA) FROM HIS FATHER IN 1968, AND TRANSFORMED IT INTO THE WORLD'S LARGEST NUDIST COLONY AND A BOOZE-SOAKED ODE TO DEPRAVITY. POPULAR WITH INDIANA REDNECKS AND TRUCKERS, THE RESORT INGENIOUSLY CATERED TO SHIT-KICKERS BY OFFERING A TRUCKSTOP WHERE THE WAITRESSES WERE NAKED. DICK ALSO HAD A GIANT SUNDIAL BUILT IN THE SHAPE OF A WOMAN'S LEG, BUT THE REAL SKEEZY SHOWCASE WAS A HUGE ANNUAL TAILGATE PARTY/PAGEANT WHERE SMILING BUCK NAKED WOMEN WERE PARADED AROUND TO THE HOOTING DELIGHT OF THOUSANDS.

AN EGOMANIAC, DROST WAS OBSESSED WITH SEEMING FAR MORE RICH AND POWERFUL THAN HE WAS. PART OF THAT WAS LIVING IN A GRAND MIRRORED GEODESIC DOME, OWNING AIRCRAFT HE COULD BARELY AFFORD, AND BUILDING AN AIRFIELD ON HIS PROPERTY. AT ONE POINT THE FAA EVEN PUT NAKED CITY'S 2300 FOOT GRASS RUNWAY ON THE CHICAGO VFR SECTIONAL CHART, BUT NEGLECTED TO WARN ABOUT THE DETERIORATED STATE OF THE FIELD. NOT LONG AFTER, A PIPER CHEROKEE AND A PACER MET THEIR UNTIMELY DEMISE.

DROST INSISTED THAT ANY OF THE NUBILE LOVELIES THAT SERVED HIM MUST GET A NAKED CITY LOGO TATTOO ON THEIR HIP, WHICH HE VIEWED AS A CATTLE BRAND OF OWNERSHIP. HE ALSO DEMANDED THAT ALL OF HIS EMPLOYEES MUST SIGN A WAIVER CONSENTING TO HONOUR ANY AND ALL OF HIS DISABLED SEXUAL NEEDS AS HE SAW FIT TO REQUEST THEM. BALLSY? THAT AIN'T THE HALF OF IT. HOW ABOUT HIS DISTURBING FASCINATION WITH UNDERAGE GIRLS, A TABOO AND CRIMINAL PROCLIVITY HE DID NOTHING TO HIDE, EVEN STARTING A "MISS NUDE TEENY-BOPPER" CONTEST TO GO WITH HIS MISS NUDE UNIVERSE PAGEANT.

NOT SURPRISINGLY, HE WAS CHARGED WITH MOLESTING A 13 YEAR OLD GIRL AND WITH SHOWING PORNOGRAPHIC FILMS AND MATERIALS TO MINORS, TO WHICH HE PLED GUILTY AND WAS

BANISHED FROM THE STATE FOR 10 YEARS. AS A RESULT, NAKED CITY CLOSED IN 1986, AND DICK JETTED OFF FOR LA-LA LAND AND STARTED NAKED CITY LOS ANGELES.

"THIS MAN SHOULD BE IN JAIL. INSTEAD, HE'S IN CALIFORNIA", LAMENTED ATTORNEY JOHN CASEY.

MATT MARANIAN, AUTHOR OF THE EXCELLENT BOOK L.A. BIZARRO, TOOK OFF HIS CLOTHES AND TOOK IN THE SIGHTS AT DROST'S NEW DIGS IN THE DESERT: "NAKED CITY WAS MORE FABULOUS THAN I COULD HAVE EVER DREAMED: A NUDIST WHITE TRASH SWINGER'S RETREAT OCCUPYING A FORMER TRAILER PARK IN THE HIGH DESERT WITH A SKANKY SWIMMING POOL AND A MIRROR-TILED CLUBHOUSE WITH WALL-TO-WALL PORN VIDEO SCREENS AND A STRIPPER'S CATWALK AND RED CARPET ON THE WALLS. ALL OWNED AND OPERATED BY A PARAPLEGIC EX-HIPPIE SWINGER WITH NUDE SECRETARIES THAT ALSO GAVE LAP DANCES! IT STILL FEELS LIKE A DREAM. NOTHING TOPPED THAT FOR ME, AND I'VE BEEN PRIVY TO SOME FAR-OUT SHIT."

AS GREAT AS MISS NUDE AMERICA IS, IT WAS AN UNMITIGATED BOX OFFICE FLOP DURING ITS INITIAL RELEASE IN THE SEVENTIES. IT WAS FAR TOO SLEAZY TO BE TAKEN SERIOUSLY AT THE ARTHOUSES, AND ALL THE FRONTAL NUDITY MEANT THE MOVIE COULDN'T BE SHOWN IN YOUR LOCAL GENERIC NEIGHBOURHOOD THEATRES EITHER. AS A SKIN FLICK IT WAS A TOTAL BUST BECAUSE IT HAD LITTLE EROTIC APPEAL, AND CERTAINLY WASN'T HOT ENOUGH TO COMPETE WITH ANY OF THE HARDCORE PORN OF ITS DAY.

REGARDLESS, THIS IS A TERRIFIC DOCUMENTARY CONSISTING OF A BEHIND-THE-SCENES GLANCE AT A VERY UNUSUAL TIME, PLACE, AND MAN -- THAT IS JUST WAITING TO BE REDISCOVERED BY A WHOLE NEW GENERATION.

— BOUGIE 2010

ILLUSTRATION FOR THIS REVIEW BY BEN NEWMAN. VISIT HIM ONLINE AT: BENNEWMANART.BLOGSPOT.COM/

NANCY SUITER

THE TAXI GIRL

YET ANOTHER R. BOUGIE JOINT 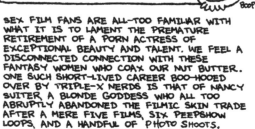 BOOP

SEX FILM FANS ARE ALL-TOO FAMILIAR WITH WHAT IT IS TO LAMENT THE PREMATURE RETIREMENT OF A PORN ACTRESS OF EXCEPTIONAL BEAUTY AND TALENT. WE FEEL A DISCONNECTED CONNECTION WITH THESE FANTASY WOMEN WHO COAX OUR NUT BUTTER. ONE SUCH SHORT-LIVED CAREER BOO-HOOED OVER BY TRIPLE-X NERDS IS THAT OF NANCY SUITER, A BLONDE GODDESS WHO ALL TOO ABRUPTLY ABANDONED THE FILMIC SKIN TRADE AFTER A MERE FIVE FILMS, SIX PEEPSHOW LOOPS, AND A HANDFUL OF PHOTO SHOOTS.

NANCY WENT TO HIGH SCHOOL IN LITTLE ROCK ARKANSAS, GRADUATED IN 1977, MOVED TO CALIFORNIA AND MADE AN INSTANT SPLASH ON THE ADULT SCENE IN THE LATE '70S. BY DECEMBER 1979 GENESIS MAGAZINE WAS REPORTING ON THE MYSTERY OF HER SUDDEN DISAPPEARANCE.

SINCE FEW KNEW WHERE SHE CAME FROM OR WHERE SHE WENT, RUMOURS RAN RAMPANT AFTER HER DISAPPEARANCE. MOST OF THEM ARE HIGHLY UNLIKELY (SOLD INTO WHITE SLAVERY IN JAPAN, GOT A SEX CHANGE) BUT ONE THEORY HOLDS SOME WATER -- THAT SHE MARRIED A FAT RICH TEXAN WHO SPIRITED HER AWAY FROM THE PUBLIC EYE. NANCY REVEALED ON AT LEAST ONE OCCASION THAT HER PHYSICAL IDEAL IN THE OPPOSITE SEX WAS "MEN WITH BIG BELLIES, LIKE STEREOTYPICAL SOUTHERN SHERIFFS", SO IT CERTAINLY FITS IN THAT RESPECT.

THE "FAT TEXAN" STORY WOULDN'T HAVE COME INTO EXISTENCE IF AUTHOR/SCREENWRITER TERRY SOUTHERN HADN'T BECOME OBSESSED WITH NANCY AND SENT SCREW MAGAZINE COLUMNIST JOSH ALAN FRIEDMAN OUT ON A QUEST TO LOCATE HER IN 1980.

"SHE HAD CHANGED HER NAME", FRIEDMAN TOLD PORN REPORTER LUKE FORD. "AND SHE'D RETIRED INTO THE PROTECTIVE ARMS OF SOME BUSINESS TYCOON (RANCHER, OILMAN OR SOMETHING) WHO THREATENED TO 'PUNCH OUT' ANYONE WHO TRIED TO LURE HER BACK

INTO THE LIFE. HER AGENT TOLD ME THE MARRIED COUPLE HAD EVEN REJECTED SMALL OFFERS FOR HER TO APPEAR IN SEVERAL HOLLYWOOD A-LIST FILMS. BUT NO MATTER, FOR TERRY AND I CAME ACROSS SOME THEN-RECENT PHOTOS OF NANCY, DISPLAYING AN OVERWORKED, NO-LONGER TIGHT SNATCH, AND HIS INTEREST BEGAN TO FIZZLE."

NANCY DIDN'T LIKE TO BE INTERVIEWED, EVEN WHEN SHE WAS IN THE MIDST OF HER SHORT-LIVED CAREER AS A CUM-GOBBLING FUCKMONKEY-FOR-HIRE. HER MAIN COMPLAINT WAS THAT SHE WASN'T TAKEN SERIOUSLY, AND THAT MEN SIMPLY LOOKED AT AN INTERVIEW WITH HER AS A CHANCE TO SLAP THEIR TEA BISCUITS AGAINST AN UNINHIBITED WOMAN. "BECAUSE I'M A PORN MODEL THEY SEEM TO THINK I'LL LAY DOWN WITH ANYBODY", SHE ONCE COMPLAINED TO A FEMALE INTERVIEWER FROM HOLLAND'S "CHICK MAGAZINE". (ISSUE #223)

ONE OF THE BEST EXAMPLES OF NANCY'S INFLUENCE OVER

HERE ARE A FEW OF THE ADULT MAGAZINES YOU CAN FIND PHOTOS OF MISS SUITER IN:

OUI (OCT. 1978) VOL.7 #10
OUI (OCT. 1980) VOL.9 #10
PLAYBOY (DEC.1981) VOL.28 #12
MAYFAIR ·UK· (NOV. 1983) VOL.18 #11
NEWLOOK (JUNE,1985) #22

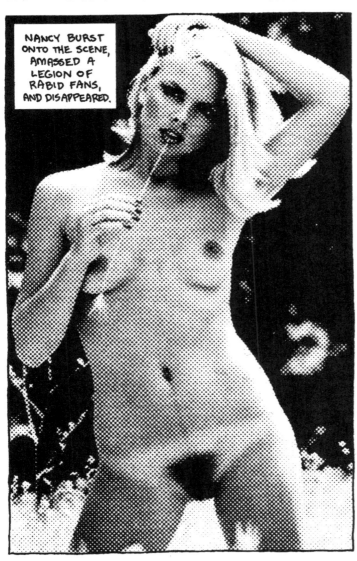

NANCY BURST ONTO THE SCENE, AMASSED A LEGION OF RABID FANS, AND DISAPPEARED.

THE GRAVY TRUMPETS OF SMUT ENTHUSIASTS WAS TO BE FOUND IN HER FIRST STARRING ROLE IN A FUN LITTLE TIME-WASTER BY ISRAELI-BORN DIRECTOR JAACOV JAACOVI. IN TAXI GIRLS, NANCY WAS MADE TO LOOK LIKE THEN-POPULAR CHARLIE'S ANGELS STAR CHERYL LADD, AND PORTRAYED A HOLLYWOOD HOOKER WHO ENDS UP IN A HOLDING CELL WHERE SHE AND THE OTHER INCARCERATED WHORES MOLEST A TINY-DICKED OFFICER OF THE LAW. THE GIRLS ESCAPE, BUT NANCY IS SICK OF THE POLICE HARASSMENT, AND DECIDES ON A CHANGE OF PROFESSIONS AFTER FINDING A CLASSIFIED AD LOOKING FOR TAXI DRIVERS.

OLD HABITS DIE HARD, HOWEVER, AND BEFORE LONG NANCY HAS TRANSFORMED HER CAB INTO A ROLLING BROTHEL WITH A STAND-UP COMEDY THEME. THAT'S RIGHT, SHE PICKS GUYS UP, TELLS THEM A FEW KNEE-SLAPPERS, AND TURNS A TRICK. IT'S A WINNING COMBINATION, ONE THAT NANCY'S PROSTITUTE PALS TAKE NOTICE OF. THE HOOKERS THEN VISIT HER BOSS, STRIP HIM NAKED, AND TRY TO CONVINCE HIM OF THE BENEFITS OF HAVING SEXED UP SLUTS ON HIS PAYROLL. UNFORTUNATELY, HE AIN'T ALL THAT IMPRESSED.

BUT THE ENTREPRENEURIAL SPIRIT CAN NOT BE CRUSHED SO EASILY. WHAT FOLLOWS IS A STEP-BY-STEP PROCESS OF HOW PROSTITUTES CAN START A THRIVING SMALL BUSINESS IN A MATTER OF DAYS. THIS INVOLVES SUCKING THE FLESH NOODLE OF A LOAN OFFICER AT THE BANK TO GET THEIR STARTUP MONEY, HUMPING A

RIDICULOUS SOUTHERN FRIED USED CAR SALESMAN TO LAND A GOOD DEAL ON A CAR, AND A SLAPSTICK MONTAGE REVEALING HOW THESE IMMORAL LADIES OF THE NIGHT STEAL FARES FROM RIVAL CAB COMPANIES USING THEIR WOMANLY WILES. I'M TALKIN' ABOUT COMMUTERS GOING FROM POINT A TO POINT B, BUT INSTEAD OF BLANKLY STARING OUT OF THE CAB WINDOW AT THE "NEON SLIME" OF SUNSET BLVD, THEY LUSTILY PLACE PALMS UPON THE BOBBING HEADS IN THEIR LAPS AND CONCENTRATE UPON THE SENSATIONS OF BLOWJOB BLISS.

BUT AS IT OFTEN DID IN SEVENTIES XXX, THE LIGHT AND FANCIFUL TONE CHANGES OH SO DRASTICALLY WHEN RIVAL CAB DRIVERS DECIDE TO GRAB NANCY AND TEACH HER A LESSON. WHAT FOLLOWS IS A ROUGH AND DISTURBING GANG RAPE -- ALTHOUGH ABOUT 80% OF THIS SCENE IS CUT IN THE MOST COMMONLY AVAILABLE VERSIONS OF THE FILM.

HIGHLIGHTS: LESBIAN RIM-JOBS AND FISTING (UNUSUAL FOR A CLASSIC ADULT MOVIE), A GUY SCREWING A BLOW-UP DOLL IN THE BACK OF A CAB, REAL-LIFE COUPLE SERENA AND JAMIE GILLIS DOING THEIR ROUGH SEX THING THEY DID SO VERY WELL, AND A SEXY CUM-DUMPING BETWEEN JOHN HOLMES AND MISS SUITER. LET ME ASSURE YOU THAT WATCHING HER NAVIGATE HER WAY AROUND THE MASSIVE PINK PYTHON OF MR HOLMES IS NOT SOMETHING FOR THE FAINT OF HEART!

FEELING FAINT MAY WELL HAVE BEEN THE REACTION OF NANCY SUITER WHEN MISS CHERYL LADD'S LAWYERS CAME CALLING, ALTHOUGH LUCKILY FOR HER THE LAWSUIT CAME DOWN ON THE HEAD OF HELM MASTER JAACOV JAACOVI. JAACOVI HAD TO PAY OVER A MILLION SMACKERS IN DAMAGES AFTER SLAPPING LADD'S NAME ALL OVER HIS TAXI GIRLS AD CAMPAIGN.

ALL TOLD, IT WAS A SHORT-BUT-SWEET CREME-COATED CAREER IN FUCK MOVIES FOR NANCY. I HOPE THAT SHE DID INDEED FIND HER CHUBBY TEXAN TO SETTLE DOWN WITH, AND THAT HE TREATS HER RIGHT.

— BOUGIE '10

AN EXAMPLE OF HOW JAACOV JAACOVI MARKETED TAXI GIRLS IN LIGHT OF THE MILLION DOLLAR LAWSUIT.

IT WAS THE FALL OF 1973 WHEN I FIRST DISCOVERED **CUT-THROATS 9** ON A DOUBLE BILL WITH THE CHINESE KUNG FU FLICK **CHINESE MECHANIC** IN A MOSTLY SPANISH LANGUAGE THEATER ON 47TH ST. IN NEW YORK'S TIMES SQUARE. IT HAD FIRST PLAYED WITH **DUEL OF THE IRON FIST** SEVERAL MONTHS PRIOR IN THE NY AREA, SO I WAS ENTHUSIASTIC AT A CHANCE TO FINALLY SEE IT. I WASN'T QUITE SURE WHAT TO EXPECT SINCE SOME WERE CALLING IT A HORROR PIC WHILE OTHERS HAD DENOTED IT AS A BADLY DUBBED SPANISH WESTERN. AS IT TURNS OUT - THEY WERE BOTH RIGHT.

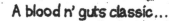

A blood n' guts classic...

THE MOVIE BEGINS WITH A GANG OF CONVICTS CHAINED TOGETHER, BEING SHIPPED TO FORT GREENE VIA COVERED WAGON WITH THE STEEL-NERVED SERGEANT BROWN PRESIDING OVER THEM - A MAN WHO FOR SOME REASON HAS ALSO BROUGHT ALONG HIS TEENAGE DAUGHTER (EMMA COHEN) ON THE TRIP. UNFORTUNATELY THE WAGON IS STOPPED ALONG THE WAY BY A GROUP OF THIEVES WHO SEEM TO THINK THE SARGE IS HIDING A SHIPMENT OF GOLD. A MELEE ENSUES WHERE ONE GUY GETS HIS THROAT CUT AND HIS NOGGIN BUSTED OPEN WITH A RIFLE BUTT. THE COACH GOES HAYWIRE WITH THE HORSES RUNNING EVERY WHICH WAY AND EVENTUALLY THE WAGON ENDS UP IN THE DITCH - FORCING THE GROUP TO MAKE THE TRIP ON FOOT.

NOW IT GETS GORY. WHEN ONE CONVICT REFUSES TO MOVE, HE'S MESSILY SHOT IN THE FACE - WHICH CAUSES HIS EYEBALL TO PROTRUDE AND GORE TO POUR OUT OF HIS HEAD. THIS PROMPTS THE SERGEANT TO HAVE A FLASHBACK OF HIS WIFE BEING MURDERED BY ONE OF THE MEN NOW CHAINED UP NEXT TO HIM - A FLASHBACK THAT INVOLVES HER GETTING STABBED MULTIPLE TIMES IN THE BELLY UNTIL LOOPS OF HER INTESTINE START FALLING OUT OF HER!

AFTER THE CONVICTS COMMIT MUTINY ONCE THE CHAINS ARE BROKEN BY A PASSING TRAIN, THE FIRST THING THEY DO IS BEAT AND RAPE THE POOR TEENAGE DAUGHTER, AND THEN BEAT HER FATHER REPEATEDLY BEFORE BURNING HIM ALIVE. AS HE ROASTS IN THE FLAMES, WE SEE A COOL CLOSE-UP OF HIS FACE TURNING SKELETAL.

THAT'S NOT ALL. BEING AS THEY ARE LOW-DOWN CONVICTS, IT DOESN'T TAKE LONG BEFORE THESE ANIMALS BEGIN TO TURN ON ONE ANOTHER. HANDS ARE HACKED OFF WITH MACHETES, BODIES BURNED, AND ONE CONVICT TAKES REVENGE ON A BIG FAT BARKEEPER BY IMPALING HIM THROUGH THE BACK WITH A LARGE MEAT HOOK BEFORE SLICING HIS STOMACH OPEN AND SPILLING MASSIVE AMOUNTS OF THE RED STUFF. BARF.

CUT-THROATS NINE WAS FILMED IN SPAIN IN 1971 UNDER THE TITLE **CONDEMNED TO LIVE**, AND WAS DIRECTED BY JOAQUIN ROMERO MARCHENT. THE ATMOSPH-ERE OF THIS FILM IS SO GRIM, COLD AND DEPRESSING - IT SENT MANY A THEATER PATRON GROANING FROM THE THEATER. IT NEARLY APPROACHES THE SHOCK LEVEL OF SUCH INFAMOUS GRINDHOUSE CLASSICS AS **CANNIBAL HOLOCAUST** AND **CANNIBAL FEROX**, AND EVEN - DARE I SAY IT - **LAST HOUSE ON DEAD END STREET**. THERE IS NO COMIC RELIEF OR HUMOR TO LIGHTEN THE IMPACT. IT'S JUST THE CINEMATIC EQUIVALENT OF WITNESSING A SERIOUS TRAFFIC ACCIDENT OR ATTENDING A FUNERAL.

AMAZINGLY, THIS FILM GOT OFF INTACT WITH AN R RATING UPON ITS INITIAL RELEASE. SOMETHING IT WOULDN'T HAVE A SNOWBALL'S CHANCE IN HELL OF DOING IN TODAY'S LAME MARKET. ABOUT A YEAR LATER I WAS ABLE TO SEE IT AGAIN ON THE DEUCE AT THE HARRIS THEATER - THIS TIME TEAMED UP WITH THE KUNG-FU WESTERN **SHANGHAI JOE** (AKA THEY CALL ME SHANGHAI JOE). SOME PEOPLE ACTUALLY LAUGHED DURING THE HEAVY MUTILATION AND EXTREME GORE! ONLY IN NEW YORK, MY FRIENDS. ONLY IN NEW YORK...

—BY SHAWN JOHNS.

YAR!!!

CUT-THROATS NINE IS PRETTY AMAZING! I'M JEALOUS THAT SHAWN GOT TO SEE IT IN A TRUE NYC GRINDHOUSE SETTING.

IS ANYONE OUT THERE AWARE OF THE EXISTENCE OF THE "CUT-THROATS NINE TERROR MASK"? THE TRAILER FOR THE FILM (AN **AWESOME** PREVIEW WHICH STATES THAT THE FILM IS "AN ADVENTURE IN VIOLENCE THAT WILL RIP YOUR HEART OUT!") MENTIONS THAT "FOR YOUR PROTECTION" THE THEATER WILL BE HANDING OUT "TERROR MASKS". CAN SOMEONE GET AHOLD OF ME AND TELL ME WHAT THIS WAS?

LOW-TECH EFFECT : REMEMBER THE SCENE EARLY ON IN **SCANNERS** (1981) WHEN LOUIS DEL GRANDE'S HEAD EXPLODES EVERYWHERE? THE AMAZING EFFECT WAS ACHIEVED BY FILLING A LATEX LOUIS HEAD WITH ALPO AND RABBIT LIVERS, AND BLASTING IT FROM BEHIND WITH A 12-GAUGE SHOTGUN! HOLY FUCKING SHIT!!

DEATH BY DRANO: ON APRIL 22nd 1974, TWO MEN ROBBED A STORE IN OGDEN UTAH, AND MADE 5 HOSTAGES DRINK DRANO BEFORE SHOOTING THEM EACH IN THE HEAD. WHEN CAUGHT, THEY ADMITTED TO GETTING THE IDEA FROM **MAGNUM FORCE** (1973).

COMMUTER GAME

1969 • b&w • directed by Fred Kamiel

SOME FILMS ARE A TRUE PRODUCT OF THEIR TIME. THIS JAUNTY LITTLE NUGGET OF LICENTIOUSNESS IS JUST THAT; AN ODE TO ALL THE SIXTIES-ERA HUSBANDS WHO WANTED TO CHEAT ON THE OL' BALL-N'-CHAINS WITHOUT GETTING CAUGHT. THANKFULLY FOR US, ALL THE PHILANDERING AND NAKED CAROUSING IS CAPTURED IN RICH GORGEOUS TONES OF BLACK, WHITE AND GREY.

ADVERTISED AS "THE FIRST INSIDE LOOK AT WHAT REALLY GOES ON INSIDE **THOSE** APARTMENTS", AND "THE SUBURBANITES' NATIONAL PASTIME", COMMUTER GAME DETAILS THE SINFUL STORY OF WHAT HAPPENS WHEN TWO SWINGIN' SUBURBAN STUDS NAMED RICHARD AND PETER RENT A "LOVE PAD" IN THE CITY AS A PLACE TO TAKE THE RACY FLOOZIES THEY BAG AFTER WORK. THE ONLY THING IS THAT THESE TWO LADY KILLERS HAVE WIVES THAT'LL "BUST 'EM IN THE HEAD" IF THEY CATCH WIND OF ANY STRAY PUSSY SNIFFIN' AROUND.

THE GENTS HAVE A STRAIT-LACED PAL NAMED JONATHAN, A HAPPILY MARRIED DOCTOR WHO RESEMBLES WOODY ALLEN AND DOESN'T GIVE A SECOND LOOK TO ANY OF THE SKIRTS THAT HIS HOMIES UNROLL TONGUE FOR. THIS IRKS OUR PLAYBOYS, AND THEY SET UP THE GOOD DOCTOR WITH A VISIT FROM THEIR SECRET WEAPON: BUBBLES LA TOUR -- THE HOTTEST, MOST CURVY STRIPPER AT 'BRANDY'S', THEIR COMMONWEALTH AVENUE BOSTON HANGOUT. BUBBLES HAS LARGE BLONDE HAIR, LONG FLUTTERY LASHES, A LUSCIOUS FULL FIGURE....AND A BIG PICTURE OF SAMMY DAVIS JR. IN HER DRESSING ROOM! **NO** MAN CAN DENY SUCH A PACKAGE!

THE WIVES, SHARON AND PAULA, KNOW SOME SHIT IS GOING DOWN, AND DESPITE SAD SUBSERVIENT ATTITUDES INDICATIVE OF THE TIMES ("I SUPPOSE I SHOULDN'T COMPLAIN AS LONG AS HE HAS ENOUGH LEFT FOR ME") IT DOESN'T TAKE THE GALS LONG TO BEGIN TO SCHEME ABOUT HOW TO GET EVEN. AND WOULDN'T YOU JUST KNOW IT? THEIR BRILLIANT PLAN INVOLVES BECOMING TRAMPY URBAN HUMPSTERS THEMSELVES!

HA HA! NEEDLESS TO SAY, THE FINALE TO COMMUTER GAME SWELLS TO A JAZZY CACOPHONY OF NUTTY HIJINX AND NICE BIG BOUNCING BOOBS!

STARRING STEPHEN ADAMS, RUTH CONTI, PETER PURE, GEORGE WADSWORTH, AND GETTI MILLER. DIRECTOR FRED KAMIEL NORMALLY WORKED AS A SOUND MIXER AND SOUND ENGINEER ON BIGGER BUDGET PICTURES. THIS IS HIS ONLY KNOWN DIRECTORIAL EFFORT.

AVAILABLE FROM:
WWW.SOMETHINGWEIRD.COM

MISS "BUBBLES LA TOUR" ♡

BOUGIE 06

HUZZAH

CHRIS ENG'S ALONE IN THE DARK

Girls Riot (MANFRED PURZER, 1983)

THERE'S SOME MISREPRESENTATION GOING ON IN THIS DUBBED GERMAN EXPORT (ORIGINALLY TITLED "RANDALE"). FIRST OF ALL, IT ISN'T SET IN A PRISON - GIRLS RIOT TAKES PLACE AT A TEEN GIRL REFORM SCHOOL (NOT THE KIND WITH WENDY O. WILLIAMS, THE KIND WHERE YOUNG GIRLS ARE SENT IF THEY DON'T LOOK LIKE A TEUTONIC GODDESS) AND SECOND, THERE ARE TWO OCCURRENCES IN THE FILM THAT COULD QUALIFY AS THE TITULAR 'RIOT'. YOU CHOOSE WHICH ONE IT IS:

1) THE SCENE WHERE THE GIRLS BANG THEIR SPOONS ON THE DINNER TABLE IN UNISON, CHANTING "WE WON'T EAT", OR...

2) THE PART WHERE A DOZEN TEENS (IN WHAT MUST BE THE MOST SINGULARLY GERMAN MOMENT IN THE MOVIE) PROTEST THE TRAGIC SUICIDE OF ONE OF THEIR FRIENDS BY DONNING PLASTER DEATH MASKS AND SMOKING SILENTLY.

IF EITHER OF THESE EVENTS QUALIFIES AS A "RIOT" IN YOUR EYES, YOU SURELY WON'T BE DISAPPOINTED WITH HOW THINGS UNFOLD. OTHERWISE YOU'RE IN FOR WHAT COULD (WITH THE EXCEPTION OF A FEW ISOLATED SWEAR WORDS AND SPORADIC PUBESCENT BOOBIES) PASS FOR A MORALISTIC MADE-FOR-TV MOVIE.

THIS SCENE DOES NOT APPEAR IN "GIRLS RIOT"

OUR PROTAGONIST ANDREA, NEWLY ARRIVED AT THE BUCHENECH SPECIAL EDUCATION HOME, IS PITTED AGAINST THE ENTIRELY TYPICAL HEADMISTRESS. IT IS THE AGE OLD ARGUMENT: DO THE GIRLS NEED TENDERNESS (ANDREA) OR DISCIPLINE (HEADMISTRESS)? WELL, IF THE APPARENT SUBTEXT IS ANYTHING TO GO BY, IT'S "DISCIPLINE". ANDREA TRIES TO MAKE A DIFFERENCE, FAILS, LOSES THE GIRLS' TRUST (FOR NO GOOD REASON), ALMOST GETS ONE OF THE GIRLS ABDUCTED BY AN EVIL PIMP THROUGH HER CARELESSNESS, AND QUITS IN THE WAKE OF IT ALL BEFORE HER SUPERIORS CAN FIRE HER. PLUS, IT'S CLEAR THAT REFORM SCHOOL LIFE ISN'T REALLY THAT BAD AND IF YOU EVER END UP IN ONE SOMEDAY AND FORSAKE THE CARING EMPLOYEES FOR THE HORRORS OF THE REAL WORLD YOU CAN EXPECT TO FIND YOURSELF A) GANGRAPED BY A GROUP OF 10 SWARTHY MEN, B) HIT BY A CAR, OR C) PITCHING YOURSELF IN FRONT OF A TRAIN. SO DON'T DO IT. DID I MENTION THE MORALITY?

...AND NEITHER DOES THIS SCENE. SORRY.

I'D RUN DOWN THE SEXY PARTS, BUT THERE REALLY AREN'T ANY. PRETTY MUCH THE ONLY TITS WE GET IN THE PICTURE ARE SONJA'S - A CRAZY, NOT-REMOTELY-LEGAL-LOOKING GIRL WHO IS SHOWING OFF HER HOMEMADE TATTOO TO ANDREA -- AND WHEN THE HEADMISTRESS BRISKLY WALKS THROUGH THE SHOWER ROOM TO DISCOVER ONE OF THE GIRLS HAS GOTTEN HER FIRST PERIOD (TO WHOM THE OTHER GIRLS ARE SINGING "FOR SHE'S A JOLLY GOOD FELLOW," WHICH CONJURES UP SOME BIZARRE QUESTIONS).

GIRLS RIOT DID CONTAIN SOME GOOD LINES OF DIALOGUE, HOWEVER, SO HERE'S A SAMPLING DEVOID OF CONTEXT: "MY GRANDMOTHER USED TO SAY IT'S BETTER TO CROUCH THEN TO BEND OVER." "YOU KNOW WHAT YOU NEED? YOU BITCHES, WELL, YOU CAN ALL GO TO HELL!". "THIS IS YOUR COLLEAGUE, GABBY DONUT." "WELL, WILL WONDERS NEVER CEASE--THIS CHILD IS GYNECOLOGICALLY INTACT." "GET A LOAD OF THOSE TWO CUNT-EATERS." "I'M NOT INTERESTED IN FINDING OUT WHO STARTED IT, I JUST WANT TO KNOW WHY THEY WERE FIGHTING LIKE CATS IN HEAT." AND PERHAPS THE BEST LINE IN THE MOVIE: "GARY COOPER, FUJIYAMA AND ASSHOLE."

ENG © 2006

INVASION OF THE BEE GIRLS (1973. DIR: DENIS SANDERS)

THEY'LL LOVE THE VERY LIFE OUT OF YOUR BODY!

"INVASION OF THE BEE GIRLS"

WILLIAM SMITH · ANITRA FORD
VICTORIA VETRI and THE BEE GIRLS

Written by NICHOLAS MEYER · Directed by DENIS SANDERS · A SEQUOIA PICTURES, INC. PRODUCTION
A CENTAUR RELEASE · COLOR by CFI.

ALSO KNOWN AS GRAVEYARD TRAMPS, A TITLE CLEARLY GIVEN BY SOMEONE WHO HAD NEVER SEEN THE MOVIE.

GOVERNMENT INVESTIGATOR NEIL AGAR (CINEMA SEWER FAVE WILLIAM SMITH, WHO IS UNFORTUNATELY SANS MOUSTACHE) IS SENT TO A SMALL TOWN IN CALIFORNIA TO INVESTIGATE A MYSTERIOUS DEATH. THE TOWN HOUSES A GOVERNMENT LAB WHERE A SCIENTIST HAS DIED, APPARENTLY OF "SEXUAL EXHAUSTION". BEFORE YOU KNOW IT, MEN ALL OVER THE GODDAMN PLACE ARE DROPPING DEAD, AND AGAR (FLANKED BY A PRETTY SCIENTIST PLAYED BY VICTORIA VETRI) USES AN ASININE LEAP OF LOGIC TO SURMISE (CORRECTLY) THAT A GROUP OF GIRLS CROSSBRED WITH BEES ARE MATING WITH, AND MASSACRING EVERYTHING IN TOWN WITH A BONER.

THE SMUTTY AND INCOMPREHENSIBLE MAD-SCIENTIST-LIKE BRILLIANCE OF INVASION OF THE BEE GIRLS REALLY TICKLES ME. ANITRA FORD (WHO ONLY MADE A HANDFUL OF FILMS), RENE BOND (MY FAVE CLASSIC PORN STAR OF ALL TIME) COLLEEN BRENNAN (THE STAR OF THE VERY FIRST PORN FILM I EVER SAW) AND ALL KINDS OF OTHER PREDATORY BEE LADIES IN GIANT SUNGLASSES AND MINI-SKIRT LAB COATS LAVISH THEE WITH WALL TO WALL SOFT CORE HUMPING, GRATUITOUS NUDE DIRT-BIKING, AND BLOODY MURDER. LACED WITH LUNATIC DIALOGUE AND UNAPOLOGETICALLY CHAUVINIST CHARACTERS, THIS DEADPAN-YET-ASININE MOVIE SEEMS TO SERVE AS A PARANOID SATIRE ON THE RISE OF THE WOMEN'S MOVEMENT IN AMERICA.

WHEN ASKED ABOUT THE MOVIE BY CHRIS POGGIALI, STAR WILLIAM SMITH LAUGHED AND REPLIED: "OH MY GOD! THAT WAS THE WEIRDEST IDEA. BUT IT WAS GREAT, ALL THESE BROADS RUNNING AROUND NAKED. SHIT, THAT PART OF IT WAS NICE -- BUT THOSE BEES WERE SOMETHIN' BAD, WEREN'T THEY?"

—BOUGIE '10

"SAY GOODNIGHT TO THE BAD GUY!"

FEATURING AN INCENDIARY AL PACINO AT THE ZENITH OF HIS POWERS, BRIAN DE PALMA'S **SCARFACE** REINVENTED THE GANGSTER MOVIE AND SET A NEW BAROMETER FOR CINEMATIC VIOLENCE, PROFANITY, AND OVER-THE-TOP DEPICTIONS OF COCAINE CULTURE.

THIS MODERN CLASSIC BEGAN AS A SCRIPT FROM OLIVER STONE WHO PENNED IT WHILE BATTLING A COCAINE ADDICTION, ALTHOUGH IT WAS WAS SIDNEY LUMET'S IDEA TO MAKE THE CHARACTERS CUBAN AND TO INCLUDE THE 1980 MARIEL HARBOUR BOAT LIFT IN THE DRAMATIC PLOT. HE WAS PRODUCER LOUIS STROLLERS FIRST PICK TO DIRECT, BUT ENDED UP BACKING OUT. BRIAN DE PALMA, SENSING A CHANCE TO STRIKE GOLD, DROPPED OUT OF DIRECTING **FLASHDANCE** (WHICH WOULD GO ON TO BE A MASSIVE HIT) TO TAKE LUMET'S SPOT IN THE CREATIVE ROSTER.

DE PALMA AND CO. COULD HAVE NEVER HAVE PREDICTED THE CULT PHENOMENON THAT DEVELOPED AROUND SCARFACE, A MOVIE THAT WAS CERTAINLY NOT BELOVED RIGHT OUT OF THE STARTING GATE. LIKE RIDLEY SCOTT'S **BLADE RUNNER** (1982) AND JOHN CARPENTER'S **THE THING** (1982), EARLY 1980S AUDIENCES AND CRITICS HAD NO CLUE WHAT TO MAKE OF SCARFACE AT THE APEX OF ITS RELEASE, AND ONLY CAME TO VIEW THESE MOVIES AS SEMINAL EXAMPLES OF THEIR GENRES MANY YEARS LATER. MOST DENOUNCED THE EXTREME, GARISH VIOLENCE OF SCARFACE IN PARTICULAR, AND THE FILM ENDED UP MAKING LESS AT THE BOX OFFICE THAN THE REVILED AQUATIC SPECTACLE THAT WAS **JAWS 3-D**.

MIAMI... 1980

PACINO

Scarface

INDEED, DEPALMA WAS NOMINATED FOR THE RAZZIE AWARD FOR WORST DIRECTOR FOR SCARFACE, WHICH ENDS UP SAYING NOTHING ABOUT THE QUALITY OF HIS WICKED-SWEET MOVIE, AND SPEAKS MORE ABOUT WHAT SEEMED TO BE A GENERAL CULTURAL DISLIKE FOR HIM AT THE TIME. HE WAS ALSO NOMINATED FOR **DRESSED TO KILL** (1980) AND **BODY DOUBLE** (1984) -- TWO EQUALLY IDIOTIC RAZZIE NOMINATIONS THAT MAKE NO SENSE.

THE ROLE OF ELVIRA HANCOCK (TONY MONTANA'S MEGA-FOXY COME-FUCK-ME GANGSTER

MICHELLE PFEIFFER

MOLL) WAS A SUBJECT OF CONTENTION AMONGST MANY YOUNG HOLLYWOOD ACTRESSES AT THE TIME. ROSANNA ARQUETTE, JENNIFER JASON LEIGH, MELANIE GRIFFITH, KIM BASINGER, KATHLEEN TURNER, JODIE FOSTER AND BROOKE SHIELDS ALL TURNED THE ROLE DOWN, WHILE KRISTY MCNICHOL, GEENA DAVIS, CARRIE FISHER, KELLY MCGILLIS AND SHARON STONE ALL TRIED OUT FOR IT AND CAME AWAY EMPTY-HANDED. AFTER THE DUST CLEARED IT WAS VIRTUAL UNKNOWN MICHELLE PFEIFFER WHO WON OVER THE PRODUCERS AND CASTING DEPARTMENT.

EARLY ON IN THE MOVIE PACINO UTTERS "YEYO" AS A SLANG TERM FOR COCAINE. NOT APPEARING IN THE SCRIPT, THE WORD WAS IMPROVISED BY PACINO AND DE PALMA LIKED IT ENOUGH TO CONTINUE SPRINKLING IT THROUGHOUT THE MOVIE. IN AN ODD CASE OF LIFE IMITATING ART, A MULTITUDE OF GANGBANGERS AND SMALL TIME CRIMINALS ACROSS THE CONTINENT WOULD GO ON TO SEE SCARFACE, PICK UP ON PACINO'S USE OF THE WORD, AND DROP IT IN THEIR DAY-TO-DAY DRUG DEALINGS.

☆ —BOUGIE 2010

DEEP RED (1975. Directed by Dario Argento)

GIALLO (DEFINITION: EURO-HORROR "WHODUNIT" THRILLER CHARACTERISED BY GORY EXTENDED MURDER SEQUENCES FEATURING UNUSUAL MUSICAL ARRANGEMENTS. A MODERN SLASHER HORROR BUT FILTERED THROUGH ITALY'S LONG-STANDING TRADITION OF OPERA AND STAGED GRAND GUIGNOL DRAMA.)

I'VE BEEN CRITICISED IN THE PAST FOR NOT GIVING THE GIALLI A FAIR SHAKE -- FOR BEING UNFAIRLY DISMISSIVE. CALL IT PERSONAL PREFERENCE IF YOU LIKE, BUT THE GENRE IS LITTERED WITH FILMS THAT WATCH LIKE SPAGHETTI VERSIONS OF AGATHA CHRISTIE'S DRY BBC TELEFILMS WITH HIGHER BLACK GLOVE, BLOOD, AND STRAIGHT RAZOR CONTENT.

THAT SAID, THE BEST GIALLO HAS TO OFFER IS AS FANTASTIC AS ANY SUBGENRE OF HORROR YOU CAN NAME, AND ONE OF THE KEY FILMS THAT ANY SELF-RESPECTING HORROR MOVIE FAN WORTH THEIR MALT LIQUOR SHOULD HAVE IMMERSED THEMSELVES IN, IS DARIO ARGENTO'S BRILLIANT DEEP RED.

When was the last time you were *REALLY SCARED!!!?*

The EXORCIST

PSYCHO JAWS

Now there's DEEP RED
You will *NEVER* forget it!!!

A Dario Argento Film Starring DAVID HEMMINGS Daria Nicolodi

ALSO KNOWN AS PROFONDO ROSSO, DEEP RED STARS A JAZZ PIANIST (PLAYED BY DAVID HEMMINGS) WHO FINDS HIMSELF CAUGHT UP IN THE INVESTIGATION OF THE VIOLENT MURDER OF A PSYCHIC MEDIUM. HIS WITNESSING OF THIS EXECUTION WEIGHS HEAVILY ON HIM, ESPECIALLY AS HE REALISES HE MAY HAVE SPOTTED THE KILLER'S FACE AMONG A GROUP OF PORTRAITS ON THE WALL OF THE VICTIM'S APARTMENT. THIS TERRIFYING MYSTERY OF MEMORY IS THE GOOEY CORE OF THE FILM, AND PROVIDES IT WITH ITS MOST CHILLING ASPECTS.

OTHER HIGHLIGHTS: A FEISTY INVESTIGATIVE REPORTER PLAYED BY THE ALWAYS ENRAPTURING DARIA NICOLODI, A VERTIGO-INDUCING SIMULTANEOUS ZOOM AND TRACK SHOT NEAR THE START, THE DISCOVERY OF A MOULDERING CORPSE WALLED UP IN A SPOOKY-ASS DERELICT HOUSE, AND A FUCKING PUPPET THAT COMES RIGHT AT THE CAMERA WITH A KNIFE GOING STABBY STABBY -- MAKING THE BOUG SHIT HIS PLUS FOURS. THIS IS A STYLISH AND EVOCATIVE MOVIE THAT DOESN'T MIND GETTING ITS HANDS DIRTY AS IT BUSTS ITS HUMP TRYING TO GET YOU EMOTIONALLY INVOLVED.

GOBLIN (THE PROG ROCK KINGS RESPONSIBLE FOR COMPOSING SCORES FOR SEVERAL OF ARGENTO'S LATER MASTERPIECES) LIGHT THIS BLOOD-DRAINER UP WITH MEMORABLE INSTRUMENTAL MUSIC. THE PLOT MAY BE CONVOLUTED AND UNREALISTIC, BUT I'M NOT SURE I'VE EVER SEEN A MOVIE WHERE MURDER WAS QUITE SO BEAUTIFUL.

SIX FROM THE SICK, SICK FINDLAYS!

APTLY DESCRIBED AS "THE MOST NOTORIOUS FILMMAKERS IN THE ANNALS OF SEXPLOITATION", HUSBAND/WIFE CREATIVE TEAM MICHAEL AND ROBERTA FINDLAY WERE GROUND LEVEL NEW YORKERS WHO SPECIALISED IN SOFTCORE ROUGHIES, WHICH, VIEWED IN THE CONTEXT OF THE TIME AND GENRE THEY WERE SHAT INTO, ARE SOME OF THE BEST FILMS OF THEIR KIND. HERE IS A LITTLE SPOTLIGHT ON THE BEST AND MOST UNFORGETTABLE WORK THEY DID TOGETHER BEFORE MICHAEL SADLY DIED (HACKED APART BY HELICOPTER ROTOR BLADES AFTER A CRASH ON THE ROOF OF THE PAN AM BUILDING IN NYC) AND BEFORE ROBERTA WENT ON TO DIRECT HARDCORE PORN IN THE LATE '70S AND EARLY '80S.

TAKE ME NAKED (1966)
THE WEAKEST OF THIS BEASTLY BUNCH, BUT STILL WORTH A HAPPY BOUGIE RECOMMENDATION SIMPLY FOR ITS OVERWROUGHT VOICE NARRATION, DISTURBING VOYEUR THEME, AND STRANGE VOYAGE INTO THE INTELLECTUALISED PHILOSOPHICAL ASPECTS OF SEEDY SLEAZE AND DEMENTED DEPRAVITY. SIMPLY PUT: THIS NO-BUDGET SEXPLOITATION MUD MUSCLE IS WONDERFULLY WEIRD.

THE TOUCH OF HER FLESH (1967)
THE FIRST OF THE FINDLAYS' FLESH TRILOGY, A SERIES OF FILMS THAT ARE SO FAR REMOVED FROM OUR POLITICALLY CORRECT WORLD OF TODAY, THEY APPEAR TO HAVE COME FROM A DIFFERENT PLANET. HERE, A MILD-MANNERED SHLUB IS CONSUMED WITH HATRED AND RAGE WHEN HIS WANTON WIFE SLUTS AROUND ON HIM. WHEN HE'S HIT BY A CAR HE GAINS AN EYEPATCH AND TURNS INTO A PUSSY-HATING PSYCHO OUT TO GET REVENGE ON BITCHES EVERYWHERE. 75 MINUTES OF BLACK AND WHITE GRIT DESIGNED TO MAKE YOUR JAW DROP.

THE CURSE OF HER FLESH (1968)
THE VILE ONE-EYED GOON (PLAYED BY MICHAEL FINDLAY HIMSELF, BY THE WAY) FROM THE FIRST MOVIE IS BACK, AND HE'S AGAIN TARGETING THE LOCAL WHORES AND GO-GO DANCERS WITH EXTREME PREJUDICE. HIS FORMS OF UNSEEMLY SAVAGERY GET MORE AND MORE CREATIVE THIS TIME, AND INCLUDE A DILDO WITH A KNIFE HIDDEN INSIDE, A MACHETE, POISON ROPES, AND MORE. GOD, I LOVE THIS DREK.

THE KISS OF HER FLESH (1968)
MY FAVE OF THE TRILOGY FINDS OUR FOUL MURDEROUS HEATHEN TOTALLY LOSING WHAT IS LEFT OF HIS MISOGYNISTIC MIND AND SLASHING AT NAKED BREASTS WITH A LOBSTER CLAW. YES, A FUCKING LOBSTER CLAW. THIS IS PRECISELY WHAT I'M TALKING ABOUT, PEOPLE. THESE MOVIES ARE TWISTED AND SICK, BUT ALSO HILARIOUSLY BIZARRE AND SILLY AS HELL.

A THOUSAND PLEASURES (1968)
I DON'T EVEN WANT TO SAY ANYTHING ABOUT THIS ONE, BECAUSE EVERY SCENE UNSPOOLS TO REVEAL SOMETHING EVEN WILDER THAN WHAT YOU PEEPED PREVIOUS, AND THE SURPRISE OF IT IS HALF THE FUN. I WILL MENTION HOWEVER, THAT FANS OF WHIPPING, TORTURE, LESBIANISM, INFANTILISM, VOYEURISM, AND BREAST MILK DRINKING WILL FIND REASONS TO BE GIDDY ABOUT THIS HARD-BOILED ROUGHIE, WHICH IS MY PERSONAL FAVE OF THE BUNCH. A MUST-SEE!

THE ULTIMATE DEGENERATE (1969)
OH MAN, THEY SAVED SOME OF THE BEST FOR LAST. GOD, I LOVE THE FINDLAYS. THIS TWISTED TRASH IS QUITE ENTERTAINING FROM THE FIRST MINUTE TO THE LAST, AND FOLLOWS AN UNDERGROUND FETISH RING IN A HOUSE FILLED WITH A HAREM OF NUBILE LESBIAN FREAKS. STICK AROUND FOR THE FINAL 10 MINUTES, BECAUSE THAT IS WHEN POOP REALLY GETS OUT OF HAND. MAN, THESE ARE THE KIND OF PERVY GRINDHOUSE FILMS THAT ABSOLUTELY THRILLED ENTIRE SALIVATION ARMIES OF SWEATY RAINCOATED MEN IN THE NINETEEN SIXTIES.

BLESS YOU MR AND MRS. FINDLAY. BLESS YOU.

☆ — BOUGIE

RENE BOND

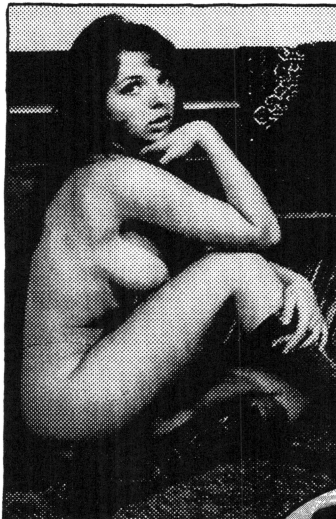

BORN RENE RUTH BOND ON OCTOBER 11th 1950 IN SAN DIEGO, RENE BOND CAME BOUNCING INTO THE PORNO LEXICON WITH HER FUNKY GROUPIE-STYLE FASHIONS, BIG ROUND DOE EYES, AND CHUBBY CHIPMUNK CHEEKS -- PROMPTLY MELTING THE HEARTS OF AN ENTIRE GENERATION OF LICENTIOUS FILM FANS.

THE GRINDHOUSE SCENE REVOLVED AROUND SOFT-CORE SEXPLOITATION IN THE LATE '60s AND EARLY '70s, BUT IN 1972 THE WILD TESTICULATION OF HARDCORE WAS POISED TO TAKE OVER -- PROMPTING MANY OF THE GIRLS TO SAY "HELL NO" TO THE NEW XXXPECTATIONS. GIRLS WERE RETIRING LEFT AND RIGHT, BUT IN A FEW CASES PERFORMERS CONTINUED MOVING BACK AND FORTH BETWEEN SOFT AND HARD SEX FILMS. THIS INITIAL SALVO OF GIRLS WERE SANDY DEMPSEY, SANDY CAREY, JANE TSENTAS, ORITA DE CHADWICK, MARIE ARNOLD AND RENE BOND.

THIS REFRESHING FREE-LOVE GENERATION WILLINGNESS TO PLEASE POISED RENE TO PERFECT THE ART OF STEALING HEARTS AS ONE OF THE ADULT INDUSTRY'S VERY FIRST FEMALE STARS. **MONA** DIRECTOR HOWARD ZIEHM WAS ONE OF THE PRIMARY DIRECTORS TO CAST INCIPIENT RENE IN A FEW OTHERWISE INSUBSTANTIAL FUCK LOOPS, AND REMEMBERED HER AS THE CUTE DOWN-TO-EARTH GIRL WITH THE SCUMMY LOW-RENT PORN-INDUSTRY BOYFRIEND WHOM SHE ALWAYS REQUESTED TO BE HER CO-STAR.

THAT BOYFRIEND WAS RIC LUTZE, WHO ALSO APPEARED WITHOUT RENE NOT ONLY IN A DOGFUCK LOOP, BUT IN SOME OTHER MORALLY DUBIOUS XXX AS WELL.

IN 1972 NICK PHILIPS FILM **LES CHIC**, RIC'S UNFLATTERING REP WAS SECURED BY THE OUTRAGEOUSLY GARISH '70s PIMP OUTFITS THAT WERE A PERMANENT PART OF HIS REAL-LIFE WARDROBE. THIS PAIR WOULD OFTEN APPEAR TOGETHER THROUGHOUT MOST OF BOND'S FILMOGRAPHY, INDICATING A COMFORT LEVEL THAT RENE NEEDED AS SHE BEGAN DOING HARDCORE MOVIES AND LOOPS.

RENE WAS ALSO A RARE INSTANCE OF AN ACTRESS USING HER REAL NAME. "SHE WAS SEEMINGLY FEARLESS. A SINFULLY SEXY AND YOUTHFUL LOOKING LITTLE STRUMPET WHOSE WELL-ROUNDED ACTING SKILLS AND VIVACIOUS APPROACH TO ON-SCREEN SEXING MADE HER AN INSTANT FAVOURITE" WRITES THE EXCALIBUR WEB SITE. "RENE HAD A BEAUTIFUL, PETULANT FACE, A YOUTHFUL AND TRIM LITTLE BODY, AND A NICE TOUCH WITH LIGHT COMEDY THAT ADDED AN EXTRA

SOMETHING SPECIAL TO EVERY ROLE SHE TOOK."

VETERAN PHOTOGRAPHER DAVID STORY HAILS
FROM KENTUCKY. HE ENTERED PORNO IN 1964,
SHOOTING FOR MILTON LUROS' PARLIAMENT NEWS
IN LOS ANGELES, AND HE REMEMBERS RENE
FONDLY: "I CAME OUT FROM KENTUCKY AND
MET RENE BOND IN 1964. I MET HER ON
HOLLYWOOD BLVD AT THE MAGIC SHOP. FOLLOWED
HER IN THERE. SHE INTRODUCED ME TO MILT
LUROS. I STARTED SHOOTING FOR HIM. ALL WE
DID WAS TOPLESS AT THE TIME, NO PUBIC HAIR.
SHE WAS ONE OF THE NICEST PERSONS I'VE
EVER MET. SHE WAS ALWAYS SWEET, ALWAYS ON
TIME. SHE
DIDN'T DO
DRUGS."

BOND WAS ONE
OF THE FIRST
PORN STARS
TO GET A
BREAST JOB,
AND REMAINS
TO THIS DAY
ONE OF THE
VERY FEW THAT
I DON'T FIND
REPELLANT
FOR IT --
PROBABLY
BECAUSE HER'S WEREN'T GROTESQUELY LARGE, JUST
ACCENTUATED. SHE APPEARED FREQUENTLY IN EARLY
'70s BONDAGE LOOPS, AND IN IT TAKES A THIEF, SHOVES
ANOTHER GIRL AROUND, TIES HER UP, AND STUFFS HER
YAPPER WITH MONEY. CONTRARY TO PORN NERD BELIEF,

RENE DID NOT WAIT UNTIL SHE RECEIVED HER SOFTBALL-SIZED
JUGGS TO MAKE THE TRANSITION FROM SOFT TO HARD. SHE WAS
CAST IN A LARGE NUMBER OF FUCK FILMS PRE-SURGERY, THOUGH
THESE DO REMAIN THE HARDEST OF HER FILMOGRAPHY TO HUNT
DOWN. ONE OF THESE RARITIES WAS KIM COMES HOME, IN
WHICH THE RAVISHING LOVELY PLAYED AN INNOCENT ART SCHOOL
STUDENT
DEBAUCHED
BY HER
CHILDHOOD
FRIEND
TURNED HOOKER.

RIC LUTZE

MISS BOND
TOOK ON FIVE
FACELESS COCKS
IN A ROW IN THE
1973 CLASSIC
TEENAGE
FANTASIES, ONE OF MY ALL-TIME FAVES. I
THINK ONE REALLY HAS TO SIT THROUGH A
LOT OF EARLY '70s SMUT TO RECOGNISE
HOW SPECIAL AND UNIQUE IT WAS FOR
RENE TO SPEAK DIRECTLY TO THE
VIEWER AS SHE SMILES AND STROKES
EACH PINK BATTER BLASTER. WHEN
SHE PANTS "MY FANTASIES ARE
MOSTLY ORAL. I ENJOY GIVING HEAD.
I ENJOY MAKING MEN CUM", YOU
FEEL EVERY GODDAMN SYLLABLE
RIGHT IN THE UNDERCARRIAGE OF

MEET
RENE
SHE'LL
PLEASE YOU IN
EVERY WAY

RENE AND FRIEND IN 1973's
TEENAGE FANTASIES

YOUR SKIN-MARBLES. SHE PROCEEDS
-- BETWEEN LICKS AND SUCKS -- TO OFFER
A BLOW-BY-BLOW ORATORY OF EACH
ASPECT OF HER SENSUAL TECHNIQUE.
AS AN EXCLAMATION POINT ON THIS
LOIN-STIRRING DISPLAY, SHE MAKES
EACH DONG ERUPT SEEMINGLY AT
WILL. NO ONE WHO WITNESSES
THIS GRAND WORM-BURPING
DISPLAY WILL FORGET IT. RENE IS
IN FULL CONTROL. SHE IS LUSCIOUS
CONFIDENT FEMININITY.

THIS DAZZLING CUM-COATED
PERFORMANCE MADE BOND

164

RENE BOND:
BELOVED SISTER OF SLEAZE

JOURNAL OF LOVE (1971)

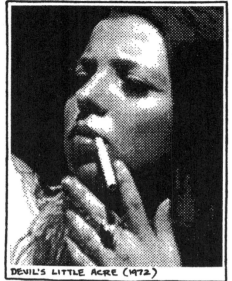

DEVIL'S LITTLE ACRE (1972)

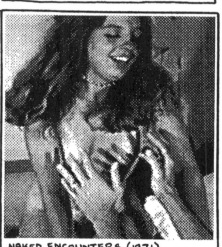

NAKED ENCOUNTERS (1971)

RENDEZVOUS IN HELL (1971)

THREE FOR ONE (1971)

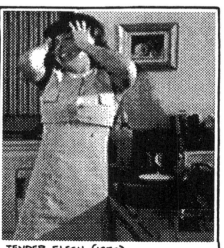

TENDER FLESH (1970)

INFAMOUS FOR HER ORAL ABILITIES, AND JOHN HOLMES WAS CAST FOR A PART IN **TEENAGE FANTASIES** PART 2. NOT MANY GIRLS COULD MANHANDLE (WOMANHANDLE ??) THAT 12 INCH MONUMENT (WITH ITS JAW-SNAPPING 2.5 INCH DIAMETER), BUT OUR GAL MADE JOHNNY SEEM LIKE HE WAS PACKING A LITTLE VIENNA SAUSAGE. THIS CHICK COULD TAME BONER, AND WOULD GO ON TO ANSWER THE TITULAR QUESTION **DO YOU WANNA BE LOVED?** (1975) WITH A RESOUNDING 'YES!' BY TAKING ON 5 GUYS ALL AT ONCE.

WORD WOULD GET AROUND THE LOW BUDGET FILM MAKING COMMUNITY THAT THE LONG-HAIRED BRUNETTE WITH THE CURVY FIGURE WAS A DEDICATED PERFORMER, AND COULD ACTUALLY REMEMBER THE DIALOGUE WRITTEN IN A SCRIPT. HER INNOCENT FACE MADE HER THE GO-TO CHOICE TO PLAY TEENAGERS OR FARMERS' DAUGHTERS, AND HER EAGERNESS TO APPEAR IN "ROUGHIES" (SO NAMED FOR THEIR RAW AND DISTURBINGLY EXPLICIT DEPICTIONS OF SEXUAL VIOLENCE) DIDN'T HURT HER RESUME EITHER. SOON SHE WAS SO BUSY SHE HAD TO TURN AWAY WORK, AND WOULD EVENTUALLY DOMINATE THE WEST COAST JIZZ BIZZ.

IN 1977 RENE DID ONE OF HER ONLY INTERVIEWS WITH A LITTLE-SEEN UNDERGROUND SEX MAG, WHICH I AM REPRINTING HERE IN THE HOPE OF KEEPING SOME OF RENE'S FEW PUBLIC WORDS ALIVE. FOR A WOMAN WHO STARRED IN ALMOST 300 MOVIES AND WITH WHOM SO MANY MASTURBATORS THROUGHOUT THE DECADES ARE INTIMATELY FAMILIAR, IT'S A SHAME SO FEW OF US EVER GOT TO HEAR HER SPEAK HER MIND. I OFTEN FEEL LIKE I KNOW RENE BETTER THAN ANY CLASSIC ADULT MOVIE STAR, AND YET, AFTER YEARS OF RESEARCH -- I ACTUALLY KNOW ALMOST NOTHING ABOUT HER.

How old were you when you began doing adult films?

RENE BOND: "I WAS NINETEEN, ALMOST TWENTY. I HAD SOME FRIENDS WHO WERE WORKING IN PORNO, AND I NEEDED THE MONEY. SO THEY SAID THEY'D INTRODUCE ME TO SOME PEOPLE, AND THEY DID. I GOT USED TO THE MONEY."

What sort of pay did you get when you were just starting out?

RB: "IT RAN ABOUT A HUNDRED DOLLARS A DAY, SOMETIMES LESS DEPENDING ON HOW MANY SEX SCENES YOU DID. I VERY SELDOM GOT MORE THAN THAT. I GET ABOUT $7,500 OR MORE TO DO A FILM NOWADAYS."

How long did it take to make your early pix?

THE FILMAKERS COMPANY presents

TEEN-AGE JAILBAIT

RB: "THEY WERE CALLED 'ONE DAY WONDERS', AND USUALLY TOOK A DAY TO SHOOT. WHEN PRODUCTION VALUES GOT BETTER, THEY WOULD TAKE TWO OR THREE DAYS TO SHOOT AND TO MAKE. SOMETIMES THEY'D SHOOT TWO FILMS BACK TO BACK AND THAT WOULD TAKE A WEEK. NOWADAYS [1977] THEY TAKE ABOUT TEN TO FIFTEEN DAYS OR LONGER, DEPENDING ON HOW GOOD THEY ARE. THERE ARE VERY FEW ONE DAY WONDERS BEING MADE ANYMORE."

Viewing your films over the past seven years, your body has changed considerably. There's been a metamorphism in your bosom. You've filled out quite a bit."

RB: "THAT'S OBVIOUSLY NOT ALL FROM GROWING. I DID HAVE [BREAST ENHANCEMENT] SURGERY, BUT THAT WAS BECAUSE I WAS TOLD THERE'S A NORTH AMERICAN BREAST FETISH, AND THAT MEN ONLY LIKE WOMEN WITH BIG BOOBS, WHICH IS NOT THE CASE ANYMORE -- BUT THEN IT WAS. AND SO I HAD IT DONE, AND IT CHANGED A LOT OF THINGS. I DID GET MORE WORK AFTER THAT."

Have you ever had any brushes with shady characters, mysterious, nefarious or suspicious persons?

RB: "WELL, AS FAR AS 'MYSTERIOUS' PERSONS, I'VE NEVER MET ANY AND I'M NOT SURE WHAT THEY'D DO. I'M SURE THERE MUST BE SOME 'UNDERWORLD CHARACTERS' AROUND, BUT MOSTLY IT'S JUST SMALL, INDEPENDENT MOVIEMAKERS WHO GO ONTO BIGGER BUDGET FILMS. I'M NOT SURE WHERE THE MONEY COMES FROM, BUT I'M SURE IT COMES FROM MANY DIFFERENT SOURCES. I DON'T THINK THAT THE UNDERWORLD HAS ANY BIG HOLD ON PORN."

How many films have you made so far?

RB: "AT LAST COUNT, ABOUT 275."

Of all of your leading men, who is your favourite?

RB: "MY BOYFRIEND RIC LUTZE IS MY FAVOURITE LEADING MAN. HE'S THE EASIEST TO WORK WITH AND I HAVE MADE THE MOST FILMS WITH HIM."

When you're making hardcore flix, are there any tricks for keeping the guy hard?

RB: "MAINLY IT'S JUST HAVING A RAPPORT WITH THE PERSON. TRY AND GIVE HIM SOMETHING. IT MOSTLY HAS TO DO WITH THE MAN HIMSELF. SOME MEN CAN GET IT UP ALMOST IMMEDIATELY AFTER CLIMAXING, WHILE OTHERS HAVE TO WAIT AWHILE."

Have you ever had any amusing incidents while filming?

RB: "THE ONLY THING THAT COMES TO MIND IS ONCE WHEN WE WERE SHOOTING IN A BATHROOM [COUNTRY CUZZINS, 1970] AND I AND ANOTHER GIRL WERE PORTRAYING TWO COUNTRY GIRLS DISCOVERING A BIDET. AND THE CREW HAD THESE LIGHTS ALL SET UP IN THE BATHROOM. WELL, WE STARTED SPLASHING

RENE AND CO-STAR RON DARBY IN 1975'S "SWINGERS MASSACRE"

MORE HARDCORE ACTION WITH MISS BOND -- THIS TIME IN 1972'S STEAMY "CITY WOMEN"

Teenage THROAT

in the surf,
in the sand and
in the sack!

in COLOR

MPAA X RATED

Starring RENE BOND   Directed by MORRIS DEAL

a fabulous flash of the '50-s

NOSTALGIA
WITH A TWIST!

HIGH SCHOOL FANTASIES

Starring LARRY BARNHOUSE
RENE BOND   TONY MAZZIOTTI
Directed by MORRIS DEAL
ADULTS ONLY   Produced by DAMON CHRISTIAN   In COLOR

A LAUGH WITH EVERY BURP!

HARRY NOVAK PRESENTS

PLEASE DON'T EAT MY MOTHER!

THE HILARIOUS TALE
OF A STRANGE
HOUSEPLANT
WHOSE APPETITE
GREW FROM THE
NEIGHBORHOOD
PETS TO MORE
SUCCULENT DISHES
—AND LOVED
EVERY PIECE!

Starring
RENE BOND

EACH OTHER WITH WATER FROM THE BIDET, AND SOME WATER GOT SPLASHED ON THE LIGHTS WHICH, BY NOW, WERE HOT, AND THE LIGHTS STARTED BURSTING. SO THERE WAS THIS STRANGE SIGHT OF TWO GIRLS JUMPING AND BOUNCING ALL OVER THE BATHROOM, TRYING NOT TO GET SPRAYED WITH FLYING GLASS. THAT WAS PRETTY FUNNY."

Are there any scenes you specifically won't do in your pictures?

RB: "I DON'T DO ANAL SEX, AND I DON'T DO SCENES WITH ANIMALS OR CHILDREN, AND THAT IS ABOUT IT. IT REALLY DEPENDS ON WHAT IT IS. THERE'S ALWAYS SOMEBODY WHO WILL THINK UP SOMETHING NEW."

Of all the films you've made, did you ever manage to get prints so you could make extra money leasing them?

RB: "WHEN YOU MAKE A PICTURE, YOU HARDLY EVER KNOW THE NAME OF IT OR WHO THE DISTRIBUTOR IS. GETTING A PRINT IS OUT OF THE QUESTION."

You have a fan club. What do your fans ask in their letters?

RB: "USUALLY MEN CONFIDE IN ME THEIR SEX PROBLEMS AND ASK MY ADVICE. I TRY TO ANSWER ALL MY LETTERS, BUT IT TAKES A LONG TIME..."

- - - - - - -

AT THE TIME OF THIS INTERVIEW, RENE WAS TAKING MORE INCENTIVE IN MAKING A LIVING OFF HER NAME, SELLING PHOTOS, SLIDES, AND USED UNDERWEAR THROUGH A MAIL ORDER COMPANY THAT WOULD ADVERTISE SMALL BLACK AND WHITE ADS IN THE BACKS OF ADULT MAGAZINES LIKE "JAGUAR" AND "CAVALIER". SOME PORN HISTORIANS CITE RENE AS THE VERY FIRST XXX GIRL TO EVER FORM HER OWN FAN CLUB.

SHE WAS ALSO PERFORMING A NOW LEGENDARY LIVE NUDE STAGE SHOW AT LEE WITTEN'S IVAR BURLESQUE THEATRE IN HOLLYWOOD FOR THE PRINCELY SUM OF $3.50. YOU GOT A FREE BREAKFAST IF YOU APPEARED BEFORE NOON. AS THE AD READ: "MEET THE WORLD'S FOREMOST EXPERT IN PERSON AND GET YOUR THUMB SUCKED!". IT WASN'T EXPLAINED WHAT SHE WAS THE FOREMOST EXPERT OF, BUT WITH ALL THAT THUMBSUCKING GOING ON, IT WASN'T HARD FOR THE IMAGINATION TO BEGIN TO RACE.

GRINNING FROM EAR TO EAR, RENE WOULD STRUT SENSUOUSLY ALONG A RED-CARPETED RUNWAY SET AMONGST THE BREATHLESS CROWD, AND WOULD

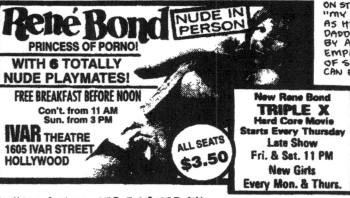
NOT ONLY DO A DAG-NASTY STRIP TEASE, BUT WOULD SING FOR HER FANS AS WELL! AS THE STORY GOES, RENE WOULD EVEN BRING HER FATHER ON STAGE WITH HER AND BELT OUT "MY HEART BELONGS TO DADDY" AS HER BIG FINALE. IN REALITY DADDY WAS PROBABLY PLAYED BY A MIDDLE AGED IVAR THEATRE EMPLOYEE, BUT THIS BUSINESS OF SHOW BEING WHAT IT IS, I CAN EASILY IMAGINE THIS NUMBER WHIPPING A ROOM FULL OF WOLFY RAINCOATERS INTO A FRENZY OF HOOTS AND WHISTLES.

AFTER EACH PERFORMANCE RENE AUTOGRAPHED GLOSSY PHOTOS FOR GUSHING ENTHUSIASTS IN THE LOBBY FOR A MERE DOLLAR EACH. AMAZING.

IS THERE ANY WONDER I NAMED MY CHERISHED HARD BMX CRUISER "RENE"? HELL, ITS THE ONLY WAY I'LL EVER GET TO RIDE HER.

RENE AND RIC RETIRED FROM 'THE LIFESTYE' TOGETHER IN THEIR LATE 20s (CIRCA 1978) AND MOVED TO LAS VEGAS TO CONCENTRATE ON RAISING A FAMILY. RENE STAYED OUT OF THE SPOTLIGHT UNTIL THE MID 1980s WHEN SHE WAS SPOTTED BY SOME OF HER EAGLE-EYE FANS AS A SMILING CONTESTANT ON THE SHORT-LIVED TV GAME SHOW **BREAK THE BANK**, WHERE SHE WAS INTRODUCED AS A "BANKRUPTCY SPECIALIST". I'M PRETTY SURE THE SHOW HAD NO IDEA WHO SHE WAS -- OR I GUESS I SHOULD SAY WHO SHE HAD BEEN. RIC LUTZE WAS NOWHERE TO BE FOUND, AS RENE HAD A NEW BEAU IN TOW, AND CLEANED UP WITH OVER $9,000 IN CASH AND PRIZES.

AFTER THAT BOND WAS SEEN AROUND LAS VEGAS THROUGHOUT THE LATE 1980s AND 1990s, AND BY ACCOUNTS SHE WAS VERY CLOSE WITH HER MOM, AS THEY WERE OFTEN SEEN TOGETHER.

ON JUNE 2ND, 1996, AT THE AGE OF 45, RENE TRAGICALLY DIED OF CIRRHOSIS OF THE LIVER, LEAVING BEHIND AT LEAST TWO CHILDREN. IN 1999 SHE WAS POSTHUMOUSLY INDUCTED INTO THE LEGENDS OF EROTICA HALL OF FAME, AND HAS

SINCE BEEN NAMED TO BOTH THE AVN HALL OF FAME AND THE X-RATED CRITICS ORGANISATION HALL OF FAME.

"IF YOU'VE LIVED IN A CAVE FOR THE LAST QUARTER CENTURY AND HAVE NEVER SEEN RENE'S WORK," WROTE AMERICA MORALIA AUTHOR DON THE DEVIATE, "THEN IT'S TIME TO COME OUT, TIME TO LEAVE THE SHADOW PLAY AND FEAST YOUR SOUL ON THE BRIGHT SUNSHINE OF REALITY."

"TECHNOLOGY IS OUR FRIEND IN THIS INSTANCE," HE PASSIONATELY PENNED. "HOME FORMATS HAVE MADE RENE, OR BETTER, THE EXPERIENCE OF RENE, AVAILABLE TO ALL WHO HAVE MISSED HER TERRIBLY SINCE HER FIRST TIME AROUND. INDEED, IF YOU ARE AT

Fugitive Girls
On
The Run...
No Prison Bars
Could Hold
Them!

A.F.P.I. PRESENTS...

JABIE ABERCROMBIE
RENEE BOND · TALIE COCHRANE
DONA DESMOND · MARGIE LANIER
IN

FUGITIVE GIRLS

Produced and Directed by A.C. STEPHEN   SCA   in EASTMANCOLOR

ALL INTERESTED IN EROTICA -- IN **TRUE** EROTICA (NOT THE HIGH-GLOSS AIRBRUSHED TEDIUM THAT PASSES FOR EROTICA TODAY) THEN DO YOURSELF A FAVOUR AND ACQUAINT YOURSELF, OR RE-ACQUAINT YOURSELF, WITH RENE BOND ASAP."

(MEOW!) ☆ — ROBIN BOUGIE

SO MAYBE YOU WANT SOME RENE, BUT YOU DON'T WANT THE WET SPLAYED PINK? HERE ARE MY PICKS FOR HER ALL-TIME BEST NON-HARDCORE ROLES:

1. FUGITIVE GIRLS (1974)
2. FRANKIE AND JOHNNIE WERE LOVERS (1975)
3. COUNTRY CUZZINS (1970)
4. SWINGERS MASSACRE (1975)
5. THE TEASER (1973)
6. PLEASE DON'T EAT MY MOTHER (1973)

TODAY For your **CRAWLING** pleasure TWO TERROR FILLED FILMS!

TIM HAS A PET RATTLESNAKE, WHEN TIM GETS MAD· STANLEY GETS DEADLY!

STANLEY ...WILL MAKE YOUR SKIN CRAWL · PG

A STANLEY PRODUCTION · A CROWN INTERNATIONAL PICTURES RELEASE · COLOR by deluxe

Distributed by MARVIN FILMS, INC.

KILLING, EATING AS THEY PROWL... GROWING LARGER AS THEY EAT.

PLUS

NO LIMIT TO THE HORROR OF... **NIGHT OF THE LEPUS**

PG · METROCOLOR · MGM Presents

AAHAHAHA! **NIGHT OF THE LEPUS** (1972). THANKS TO THE AMAZING FRED ADELMAN AND HIS COLLECTION OF MEMORABILIA, I HAVE NOW GOTTEN MY LEATHERY MITTS ON ONE OF MY FAVOURITE NEWSPAPER AD-MATS OF ALL TIME (SEE ABOVE), AND PRESENT IT HERE WITH SOME VAGUELY INTERESTING TRIVIA MORSELS YOU MIGHT LIKE TO BE SEEING WITH YOUR LOOKING EYES.

YES, IT IS A SERIOUS HORROR MOVIE ABOUT GIANT KILLER BUNNIES, NOT A COMEDY -- A WHITE-KNUCKLER THAT'S SUPPOSED TO **SCARE** YOU. I'M SERIOUS. WHEN PUT INTO SECOND RUN, THIS BOX OFFICE EMBARRASSMENT WAS DOUBLED UP WITH **STANLEY**, AN EQUALLY UNSCARY MOVIE ABOUT A FREAKY INDIAN WITH A SNAKE. I RECOMMEND THEM TO BE VIEWED WHILE HAPPILY DRINKING WITH FRIENDS AND EATING "COMBOS" OUT OF A SALAD BOWL.

COBBLED UP BY THE LEGENDARY MGM STUDIOS WHILE IN THE MIDDLE OF FALLING APART AND BEING SCHOOLED AT THE BOX OFFICE BY INDEPENDENTS WITH FAR LESS MONEY AND INDUSTRY POWER. DESPITE A FAIR AMOUNT OF GORE, VISCERA, AND REAL RABBIT KILLING (ONE IS EVEN SET ON FIRE!), THE MPAA GAVE LEPUS A PG RATING. I GUESS THEY DIDN'T WANT ANYONE TO MISS IT, NO MATTER HOW OLD THEY WERE.

THE EFFECTS ARE ACHIEVED BY FILMING NORMAL SIZED RABBITS ON LITTLE MINIATURE SETS. ADDITIONALLY, A DUDE IN A FUCKING RABBIT SUIT JUMPS ON THE ACTORS FOR CLOSE UPS. FOR PROMO, LUCKY RABBIT FEET DIPPED IN RED PAINT WERE DISTRIBUTED! CLASSY!

THE SLAVE

written by **Robin Bougie**

drawn by **David Paleo**

Lovely Evelyn and her boy-toy Bob are happily enjoying an extramarital French-countryside romp when her older brother Maurice and his spooky sex-bomb girlfriend come sauntering in. They're on the run from the law, and don't have much to lose.

Maurice is a skuzzy little warthog of a man with a gun, a briefcase full of cash, and some naked pictures of his sis when she was a desperate young starving model.

Within an hour of arriving the gangster has instructed his gal to seduce Bob while he slyly blackmails his poor sister with his dirty-photo collection.

This control he exerts over his kin is purely mental, and plays out like a sick little game of tit for-tat as he laughs and hands over a fleshy photo for each article of clothing she sheds.

SOON SHE STANDS TOTALLY NAKED AND DEFENCELESS BEFORE HIS LEERING EYES. IN ORDER TO KEEP THINGS QUIET AND SAVE HER MARRIAGE, EVELYN SIMPLY MUST SUBMIT TO HIS DEBAUCHED WHIMS.

THE INTRIGUES GET BEEFIER AND MORE SENSATIONAL AND SOON A MYSTERIOUS BALD YUL-BRYNNER-WANNABE WITH AN INTERESTING CONNECTION TO THE STOLEN MONEY MAKES THE SCENE IN AN AMBULANCE.

HIS NAME IS MARCO, HE'S PISSED, HE'S GOT A SERIOUSLY KINKY GIRLFRIEND, AND HE DROPS SOME SAVAGE N' HEADY DIALOGUE BEFORE ROCKETING THE FILM INTO A VIOLENT FINALE.

HAVE YOU EVER HATED ANYONE WITH A HATE THAT'S ALMOST LOVE? YOU CAN FEED YOURSELF WITH IT FOR MONTHS!

THIS BLACK AND WHITE 1967 BONER-COAXER IS A RIPE EXAMPLE OF THE 1960S FRENCH ART-HOUSE / SEXPLOITATION HYBRID.

DIRECTOR MAX PECAS (A TRAIL BLAZER IN EACH STAGE OF CLASSIC EUROPEAN SKIN-TRASH) KICKS IT OUT ROGER-VADIM STYLE -- ONLY WITH A PULSE.

ANAL FUCKING DESECRATES HOLY GROUND

WRITIN': ROBIN BOUGIE • DRAWIN': JOSH SIMMONS

IN 1998 A CHURCH IN ITALY WAS OUTED AS THE BACKDROP FOR A PORN FILM SHOT CALLED **IL CONFESSIONALE** ("THE CONFESSIONAL BOX") STARRING POPULAR ITALIAN PORN GODDESS MONICA ROCCAFORTE.

A GOD-FEARING RESIDENT WHO LIVED NEAR THE 13th CENTURY CHURCH OF SAN VICENZO DOWNLOADED THE XXX FILM, AND EITHER BEFORE OR AFTER USING IT AS INSPIRATION TO BEAT HIS MEAT, RECOGNIZED HIS BELOVED HOUSE OF WORSHIP ON DISPLAY AND CALLED THE POLICE.

IN THE SCENE IN QUESTION 27-YEAR-OLD ROCCAFORTE (WHO IS NO STRANGER TO THE POPULAR SUBGENRE OF ITALIAN PORN THAT MIXES RELIGION AND HARDCORE PORKING) GETS HER ASSHOLE REAMED OUT BY A PRIEST PLAYED BY JOEY CALZONE.

IN LIGHT OF THE "UNHOLY UNION," AND TO KEEP HUNDREDS OF MARRIAGES CARRIED OUT ON THE HOLY PROPERTY IN THE CENTRAL REGION OF ABRUZZO IN THE PREVIOUS FIVE YEARS FROM BEING DEEMED INVALID, THE BISHOP OF MARSI HAD TO RECONSECRATE THE CHURCH ITSELF AND ALL SERVICES (WEDDINGS, CHRISTENINGS, ETC) HELD IN SAN VICENZO'S SINCE THE FILMING OF THE SCENE.

PROSECUTORS INVESTIGATED THE POSSIBILITY OF BRINGING "BLASPHEMY CHARGES" AGAINST THE PRODUCERS OF THE XXX-RATED FILM, A CHARGE NOT UNCOMMON IN ITALY, A COUNTRY WHERE CHURCH AND STATE ARE NOT NEARLY AS FAR SEPARATED AS THEY ARE IN MANY OTHER DEVELOPED NATIONS.

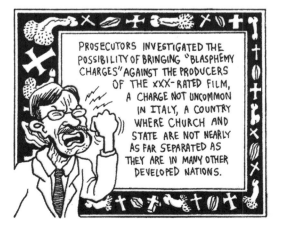

AS THE STORY BROKE, MEMBERS OF THE ITALIAN CHURCH WERE VISIBLY SHAKEN, AND DEMANDED ANSWERS. OBVIOUSLY THE SINFUL PORNOGRAPHERS DIDN'T REALIZE THAT ONLY PEDOPHILIC PRIESTS WERE ALLOWED TO ASSFUCK ON CHURCH PROPERTY.

THE PARISH PRIEST AT THE TIME, ONE FATHER AR-TEMIO DE VINCENTIIS TOLD REPORTERS THAT HE HAD HANDED OVER THE KEYS TO THE OWNER OF A RESTAURANT NEXT DOOR TO THE CHURCH, WHO IN TURN HAD LOANED THE SPACE TO A CREW LOOK-ING TO "FILM A WEDDING SCENE."

THE SOFTCORE VERSION OF THIS GENRE - BETTER KNOWN TO EURO-TRASH MOVIE NERDS AS "NUNSPLOI-TATION"- HAS A GRAND AND RICH TRADITION DATING BACK TO THE LATE 60s, POPULATED BY MISCHIEVOUS LESBIAN NUNS SPENDING MUCH OF THEIR TIME CAR-PET-MUNCHING EACH OTHER OR GETTING CORNHOLED BY EARTH-BOUND DEMONS AND DEVILS.

MANY OF THE NUNS IN TRASHY CLASSICS LIKE FLAVIA THE HERETIC (1974), MALABINBA: THE MALICIOUS WHORE (1981), AND IMAGES IN A CONVENT (1979) ARE PRISONERS IN THEIR OWN BELIEF STRUCTURE. THE VERY RELIGION THAT GIVES THEM SPIRITUALITY, IN TURN PERVERTS THEM AND MAKES THEM EITHER SUBMISSIVE MASOCHISTS, OR VIOLENTLY AND INSANELY SADISTIC.

THE SHOCK AND TABOO OF MIXING PORN AND RE-LIGION IS AN EYE-OPENING MIX OF CONCEPTS THAT HAS AND FOREVER WILL WIN OVER PORN AUDIENCES. YOU DON'T HAVE TO BE THE POPE TO FIGURE OUT WHY NUN PORN IS FREAKIN' HOT!

JHS 3/4-05

YOUNG DUMB AND FULL OF CUM

THE SAUCY STORY OF DESIREÉ COUSTEAU

BORN DEBORAH A. SCHEER, DESIREE COUSTEAU LAUNCHED HER FILM CAREER ON A HIGH NOTE WITH A BIT PART IN JONATHAN DEMME'S CULT-FAVOURITE WOMEN-IN-PRISON FILM, CAGED HEAT. WITHIN MONTHS SHE WAS DOING HARDCORE SEX FILMS, WOULD GO ON TO BECOME ONE OF THE MOST DISTINCTIVE ADULT STARS OF THE SEVENTIES, AND BESTOW THIS PARTICULAR BOUGIE WITH COUNTLESS BONERS.

HORNED-UP SINCE SHE SQUEEZED INTO HER FIRST TRAINING BRA, YOUNG DEBORAH WAS A TEENAGE NYMPHET WHO GOT AN URGENT AND ENTHUSIASTIC START IN THE MYSTIC ART OF HAM-SLAMMIN'. "THE FIRST TIME I HAD SEX IT HURT A LITTLE, BUT I WAS SO EXCITED TO FINALLY GET GOING INTO THAT WHOLE BEING-A-WOMAN THING, I DIDN'T REALLY CARE."

"I WAS 17 AND I TOLD HIM I WANTED IT. HE WAS SHY AND HESITANT, BUT GOT ON TOP OF ME AND WE WENT AT IT. I CAME AND HE CAME, AND IT WAS OVER IN 5 MINUTES. BUT I'D LIKE TO ADD THAT MY REAL SEX LIFE STARTED WHEN I WAS ABOUT 20 AND MY PUSSY WAS EATEN OUT FOR THE FIRST TIME."

GRACED WITH AMAZING FULL-FIGURE CURVES AND AN ALWAYS PERFECTLY COIFED HEAD OF HAIR, COUSTEAU APPEARED BUBBLY AND EFFERVESCENT. IT SEEMED SHE WAS BLESSED WITH THE X-FACTOR THAT MADE MOST OF HER CO-STARS SEEM LIKE BIT PLAYERS, NO MATTER WHAT THEIR BILLING WAS.

AS SHE ONCE STATED TO AN INTERVIEWER; "IF NATURE IS GENEROUS WHERE IT COUNTS, A YOUNG LADY MAY AS WELL MAKE DUE WITH THE GIFTS THAT GOD HAS GIVEN HER." IT WAS A PRINCIPLE TO WHICH SHE READILY ADHERED ALL THROUGH HER LUSTY ORIFICE-PACKED FILM ROLES AND HER TENURE ON THE STRIP CIRCUIT.

DESIREE BEGAN HER SMUT CAREER LIKE SO MANY YOUNG WOMEN; SHE WAS DUTIFULLY TRYING TO PUT HERSELF THROUGH COLLEGE AND COULDN'T PAY THE RENT. TAKING UP NUDE MODELLING IN ATHENS GEORGIA DID THE TRICK FOR A LITTLE WHILE, BUT PRETTY SOON THE ALLURE OF THE EASY MONEY WAS TOO MUCH, SO SHE SHACKED UP WITH A STAGE ACTOR AND DITCHED THE HIGHER EDUCATION. WHEN HE MOVED TO THE WEST COAST TO GET MORE ACTING JOBS, SHE TAGGED ALONG AND BECAME A MODEL FOR MEN'S MAGAZINES AND A TOPLESS DANCER. HER FIRST JOB WAS AT THE 'CLASSIC CAT' GO-GO CLUB IN HOLLYWOOD, AND SHE QUICKLY BUILT UP A LOYAL FOLLOWING OF DROOLING WOLVES.

ONE HER FIRST MODELLING GIGS WAS FOR HUSTLER MAGAZINE. IN THE SHOOT, A NUDE DESIREE AND A BRAWNY, WELL-HUNG (14 FUCKING INCHES) BLACK FELLAH FROLIC AND HUMP IN A FOREST, ROLL AROUND ON THE BEACH, AND TENDERLY EMBRACE THE WAY LOVERS ARE INCLINED TO DO. NONE OF THIS SHOULD BE PARTICULARLY NOTEWORTHY, BUT ONCE YOU PLACE IT WITHIN THE RACIALLY INTOLERANT CONTEXT OF AMERICA IN DECEMBER 1975, THE PLOT BECOMES EASIER TO FOLLOW. THE PICTORIAL WAS ENTITLED "BUTCH AND PEACHES", AND IT PROMPTED BAGS OF HATEMAIL. IT REMAINS TO THIS DAY THE MOST TALKED ABOUT PICTORIAL IN HUSTLER HISTORY, AND IS CONSIDERED BY SOME TO BE THE FLASH POINT FOR THE ASSASSINATION ATTEMPT ON (NOW WHEELCHAIR-BOUND) PUBLISHER LARRY FLYNT.

ASIDE FROM THE "BUTCH AND PEACHES" DEBACLE, BREAKS CAME HER WAY HERE AND THERE, BUT IT WASN'T UNTIL PORN DIRECTOR ALEX DE RENZY DROPPED IN ON A LIVE 3-GIRL LESBIAN SEX SHOW AT THE PLAYPEN IN SAN FRANCISCO THAT SHE COULD SAY THAT SHE HAD ARRIVED AS AN EROTIC PERFOMER. HE LIKED THIS "PEACHES" GIRL EVERYONE WAS TALKING ABOUT.

"HE ASKED ME IF I'D LIKE TO MAKE A MOVIE, AND SO WE MADE PRETTY PEACHES. THAT WAS MY FIRST STARRING ROLE", RECOUNTED DESIREE IN 1979. IT WASN'T EXACTLY THE KIND OF MOVIE STAR I WAS HOPING TO BECOME. I THOUGHT ONE OF THE STUDIOS WOULD TAKE ME IN AND SHAPE ME UP. OF COURSE, IT DOESN'T WORK LIKE THAT, BUT I BELIEVED THE OLD LEGENDS. I EVEN HUNG AROUND SCHWAB'S DRUGSTORE (WHERE LANA TURNER WAS DISCOVERED WHILE SIPPING A SODA) IN A TIGHT SWEATER AND HAD A COKE, BUT I WASN'T DISCOVERED."

AT VARIOUS POINTS IN HER CAREER, DESIREE REVEALED THAT SHE HAD A SINCERE PASSION FOR DANCE AND THE THEATRE. ALTHOUGH SHE PUT ON A BRAVE FUCK-ME FACE WHENEVER IN PUBLIC, SHE MUST HAVE FELT FRUSTRATION FOR NOT GETTING A CHANCE TO EXPLORE THOSE AVENUES OUTSIDE OF JIZZ-COAXING, A VOCATION WHERE ONE CERTAINLY DOES NOT GET AS MUCH RESPECT AS A STAGE ACTRESS OR A BALLERINA.

HER PARENTS CERTAINLY DIDN'T RESPECT HER CHOICE OF CAREER. "THEY SAW MY PICTURES ADVERTISED IN THE NEWSPAPERS AND THEY FREAKED. THEY'RE VERY CONSERVATIVE BAPTIST PEOPLE. MY DAD DOESN'T LIKE IT, MY MOM CRIES A LOT. WHEN I GO HOME IT'S KIND OF EMBARRASSING."

THE RECEPTION IN HER HOME TOWN WAS NOT THE ONLY TRAUMATIC EXPERIENCE TO BE HAD. ON SEPTEMBER 16TH 1981 IN FORT WAYNE INDIANA, SHE FELT THE STING OF WHAT IT MEANT TO BE A DISREPUTABLE WHORE IN THE EYES OF SOCIETY AND THE LAW. HER AGENT HAD BOOKED AN APPEARANCE AT THE CINEMA BLUE THEATER TO PROMOTE ONE OF HER FILMS, AND AS A BONUS DESIREE PRANCED AROUND THE THEATRE NAKED AND SAT ON LAPS WHILE HER MANAGER TOOK SNAPSHOT KEEPSAKES, FOR WHICH THE THRILLED FANS WOULD THEN PAY $5 EACH.

UNFORTUNATELY, AN UNDERCOVER VICE OFFICER WAS ONE OF THE FANS SHE ROOSTED ON, AND COUSTEAU WAS UNCEREMONIOUSLY HUSTLED OFF TO JAIL, CHARGED WITH PUBLIC INDECENCY, AND WASN'T RELEASED UNTIL HER FRIENDS AND MANAGER COULD COME UP WITH $750 BOND. THAT IS OVER $2000 TODAY, WHEN YOU ADJUST FOR

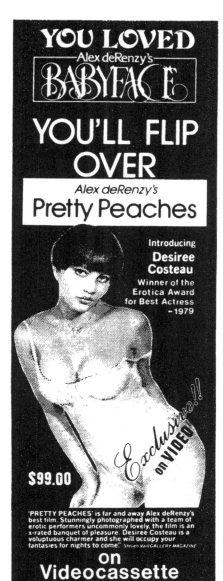

INFLATION. DESIREE LEFT THE JAIL HOUSE IN TEARS.

DESPITE THE INCIDENT AT THE CINEMA BLUE, DESIREE REALLY ENJOYED THE ATTENTION AND MONEY THAT CAME FROM INTERACTING WITH HER FANS IN MORE LIBERAL CITIES, SUCH AS AT THE INFAMOUS MELODY BURLESQUE THEATRE IN NEW YORK. THERE, SHE WOULD DANCE, AND DO LIVE SEX SHOWS WITH OTHER GIRLS. WHEN ASKED ABOUT THE EXPERIENCE IN 1981 BY VIDEO X MAGAZINE, SHE SPOKE QUITE CANDIDLY:

"IT'S A LOT LIKE PERFORMING IN A MOVIE BECAUSE THERE IS AN AUDIENCE TO PERFORM FOR WITH THE BIG DIFFERENCE BEING THAT IT IS ALIVE INSTEAD OF ON FILM. LIKE WHEN I'M FILMING, I PUT MY HEART AND SOUL INTO MY WORK AND I WANT TO GIVE THEM THEIR MONEY'S WORTH. THIS IS MY JOB, MY CAREER, AND LIKE ANY OTHER LINE OF WORK YOU'VE GOT TO GIVE THE CUSTOMER WHAT HE WANTS IF YOU EXPECT TO MAKE MONEY. AT PLACES LIKE THE MELODY THE GUYS SIT RIGHT AROUND THE STAGE ONLY A FEW FEET AWAY. IT'S IMMEDIATE REACTION TO WHAT I'M DOING IN MY ACT, AND I CAN SEE BY THEIR FACES WHAT THEY THINK OF ME AND I CAN CHANGE MY ACT TO SUIT THE ATMOSPHERE. WHAT THEY SEEM TO LIKE THE BEST IS WHEN I STAND RIGHT OVER THEM ON THE STAGE SO THEY CAN LOOK RIGHT UP INTO MY CUNT. I LOVE MAKING MOVIES, BUT I THINK I LIKE DANCING LIVE BETTER. AND I THINK THE MEN LIKE IT BETTER, TOO."

ONE OF THE BIGGEST HITS SHE WAS A PART OF WAS **THE ECSTASY GIRLS**, AND SHE SHARED THE LIMELIGHT WITH SOME OF THE BIGGEST NAMES IN SMUT AT THE TIME. THE FILM WAS A LAVISH PRODUCTION (FOR XXX PORN ANYWAY) THAT RANKS AS DIRECTOR GARY GRAVER'S BEST. IT PROMPTED ITS DISTRIBUTOR LEISURE TIME BOOKING, TO POUR $250,000 (AN UNHERALDED AMOUNT) INTO THE FIRST ALL-OUT NATIONAL ADVERTISING, PROMOTIONAL CAMPAIGN, AND A NATION-WIDE INSTANTANEOUS XXX RELEASE.

ITS RED CARPET GALA HOLLYWOOD OPENING DREW OVER 600 GUESTS AND DOZENS OF PORN INDUSTRY REPORTERS. THE EVENT WAS FOLLOWED BY A PARTY AT PLATO'S RETREAT WEST, WHERE DESIREE AND CO-STAR JAMIE GILLIS GOT NAKED AND TOOK PART IN DISCO-DANCING, SWIMMING, AN ENORMOUS BUFFET OF QUICHE AND SALMON, AND THEN TOPPED IT OFF WITH SOME VERY DIRTY ANTICS IN THE NOT-SO-PRIVATE SWINGER ROOMS.

HER DELIGHTFUL DOPINESS (IMAGINE A PORN VERSION OF JENNIFER TILLY) IN **PRETTY PEACHES** IS ONE OF THE REASONS THE FILM STANDS AS

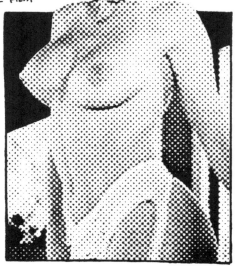

MY PERSONAL FAVOURITE OF HER FILMOGRAPHY. IT'S AS IF THE ENTIRE BIG OL' WORLD IS OUT TO TAKE ADVANTAGE OF HER INNOCENCE. FROM HER DELICATE UNCONSCIOUS POST CAR-CRASH MOLESTATION SCENE, TO THE MEMORABLE MAD DOCTOR WHO FORCES UPON HER A HIGH-PRESSURED ENEMA THAT EXPLODES OUT OF HER BUTT (DON'T WORRY KIDS, THE WATER JETS OUT CLEAN -- NOT BROWN AND CHUNKY), TO THE MOVIE'S CLIMACTIC FULL-BLOWN OIL ORGY, PRETTY PEACHES IS <u>EXCEPTIONAL</u> FILTH.

"MY BOYFRIEND AND I USED TO GIVE EACH OTHER ENEMAS", COUSTEAU TOLD STAG MAGAZINE. "WE LIKED IT, AND WE DID IT FOR HEALTH REASONS. THAT WAS ACTUALLY HOW I GOT THE NAME COUSTEAU. MY BOYFRIEND GAVE ME THAT NAME BECAUSE HE SAID I WAS ALWAYS UNDER WATER."

WINNING THE 'BEST ACTRESS' AWARD AT THE 1979 EROTICA AWARDS FOR HER ROLE AS THE NAIVE PEACHES, DESIREE CLIMBED THE STAGE AT THE HOLLYWOOD PALLADIUM, AND HAPPILY COOED INTO THE MIC: "THANK YOU ALEX DE RENZY. I ENJOYED BEING IN YOUR FILM VERY MUCH, AND I ENJOYED ALL THE FRIENDS THAT I MADE."

I'M SURE THEY ENJOYED MAKING HER TOO.

WHICH ISN'T TO SAY SHE WAS TOTALLY BELOVED BY ALL HER CO-STARS. "SHE DIDN'T LIKE BEING IN THE BUSINESS", RECALLED JOHN SEEMAN. "I HAD TROUBLE GETTING IN A RHYTHM WITH HER DURING SEX. I DID A FEW SCENES WITH HER BUT NEVER COULD FEEL COMFORTABLE." DESIREE HAD AN ONGOING FEUD WITH ANNETTE HAVEN, AND THE TWO SHARED A MUTUAL DISLIKE DESPITE HAVING TO CHOW ON EACH OTHERS MUFFS FOR THE CAMERA. "I WAS DOING A MENAGE-A-TROIS WITH DESIREE COUSTEAU" HAVEN TOLD A REPORTER IN 1980. "WE WERE SUPPOSED TO EAT EACH OTHER AND FONDLE EACH OTHER'S PUSSIES, YOU KNOW. THE DIRECTOR WAS GIVING US INSTRUCTIONS AND DESIREE WOULD NOT LET ME TOUCH HER BODY! IT WAS AWFUL! I WOULD NOT WANT TO WORK WITH HER AGAIN."

"SHE IS SO **COLD**", COMPLAINED DOROTHY LEMAY, DESIREE'S

That "PEACHES" Girl Is Back!!!

Hot & Saucy Pizza Girls

X

WE DELIVER!

STARRING DESEREE COUSTEAU with JOHN C. HOLMES

COSTAR ON 1978'S A **FORMAL FAUCETT**. "THE CAMERAMAN SAID CUT, AND I CONTINUED EATING HER PUSSY. SHE PUSHED ME AWAY! I SAID 'OK, IF THAT IS THE WAY YOU WANT IT', BUT FOR THE REST OF THE SCENE I WAS DISTURBED BY THAT. I DON'T WORK THAT WAY."

DE RENZY ADORED HIS BUSTY, LUSTY, STARLET, THOUGH. "DESIREE WAS MY ALL-TIME GREATEST ACTRESS," THE LATE DIRECTOR UNEQUIVOCALLY STATED IN AN AVN INTERVIEW. "THE BIGGEST STAGE PRESENCE I EVER HAD. AND THAT'S WHAT I LOOK FOR IN A GIRL, SOMEONE WHO CAN REALLY CARRY THE BALL. THE GIRLS I SHOOT HAVE TO BE REALLY GOOD SPORTS, HAVE BIG PERSONALITIES AND BE SEX-MANIACS. IT'S A TOUGH COMBINATION."

COUSTEAU MAY HAVE BEEN A "SEX-MANIAC" FOR DE RENZY, BUT SHE WAS NOT GAME FOR EVERYTHING. ONLY TWO DESIREE ANAL FUCK SCENES ARE KNOWN TO EXIST. SWEDISH EROTICA 8MM LOOPS #152 ENTITLED "CLOSE ENCOUNTERS OF THE BREAST KIND" AND #154, IN BOTH OF WHICH SHE IS SODOMISED BY WELL-HUNG BLACK STUD, JONATHAN YOUNGER. AS YOUNGER PULLS OUT OF HER ASS AND BLOWS HIS GOOPY GUNK ALL OVER HER FACE IN #152, ONE CAN SENSE HER DISCOMFORT.

IN 1979 SHE GOT MARRIED, AND AT THE NEW YORK PUSSYCAT THEATRE PREMIERE OF HER FILM **DEEP RUB**, CAST A BITTERSWEET PALL OVER THE EVENT BY ANNOUNCING THAT SHE WAS LEAVING PORN. FLASHBULBS POPPED AND AN ANGUISHED FAN CRIED OUT "OH NO! YOU MEAN YOU'RE LEAVING FOR GOOD?". DESIREE SMILED AND NODDED HER HEAD. "BUT DON'T FRET, I MADE A FEW MORE THAT ARE IN THE CAN AND WILL BE COMING OUT IN THE NEXT FEW MONTHS. YOU'LL SEE ME AGAIN."

DESIREE GETS INTIMATE WITH SUPERSTUD JOHN HOLMES

DESIREÉ COUSTEAU, 40.

INDEED WE WOULD. DESIREE DASHED OFF FROM THAT PRESS EVENT TO THE MELODY BURLESQUE THEATRE, PROVING THAT OLD HABITS WERE GOING TO BE TOUGH TO BREAK. SHE WOULD CONTINUE TO DO LIVE SEX SHOWS FOR ANOTHER 3 YEARS, AND WOULD ALSO GOBBLE DONG ON-SCREEN FROM TIME TO TIME -- BUT THAT ALL CAME TO AN END WHEN SHE FOUND OUT THAT HER NEW HUSBAND HAD A FLING WITH HATED ADVERSARY ANNETTE HAVEN. DUN DUN DUNNNNN !

"EVEN THOUGH WE'VE BEEN MAKING GOOD MONEY, HE GETS JEALOUS ABOUT ME BEING WITH ALL THE GUYS IN SEX SCENES," DESIREE COMPLAINED. " AND I'M JEALOUS OF ALL THE GIRLS HE MEETS AROUND PORN MOVIE SETS, LIKE ANNETTE HAVEN. HE'S IN LOVE WITH HER. WE FIGHT A LOT."

IN EARLY 1983, AMID REPORTS OF

MS. MAGNIFICENT WAS ORIGINALLY MARKETED AS "SUPERWOMAN", AN AUDACIOUS MOVE THAT GOT THE PRODUCERS SUED BY DC COMICS.

HEAVY SUBSTANCE ABUSE AND A NASTY BREAKUP WITH HER HUSBAND, DESIREE LEFT L.A. AND WAS NEVER SEEN OR HEARD FROM AGAIN. IT WAS A CLEAN BREAK THIS TIME.

SCREW'S AL GOLDSTEIN CLAIMED THAT SHE BECAME MENTALLY ILL, AND WAS FORCIBLY PLACED IN AN INSTITUTION. A MUCH HAPPIER ENDING WAS TOLD BY INTERNET REPORTER LUKE FORD, WHO CIRCULATED A STORY THAT SHE HAD GONE BACK TO SCHOOL IN SAVANNAH GEORGIA, AND HAD EMERGED WITH A DEGREE IN MENTAL HEALTH.

IN MID 2007 A BLOGGER BY THE HANDLE OF SCARAMOUCHE RAN AN INTERVIEW ON HIS (NOW DECEASED AS OF 2010) WEBSITE WITH THE SUPPOSEDLY DEAD STAR OF DEBBIE DOES DALLAS, BAMBI WOODS. MANY WEREN'T SURE OF ITS VALIDITY, BUT THE SHENANIGANS TIP-OFF FOR ME IS THAT THE HOAXER HAD THEIR "DEBBIE" REVEAL (UNPROMPTED) THAT DESIREE COUSTEAU IS ALSO ALIVE AND WELL, AND THE TWO FORMER SPERM-STARLETS' KIDS PLAY TOGETHER .

I MEAN, C'MON, THE TWO MOST WONDERED-ABOUT PORN STARS FROM THE CLASSIC ERA BOTH DROPPED OF THE FACE OF THE PLANET TOGETHER? IT'S THE EQUIVALENT TO FINDING OUT THAT D.B. COOPER IS NOT ONLY STILL ALIVE, BUT THAT HE WAS DISCOVERED DRIVING JAMES DEAN'S LOST 1955 PORSCHE SPYDER DEATH-CAR.

WHILE TRYING TO DESCRIBE THE IRRESISTIBLE

QUALITIES SHE BROUGHT TO HER ROLES, ADAM FILM WORLD MAGAZINE GUSHED ABOUT THE LONG-MISSING SPOOGE-GARGLER: "ONE OF THE FIRST DOUBLE-BARRELLED BLASTS OF PASSION AND FUN TO GRACE THE SCREEN WITH DIZZY DELIGHTS WAS A SAUCER-EYED BABY-POUT BEAUTY NAMED DESIREE COUSTEAU."

LUSTED AFTER BY MULTITUDES, SHE WAS THE ORIGINAL "YOUNG, DUMB, AND FULL OF CUM" GIRL -- A TALENTED ADULT PERFORMER WHO SO EXCELLED AT THE DITZY BIMBO ROLE, THE CHARACTER BECAME SYNONYMOUS WITH HER OWN SHY, YET CLEARLY EXHIBITIONISTIC PERSONA.

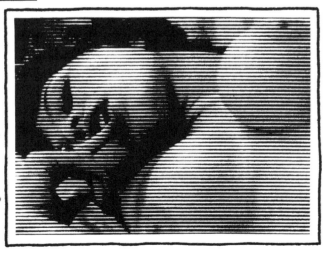

DESIREE'S THEATRICAL FILMS:

CAGED HEAT (1974)
PRETTY PEACHES (1978)
EASY (1978)
TELEFANTASY (1978)
HOT LUNCH (1978)
BOILING POINT (1978)
  AKA "INTIMATE ILLUSIONS"
A FORMAL FAUCETT (1978)
CHINA CAT (1978)
THE ECSTASY GIRLS (1979)
SUPERWOMAN (1979)
  AKA "MS. MAGNIFICENT"
HOT RACKETS (1979)
800 FANTASY LANE (1979)
BLUE'S VELVET (1979)
CANDY GOES TO HOLLYWOOD (1979)
GETTING OFF (1979)
INSIDE DESIREE COUSTEAU (1979)
SUMMER IN HEAT (1979)
HOT AND SAUCY PIZZA GIRLS (1979)
DEEP RUB (1979)
FEMALE ATHLETES (1980)
RANDY, THE ELECTRIC LADY (1980)
VANESSA'S HOT NIGHTS (1980)
BODY LUST (1981)
  AKA "THE TALE OF TIFFANY LUST"
FRENCH FINISHING SCHOOL (1981)
CALL GIRLS DELUXE (1981)
DELICIOUS (1981)
CENTER SPREAD GIRLS (1982)
FLIGHT SENSATIONS (1983)
SWEET ALICE (1983)
APHRODESIA'S DIARY (1983)
BEHIND THE SCENES OF AN ADULT MOVIE (1984)

It Sure Feels Good!

HOT RACKETS

Starring
CANDIDA ROYALLE
DESIREE CLEARBRANCH
and
JON MARTIN

Ⓧ

ACCORDING TO THAT DIRTY-MOUTH PORN MAGAZINE COPY (YOU KNOW, THE KIND THAT RUNS ALONGSIDE THE SPLIT BEAVER SHOTS), DESIREE COUSTEAU:

♡ LOVES: ALMOND ROCCA (HER FAVOURITE CANDY), RAISING DOBERMAN PINSCHERS, WAYLON JENNINGS, BAKING BREAD, WATCHING GOOD X-RATED FLICKS.

☹ HATES: MEN WHO WHINE, DISHONESTY, VIOLENCE IN MOVIES.

MIND YOU, MOST OF THAT KINDA STUFF IS TOTALLY FABRICATED BY DUDES WHOSE JOB IT WAS TO WRITE THE HOT SEXY QUOTES THAT WENT WITH THE PICS. IMAGINE HOW SHOCKED I WAS TO DISCOVER THIS FACT AFTER GETTING WORK WRITING FOR ADULT MAGAZINES MYSELF. ALL I COULD THINK OF WAS MYSELF AS A YOUNG BUCK WHO THOUGHT OF THIS ELECTRIC TEXT AS A FORM OF SOFT COOING IN MY EAR BY THE PINK, EXPOSED WOMEN STARING DOE-EYED AT ME WHILE I FURIOUSLY YANKED ON MY DINGUS. OH WELL.

-AND THOSE, MY FRIENDS, ARE THE **TEACHES OF PEACHES!!**

YE OLDE BOUG MAN

STOP

Alex deRenzy's "Pretty Peaches"

AT THE ADULT EXPO BACK IN 2003 THE SALIVATION ARMY WHO HAD ARRIVED TO CUE UP IN LONG LINES TO CATCH A GLIMPSE OF THE PLASTIC LOOKING HO'S AT THE VIVID TABLES, PAID LITTLE ATTENTION TO HER.

A YEAR LATER ALMOST TO THE DAY SHE TROTTED UP TO THE STAGE AT THE **AVN** AWARDS IN LAS VEGAS AND MADE A SHORT DEEP THROAT JOKE BEFORE ACCEPTING THE HONOR OF "FEMALE PERFORMER OF THE YEAR".

ASHLEY BLUE!!

CINEMA SEWER

BLUE'S CAREER IS ONE OF THE FASTEST RISING IN THE BUSINESS, A BREATH OF FRESH·YET·FILTHY AIR, AND CINEMA SEWER'S PICK FOR ONE OF THE CUTEST AND MOST REFRESHINGLY HONEST YOUNG WOMEN TO ENTER HARD CORE IN YEARS.

SHE CREDITS DIRECTOR SKEETER KERKOVE FOR TRAINING HER TO FIST HER OWN ASS, ADMITS SHE DOESN'T REALLY LIKE TO MASTURBATE ON CAMERA, OR THE TASTE OF CUM -- BUT SHE REALLY, HONESTLY DOES LIKE TO SUCK COCK AFTER IT HAS BEEN DRILLED IN HER BUNG·HOLE. WHEN ASKED WHY IT TOOK HER SO LONG TO DO A LESBIAN SCENE?

I NEVER BANGED A CHICK AT HOME AND I DIDN'T WANT TO LOOK LIKE A DUMB·ASS!

BORN JULY 8TH, 1981 BLUE'S SMALL BREASTED ALL·NATURAL FIGURE AND DAZZLINGLY ADORABLE FACE GIVE HER THE KIND OF GIRL·NEXT·DOOR LOOK THAT NEVER GOES OUT OF STYLE.

BLUE FIRST GOT INTO HARD·CORE AT THE URGING OF HER THEN REAL·LIFE BOYFRIEND, PORN ACTOR TRENT COCKER (AKA TRENT TESORO)

FAP! FAP! FAP!

THE COUPLE CAN BE SEEN PASSIONATELEY BOFFING IN SOME OF ASHLEY'S BETTER EARLY SCENES... AMONG THEM: "BARELY LEGAL #27" AND THE RAUNCHY 3·WAY DEBAUCHERY OF "TRY·A·TEEN #16"

AFTER A 4·5 DAY PORN WORK WEEK FOR SEVERAL YEARS AND NEARLY 300 FILMS TO HER CREDIT, THERE ARE SOME HIGHLIGHTS TO SPEAK OF. BLUE OUT-DID HERSELF WITH AN ASS-TONISHING DP EXTRAVAGANZA WITH WESLEY PIPES AND THE BIGGEST COCK IN PORN --MANDINGO, IN: "LITTLE WHITE CHICKS AND BIG BLACK MONSTER DICKS #16!"

BUT THE SERIES THAT BLUE IS BEST KNOWN FOR HAS GOT TO BE JM PRODUCTIONS "GIRLVERT." IN PART 2 SHE SHOWS THAT SHE CAN ALSO DISH IT OUT WHILE ANGRILY DOMINATING SUBMISSIVE GIRLS BY STUFFING HER TOES IN THEIR MOUTHS, PULLING HAIR AND GROWLING WHILE HATE-PLOWING THEIR FACES INTO HER JUICED-UP GROIN.

THIN SKINNED PORN FANS NEED NOT APPLY

SPEAKING OF PERVERSE, ACCORDING TO HER WEBSITE (WWW. ASHLEYBLUE.NET) BLUE'S MOST CONTROVERSIAL SCENE CAN BE FOUND IN "SERVICE ANIMALS #10" WHERE SHE PLAYS A HITCH-HIKER WHO GETS PICKED UP AND MISTREATED IN A ROUGH-EDGED PSUEDO-RAPE SESSION.

BUT TRUE BLUE FANS KNOW THAT THIS IS FAR FROM THE MOST CONTROVERSIAL SCENE SHE'S BEEN IN. THAT DISTINCTION GOES TO WHAT MIGHT BE THE HARDEST-TO-WATCH SCENE IN MODERN PORN HISTORY: A HARD-CORE CHOKE-OUT AT THE HANDS OF INFAMOUS MISOGYNIST KHAN TUSION, WHO FACE-FUCKED BLUE ON CAMERA UNTIL SHE PASSED-OUT FROM LACK OF OXYGEN!

KAF! KAF!

WHEN SHE WAKES UP, SHE BEGINS TO SOB UNCONTROLLABLY WHILE TUSION LOOMS AND SEEMS THRILLED BY THE FACT THAT HE'S NEARLY MURDERED HIS CO-STAR. THIS IS NOT YOUR USUAL FAKE "REALITY" ADULT ENTERTAINMENT THIS IS GAG-STYLE ORAL GONE HORRIBLY WRONG, AND AFTER KHAN PROUDLY POSTED IT ON HIS SITE (WWW.MEATHOLES.COM), CHIN-WAGGERS IN THE INDUSTRY BEGAN TO VOICE THEIR ANGER. WITHIN WEEKS THE CLIP WAS GONE NEVER TO BE SEEN AGAIN.

RECENTLY BLUE MADE HER DEBUT ON DAY-TIME T.V. THE WB'S "JUDGE MATHIS". A TELEVISED TRAVESTY IN THE VEIN OF "THE PEOPLES COURT" SAW BLUE FILING A SMALL CLAIMS PETITION AGAINST HER EX --TRENT TESORO IN AN ATTEMPT TO RECOUP APPROXIMATELY $3,650 THAT SHE HAD LOANED HIM.

ACCORDING TO AVN.COM SHE WANTED JUDGE JUDY BUT MADE DO WITH THE LESSER KNOWN MATHIS INSTEAD WHO RULED IN HER FAVOR.

TEXT: ROBIN BOUGIE   ART: SEAN ESTY   VISIT: MR-ESTY.LIVEJOURNAL.COM

COREY HAIM: ME MYSELF AND I (1989)

IMAGINE SPENDING A QUIET VACATION ALONE NEAR AN ISOLATED LAKE IN THE MIDDLE OF THE FOREST. FOR ONCE YOU'RE COMPLETELY AND TOTALLY ALONE. BUT ONE NIGHT AS YOU SLOWLY DRIFT ASLEEP YOU NOTICE TWO FIGURES STUMBLING OUT OF THE WOODS LOUDLY BRAGGING OVER THE EXTRA WAFFLES THEY RECEIVED WHEN THE DENNY'S WAITRESS FINALLY RECOGNIZED THEM. AS THEY DRUNKENLY INCH CLOSER TO THE LAKE YOU RECOGNIZE THESE MYSTERIOUS FIGURES AS COREY FELDMAN AND COREY HAIM. UNFORTUNATELY, THINGS QUICKLY GET OUT OF HAND AS HAIM PLAYFULLY KNOCKS FELDMAN'S SMOOTH CRIMINAL FEDORA OFF HIS HEAD THEY BOTH LOSE THEIR BALANCE AND FALL INTO THE LAKE. AS THE TWO STRUGGLE IT BECOMES ALL TOO CLEAR THAT NEITHER '80S ICON CAN SWIM, AND IT LOOKS AS IF YOU'LL ONLY HAVE TIME TO SAVE A SINGLE COREY. SO WHICH STAR OF **NATIONAL LAMPOON'S LAST RESORT** WILL IT BE?

WELL, BEFORE YOU ANSWER THAT QUESTION, LET'S TAKE A CLOSER LOOK AT OUR SINKING DREAMBOATS. ON THE ONE HAND THERE'S FELDMAN, A WALKING EMBARRASSMENT WHO ISN'T ABOVE NAMING HIS SHITTY BAND "THE TRUTH MOVEMENT", OR WANDERING AROUND MAGIC MOUNTAIN IN A BLACK LEATHER OUTFIT IN 90 DEGREE WEATHER. THE ONLY POSITIVE THING TO BE SAID OF THE GUY IS THAT ALL AROUND REPULSIVENESS MEANT THAT HIS FRIENDSHIP WITH MICHAEL JACKSON WAS SIMPLY THAT. ON THE OTHER HAND, IF WE LET FELDMAN DIE, THAT WOULD LEAVE ONLY HAIM. ALTHOUGH HE MAY SEEM PREFERABLE TO THE OTHER LESSER COREY, HE STILL LEADS SUCH A THOROUGHLY PATHETIC LIFE THAT MAYBE DEATH ISN'T SUCH A HORRIBLE OPTION. BETTER HAS BEENS HAVE KILLED THEMSELVES FOR A LOT LESS.

"YEEEAH-BOYEEEE"

OF COURSE BEING PITIFUL ISN'T ALWAYS THE BEST REASON TO WATCH SOME POOR BASTARD DROWN. IN FACT, IT'S NEVER A GOOD REASON. HOWEVER, IF SAID BASTARD SOMEHOW MANAGED TO STAR IN SOMETHING CALLED **COREY HAIM: ME, MYSELF AND I**, THEN IT ISN'T JUST COMMON COURTESY TO WATCH THEM DROWN - YOU'LL ALSO BE EXPECTED TO HURL EMPTY BEER BOTTLES AT THEIR HEAD AS THEY GO UNDER.

FOR THOSE UNFAMILIAR WITH **COREY HAIM: ME, MYSELF AND I**, IT WAS A "DOCUMENTARY" REVOLVING AROUND THE DAY TO DAY ACTIVITIES OF HAIM. IT INTENDED TO PROVE TO AUDIENCES (AS WELL AS FILM PRODUCERS) THAT HAIM WAS JUST AN AVERAGE KID THAT WOULD RATHER EAT A BIG OL' BUG THAN TAKE SOME NASTY DRUG. THE ONLY PROBLEM WITH **ME MYSELF AND I** WAS THAT NONE OF IT WAS TRUE, AND NO ONE INVOLVED EVEN TRIED TO HIDE THAT FACT. EVERYTHING IS FAKE. THEY DIDN'T EVEN BOTHER TO CUT THE FOOTAGE WHERE HAIM IS INSTRUCTED ON WHAT TO SAY DURING THE VIDEO'S "SPONTANEOUS" MOMENTS.

THE RANCID CHARM OF **COREY HAIM: ME, MYSELF AND I** BEGINS IMMEDIATELY AS HAIM SLOWLY WRITES THE TITLE ON A WHITE WALL IN CRAYON. THIS IS AN IMPORTANT MOMENT MAINLY BECAUSE IT SILENCED CRITICS THAT CLAIMED THAT HAIM COULD NOT SPELL HIS OWN NAME WITHOUT INTENSIVE COACHING. TO FURTHER ILLUSTRATE THE VIDEO'S BOTTOM OF THE BARREL PRODUCTION VALUES, THE SCENE IS PUNCTUATED BY A SAD SOLARIZATION EFFECT RARELY SEEN OUTSIDE PUBLIC ACCESS PROGRAMS STARRING TAP DANCERS WITH DOWNS SYNDROME.

FROM HERE, HAIM TAKES US ON A TEN MINUTE CAR RIDE IN WHICH HE BARELY SPEAKS AND TREATS THE CAMERA AS IF IT WERE AN EVIL SPIRIT HELL BENT ON STEALING HIS SOUL THE MOMENT HE LOOKS INTO THE LENS. THEN HE PUTS ON AN IMPROMPTU FASHION SHOW WHERE HE PERFORMS LIMP KARATE KICKS IN CLOTHES DESIGNED FOR LESBIAN GOLF PROS. HE ALSO "DIBBLE DABBLES" AT HIS KEYBOARD, WHATEVER THE HELL THAT MEANS. FROM THE LOOKS OF IT I GUESS IT MEANS TO NOD ARRYTHMICALLY WITH YOUR MOUTH WIDE OPEN.

BUT AS SOUL CRUSHING AS "DIBBLE DABBUNG" MIGHT SOUND, IT'S MERELY A PRELUDE TO THE TRUE HEART OF DARKNESS: THE INTERVIEW SESSION. IN THIS INSIGHTFUL SEGMENT "THE HAIMSTER" CANDIDLY REVEALS HIS STRUGGLES WITH SCHIZOPHRENIA, OR AS HE PUTS IT: "YOU ARE WHAT YOU WEAR. I WEAR SOMETHING DIFFERENT EVERY DAY." A STATEMENT ONLY SLIGHTLY LESS STUPID THAN "I LOVE TO WEAR AN EYEPATCH WHEN I SHRIEK ARR MATEY AT PASSING CARS."

HE ALSO REFLECTS ON THE JOYS OF LOVE WHICH HE COMPARES TO "DOLPHINS SWIMMING THROUGH YOUR BLOODSTREAM." BUT MOST IMPORTANTLY HE LOOKS TOWARDS A PROMISING FUTURE IN WHICH HE LIVES "IN TAHITI WATCHING THE SEA HORSES GO BY". THIS QUOTE IS ACTUALLY QUITE PROPHETIC ONCE YOU REPLACE "IN TAHITI" WITH "MY MOM", AND "WATCHING THE SEAHORSES GO BY" WITH "WHO SELLS MY HAIR AND MOLARS ON E-BAY". NEEDLESS TO SAY, WHATEVER BLAND STATEMENTS THEY PREPARED FOR HIM WERE CLEARLY MANGLED AND DISTORTED IN HAIM'S FIDGETY, DRUG-ADDLED BRAIN PAN.

BUT THAT'S NOT ALL. THERE'S MORE TO **COREY HAIM: ME, MYSELF AND I**. MUCH, MUCH, MORE. SUCH AS: HAIM TWIRLING SPASTICALLY WHILE ASKING WHERE HIS ROBOT IS, A BRIEF ONE MAN PERFORMANCE OF A **THREE'S COMPANY** EPISODE, AND OF COURSE THE PADDING, THE ENDLESS, POINTLESS PADDING. IT'S 40 SOLID MINUTES OF PAINFUL, CRINGE

* CONTINUED FROM PREVIOUS PAGE *

INDUCING KITSCH THAT PLAYS LIKE A SNUFF FILM FOR PEOPLE WHO LIKE TO WATCH CAREERS KILLED ON CAMERA. OH, AND BEFORE I FORGET, HERE'S THE SOLUTION TO MY "GET COREY TO THE SHORE-Y" RIDDLE ABOVE: IGNORE THE TWO COREY'S AND INSTEAD SAVE THAT WEIRD KID WHO PLAYED PAUL ON **WONDER YEARS** FROM THE RABID GRIZZLY NEAR THE LOG CABIN. THANKS FOR PLAYING.

REVIEW BY: MIKE SULLIVAN

MEANWHILE: DURING THE CREATIVE PROCESS, DOUBT REARS ITS DISGUSTING HEAD.

WHAT AM I **DOING** HERE!? IS THIS JUST A BIG STUPID VANITY PROJECT? AM I THIS **FUCKING** DESPERATE FOR ACCEPTANCE AND ATTENTION? AM I JUST WASTING MY LIFE? JESUS, I'M GOING TO BE DEAD SOON... WHAT WILL BE LEFT WHEN I'M GONE? ETC ETC, ETC, ETC

KING CAT

WHAT THE ☆FUCK?☆

A FEW SHORT WEEKS AFTER I DREW THIS, WE ENDED UP CASTING MAYA IN THE FIRST CINEMA SEWER XXX PRODUCTION: **THE CUMMING OF JIZZUS** (NOW AVAILABLE ON DVD FROM WWW.CINEMASEWER.COM) IN HER SCENE (WHICH WE SHOT THE VERY EVENING THAT I'M WRITING THIS, ACTUALLY) THE LOVELY MAYA UTTERLY ROCKED OUR BIBLICAL TEMPLE SET TO ITS VERY FOUNDATIONS WITH AN ASS-GRINDING, BALL-SUCKING, ANUS-LICKING, PISS-DRINKING PERFORMANCE ON PAR WITH THE GREATS OF EROTIC CINEMA. CAN YOU SENSE MY ENTHUSIAM?!! I WITNESSED **GREATNESS** TONIGHT, MY FRIENDS.

UNDERAPPRECIATED FUCK STARS: MAYA

A SEXY SLUT WHO ALWAYS HAS A SWEET SMILE, MAYA IS ONE OF THE MOST OUTRAGEOUS PERFORMERS IN THE CANADIAN PORN SCENE. PISS DRINKING, FISTING, BASEBALL BATS, YOU NAME IT... SHE'S DONE IT, AND MORE IMPORTANTLY... SHE SEEMS TO BE HAVING A BLAST DOING IT! TOP MARKS!

BOUGIE '06

OBSCURE CRUSH OF THE ISSUE:

"JANET"

WITH HER ADORABLE TATUM O'NEAL HAIR CUT AND HEART-SHAPED PUBE CUT, "JANET", (PROBABLY NOT HER REAL NAME) APPEARED IN A PULP MAGAZINE FOR MEN CALLED **TRUE** BACK IN APRIL 1976. I'VE NEVER FOUND HER IN ANOTHER NUDE LAYOUT OR A PORN FILM -- BUT I WON'T STOP LOOKING. NEVER, YOU HEAR?

ACCORDING TO THE PATTER IN HER LAYOUT, "SHE'S SHY, LOVES AGGRESSIVE MEN, LIVES IN ATLANTA, AND WORKS AS A TRAVEL WRITER FOR YOUTH ORIENTATED FASHION MAGAZINES. BE STILL, MY BEATING HEART! ♡♡♡

CHERYL DUNYE'S **STRANGER INSIDE** (2001) WAS TOUTED AS A "REALISTIC PORTRAYAL OF LIFE INSIDE A WOMEN'S PRISON AND ALLOWS FOR A DECENT DISPLAY OF ILLICIT DRUGS, VIOLENCE, RACIAL TENSIONS, OFFICER CORRUPTION, AND WOMEN-HAVING-SEX-WITH-WOMEN. THIS LACKS A LOT

OF WHAT MADE THE 1970S FEMALE PRISON MOVIES SO GRITTY N' SLEAZY, BUT WHAT IS SO COOL IS THAT THIS IS ONE OF THE FEW W.I.P FILMS TO TELL THE STORY FROM A BLACK FEMALE PERSPECTIVE -- WHICH IS APT, SEEING AS MOST WOMEN IN U.S.A JAILS ARE BLACK.

WOMEN'S PRISON MASSACRE (1983)

OH ME OH MY, THAT LORD OF NASTINESS BRUNO MATTEI STRIKES AGAIN, AND THIS IS ONE OF MY FAVOURITE ALL TIME FEMALE PRISON FILMS! THIS BAD-GIRL STARS LAURA "EMMANUELLE" GEMSER, FEATURES ALL OUT BRAWLS WITH SWITCHBL-ADES, GRUNGY PRISON SEX, SICKENING OVER THE TOP VIOLENCE, KUNG-FU SOUND FX, THROAT BITING,

BITTER VENGENCE, HOSTAGE TAKINGS, A DEADLY GAME OF RUSSIAN ROULETTE, MEGA AMOUNTS OF EXPOSED TITTIES, AND A FEMALE INMATE PUTTING A RAZORBLADE CONTRAPTION IN HER PUSS SO THAT A RAPIST SLICES HIS PENIS IN HALF WHEN HE BANGS HER!

MOST OF THE GALS LOOK AS NASTY AND BALLS OUT SAVAGE AS YOU'D EXPECT (GIVEN THE STATE OF THE PRISON), AND IT MAKES THE MOVIE THAT MUCH BETTER FOR IT! THIS, MY FRIENDS, IS 100% CINEMA SEWER BLISS! BUY IT ON DVD TODAY!

index

(Note: Entries in bold refer exclusively to illustrations.)

index

index

More Quality Books for Cult Connoisseurs from FAB Press